Malaysia, Singapore & Brunei

a travel survival kit

Crowther, Geoff.

Malaysia, Singapore & Brunei – a travel survival kit
Second edition

Published by
  Lonely Planet Publications
  PO Box 88, South Yarra, Victoria 3141, Australia
  Lonely Planet Publications
  PO Box 2001A, Berkeley, California, USA 94702

Printed by
  Colorcraft, Hong Kong

Photographs by
  Tony Wheeler and Geoff Crowther

First published
  May 1982

This edition
  April 1985

National Library of Australia
Cataloguing in Publication Data

Crowther, Geoff, 1944-.
  Malaysia, Singapore & Brunei, a travel survival kit.

  2nd ed.
  Includes index.
  ISBN 0 908086 65 2.

  1. Malaysia – Description and travel – Guide-books.
  2. Singapore – Description and travel – Guide-books.
  3. Brunei – Description and travel – Guide-books.
  I. Wheeler, Tony, 1946-. II. Title.

915.95

Copyright © Geoff Crowther, Tony Wheeler, 1982, 1985

The Authors

Geoff Crowther was born in Yorkshire, England and started his travelling days as a teenage hitch-hiker. Later, after many short trips around Europe, two years in Asia and Africa and short spells in the overgrown fishing village of Hull and on the bleak and beautiful Cumberland fells, Geoff got involved with the London underground information centre BIT. He helped put together their first, tatty, duplicated overland guides and was with them from their late '60s heyday right through to the end. Since his first Lonely Planet guide, to Africa, Geoff has written or collaborated on numerous other guides in the series. Geoff now lives with Hyung Pun, whom he met in Korea, on an old banana plantation in the rainforests near the New South Wales/Queensland border. In between travel he spends his time pursuing noxious weeds, cultivating tropical fruit and brewing mango wine.

Tony Wheeler Tony Wheeler was born in England, but spent most of his younger years overseas due to his father's occupation with British Airways. Those years included a lengthy spell in Pakistan, a shorter period in the West Indies and all his high school years in the US. He returned to England to do a university degree in engineering, worked for a short time as an automotive design engineer, returned to university again and did an MBA then dropped out on the Asian overland trail with his wife Maureen. They've been travelling, writing and publishing guidebooks ever since having set up Conely Planet Publications in the mid-70s. In 1985 Tony and Maureen are temporarily living in the San Francisco bay area, establishing a Lonely Planet US office. Travel for the Wheelers is now considerably enlivened by their daughter Tashi and son Kieran, who have already made several Asia trips.

Mark Lightbody was born and grew up in Montreal. Educated there and in London, Ontario he holds a degree in journalism and has worked as a writer and editor. Mark has travelled in 45 countries on five continents, most extensively throughout all the Americas. Now a resident of Toronto, Mark first wrote Lonely Planet's guide to Canada and has recently worked on updating this book and the Lonely Planet guide to Papua New Guinea.

Producing this Book

Researching this guide was originally a two part operation. While Geoff Crowther covered Sarawak, Sabah and Brunei in north Borneo, Tony and Maureen Wheeler roamed around Singapore and up and down the Malay peninsula. For Tashi Wheeler, at that time seven months old, Malaysia was her first Asian jaunt. When it came to researching this second edition, however, both Geoff and Tony were tied up with other projects so Mark Lightbody stepped in and covered both the peninsula and north Borneo.

Final integration of Mark's new material and the previous book took place at Lonely Planet's Berkeley, California office. Special thanks to Elizabeth Kim for her assistance there. Thanks must also go to Tony Jenkins, whose delightful cartoons and sketches you can also see in *India – a travel survival kit*. To Murray D Bruce and Constance S Leap Bruce who wrote the section on national parks. And to all the workers at Lonely Planet in Melbourne, Australia, who typeset, drew maps, designed and put together this new edition.

Last, but as ever not least, a special thanks to 'our travellers' who took the time and energy to write to us from places large and small all over the region and tell us where we went wrong or where we could go better. Particular thanks to Dr Ann Faraday and Professor John Wren Lewis for their long and detailed letter, particularly for information on the 'coast to coast' routes across the peninsula. And to prolific writers Fabian Pedrazzini, Jan King and Tom Harriman.

Many others deserve thanks too. They are listed at the back of the book.

A Warning & a Request

Things change – prices go up, good places go bad, bad ones go bankrupt, nothing stays the same. So if you find things better, worse, cheaper, more expensive, recently opened or long ago closed please don't blame us but please do write and tell us. The letters we get from 'our' travellers out there on the road are some of the nicest things about doing these guides for a living. As usual the best letter writers will be rewarded with a free copy of the next edition (or any other Lonely Planet guide if you prefer).

Contents

Introduction

Malaysia, Singapore and Brunei are three independent South-East Asian nations offering the visitor a taste of Asia at its most accessible. In all of Asia only Japan has a higher per capita income than these countries so, as you might expect, they are relatively prosperous and forward looking. Transport facilities are good, accommodation standards are high, the food excellent (often amazingly good in fact) and for the visitor there are very few problems to be faced.

Yet despite these high standards these are not expensive countries – Singapore may be able to offer all the air-conditioned comforts your credit cards can handle and East Malaysia may at times be a little pricey due to its jungle-frontier situation, but in Peninsular Malaysia the costs can be absurdly cheap if you want them to be.

More important than simple ease of travel this region offers amazing variety both geographically and culturally. If you want beaches and tropical islands it's hard to beat the east coast of the peninsula. If you want mountains, parks and wildlife then you can climb Mt Kinabalu, explore the rivers of Sarawak or watch for wildlife in the huge Taman Negara (National Park) on the peninsula.

If you want city life then you can try the historic old port of Melaka, the easy going back streets of Georgetown in Penang or the modern-as-tomorrow city of Singapore. When it comes to people you've got Malays, Chinese, Indians and a whole host of indigenous tribes in Sabah and Sarawak. Last, but far from least, you've got a choice of food which alone brings people back to the region over and over again; there's no question in many people's minds that Singapore is deservedly the food capital of Asia.

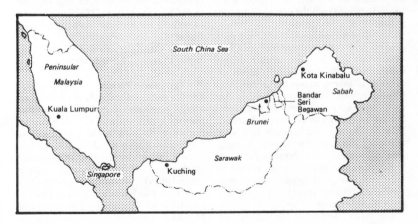

Facts about the Country

HISTORY

It is only since WW II that Malaysia, Singapore and Brunei have emerged as three separate independent countries. Prior to that they were all loosely amalgamated as a British colony, Sarawak excepted, and earlier still they might have been independent Malay kingdoms, or part of the greater Majapahit or Srivijaya empires of what is now Indonesia. In the dim mists of time it's possible that Malaysia was actually the home for the earliest homo sapiens in Asia. Discoveries have been made in the gigantic Niah Caves of Sarawak which indicate that stone age man was present there, and in other caves of north Borneo and the Malay peninsula, as long as 40,000 years ago.

Early Trade & Empires

Little is known about these stone age Malaysians, but around 10,000 years ago the aboriginal Malays, the Orang Asli, began to move down the peninsula from a probable starting point in south-west China. Remote settlements of Orang Asli can still be found in parts of Malaysia, but 4000 years ago they were already being supplanted by the Proto-Malays, ancestors of today's Malays, who at first settled the coastal regions, then moved inland. In the early centuries of the Christian era Malaya was known as far away as Europe. Ptolemy showed it on his early map with the label 'Golden Chersonese'. It spelt gold not only to the Romans for soon Indian and Chinese traders also arrived in search of that most valuable metal and Hindu mini-states sprung up along the great Malay rivers.

The Malay people were basically similar ethnically to the people of Sumatra, Java and even the Philippines and from time to time various South-East Asian empires extended their control over all or part of the Malay peninsula. Funan, a kingdom based in modern day Kampuchea, at one time controlled the northern part of the peninsula, but from the 7th century the great Sumatran based Srivijaya empire, with its capital in Palembang, held the whole area and even extended its rule up into Thailand.

In turn the Srivijayans fell to the Java based Majapahit empire, then in 1403 Paramesvara, a Sumatran prince, established himself at Melaka which soon became the most powerful city state in the region. At this time the spice trade from the Moluccas was beginning to develop and Melaka, with its strategic position on the straits which separate Sumatra from the Malay peninsula, was a familiar port for ships from the east and west.

In 1405 the Chinese Admiral Cheng Ho arrived in Melaka with greetings from the 'Son of Heaven' and, more important, the promise of protection from the encroaching Siamese to the north. With this support from China the power of Melaka extended to include most of the Malay peninsula. Cheng Ho brought something else to Melaka – the Islamic religion which also began to spread through Malaya.

The Portuguese Period

For the next century Melaka's power and wealth expanded to such an extent that the city became one of the wealthiest in the east. So wealthy in fact that the Portuguese began to take an over-active interest in the place and after a preliminary skirmish in 1509 Alfonse de Albuquerque arrived in 1511 with a fleet of 18 ships and overpowered Melaka's 20,000 defenders and their war elephants. The Sultan of Melaka fled south with his court to Johore where the Portuguese were unable to dislodge him. Thus Melaka came to be the centre of European power in the region while Johore grew to be the main Malay city state, along with other Malay centres at Brunei in north Borneo and Acheh in the north of Sumatra.

The Portuguese were to hold Melaka for over 100 years although they were never able to capitalise on the city's fabulous wealth and superb position. Portuguese trading power and strength was never great enough to take full advantage of the volume of trade that used to flow through Melaka but, more important, the Portuguese did not develop the complex pattern of influence and patronage upon which Melaka had based its power and control. Worse, the Portuguese reputation for narrow-mindedness and cruelty had preceded them and they gained few converts to Christianity and little support for their rule.

Thus the other Malay states were able to grow into the vacuum created by the Portuguese takeover of Melaka and while they squabbled and fought between themselves they also had the strength to make attacks on Melaka. Gradually Portuguese power declined and after long skirmishes with the Dutch, who supported the rulers of Johore, Melaka eventually fell, after a long and bitter siege, in 1641.

The Dutch Period

Like the Portuguese the Dutch were to rule Melaka for over a century but, also like the Portuguese, the Dutch failed to recognise that Melaka's greatest importance was as a centre for entrepot trade. To an even greater extent than their predecessors the Dutch tried to keep Melaka's trade totally to themselves and as a result Melaka continued to decline. Also the greatest Dutch interest was reserved for Batavia, modern day Jakarta, so Melaka was always the poor sister to the more important Javan port.

The British Arrive

Meanwhile the British were casting eyes at Malaya again. They had shown an interest in the area then decided to concentrate on their Indian possessions,

but in 1786 Captain Francis Light arrived at Penang and this time British intentions were firm ones. Light followed a free trade policy at Penang, a clear contrast to the monopolistic intentions of the Portuguese and then the Dutch in Melaka. As a result Penang soon became a thriving port and by 1800 the population of the island, virtually uninhabited when Light took over, had reached 10,000.

While Penang was a success story locally it did not meet the high expectations of the British East India Company and in 1795 the company also found itself controlling Melaka due to events in Europe. When Napoleon overran the Netherlands the British temporarily took control of first Melaka and later the other Dutch possessions in the region. In 1814, with Napoleon defeated, an agreement was reached on the return of these possessions and by 1818 Melaka and Java had been returned to Dutch control.

During the years of British rule, however, there had been a number of advocates for greater British power in the region – one of the most outspoken being Thomas Stamford Raffles. He had decided that Britain, not the Dutch, should be the major power in the region, but was unable to convince his superiors in London that this was a wise plan. In 1818, however, the re-establishment of Dutch power had caused sufficient worry to the company officials in Calcutta that Raffles was told to go ahead and establish a second British base further south than Penang. In early 1819 Raffles arrived in Singapore and decided this should be the place.

Raffles' Singapore

Over a thousand years earlier Singapore, then known as Temasek or 'Sea Town', had been a small outpost of the Srivijaya empire and around 1100 AD the place had been renamed Singapura or 'Lion City' by a visiting Sumatran prince who fancied he had seen a lion there. Later other Malay kings ruled the swampy island, but with the defeat of Singapura's last Sumatran prince, Iskandar Shah, in the mid-1300s Singapore sank into backwater oblivion.

Thus when Raffles arrived the population of the island consisted of little more than a few sea gypsies and some Chinese farmers. Raffles' first problem was to find somebody to buy the island from since his instructions were not to provoke any dispute with the Dutch and if anyone could lay claim to Singapore it would probably be a sultan who owed allegiance to the Dutch. Raffles turned up an uncommitted local ruler, announced that he was the ruling sultan and then contracted to pay him a yearly stipend for ownership of the island. Thus Singapore became the second British settlement in Malaya and the Dutch became highly annoyed.

Fortunately for Raffles communications were slow and by the time a few letters had crawled their way back and forth between Singapore, Calcutta, London and Amsterdam a new agreement had been hammered out between the British and Dutch. Bengkulu in Sumatra was transferred to the Dutch in exchange for Melaka. In 1826 Singapore, which by this time had a population already approaching 100,000, became part of the British Straits Settlement, governed from Bengal in India along with Melaka and Penang. The agreement with the Dutch had a further effect on the region – the Malay peninsula and Sumatra, so long connected by a common culture, religion and language and often politically connected as well, were now divided. Sumatra was clearly under Dutch control and Malaya was equally clearly destined to be ruled by the British.

The British Period

Despite British rule the straits continued to be a fairly frontier-like area. Piracy, long a popular activity, still thrived although the British eventually got around to cracking down on it. Curiously piracy has had a revival in the 1980s. A number of ships have been boarded and their safes ransacked or the crew robbed as they neared the islands around Singapore!

In Singapore and Malaysia the developments through the balance of the 19th century were chiefly economic ones, but in their wake they brought enormous changes to the racial make up of the region. There had been Chinese settlers in Malaya from the time of Cheng Ho's visit to Melaka in the early 1400s, but in the 1800s they began to flood in in much greater numbers. The main attraction was tin and at mining towns around Kuala Lumpur and Perak fortunes were quickly won and lost. In 1877 rubber plantations began to spring up all over the peninsula. Since the Malays were unwilling to work the long hard hours necessary to tap the rubber the British plantation owners brought in labourers from India. Thus by the turn of the century Malaya had a burgeoning economy, but also a vastly different racial mix than a century before. Whereas Malaya had been predominantly populated by Malays now it also had large groups of Indians and Chinese. Furthermore with the arrival of women settlers the labourers who had come there only to work now began to think of settling down and remaining.

As in India the British managed to bring more and more of the country under their control without having to fight for it or even totally govern it. Internal government was left up to the local sultans while the British provided 'advisers' and managed external affairs. In 1867 the Straits Settlements became a crown colony and was no longer governed from India. In 1895 Perak, Selangor, Negri Sembilan and Pahang became the Federated Malay States. Johore refused to join the federation while Kelantan, Trengganu, Perlis and Kedah were still controlled by the Thais until 1909.

Meanwhile in Borneo

Across in north Borneo events sometimes read more like Victorian melodrama than hard fact. In 1838 James Brooke, a British adventurer, arrived in Borneo with his armed sloop to find the Brunei aristocracy facing rebellion from the dissatisfied inland tribes. He quelled the rebellion and in gratitude was given power over part of what is today Sarawak. Appointing himself 'Rajah Brooke' he successfully cooled down the fractious tribes, suppressed head hunting, eliminated the dreaded Borneo pirates and founded a personal dynasty that was to last for over a hundred years. The Brooke family of 'White Rajahs' gradually brought more and more of Borneo under their power until the Japanese arrived in WW II.

The development of British power in Sabah was much more prosaic. Once part of the great Brunei empire, Sabah came under the influence of the British North Borneo Company after centuries of being avoided due to its unpleasant pirates. At one time Kota Kinabalu was known as Api Api, 'Fire, Fire', from the pirates' tiresome habit of repeatedly burning it down. Eventually in 1888 the whole North Borneo coast was brought under British protection although Mat Salleh, a Sabah rebel, held out against British power until his death in 1900.

World War II

From the turn of the century until WW II Malaya became steadily more prosperous although the peninsula continued to forge ahead of the north Borneo states. The various peninsula states came more and more under British influence, but more and more Chinese and Indian immigrants flooded into the country and eventually outnumbered the indigenous Malays. By the time WW II broke out in Europe Malaya supplied nearly 40% of the world's rubber and 60% of its tin.

When the war arrived in Malaya its impact was sudden and devastating. A few hours before the first Japanese aircraft was sighted over Pearl Harbor the Japanese landed at Kota Bahru in the north of Malaya and started their lightning dash down the peninsula. British confidence that they were more than a match for the Japanese soon proved to be

sadly misplaced and it took the Japanese little over a month to take Kuala Lumpur and a month after that they were at the doors of Singapore. On 15 February 1942 Singapore fell and the remaining British inhabitants who had not managed to escape were to spend the rest of the war in prison camps. North Borneo had fallen to the Japanese with even greater speed.

The Japanese were unable to form a cohesive policy in Malaya since there was not a well organised Malay independence movement which they could harness to their goals. Furthermore many Chinese were bitterly opposed to the Japanese who had invaded China in the 1930s. Remnants of the British forces continued a guerilla struggle against the Japanese throughout the war and the predominantly Chinese communist Malayan People's Anti-Japanese Army also continued the struggle against the Japanese.

Post War & the Emergency

Following the sudden end of WW II Britain was faced with reorganising its position in Malaya. There had not been the same concerted push towards independence which India had been through in the inter-war years so while independence and the end of colonial rule was clearly a long term programme, in the short term British rule was likely to continue.

At first the plan was to take over the rule of Sabah, Sarawak and Brunei, to form the Malay states into a Malay Union and to rule Singapore as a crown colony. This plan faced one major obstacle – all prior British plans for Malaya had been based on the premise that the country was Malayan even though, with the increasing percentage of the population of either of Indian or Chinese descent, this became less and less realistic. Through WW II the population of Indians and Chinese had become much more settled than before and now there was even less likelihood of them returning to their 'homelands'. British acceptance of this fact of life naturally provoked strong Malay opposition.

Faced with these difficulties the British soon had an even greater problem to grapple with – the Emergency. In 1948 the Malaysian Communist Party, which had fought against the Japanese throughout the war, decided the time had come to end British colonial rule and launched a guerrilla struggle which was to continue for 12 years. Although there are still sporadic outbreaks of communist violence the threat was eventually declared over in 1960. In part this was because the communists were never able to gain a broad spectrum of support. They were always predominantly a Chinese grouping and while the Malays might have wanted independence from Britain they certainly did not want rule by the Chinese. Nor were all Chinese in favour of the party, it was mainly an uprising of the peasantry and lower classes.

Independence

In 1955 Britain agreed that Malaya would become fully independent within two years, but in the same year Singapore was torn by strikes, riots and demonstrations over low wages, terrible housing conditions, unemployment and education. Nevertheless in 1956 Britain also agreed that Singapore should have internal self government by 1959. Malaya duly achieved independence (merdeka) in 1957 despite unsuccessful meetings with Chin Peng, leader of the communist forces, in an attempt to end the now merely smouldering Emergency. Tunku Abdul Rahman was the leader of the new nation which came into existence with remarkably few problems.

In Singapore things went nowhere near as smoothly and politics became increasingly radicalised. The election in 1959 swept Lee Kuan Yew's People's Action Part (PAP) into power, but they faced a whole series of major problems. When the Federation of Malaya was formed in 1948 the Malay leaders were strongly opposed to including Singapore because this would

have tipped the racial balance from a Malay majority to a Chinese one. Furthermore while politics in Malaya were orderly, upper class and gentlemanly, in Singapore they were anything but.

Nevertheless to Singapore merger with Malaya seemed to be the only answer to high unemployment, a soaring birthrate and the loss of its traditional trading role with the growth of independent South-East Asian nations. Malaya was none too keen to inherit this little parcel of problems, but when it seemed possible that the moderate PAP party might be toppled by its own left wing the thought of a moderate Singapore within Malaysia became less off-putting than the thought of a communist Singapore outside it. Accordingly in 1961 Tunku Abdul Rahman agreed to work towards the creation of Malaysia which would include Singapore. To balance the addition of Singapore, discussion also commenced on adding Sarawak, Sabah and Brunei to the union. This proposal was welcomed by Britain who had been facing the problem of exactly what to do with their north Borneo possessions.

Confrontation

Accordingly in 1963 Malaysia came into existence although at the last moment Brunei, afraid of losing its oil wealth, refused to join. No sooner had Malaysia been created than problems arose. First of all the Philippines laid claim to Sabah, which had been known as North Borneo prior to the union. More seriously Indonesia laid claim to the whole place and Sukarno, now in the final phase of his megalomania, commenced his ill-starred 'Confrontation'. Indonesian guerrilla forces crossed the borders from Kalimantan (Indonesian south Borneo) into Sabah and Sarawak and landings were made in Peninsular Malaysia and even in Singapore. British troops, having finally quelled the Emergency only four years earlier, now found themselves back in the jungle once again.

Singapore Departs

At the same time relations between Malaya and Singapore soured almost as soon as Malaysia was formed. The ogre of Chinese domination reared its ugly head, and Singapore refused to extend the privileged position held by Malays in Malaya to Malays in Singapore. In August 1965, exactly two years after Malaysia was created, Singapore was kicked out.

Fortunately for Singapore the breathing space had been a valuable one. Lee Kuan Yew had tamed the PAP's left wing and Singapore radicals who spoke out against his policies soon found themselves off the streets indefinitely. The economy had started to grow and with Sukarno's dramatic fall from power and the end of Confrontation Singapore was soon able to plot a path towards prosperity.

Lee Kuan Yew went all out on his campaign to turn Singapore into a tough, resilient country where enterprise and hard work would win the day. It worked – by the late '70s Singapore, a country devoid of natural resources and with massive problems of unemployment and squalid living conditions, had become the second most prosperous country in Asia with negative unemployment and a much praised government housing plan. Nor was Malaysia doing so badly – abundant natural resources, self-sufficiency in oil and a reasonable population level all helped to give Malaysia economic prospects not far behind Singapore.

Problems in Malaysia

By 1968 the PAP in Singapore had changed their precarious electoral position at the beginning of the decade so dramatically that they now held every single seat in the Singapore parliament! When a solitary opposition representative was elected in 1981 it made headlines. Despite its economic stability, things were not so smooth politically in Malaysia. One of the government's major policies had been to right the imbalance between various elements of the population.

In 1969 only 1.5% of company assets in Malaysia were owned by Malays and per capita income amongst Malays was less than 50% of that of non-Malays. Attempts to unify Malaysia by making Bahasa Malay the one national language also created resentment amongst the non-Malays as did the privileges Malays had in land ownership, business licences, educational opportunities and government positions. In 1969 violent inter-communal riots broke out, particularly in Kuala Lumpur, and hundreds of people were killed.

Following these riots the government moved to improve the position of Malays in Malaysia with much greater speed. The title *bumiputra* or 'sons of the soil' was created to define the indigenous Malay people; this meant not only Malays, but also the aboriginal inhabitants and the indigenous peoples of Sarawak and Sabah. New guidelines were instituted stipulating how much of a company's shares must be held by *bumiputras* and in other ways enforcing a Malay share in the nation's wealth.

Although many Chinese realised that Malaysia could never attain real stability without an equitable distribution of the country's wealth there was also much resentment and many talented people either left the country or simply withdrew their abilities and capital. Fortunately Malaysia's natural wealth has enabled it to absorb these inefficiencies, but the problems of bringing the Malays to an equal position in the nation, economically as well as politically, remains a thorny one. Travellers in Malaysia will have ample opportunity to discuss the problem – either with expats or with Malaysians, when they know there is no possibility of them being overheard.

Malay, Malays & Malaysia

Malays are the indigenous people of Malaysia although they are not the original inhabitants. Malaya is the old name for the country which, prior to 1963, consisted only of peninsular

Malaya. With the amalgamation of Malaya, Sarawak and Sabah the title Malaysia was coined for the new nation and the peninsula is now referred to as Peninsular Malaysia while Sarawak and Sabah is referred to as East Malaysia.

PEOPLE

The populations of Singapore and Malaysia are essentially the same peoples – Malays, Chinese, Indian, indigenous orang asli and the various tribes of Sarawak and Sabah. The Malays are the majority indigenous people of the region although they were preceded here by aboriginal people, small pockets of whom still survive. The Malays are Muslim and despite major changes in the last decades are still to some extent 'country' rather than 'city' people.

The Chinese are later arrivals. Although some have been here since the time of Admiral Cheng Ho's visit to Melaka in 1403, the vast majority of the region's Chinese settlers have arrived since the beginning of the 19th century. The biggest group of Chinese are Hokkiens who comprise 40% of the population of Singapore. Another 20% are Teochew's and slightly less than that percentage, Cantonese. The remainders are Hakkas, Hainanese and other groups. Although all Chinese use a similar script the dialects can be quite different and a Hokkien and a Hakka speaker may well have to resort to English to communicate!

The region's Indian population arrived later still and in a more organised fashion. Whereas the Chinese flooded in of their own volition the Indians were mainly brought in to provide plantation labour for the British colonists. In Singapore approximately 60% of the Indian population are Tamils and a further 20% are Malayalis from the other southern state of Kerala. The remainder include Kashmiris, Sikhs, Punjabis and Bengalis.

There are still small scattered groups of orang asli, 'original men', in peninsular Malaysia. The indigenous people of Sarawak and Sabah are much greater in number, approaching one million in total. They include Ibans and Land Dyaks in Sarawak and the Muruts of Sabah – all of whom are noted for the longhouses they live in. In this form of communal living a whole village effectively shares one 'long house' with individual houses opening out onto the shared verandah. The Kadazan of Sabah and the Punan of Sarawak are other groups. Of course there are also other minority groupings including expatriate westerners, Japanese, Filipinos and Sri Lankans.

GEOGRAPHY

Malaysia, Singapore and Brunei consist of two distinct parts. Peninsular Malaysia is the long finger of land extending down from Asia as if pointing towards Indonesia and Australia. Singapore is the island at the very tip of this peninsula. Much of the peninsula is covered by dense jungle, particularly in its northern half where there are also high mountains, and the central area is very lightly populated. While on the western side of the peninsula there is a long fertile plain running down to the sea, the mountains descend more steeply on the eastern side where there are also many more beaches.

The other part of the region, making up more than 50% by area, is East Malaysia – the northern part of the island of Borneo. The larger, southern part is the Indonesian state of Kalimantan. East Malaysia is divided between Sarawak and Sabah with Brunei a small enclave between them. Both parts are covered by dense jungle with many large river systems, particularly in Sarawak. Mt Kinabalu in Sabah is the highest mountain in South-East Asia; indeed it is the highest mountain from Papua New Guinea to the Himalaya.

RELIGIONS

Malaysia and Singapore have religions in as great a variety as they have races. Although Islam is the state religion of Malaysia, freedom of religion is guaranteed. The Malays are almost all Muslims and there are also Muslims amongst the Indian population. The Chinese predominantly follow their peculiar blend of Confucianism and Buddhism although there are also small pockets of pure Buddhism, particularly close to the Thai border. The majority of the region's Indian population is from the south and are Hindu. Although Christianity has made no great inroads into Peninsular Malaysia it has had a much greater impact upon Sarawak and Sabah where many of the indigenous people have converted to Christianity.

FESTIVALS & HOLIDAYS

With so many cultures and religions there is a quite amazing number of occasions to celebrate in Malaysia and Singapore. Although some of them have a fixed date each year, the Hindus, Muslims and Chinese all follow a lunar calendar which results in the dates for many events varying each year. In particular Muslim festivals can change enormously.

The major Muslim events each year are connected with Ramadan during the 30 days of which Muslims cannot eat or drink from sunrise to sunset. Fifteen days before the commencement of Ramadan the souls of the dead are supposed to visit their homes on Nisfu Night. During Ramadan Lailatul Qadar, the 'Night of Grandeur', celebrates the arrival of the Koran on earth from heaven before its revelation by Mohammed. A Koran reading competition is held in Kuala Lumpur (and extensively televised) during Ramadan. Hari Raya Puasa marks the end of the month-long fast with three days of joyful celebration. This is the major holiday of the Muslim calendar and it can be difficult to find accommodation in Malaysia, particularly on the east coast.

January 14

Thai Pongal A Hindu harvest festival marking the beginning of the Hindu month of Thai, the luckiest month of the year.

January-February

Chinese New Year Dragon dances and pedestrian parades mark the start of the new year. Families hold open house, children receive ang pows (money in red packets), businesses traditionally clear their debts and everybody wishes you a Kong Hee Fatt Choy (a happy & prosperous new year).

January-February

Birthday of Chor Soo Kong Six days after the new year the number of snakes at Penang's snake temple, dedicated to Chor Soo Kong, is supposed to be the greatest.

January-February

Birthday of the Jade Emperor Nine days after the new year a Chinese festival honours Yu Huang, the Supreme Ruler of Heaven, with offerings at temples.

January-February

Ban Hood Huat Hoay A 12-day celebration for the Day of Ten Thousand Buddhas is held at the Kek Lok Si Temple in Penang.

January-February

Chap Goh Meh On the 15th day after Chinese New Year the celebrations officially end.

January-February

Chingay In Singapore and Johore Bahru processions of Chinese flag bearers, balancing bamboo flag poles six to 12 metres long, can be seen on the 22nd day after the new year.

January-February

Thaipusam One of the most dramatic Hindu festivals in which devotees honour Lord Subramaniam with acts of amazing masochism. In Singapore they march in a procession to the Chettiar Temple carrying 'kavadis', heavy metal frames decorated with peacock feathers, fruit and flowers. The kavadis are hung from their bodies with metal hooks and spikes driven into the flesh. Other devotees pierce their cheeks and tongues with metal skewers or walk on sandals of nails. Along the procession route the kavadi carriers dance to the drum beat while spectators urge them on with shouts of 'Vel, Vel'. In the evening the procession continues with an image of Subramaniam in a temple car.

In Penang Thaipusam is celebrated at the Waterfall Temple; in KL at the Batu Caves. This festival is now banned in India.

late February
Kwong Teck Sun Ong's Birthday Celebration of the birthday of a child deity at the Chinese temple in Kuching.

March-April
Tua Peck Kong Paper money and paper models of useful things to have with you in the after life are burnt at the Sia Sen Temple in Kuching.

March-April
Easter On Palm Sunday a candlelight procession is held at St Peter's in Melaka. Good Friday and Easter Monday also witness colourful celebrations at St Peter's and other Melaka churches and in the Church of St Joseph in Singapore.

March-April
Panguni Uttiram On the full moon day of the Tamil month of Panguni, the marriage of Shiva to Shakti and of Lord Subramaniam to Theivani is celebrated.

March-April
Birthday of the Goddess of Mercy Offerings are made to the very popular Kuan Yin at her temples in Penang, Kuala Lumpur and Singapore.

March-April
Cheng Beng On All Soul's Day Chinese traditionally visit the tombs of their ancestors to clean and repair them and make offerings.

March-April
Sri Rama Navami A nine day festival held by the Brahman caste to honour the Hindu hero of the Ramayana, Sri Rama.

March-April
Birthday of the Monkey God The birthday of T'se Tien Tai Seng Yeh is celebrated twice a year. In Singapore mediums pierce their cheeks and tongues with skewers and go into a trance during which they write special charms in blood.

March-April
Birthday of the Saint of the Poor Kong Teck Choon Ong is honoured with a procession from the White Cloud Temple on Ganges Avenue in Singapore.

April-May
Songkran Festival A traditional Thai Buddhist new year in which Buddha images are bathed.

April-May
Chithirai Vishu Start of the Hindu new year.

April-May
Puja Pantai A large three-day beach festival held five km south of Kuala Trengganu.

April-May
Birthday of the Queen of Heaven Ma Cho Po, the Queen of Heaven and Goddess of the Sea, is honoured at her temples.

April-May
Vesak Day Buddha's birth, enlightenment and death are celebrated by

various events including the release of caged birds to symbolise the setting free of captive souls.

early May
Sipitang Tamu Besar Annual market celebration at Sipitang near Beaufort in Sabah. Blowpipe competitions feature among the events.

May
Start of the turtle season; from now through September giant turtles come ashore along the beach at Rantau Abang on the east coast of the peninsula each night to lay their eggs.

May 10-11
Kadazan Harvest Festival A thanksgiving harvest festival by the Kadazan farmers of Sabah, marked by the sumazau Kadazan dance.

May 30-31
Kota Belud Tamu Besar Bajau horsemen feature in this annual market festival at Kota Belud, near Kota Kinabalu in Sabah.

May-June
Birthday of the Third Prince The child-god is honoured with a procession from the Taoist temple dedicated to him in Singapore – it's near the junction of Clarke St and North Boat Quay.

June 1-2
Gawai Dayak Annual Sarawak festival of the Dayaks to mark the end of the rice season. War dances, cockfights and blowpipe events all take place.

June 4
Birthday of the Yang di Pertuang Agong Celebration of the official birthday of Malaysia's Supreme Head of State.

June 29
Festa de San Pedro Christian celebration in honour of the patron saint of fishermen, particularly celebrated by the Eurasian-Portuguese community of Melaka.

June
Birthday of the God of War Kuan Ti, who has the ability to avert war and protect people during a war, is honoured on his birthday.

June-August
Dragon Boat Festival Commemorating the death by drowning of a Chinese saint this festival is celebrated with boat races in Singapore.

June-September
Isra Dan Mi'Raj A Muslim holiday in mosques and homes to celebrate the prophet's ascension.

July 1
Keningau Tamu Besar Market festival at Keningau in Sabah with buffalo races, blowpipe competitions and other events.

July 29
Tuaran Tamu Besar Tuaran, only 35 km from Kota Kinabalu, celebrates its annual market festival with boat races as well as Bajau horsemen and other events.

late July
Lumut Sea Carnival At Lumut, the port for Pangkor Island, boat races, swimming races and many other events are held.

July
Birthday of Kuan Yin The Goddess of Mercy has another birthday!

July-August
Sri Krishna Jayanti A 10-day Hindu festival celebrating events in Krishna's life, highlighted on the day eight by his birthday. The Laxmi Narayan Temple in Kuala Lumpur is a focal point.

July-September
Market Festival Month long festival in the markets of Singapore with wayangs (street operas).

August 9
Singapore National Day A series of military and civilian processions and an evening firework display celebrate Singapore's independence in 1965.

August 31
National Day Hari Kebangsaan Malaysia celebrates Malaysia's independence with events all over the country, but particularly in Kuala Lumpur where there are parades and a variety of performances in the Lake Gardens.

August 31
Beaufort Tamu Besar Another annual market festival in Sabah.

August
Festival of the Seven Sisters Chinese girls pray to the Weaving Maid for good husbands.

August
Festival of the Hungry Ghosts The souls of the dead are released for one day of feasting and entertainment on earth. Chinese operas and other events are laid on for them and food is put out, which the ghosts eat the spirit of but thoughtfully leave the substance for mortal celebrants.

August-September
Vinayagar Chathuri During the Tamil month of Avani prayers are offered to Vinayagar, another name for the extremely popular elephant-headed god Ganesh.

September 1-22
Feast of Santa Cruz A month long pilgrimage season at the Church of Santa Cruz at Malim, Melaka.

September 15-20
Papar Tamu Besar Annual market festival in an area of Sabah renowned for its beautiful Kadazan girls.

September
Moon Cake Festival The overthrow of the Mongol warlords in ancient China is celebrated by eating moon cakes and lighting colourful paper lanterns. Moon cakes are made with bean paste, lotus seeds and sometimes a duck egg.

September-October
Thimithi – Fire Walking Ceremony Hindu devotees prove their belief by walking across glowing coals at the Gajah Berang temple in Melaka or the Sri Mariamman Temple in Singapore.

September-October
Navarathri In the Tamil month of Purattasi the Hindu festival of 'Nine Nights' is dedicated to the wives of Shiva, Vishnu and Brahma. Young girls are dressed as the goddess Kali. The Chettiar Temple in Singapore is a centre of activities.

September-October
Festival of the Nine Emperor Gods Nine days of Chinese operas, processions and other events honour the nine emperor gods. At the Kau Ong Yah temple in KL a fire walking ceremony is held on the evening of the ninth day.

September-November
Pilgrimage to Kusu Island Tua Pek Kong, the God of Prosperity, is honoured by Taoists in Singapore by making a pilgrimage to the shrine on Kusu Island.

October 1-31
Puja Ketek Offerings are brought to Buddhist shrines or keteks in the state of Kelantan. Traditional dances are often performed.

October 1-31
Menggatal Tamu Besar Another Sabah
market festival.

October 7
Universal Children's Day A rally for
children in Kuala Lumpur.

mid-October
Kudat Tamu Besar And another Sabah
market festival.

October-November
Kantha Shashithi Subramaniam, a
great fighter against the forces of evil,
is honoured during the Hindu month of
Aipasi.

October-November
Deepavali Later in the same month
Rama's victory over the demon King
Ravana is celebrated with the 'Festival
of Lights' where tiny oil lamps are lit
outside Hindu homes.

October-November
Birthday of Kuan Yin The birthday of
the popular Goddess of Mercy is
celebrated yet again.

October-November
Kartikai Deepam Huge bonfires are lit
to commemorate Shiva's appearance
as a pillar of fire following an argument
with Vishnu and Brahma. The Thanday-
uthapani Temple in Muar is a major
site for this festival.

November 22
Guru Nanak's Birthday Celebration of
the birthday in 1496 of the founder of
the Sikh religion.

December
Pesta Pulau Penang Month long
carnival on Penang Island featuring
many water events including dragon
boat races towards the end of the
festival.

December
Winter Solstice Festival Chinese festival
to offer thanks for a good harvest.

December 25
Christmas

LANGUAGE
You can get along quite happily with
English throughout Malaysia and Singapore.
Although it is not the official language in
either country it is still the linking
language between the various populations.
When a Tamil wants to speak to a Chinese
or a Chinese to a Malay it's likely to be
English they'll use. Officially Bahasa
Malay or 'bahasa' is the language in both
countries. In Malaysia the government is
trying to make that edict a reality, but in
Singapore only lip service is paid to it.
There the everyday languages are either
English or one of the Chinese dialects like
Hakka or Hokkien. The government is,
however, waging a campaign to persuade
people to speak Mandarin, the main non-
dialectal Chinese language. The majority
of the region's Indians speak Tamil
although there are also groups who speak
Malayalam, Hindi or other Indian languages.

Bahasa is, as near as makes no difference, the same as Indonesian. So if you
are also visiting that country you'll find a
little knowledge worthwhile since English
is much less widely spoken there. Equally
important picking up enough bahasa to
get by on is remarkably easy and also good
fun. Bahasa is, at least in its most basic
form, very simple. There are no tense
changes for example – you just add *suda*
(already) to make anything past, or by
using words such as yesterday or tomorrow
indicate the tense to be used. Many nouns
are pluralised simply by saying them twice
– thus *buku* is 'book', *buku buku* is 'books'.
Or *anak* is 'child', *anak anak* is 'children'.
They are often written *buku 2* or *anak 2*.

The everyday street language is often
referred to as *pasar* or market language.
Other language simplifications include
the omission of the articles 'the', 'a' or 'an'.

Thus you just say *buku baik* rather than "a good book' or 'the good book'. The verb 'to be' is also omitted so again it would be *buku baik* rather than 'the book is good'. Bahasa is also a very musical and evocative language – 'the sun', for example, is *mata hari* or 'the eye of the day'!

Indonesia Phrasebook is a handy introduction to bahasa. It's the first Lonely Planet 'language survival kit' and if you can't find a copy in bookshops you can order it directly from Lonely Planet.

As in India many Malay terms find their way into everyday English. You'll often read in the papers or see ads with the word *bumiputra*, which literally means 'sons of the soil' but is used to specify that the job or whatever is open only to Malay-Malays not Indian-Malays or Chinese-Malays. Papers occasionally complain about *jaga keretas* – they're people who operate car parking rackets; pay them to 'protect' your car while it's parked or you'll wish you had. Or you may hear of a couple being accused of *khalwat* – literally 'close proximity' and something unmarried Muslims should not be suspected of!

Civilities

thank you (very much)
  terima kasih (banyak)
please
  silakan
good morning
  selamat pagi
good day
  selamat siang
goodbye (to person staying)
  selamat tinggal
goodbye (to person going)
  selamat jalan
good afternoon/evening
  selamat sore
good night
  selamat malam
sorry
  ma'af
excuse me
  permisi

how are you?
  apa khabar?

Questions
what is this?
  apa ini?
how much (money)?
  berapa (harga)?
expensive
  mahal
what is your name?
  siapa nama saudara?
my name is . . .
  nama saya . . .
how many kilometres?
  berapa kilometre?
where is/which way?
  dimana ada/kemana?

Travelling

ticket	*tikit*
ticket window	*tempat tikit*
bus	*bus*
train	*kereta-api*
ship	*kapal*
town	*pekan*
city	*negri*

Numbers

1 – *satu*
2 – *dua*
3 – *tiga*
4 – *empat*
5 – *lima*
6 – *enam*
7 – *tujuh*
8 – *delapan*
9 – *sembilan*
10 – *sepuluh*
11 – *sebelas*
12 – *duablas*
20 – *duapuluh*
21 – *duapuluh satu*
30 – *tigapuluh*
53 – *limapuluh tiga*
100 – *seratus*
1000 – *seribu*
1/2 – *setengah (say 'stinger')*

Time

when?	*kapan?*
tomorrow/yesterday	*besok/semalam*
week/year	*minggu/tahun*
hour	*pukul*
what time	*pukul berapa?*
how long?	*berapa pukul?*
7 o'clock	*pukul tujuh*

Days of the Week

Monday	*Hari Senen*
Tuesday	*Hari Selasa*
Wednesday	*Hari Rabu*
Thursday	*Hari Kamis*
Friday	*Hari Jum'at*
Saturday	*Hari Sabtu*
Sunday	*Hari Minggu*

Useful Words & Phrases

I want to go to ...	*saya mau ke ...*
Bank	*bank*
Street	*jalan*
Post Office	*pejabat pos*
Immigration	*immigrasi*
How much for ...	*berapa harga*
one night?	*satu malam*
one person?	*satu orang*
sleep	*tidur*
bed	*tempat tidur*
room	*bilik*
bathroom	*bilik mandi*
toilet	*WC ('way say')*
soap	*sabun*
I don't understand	*saya tidak mengerti*
this/that	*ini/itu*
big/small	*besar/kechil*
here	*disini*
stop	*berhenti*
another	*satu lagi*
no, not, negative	*tidak*
shop	*toko, kedai*
open/closed	*buka/tutup*
see	*lihat*
good, very nice	*bagus* (+ big smile)

no good	*tidak baik*
alright, good, fine	*baik*
finished	*habis*
dirty	*kotor*

Food – makan

fried rice	*nasi goreng*
boiled rice	*nasi putih*
rice with odds 'n ends	*nasi campur*
fried noodles	*mee goreng*
noodle soup	*mee kuah*
soup	*soup*
fried vegetables	*cap cai*
with crispy noodles	*tami*
sweet 'n sour omelette	*fu yung hai*
fish	*ikan*
chicken	*ayam*
egg	*telur*
pork	*babi*
frog	*kodok*
crab	*kepiting*
beef	*daging lembu*
prawns	*udang*
potatoes	*kentang*
vegetables	*sayur*

Drink – minum

drinking water	*air minum*
orange juice	*air jeruk*
coffee	*kopi*
sweet tea	*teh manis*
plain tea	*teh-O*
milk	*susu*
cordial	*stroop*

additions

butter	*mentega*
sugar	*gula*
salt	*garam*
ice	*air batu*
hot peppers	*sambel*

description

sweet	*manis*
no sugar	*pahat*
hot hot	*panas*
hot spicy	*pedas*
cold	*sejoh*
delicious	*enak*
special, usually means an egg on top	*istemiwa*

Finally for vegetarians *tidak mahu ikan, ayam, daging* means 'I do not want fish, chicken or meat'.

NATIONAL PARKS

Malaysia, Singapore and Brunei are part of the region possessing the most ancient rain forests in the world, having remained virtually unchanged for many millions of years. Particularly in Malaysia we can see the entire spectrum – from the extensive, lowland rain forest tracts, to the summits of several mountainous areas (Mt Kinabalu in Sabah is the highest mountain between the Himalaya and New Guinea at 4101 metres). West Malaysia sits at the centre of what has evolved into the most complex, diverse animal and plant communities ever known. Situated along the north of the great island of Borneo, East Malaysia and Brunei are more on the periphery of this tropical lushness, but it has not missed much of this diversity.

It is the remarkable climatic stability of this region which has made its forests such a major focal point of scientific interest for many years. Within these vast jungles nature has run rampant for so long that just about every type of bizarre animal or plant known today has survived somewhere here. In fact, scientists are still far from knowing even a significant percentage of the mysteries concealed in these forests. Regrettably, the focal point has shifted to one of concern to understand this living laboratory before it is irretrievably consumed by uncontrolled development and inadequate conservation measures.

In Peninsular Malaysia alone there are over 8000 species of flowering plants, including 2000 trees, 800 orchids and 200 palms. Here is found the world's tallest tropical tree species, the Tualang, reaching to a height of 80 metres, with a base diameter of over three metres. The *Rafflesia* is the world's largest flower measuring up to one metre across and weighing up to nine kg.

There are over 200 species of mammals, 450 of birds, 250 of reptiles (including 100 snakes, 14 tortoises and turtles and three crocodiles), 90 frogs, and 150,000 insects (including the giant birdwing butterflies and the Atlas Moth). There are snakes, lizards and frogs which can 'fly', spiders that eat birds, giant (as well as flying) squirrels, and many smaller creatures which have 'giant' versions. Even the leeches can seem huge after a day on some of the jungle trails!

Mammals include elephants, rhinos (very rare now), tapirs, tigers, leopards, honey bears, several kinds of deer, seladang (forest cattle), various gibbons and monkeys (including in Borneo the orang utan and the bizarre proboscis monkey in which the male has a huge, pendulous nose), scaly anteaters (pangolins) and porcupines, to name a few.

The birdlife features spectacular pheasants, hornbills (including the rare helmeted hornbill, prized for its 'ivory' – actually the base of its 'horn' or casque), and many groups of colourful birds, such as kingfishers, sunbirds, pittas, woodpeckers, trogons and barbets. Snakes include cobras, notably the spitting cobra, which shoots venom into the eyes of its prey, vipers (the kind seen in snake temples), pythons (including the reticulated python, the world's longest snake, with some growing over 10 metres), and colourful tree snakes (most are harmless to man).

The orang asli (original people) still living in the forests survive in scattered groups. They are allowed to hunt in protected areas, such as parts of Taman Negara, as long as they only practise traditional hunting methods, such as the blowgun, with darts poisoned by the sap of the ipoh tree, a relative of the South American curare.

The British had established the first national park, in Malaysia, in 1938, which is now included in Taman Negara, Malaysia's major (and Peninsular Malaysia's only) national park. Its future is still not secured as sections are threatened by various development plans. East Malaysia has several national parks, forming a valuable, but still inadequate, network. Singapore contains several nature reserves, particularly for the protection of water catchment areas, while Brunei is in the stage of developing a protected areas system.

The greatest concern today is to see more areas protected in Peninsular Malaysia, because the diversity of the flora and fauna is the richest, containing much that does not extend to Borneo. Many areas have been proposed here for protection, with the most important area being the lowland forests of Endau-Rompin (perhaps the last refuge for the Sumatran rhinoceros, photographed in the wild only in December 1983), straddling the borders of Pahang and Johore. Today we can see an increase in public awareness of these and other environmental problems. In the 1970s the region of Gunung Mulu, in east Sarawak, was the centre of what became the most intensively studied tropical forest area in the world, leading to the establishment of a national park there. Visitor facilities, however, are still underdeveloped.

For those who wish to experience the primeval world of the ancient rain forests, Taman Negara offers a spectacular introduction, but there are other places which can be visited in Peninsular Malaysia, and a visit to East Malaysia is recommended, if only to see (and perhaps climb) Mt Kinabalu. Details are provided here for the main national parks and several other places.

Accommodation is not a problem when visiting most national parks, and various categories, from hostel to chalet, are available. For arrangements in Peninsular Malaysia contact the Wildlife & National Parks Department (tel 03-941056/941272), Block K20, Government Offices Building, Jalan Duta, Kuala Lumpur by a visit or letter to arrange your dates and cover fees. Best times: June through September (east coast, including Taman Negara); October through March (west coast).

In Sabah contact the National Park Office (tel 211585), Box 626, Kota Kinabalu, and in Sarawak contact the National Parks & Wildlife Office (tel 24474), Jalan Gertak, Kuching. It is always advisable to settle all arrangements and fees in advance. Best time is April through October. Basic and other information is available in all areas, and may be found in tourist offices also.

Taman Negara

A scenic region of forested plateau, hills and mountains covering 434,340 hectares, the national park ranges from 120 to 2150 metres (the summit of Gunung Tahan, the highest mountain in Peninsular Malaysia). It is traversed by several rivers, and of these, the Tembeling provides access to the park headquarters. From Kuala Lumpur take a bus or taxi to Kuala Tembeling via Jerantut. Here you meet the park boat for the 60 km trip into the park, taking three to four hours. Around the headquarters are several trails, and a number of observation hides can be visited. For the adventurous, it's a nine-day return trip to Gunung Tahan; otherwise there is much to do walking the trails, watching at the hides, or arranging a river trip.

Templar Park

This park of 1214 hectares was originally established as a botanical reserve in 1955, but is now a fully protected area, about 30 minutes from Kuala Lumpur. Signs of former tin-mining operations can be seen but today it is a popular place for a day trip. The dominant feature of the area is the 305-metre limestone hill Bukit Takun. The main trail to the summit is the centre of activity for many visitors and offers good views. There are many caves here, too, with little known about them. A good place to go if you're contemplating Kinabalu. It is reached on the Rawang road, turning off at the 13th milestone. The road forks ahead, with a right turn indicating the main Templar Park area, while Bukit Takun is straight ahead. Also near here are the Kancing Falls and Serendah Forest Reserve.

Bukit Lagong Forest Reserve

This 607 hectare reserve, close to Kuala Lumpur, includes a Forest Research Institute. There are several attractions for visitors, including a picnic area near a waterfall, a small museum and an arboretum. The 300 metre peak of Bukit Lagong can be climbed on a good trail through undisturbed forest (about two hours up). A visit may be arranged by contacting the Director, Forest Research Institute, Kepong, Selangor. (A guide is needed for Bukit Lagong.)

Bukit Timah Nature Reserve

A piece of primary forest measuring 75 hectares, the nature reserve is located at the south-west fringe of the catchment area in Singapore. In land-short Singapore this and other small reserves are being increasingly used for public recreation. Facilities are much improved and access is easy to organise through the island's efficient bus services.

Bako National Park

A small park of 2550 hectares in west Sarawak, the Bako National Park is located on a peninsula at the mouth of the Bako River. It features sandstone cliffs and sandy bays, with a range of forest types, including mangroves. Access is only by boat, about 30 minutes from Kuching to Kampung Bako, from where you take another boat into the park. The park has beach areas and a network of paths. Camping gear can be hired, but all food must be brought with you. A pleasant way to spend a few days.

Niah National Park

This 3102 hectare park has only recently been established to protect the valuable Niah caves, made famous by the discoveries of traces of early man dating back 35,000 years. The caves are also remarkable for the millions of bats and swiftlets which roost here. The swiftlets are famous, as their nests made of saliva are collected for bird's nest soup. The mass movements of these bats and swiftlets through the mouth of the Great Cave are a spectacular sight at dawn and dusk. Other examples of cave life can be seen, and if you are lucky you may see the black-and-white bat hawk at the entrance waiting to pounce on a bat or swiftlet.

The park, in east Sarawak, can be reached from Bintulu or Miri via nearby Batu Niah. Hostel space and boat access can be arranged in advance, or just stay at Batu Niah and walk in. The walk includes the famous plank trail, which can take 45 minutes to one hour, if not too slippery. (If you're not sure about your shoes you can walk the planks barefoot.) There are other trails in the park and a longhouse nearby. It's a good detour if you're travelling overland to Brunei and Sabah.

Tunku Abdul Rahman National Park

This park covers five islands off Kota Kinabalu, Sabah, and has an area of about 4930 hectares. The attractions here are coral reefs and beaches, which can only be visited by making arrangements with private boat operators – good if you can organise a small group. Park headquarters are on Pulau Gaya, the largest island. There are also forest trails, and camping can be arranged, but all food must be brought in. Facilities for day visitors are available and plans to increase tourism, such as a rest house on Pulau Mamutik, are well underway.

This park partly developed from the notion that protecting offshore islands also protected the flora and fauna of Sabah until it was demonstrated that most is not found off the mainland. Fortunately, it led to the establishment of the first valuable marine park, with the hope that Malaysia will protect more of its marine resources.

Kinabalu National Park

This magnificent park of about 77,000 hectares was established in 1964 to protect the massif of Mt Kinabalu and its environs. The region has been a focal point of exploration and scientific investigation in Borneo for over a century. Today the focus has shifted more towards tourism as the climb to the summit offers an exciting enticement to the visitor.

The park headquarters (1560 metres) is about 50 km from Kota Kinabalu at Simpangan. Getting there takes about two hours, it's close to the road. Buses stop there on the way to Ranau or Sandakan, but there are also minibuses and Land-Rovers available. It is advisable to book ahead for accommodation at the headquarters in case large groups of summit seekers may be arriving. Also, the army uses the mountain for hiking exercises and can quickly fill up the available space. While it is not so essential to book ahead for the high-altitude huts, it is worth checking at headquarters about groups which may have gone up just before you arrived.

There is plenty of information available at park headquarters for planning your ascent, including a recently published book by the Sabah Society. Plan to spend at least two or more nights on the mountain in case fickle weather conditions force you to wait for a clear morning to reach the top. The best time to be there is at or near sunrise. On a clear morning the vista is incredible and exhilarating and worth all the time spent getting there.

The trail, starting on a road, is well marked all the way up, with steeper

sections graded and other aids provided nearer the top. The Panar Laban huts and those just below it (around 3340 metres) are the main stop for climbers and a good base for exploring the upper terrain, but Sayat Sayat hut (3800 metres), although smaller, can give you more time to reach the summit and await the sunrise. All food, and cooking fuel, must be carried up, so it is always better to allow for at least one extra day there. Also be sure to have enough warm clothing and sleeping gear. Guides are recommended for all visitors, but it is possible to join others once you're at the upper huts.

At least a week is needed at the park. Around the headquarters are several shorter trails, and a day or overnight trip can be made to the Poring Hot Springs, about 20 km by road on the other side of Ranau. Kinabalu offers one of the best opportunities to see the changes in the forests, which become very stunted near the top. The famous pitcher plants can be seen along the trail, with the largest ones capable of holding two litres of water. There are many fascinating animals found in the upper levels of Kinabalu, with the most obvious being squirrels and birds, notably the mountain blackbird and the Kinabalu friendly warbler. A native rat species has found the huts to be a good food source and some have learned to lift the lid on rice pots and steal leftovers.

Sepilok Reserve & Orang Utan Rehabilitation Centre

If you go to Sandakan, it is worth visiting this centre. Take a Batu 14 bus. This centre was originally designed for looking after orang utans before releasing them back into the wild, but it has become a little touristy and the animals are the main attraction. Some other animals are also kept here, and there is a very good visitor centre. Through the compound there are some forest trails which offer good walking in lowland forest. The forest on the seaward side of the reserve contains proboscis monkeys and it is possible to organise a boat to try and see them. Check with the centre or at the National Parks office in Sandakan.

What may have been the most devastating fire of modern times burned for six months of 1983 in east Borneo, including parts of east Sabah and the extent of damage in the region is uncertain, so this unhappy event may discourage many visitors.

Murray D Bruce & Constance S Leap Bruce

Facts for the Visitor

VISAS & IMMIGRATION – SINGAPORE

Commonwealth citizens, western Europeans and Americans do not require a visa to visit Singapore. In general you will be given a 14-day stay permit on arrival and this can be extended at the Immigration Department (tel 324031) at Empress Place. Recent reports, however, indicate that the Singapore government has decided that 14 days is enough for anybody to get their duty free shopping done and unless you can provide a guarantee from a Singapore sponsor you'd better plan on being on your way by day 14.

Singapore used to be famed for its 'anti-long hair and hippy' attitudes but these have somewhat relaxed of late. You're unlikely to be given a free haircut on arrival unless you look really outrageous. Nor, despite the signs in post offices and the like announcing that 'long haired males will be served last', are you likely to find yourself perpetually at the end of the queue if your hair reaches to your collar. Nevertheless it's wise not to look too scruffy on arrival in Singapore – but that's simple good manners in any Asian country.

Some relevant Singaporean consulates and embassies overseas include:

Australia
    81 Mugga Way, Red Hill, Canberra ACT 2603
Germany
    Ubierstrasse 45, 5300 Bonn-Bad, Godesberg
Hong Kong
    19th floor, Wang Kee Building, 36 Connaught Rd, Central
India
    48 Golf Links, New Delhi 110003
Indonesia
    23 Jalan Proklamasi, Jakarta
    3 Jalan Suryo, Medan
Japan
    12-2 Roppongi, 5 chome, Minato-ku, Tokyo
Malaysia
    5th floor, Straits Trading Building, Leboh Pasar Besar, Kuala Lumpur

New Zealand
    17 Kabul St, Khandallah, Wellington
Philippines
    6th floor, ODC International Plaza, 217-219 Salcedo St, Legaspi Village, Makati, Rizal
Sweden
    Banergathan 10, 5 Tr S-11522 Stockholm
Thailand
    129 Sathorn Tai Rd, Bangkok
UK
    2 Wilton Crescent, London SW1
USA
    1824 R St NW, Washington DC 20009

VISAS & IMMIGRATION – MALAYSIA

Commonwealth citizens, western Europeans and Americans do not require a visa to visit Malaysia. Recently the immigration regulations for visitors have been eased and you now normally get a 30-day stay permit on arrival. Previously you only got 14 days and if you wanted to stay longer had to hunt out an immigration office, fill in a form, hand in your passport and hang around for half an hour to have your length of stay extended. The extension was quite straightforward, just a little time consuming.

Note that Sabah and Sarawak are treated in some ways like separate countries. Your passport will be checked again on arrival in each state and a new stay permit issued. Travelling directly from either Sabah or Sarawak back to Peninsular Malaysia, however, there are no formalities and you do not start a new entry period.

Malaysia is very unhappy about 'hippy' visitors. The regulations state that:

Malaysia welcomes bona fide tourists but not hippies. If you are found dressed in shabby, dirty or indecent clothes, or living in temporary or makeshift shelters you will be deemed a hippy, your visit pass will be cancelled and you will be ordered to leave Malaysia within 24 hours, failing which you will be prosecuted under the immigration laws, furthermore you will not be permitted to enter Malaysia again.

In the mid-70s this ruling was used on a number of occasions as a pretext to round up westerners staying with villagers at the kampong at Batu Ferringhi in Penang since they were in 'makeshift' shelters. Similar events have occurred at Telok Bahang in Penang and at the Tangjong Kling beach centre near Melaka. Fortunately this attitude seems to have improved today, but backpackers and shoestring travellers should follow the sensible policy of dressing and behaving in a manner that fits in with local attitudes. Malaysia is a predominantly Muslim country with the conservative attitudes towards dress and behaviour that go with that religion.

Some relevant Malaysian consulates and embassies overseas include:

Australia
71 State Circle, Yarralumla, Canberra ACT 2600
Canada
60 Betelel St, Ottawa, Ontario KLN 8Y7
Germany
Rheinallee 23, 5300 Bonn 2
Hong Kong
24th floor, Lap Heng House 47-5, Gloucester Rd, Wanchai
India
50M Satya Marg, Chanakyapuri, New Delhi 110021
23 Khader Nawaz Khan Rd, Madras
Indonesia
17 Jalan Imam Bonjol, Jakarta
11 Jalan Diponegoro, Medan
Japan
20/16 Nempedai Machi, Shibuya-ku, Tokyo
Netherlands
Adries Bickerweg 5, The Hague
New Zealand
Chase-NBA House, 163 The Terrace, Wellington
Philippines
2nd & 3rd floor, Republic Glass Building, Tordesillas & Galardo Sts, Salcedo Village, Makati
Singapore
301 Jervois Rd, Singapore 1024
Thailand
35 South Sathorn Rd, Bangkok
4 Sukum Rd, Songkhla

UK
45 Belgrave Square, London SW1
USA
2401 Massachusetts Avenue NW, Washington DC 20008

VISAS & IMMIGRATION – BRUNEI

Visas are not required by citizens of Commonwealth countries, most western European nations or the USA. Those requiring visas must obtain them from the nearest British embassy or consulate. There is an honourary Brunei representative in KK but he cannot issue visas. If you're in KK and need a visa for Brunei (for example if you're Japanese) your passport will have to be sent to the British High Commission in Kuala Lumpur! And this can take a month or more! In other words forget it.

If entering from Sarawak or Sabah there's no fuss on arrival – no money showing, no requirement for an onward ticket and it's unlikely your bags will even be looked at – and a one-week stay permit is more or less automatic. If you ask you can usually get two weeks; it might be useful, you never know. At the Brunei/Sarawak border there are some yellowing-with-age and quite hilarious sketches of 'acceptable' and 'unacceptable' hair styles, but no-one cares.

MONEY

A$1	=	S$1.80	M$2.00
US$1	=	S$2.17	M$2.40
£1	=	S$2.57	M$2.86
DM1	=	S$0.70	M$0.78
NZ$1	=	S$1.05	M$1.16
HK$1	=	S$0.28	M$0.31

The Brunei dollar is on par with the Singapore dollar. Coins in use in Malaysia, Singapore and Brunei are 1c, 5c, 10c, 20c and 50c while notes are $1, $5, $10, $50, $100, $1000 and Singapore also has a S$10,000 note – not that you'll see too many. All major credit cards are widely accepted in Singapore and Malaysia although you're not going to make yourself too popular after a hard bargaining session for a new camera if you then try to pay for it with your Amex card.

Originally the Singapore, Malay and Brunei currencies were all directly interchangeable, but a fixed exchange rate is no longer maintained between them, although they tend to remain fairly comparable in value. Of late the Singapore dollar has become somewhat stronger than the Malay dollar or ringgit. The end result is that while Singapore currency is generally acceptable in Malaysia you won't find many Singaporeans keen on accepting Malay money.

At present coins present no problem, however. They're identical in size and shape so even if they weren't acceptable you could use them in pay phones or other coin operated devices. Currencies in these countries are strong, stable and easily exchanged. The banks are efficient and there are also plenty of money changers, but see the special notes in the Singapore section about service charges on travellers' cheques and varying exchange rates. For cash you'll generally get a better rate at a money changer than in a bank – quicker too. Singapore is also an excellent place to buy other foreign currencies, should you want to arrive (illegally) in India with pocketfuls of rupees.

Normal banking hours in Singapore are 10 am to 3 pm from Monday to Friday and 9.30 to 11.30 am on Saturdays. The Development Bank of Singapore branches stay open until 4.30 pm on Saturdays. There's 24 hours banking at Changi Airport and the bank at the Singapore Tourist Promotions Board Office is open 9.30 am to 4 pm on weekdays, 9.30 am to noon on Saturdays – but closed for an unspecified time at lunch time.

In Malaysia banking hours are the same except that Sabah banks open 30 minutes earlier and on weekdays they also close 30 minutes earlier. Money changers are open much longer hours and generally offer equally good or better rates for cash than banks, but will not (usually) change travellers' cheques. Note that the exchange rate for cash in banks is usually considerably inferior to that offered for travellers' cheques. Major hotels and some major shops will also change cash and travellers' cheques, but usually at a very poor rate.

COSTS

Singapore and Malaysia can pretty much cost you what you want. If you're travelling on a shoestring then Malaysia has lots of hotels where a couple can get a quite decent room for around US$6 (more like US$10 in Singapore), but if you want to spend US$100 a night that's no problem either, especially in Singapore.

Food is a delight, and an economical delight at that, in Singapore and Malaysia. There's a quite amazing variety of restaurants, particularly in Singapore, offering excellent food at amazingly cheap prices. You'll wonder if anyone ever eats at home when you can get an excellent meal in a small restaurant for not much over US$1 – in Singapore chicken rice with soup, a soft drink, a cup of coffee and a couple of varieties of tropical fruit to finish up with will set you back less than US$1.50 in any food centre. Meanwhile at the other end of the scale the fancy hotels and restaurants offer French cuisine at Parisian-style prices.

It's the same story when it comes to getting around. If you want to travel by chauffeur-driven air-conditioned car you can, but there are lots of cheaper and quite comfortable means of getting around. In Malaysia and Singapore there are plenty of reasonably priced and reasonably honest taxis for local travel – there's no need to get into the frantic bargaining sessions or fear the subsequent arguments that taxi travel in some Asian countries entails. Longer distance, Malaysia has excellent buses, trains and surprisingly economical long distance taxis, all at very reasonable prices.

On top of these travel essentials – accommodation, food and transport – you'll also find non-essentials and luxuries are reasonably priced, even downright cheap. After all shopping is what a lot of people come to Singapore for?

CLIMATE

Malaysia and Singapore have a typically tropical climate – it's hot and humid year round. Once you've got used to the tropics it never strikes you as too uncomfortable though, it's simply almost always warm and sunny. The temperature rarely drops below 20°C even at night and usually climbs to 30°C or more during the day. Rain, when it comes, tends to be short and sharp and is soon replaced by more of that ever present sunshine. At certain times of year it may rain every day but it's rare that it rains all day. Although the region is monsoonal it's only on the east coast of Malaysia that you have a real rainy season – elsewhere it's just a time of year when the average rainfall is heavier than at other times of year.

Singapore is wettest from November through January, west coast Malaysia gets heavier rainfall from September through December. On the east coast, and also in Sarawak and Sabah, October through February is the wet season. Throughout the region the humidity tends to hover around the 90% mark, but on the peninsula you can always escape from heat and humidity by retreating to the delightfully cool hill stations.

NEWSPAPERS & MEDIA

There are Chinese, Tamil, Malay, Malayalam and even English papers in Singapore and Malaysia. The *Nanyang Siang Pau*, a Singapore Chinese language daily, is the most widely read but for visitors the *Straits Times* (Singapore) and the *New Straits Times* (Malaysia) are the two main dailies. Although they look remarkably alike they're actually quite separate and, believe it or not, the customs officials at the causeway will confiscate copies of the *Straits Times* as you cross into Malaysia. Other English language papers include the popular *New Nation* in Singapore.

Asian and western magazines are readily available throughout the region. Radio and television are equally cosmopolitan in their languages and programming. Singapore and Malaysia each have two TV channels and in Singapore you can generally receive all four. Programmes range from local productions in the various languages to imports from the US and UK. Hardly surprisingly *Dallas* is very popular in Singapore!

BOOKS & BOOKSHOPS

There are a wide variety of books available on the region and a number of good bookshops to look for them in. Singapore's main bookshop chain is MPH and their shop at 71-77 Stamford Rd is probably the best general bookshop in the region. They have others on Robinson Rd, at Changi Airport, in the basement level at Plaza Singapura on Orchard Rd and other places around the city. Select Books, 215 Tanglin Shopping Centre (near the Tourist Office) has an excellent collection specialising in South-East Asia.

Other good bookshops include Times Bookshops at Lucky Plaza on Orchard Rd, in Robinson's department store in the Specialists' Centre also on Orchard Rd and at other locations. Marican have branches at DBS Building on Shenton Way and Supreme House on Penang Rd. In Plaza Singapura Shizuoka Yajimaya is another excellent bookshop. There are also book and magazine stalls in many of the larger hotels. Along Bras Basah Rd there are a number of small bookshops, some specialising in secondhand books.

In Malaysia there are again several branches of MPH including the main one on Jalan Tuanka Abdul Rahman in Kuala Lumpur. There is also a good bookshop in the Jalan Raja Chulan supermarket in KL. In Penang there are several good bookshops along Beach Rd (Pantai St) and the E&O Hotel also has a good bookshop. Major hotels also often have book stalls, but on the east coast the selection of bookshops is not as good as elsewhere.

Guidebooks

The Apa series includes *Insight Singapore* and *Insight Malaysia* with their usual collection of text and photographs. Also from this Singapore based company there's a coffee table book on Malaysia titled *Jalan Jalan*. It's as much a photographic book as a travel book since it covers Malaysia with a series of photographs taken with a 8 x 10 large format studio camera. The description of how the photographs were taken and the travels around Malaysia (by motorcycle) to take them is as interesting as the pictures themselves.

If you're travelling further through the region there are other Lonely Planet guides to most South-East Asian countries as well as the overall guidebook *South-East Asia on a Shoestring*.

History

There are a great number of books on the history of Singapore and Malaysia. If you simply want a straightforward and not over-long history from early civilisation to modern politics then *A Short History of Malaysia, Singapore & Brunei* by C Mary Turnbull (Cassell Australia, 1980) may fit the bill. Other standard histories include *A History of Malaya* by R Winstedt (Porcupine Press, 1979). Read *Raffles* by Maurice Collins (Day, 1968) for the story of the man who founded Singapore.

Recently there has been a great deal of interest in the fall of Malaysia and Singapore and the subsequent Japanese occupation and the internal and external struggles of the '50s and '60s. These include *Sinister Twilight – The Fall of Singapore* by Noel Barber, originally published in 1968 and now available in a Fontana paperback. It recounts the bunglings, underestimations and final heroics that culminated in the rapid collapse of Singapore.

Two interesting books then tell of different sides of the war years that followed. *The Jungle is Neutral* by F Spencer Chapman was originally published

in 1949 and now is available in a Mayflower paperback. It recounts the hardships and adventures of a British guerrilla force that fought on in the jungles of Malaya for the rest of the war. *Out in the Midday Sun* by Kate Caffrey (Andre Deutsch, 1973) tells of the hardships of those who were captured and spent the rest of the war years in prison camps like the notorious Changi camp.

The events of the long running communist insurrection are recounted in *The War of the Running Dogs – Malaya 1948-1960* by Noel Barber. Originally published in 1971 it too is now available in a Fontana paperback. No sooner had that struggle ended than the confrontation with Indonesia commenced. The events of that strange and disorganised argument are told in *The Undeclared War – The Story of the Indonesian Confrontation* by Harold James and Denis Sheil-Small which was originally published in 1971 and is now available in a paperback from the University of Malaya Co-Operative Bookshop.

Lee Kuan Yew – The Struggle for Singapore by Alex Josey was originally published in 1968 and has been brought up to date and republished on a number of occasions since. It covers all the twists and turns of Lee Kuan Yew's rise to power and the successful path which his People's Action Party has piloted Singapore along. *The Malay Dilemma* was written in 1970 by Mahathir bin Mohamed who became Prime Minister in 1981. It is interesting both for its not altogether optimistic analysis of the problems facing Malaysia and the fact that it was banned for a number of years. It has now been republished in a Federal Publications paperback.

Fiction

Singapore and Malaysia have always provided a fertile setting for novelists and Joseph Conrad's *The Shadow Line* and *Lord Jim* both use the region as a setting. Somerset Maugham also set many of his classic short stories in Malaya – look for the *Borneo Stories*. More recently Anthony Burgess' *The Malayan Trilogy* (available in Penguin paperback) is a classic series of long stories of life in Malaya during the declining years of Britain's colonial management. Paul Theroux's very readable collection of short stories *The Consul's File* is set in, of all places, Ayer Hitam near KL. Theroux's *Saint Jack* is set in Singapore

The Singapore Grip by J G Farrell (Fontana paperback, 1979) was a local bestseller and provides an almost surreal view of life in Singapore as the Japanese stormed down the peninsula in WW II – a certain amount of 'fiddling while Rome burnt' appeared to be going on. Blanche d'Alpuget's Australian award winning novel *Turtle Beach* (Penguin, 1981) is an interesting insight on the impact of the Vietnamese boat peoples' arrival on Malaysia and the racial tension these events engendered – with flashbacks to the horrors of 1969.

North Borneo

The best book on the fascinating history of Sarawak, Sabah and Brunei is *Nineteenth Century Borneo – A Study in Diplomatic Rivalry* by Graham Irwin (Donald Moore Books, Singapore). If you want to know more about the white rajahs then look for *Rajah Charles Brooke – monarch of all he surveyed* (Oxford University Press, 1978) by Colin N Criswell.

Vanishing World, the Ibans of Borneo by Leigh Wright (Weatherhill, 1972) has some beautiful colour photographs. James Barclay's *A Stroll Through Borneo* (Hodder & Stoughton, 1980) is a delightful tale of a long walk and river trip through Sarawak, Sabah and Indonesian Kalimantan. The contrasts between Malaysian bureaucracy and the Indonesian variety are enlightening, the Malaysian variety comes off distinctly second best.

A Few Insights

A delightful introduction to Malay life can be found through the cartoons of Lat.

Straits Times Publishing have produced *Kampong Boy* and more recently *Town Boy*, a humourous autobiographical cartoon series on growing up first in a village (kampong) and then in the town of Ipoh.

For quick, easy reading with some informative details on Chinese life try *Tales of Chinatown* by Sit Yin Fong (Heineman Asia, 1983). Fong was a newspaper man in Singapore for many years and writes anecdotal short stories about Chinese customs and beliefs.

Culture Shock by JoAnn Craig (Times Books International, 1979) is an attempt to explain the customs, cultures and lifestyles of Singapore's polyglot population to expatriates working there. Westerners setting up house in Singapore may also find *Living in Singapore* (American Association of Singapore, 1979) a useful introduction to life in the tropical city-state.

MAPS

It's not possible to get the detailed maps of Malaysia available during the colonial period because of fears that they will fall into communist hands. You can, however, get good road maps from petrol stations. Probably the best is the Shell one which is larger scale since it is two-sided. On the other hand the Mobil map also shows relief. Check a map's age by seeing if it still shows the old ferry crossings on east coast rivers. The last crossing was only bridged in the mid-70s. Or look for the recently completed east-west highway in the north.

A very good map, particularly for roads, is the *Asian Highway Route Map – Singapore, Malaysia, Thailand, Laos* which is published by the United Nations, Escap, Transport & Communications Division. It's available from the Singapore Automobile Association headquarters for just one dollar.

FILM & PHOTOGRAPHY

Singapore and Malaysia are, of course,

Top: fruit stall, Singapore (TW)
Bottom: chicken rice stall, Georgetown, Penang (TW)

Top: a sign in Chinatown, Singapore (TW)
Bottom: shop blind, Kuantan (TW)

delightful areas to photograph. There's a lot of natural colour and activity and the people have no antipathy to being photographed. It is, of course, polite to ask permission before photographing people or photographing in mosques or temples. There is usually no objection to taking photographs in places of worship, in Chinese temples virtually anything goes.

The usual rules for tropical photography apply: Try to take photographs early in the morning or late in the afternoon. By 10 am the sun will already be high in the sky and colours are easily washed out. Try to keep your camera and film in a happy environment – don't leave it out in direct sunlight, try to keep film as cool as possible, have film developed as soon as possible after use. Colour film can be developed quickly, cheaply and competently, but Kodachrome colour slides are usually sent to Australia for developing. Ektachrome, however, can be developed in Singapore.

Film is readily available in both Singapore and Malaysia, but there is a considerable price difference. Even 'duty free' a Kodachrome 64 36-exposure slide film costs 50% more in Malaysia than in Singapore. If you buy a reasonable number of films at a time the price in Singapore will probably beat anything you could do in the west – as low as S$15 for Kodachrome 64 36-exposure including developing. Singapore is, of course, an excellent place for camera equipment and there are competent camera shops in both countries.

HEALTH

Singapore and Malaysia are both healthy countries with good standards of cleanliness. In Singapore you can safely eat in virtually any street food stall and tap water is drinkable. You can drink tap water in major towns and cities in Malaysia but it is still wise to ensure that water has been boiled in kampongs or off the beaten track.

Vaccinations against cholera or yellow fever are only required if you've recently come from an infected area – there are no other health requirements on arrival. Although Singapore and Peninsular Malaysia are not malarial you should take precautions if you're visiting Sarawak or Sabah, particularly if you will be travelling up-river. Your doctor will prescribe a daily or weekly anti-malarial drug. Keeping mosquitoes away also helps – insect repellants, mosquito coils and mosquito nets are all extra protection.

The usual rules for healthy living in a tropical environment apply. Ensure that you do not become dehydrated, particularly before you have acquired some acclimatisation, by keeping your liquid intake up. Wear cool, lightweight clothes and avoid prolonged exposure to the sun. Treat cuts and scratches with care since they can easily become infected.

Dr Ann Faraday and Professor John Wren-Lewis recommended that:

If you are in need of medical services in any of the smaller towns, we strongly recommend the government hospitals, which are either completely free or make a nominal M$1 charge and go out of their way to be helpful to travellers. Medical staff and most of the senior nursing staff speak good English and there is rarely any need to wait for long. We especially commend the staff at the General Hospitals in Tapah, Tanah Rata (Cameron Highlands) and Kuala Lipis.

In major cities the queue situation is likely to be a very different story, though staff are in our experience no less helpful and may help a helpless-looking foreigner to jump the huge lines. However, it may be simpler (especially in Kuala Lumpur) to resort to a private clinic, in which case the minimum charge for a visit is about M$20. If you are contemplating visits to jungle areas you should certainly go to a hospital for anti-malarials.

DRUGS

In both Singapore and Malaysia the answer is simple – don't. Drug trafficking can result (and has) in the death penalty in either country. Mere possession can bring down a lengthy jail sentence and a beating with the rotan into the bargain. The penalties are severe and the authorities seem to catch a steady stream of unsuccessful peddlers and smugglers. There was a period in the '70s when Malaysia was a major staging post for heroin coming down from Thailand and continuing on to the west and also had manufacturing laboratories in its own right. There still seems to be plenty of it around, especially in Penang where numerous trishaw riders offer to pedal far more than their bicycles.

Recently, due to bumper opium crops, local use has also become a problem. The odd old opium den still continues a precarious existence too. Due to these factors baggage of travellers coming from South-East Asia has become particularly suspect to customs inspectors.

POST

Singapore and Malaysia have efficient postal systems with good poste restantes at the major post offices. In Singapore the GPO is open 8 am to 6 pm Monday to Friday, 9 am to 1 pm on Saturday. The Killiney Rd post office is open 8 am to 9 pm daily. In Malaysia post offices are open 8 am to 6 pm from Monday to Friday and 8 am to 12 noon on Saturdays. Costs for aerograms and postcards are as follows, light air letters cost the same as aerograms from Singapore:

	Malaysia	Singapore
aerogram	35c	30c
postcard –		
Australasia	25c	25c
Americas	55c	55c
Europe	40c	40c

TELEPHONE

There are good telephone communications throughout Singapore and Malaysia. You can direct dial long distance calls between all major towns in Malaysia. Local calls cost 10c for three minutes in Singapore, unlimited time in Malaysia from phone boxes, but in Singapore local calls are free from private phones. A trunk call to

Singapore from KL costs M\$5 before 6 pm, M\$2.50 after 6 pm.

Overseas calls can be direct dialled from Singapore or Kuala Lumpur. In Singapore there are a number of telecom offices from where you can make international calls and pay by time rather than in three minute blocks. Dialling codes in Malaysia include Singapore 02, Kuala Lumpur 03, Penang 04, Ipoh 05, Melaka 06, Kuantan 095, Kuala Trengganu 096, Kota Bahru 097, Sarawak 082, Sabah 088.

BUSINESS HOURS

In Singapore government offices are usually open Monday to Friday and Saturday mornings. Hours vary, starting around 7.30 to 9.30 am and closing between 4 and 6 pm. On Saturdays closing time is 11.30 am to 1 pm. Hours are similar in Malaysia. Shop hours are also somewhat variable although Monday to Saturday from 9 am to 6 pm is a good rule of thumb. In Singapore major department stores, Chinese emporiums and some stores catering particularly to tourists are open until 9 pm seven days a week. The story is similar in Malaysia.

TIME

Singapore and Malaysia are on the same time, three hours behind Australian eastern standard time (Sydney and Melbourne), one hour behind Australian western standard time (Perth), seven hours ahead of GMT (London), 11 hours ahead of American eastern standard time (New York) and 14 hours ahead of American western standard time (San Francisco and Los Angeles). Thus 12 noon in Singapore is 3 pm in Sydney, 1 pm in Perth, 5 am in London, 1 am in New York and 10 pm the previous day in Los Angeles.

ELECTRICITY

Electricity supplies are dependable throughout Singapore and Malaysia. Supply is 220-240 volts, 50 cycles.

TIPPING

Tipping is not normally done in Singapore or Malaysia. More expensive hotels and restaurants have a 10% service charge. In that case in Singapore tipping is actually prohibited, as it is at Singapore airport. You do not tip taxi drivers.

INFORMATION

Both Singapore and Malaysia have efficient tourist offices with a wide range of literature and brochures available and offices around the world. In Malaysia there are also a number of local tourist promotion organisations, such as the Penang Tourist Association, who back up the national Tourist Development Corporation's activities. Some offices of the Singapore Tourist Promotion Board and the Malaysian Tourist Development Corporation include:

Singapore Tourist Promotion Board

Australia
   8th floor, Goldfields House, 1 Alfred St, Circular Quay, Sydney 2000 (tel 02 241-3771)
   2nd floor, Grainpool Building, 172 St George's Terrace, Perth 6000 (tel 06 322-6996)
Germany
   Poststrasse 2-4, D-6000 Frankfurt/Main (tel 0611 231456)
Hong Kong
   19th floor, Wang Kee Building, 36 Connaught Rd Central, Hong Kong (tel 5-268538)
New Zealand
   c/o Rodney Walsh Ltd, 2nd floor, Dingwall Building, 87 Queen St, Auckland 1 (tel 9 793 708)
Singapore
   131 Tudor Court, Tanglin Rd, Singapore 1024 (tel 2356611)
UK
   33 Heddon St, off Regent St, London W1R 7LB (tel 01 437 0033)
USA
   Suite 1008, 10th floor, 342 Madison Ave, New York, NY 10017 (tel 212 687-0385)
   251 Post St, San Francisco, CA 94108 (tel 415 391-8476)

Malaysian Tourist Development Corporation

Australia
   12th floor, R&W House, 92 Pitt St, Sydney 2000 (tel 02 232-3751)
Germany
   Rossmarkt 17, Am Salzhaus 6, 6000 Frankfurt/Main (tel 0611 283782)
Hong Kong
   Ground Floor, Shop 1, Malaysia Building, 47-50 Gloucester Rd (tel 5 285810)
Singapore
   G3 Ocean Building, Collyer Quay, Singapore 0104 (tel 02 96351)
Thailand
   285/9 Silom Rd, Bangkok 10500 (tel 2349808)
UK
   17 Curzon St, London W1 (tel 01 499-7388)
USA
   c/o MAS, Suite 2148, 420 Lexington Ave, New York, NY 10017 (tel 212 697-8994)
   36th floor, Transamerica Pyramid Building, 600 Montgomery St, San Francisco, CA 94111 (tel 415 788-3344)
   c/o MAS, Suite 417,510 West Sixth St, Los Angeles, CA 90014 (tel 213 627-1301)

PLACES TO STAY

Malaysia and Singapore have a very wide range of accommodation possibilities – you can still find many places to stay for less than US$3 per person per night while at the other end of the scale some of Singapore's more luxurious 'international standard' hotels now run over US$100 a night for a room. Student Travel have special discount rates negotiated at a number of hotels in Malaysia and Singapore. These hotels tend to be rather more expensive than most real students could afford since they are predominantly upper bracket places. Check with Student Travel in KL or Singapore. Accommodation possibilities include:

International Hotels

There are modern, multi-storey, air-con, swimming pool, all mod-cons hotels of the major international chains (Hyatts, Holiday Inns, Hiltons) and of many local chains (the Singapore Goodwood group, the

Merlin Hotels found all over Malaysia). In these hotels nightly costs are generally from S$100 and up for a double in Singapore with standard doubles in the upper notch establishments running to well over S$200. Although you can approach these levels in Kuala Lumpur or Penang you'll generally find Malaysia hotel prices somewhat lower. In most places it's possible to get an air-con, fully equipped room in a modern hotel for as low as M$50 and rarely do prices go over M$100.

Traditional Chinese Hotels

At the other end of the price scale are the traditional Chinese hotels found in great numbers all over Malaysia and Singapore. They're the mainstay of the budget travellers and backpackers and in Malaysia you can generally find a good room for M$10 to 16, in some places even less than M$10. In Singapore they will start somewhat more expensive, there's not much available for less than S$20 these days.

Chinese hotels are generally fairly spartan – bare floors, just a bed, a couple of chairs and a table, a wardrobe and a sink. The showers and toilets (which will almost inevitably be Asian squat style) will generally be down the corridor. A couple of catches and points to watch for: couples can generally economise by asking for a single since in Chinese hotel language single means one double bed, double means two beds. Don't think this is being tight, in Chinese hotels you can pack as many into one room as you wish.

The main catch with these hotels is that they can sometimes be terribly noisy. They're often on main streets and the bottom rung of the Chinese hotel ladder has a serious design problem – the walls rarely reach the ceiling. The top is simply meshed or barred in. This is great for ventilation but terrible for acoustics. Every noise carries throughout the hotel and Chinese hotels all awake to a terrible dawn chorus of hawking, coughing and

spitting like only the Chinese know how.

That apart these hotels are delightfully traditional in style (all swishing ceiling fans and old furniture), are almost always spotlessly clean (there are exceptions) and they're great fun to stay in. They're very often built on top of coffee bars or restaurants so food is never more than a few steps away. And they're cheap.

There are also many older style Chinese places a notch up from the most basic places, where M$10 to 20 will get you a fan-cooled room with common facilities. For M$20 to 30 you can often find air-con rooms with attached bathroom – but still basically Chinese in their spartan style.

Other Possibilities – Singapore

In Singapore there are a number of YMCAs and YWCAs, but for the budget traveller the crash pads are the important accommodation story. In part these are a result of the frantic pace of Singapore's modernisation. As more and more of the traditional old parts of Singapore disappear the traditional old hotels disappear with it. There are certainly no plans in Singapore to build new hotels not equipped with swimming pools, air-con and wall-to-wall carpet – which leaves budget travellers out in the cold.

Naturally some bright young entrepreneurs have jumped into this yawning gap in the accommodation market. Their answer is to get a large flat or apartment and divide the rooms up into smaller rooms and dormitories into which they pack lots of backpackers at rock bottom prices. Of course this is probably mildly illegal but in free enterprise Singapore who cares? Some people enjoy the atmosphere, informality and useful exchange of information these handy meeting places provide but other travellers still prefer the less crowded atmosphere of the old hotels.

Other Possibilities – Malaysia

There are also a number of alternatives to the cheap hotels in Malaysia. For a start some of the old British-developed rest houses are still in operation. During the colonial era these were set up to provide accommodation for travelling officials and later provided excellent shelter for all types of tourists and travellers. Now the remaining rest houses are all privately operated although still government owned. Many have now closed down but there are still a number of rest houses offering excellent accommodation standards in traditional style and often at pleasantly low prices.

There are a number of YMCAs and YWCAs around Malaysia and at one time there were also a string of youth hostels. Unfortunately some of them were inconveniently situated and almost all of them suffered from extremely indifferent operators. Combined with the competition from cheap hotels most of the hostels have now closed; a shame since some of them were very pleasant.

Finally Malaysia has a number of cheap local accommodation possibilities, usually at beach centres. Unfortunately some of this village level accommodation has suffered from official harassment. Immigration regulations describe in detail how unpopular 'hippies' are in Malaysia and how you can be unceremoniously hustled out of the country if they should decide you are a 'hippy'. One definition of this unwanted creature is 'a person who stays in temporary or makeshift shelter'. Since many of these village level places are not government registered, local officials could, if the mood was upon them, accuse people staying there of being in 'temporary or makeshift shelter'.

In the mid-70s a series of highly publicised raids were made on the Penang village of Batu Ferringhi and many travellers were given orders to depart Malaysia immediately. Fortunately these policies have been curbed today but it's worth bearing in mind. Places with village level accommodation include Batu Ferringhi and Telok Bahang on Penang Island, Tanjong Kling near Melaka, Cherating village on the east coast and Tioman Island off the east coast.

Taxes & Service Charges In Singapore the more expensive hotels are all subject to a government 3% tax. In Malaysia there's a 5% tax and it applies to all hotels. In both countries a 10% service charge is tagged on in the more expensive place – in that case tipping is actively discouraged. More expensive places always quote prices exclusive of service charge and tax so you can add 13% in Singapore, 15% in Malaysia to get the real nightly cost.

Cheap Malaysian hotels, however, generally quote a price inclusive of the 5% government tax – hence prices like M$7.35 or M$16.80. Most hotel prices quoted in this guide have been rounded off to the nearest dollar. This 10% plus 5% business also applies to food and drink in the more expensive places – a cup of tea or coffee in an expensive place might cost you M$1.80 plus 18c plus 9c whereas in a cheap hotel coffee bar it would be 30 or 40c with no additions.

FOOD & DRINK
While travelling around some parts of Asia is as good as a session with weight watchers Singapore and Malaysia are quite the opposite. The food is simply terrific, the variety unbeatable and the costs pleasantly low. Whether you're looking for Chinese food, Malay food, Indian food, Indonesian food or even a Big Mac (巨無霸) you'll find happiness!

Chinese Food
You'll find the full range of Chinese cuisines in Singapore and Malaysia although if you're kicking round the backwoods of Sabah or Sarawak Chinese food is likely to consist of little more than noodles and vegetables. In Singapore you'll find variety to send any epicure into raptures.

Cantonese When people in the west speak of Chinese food they probably mean Cantonese food. It's the best known and most popular variety of Chinese cooking even in Singapore where the majority of Chinese are not Cantonese, as they are in Hong Kong. Cantonese food is noted for the variety and freshness of its ingredients. The food is usually stir-fried with just a touch of oil to ensure that the result is crisp and fresh. All those best known 'western Chinese' dishes fit into this category – sweet & sour dishes, won ton soup, chow mein, spring rolls.

With Cantonese food the more people you can muster for the meal the better because dishes are traditionally shared so that everyone manages to sample the greatest variety. A corollary of this is that Cantonese food should be balanced – traditionally all foods are said to be ying or 'cooling' (like vegetables, most fruits, clear soups) or yang or 'heaty' (starchy foods and meat). A cooling dish should be balanced by a heaty dish, too much of one or the other is not good for you.

Another Cantonese speciality is tim sum or 'little heart'. Tim sum is usually eaten at lunchtime or as a Sunday brunch. Tim sum restaurants are usually large, noisy affairs and the tim sum, little snacks, fried, steamed, dumplings, buns, small bowls or whatever, are whisked around the tables on individual trolleys or carts. As they come by you simply ask for a plate of this or a bowl of that. At the end of the meal your bill is toted up from the number of empty containers on your table. Eating tim sum is generally fun as well as tasty.

Cantonese cuisine can also offer real extremes – shark's fin soup or bird's nest soup are expensive delicacies from one end of the scale; mee (noodles) or congee (rice porridge) are cheap basics from the other end.

North & West China Far less familiar than the dishes of Canton are the cuisines from the north and west of China – Szechuan, Shanghainese and Peking cooking. Szechuan food is the fiery food of China, the food where the peppers really get into the act. Whereas the tastes of Cantonese food are

delicate and understated, in Szechuan food the flavours are strong and dramatic – garlic and chillies play their part in dishes like diced chicken or sour & hot soup.

Peking food is, of course, best known for the famous Peking duck where the specially fattened ducks are basted in syrup and roasted on a revolving spit. The duck skin is served as a separate first course. Like the other northern cuisines Peking food is less subtle, more direct than Cantonese food. Although Peking food is usually eaten with noodles or steamed buns in China, because rice does not grow in the cold northern Peking region, in Singapore it's equally likely to come with rice.

Food from Shanghai is to some extent a cross between northern and Cantonese cuisines – combining the strong flavours of the north with the ingredients of Canton. It is not easy to find, however, in Singapore.

South China Cantonese is, of course, the best known southern Chinese cuisine but it is quite easy to find a number of other regional styles in Singapore – particularly since so many of the region's Chinese are Hokkiens or Hakkas. One of the best known of these southern dishes comes from the island of Hainan. Throughout Singapore and Malaysia one of the most widespread and also most economical meals you can find is Hainanese chicken rice. It's one of those dishes whose very simplicity ensures its quality. Chicken rice is simply steamed chicken, rice boiled or steamed in the chicken stock, a clear soup and slices of cucumber. Flavour this delicate dish with soy or chilli sauce and you've got a delicious meal for Singapore or Malay $1.50 to 2.50. The Hainanese also produce steamboat, a sort of oriental variation on a Swiss fondue where you have a boiling stockpot in the middle of the table into which you dip pieces of meat, seafood or vegetables.

The Hokkiens come from Fukien province and make up the largest dialect group in

Singapore. Although Hokkien food is rated way down the Chinese gastronomic scale they have provided the unofficial national dish of Singapore – Hokkien fried mee. It's made of thick egg noodles cooked with pork, seafood and vegetables and a rich sauce. Hokkien popiah spring rolls are also delicious.

Teochew food, from the area around Swatow, is another style noted for its delicacy and natural flavour. Teochew food is also famous for seafood and a popular food-centre dish is Char Kway Teow – broad noodles, clams and eggs fried in chilli and black bean sauce. Hakka food is noted for its simple ingredients and the best known Hakka dish, again easily found in food-centres, is Yong Tau Foo – beancurd stuffed with minced meat.

Taiwanese food includes rice porridge, a healthy and economical meal, often with small side dishes of oysters, mussels or pork stewed in a rich sauce.

Indian Food

Indian food is one of the region's greatest delights, indeed it's easier to find really good Indian food in Singapore or Malaysia than in India! Very approximately you can divide Indian food into south and north – from the south the food tends to be hotter with the emphasis more on vegetarian food while from the north the food tends to be more subtle in its spicing, more Muslim in its influences and uses more meat. Common to all Indian food are the spices or masala, the lentil soup known as dahl, the yoghurt and water drink known as lassi and the sauces or condiments known as chutneys.

The typical south Indian dish is a rice plate. If you ask for one in a vegetarian restaurant you won't get a plate at all, instead a large banana leaf is placed in front of you and on this a large mound of rice is placed then scoops of a variety of vegetable curries are added around the rice and a couple of papadums tossed in for good measure. With your right hand,

for south Indian vegetarian food is never eaten with utensils, you then knead the curries into the rice and eat away. When your banana leaf starts to get emptier you'll suddenly find it refilled – for rice plate is always an 'as much as you can eat' meal. When you've finished fold the banana leaf in two, with the fold towards you, to indicate that you've had enough.

Other vegetarian dishes include the popular masala dosa. A dosa is a thin pancake which, when rolled around the masala (spiced vegetables) with some dahl on the side, provides about the cheapest light meal you could ask for. An equivalent snack meal in the north would be a murtabak, made from a paratha (paper thin dough) which is then folded around egg and minced mutton and lightly grilled with oil. Or a roti chanai – simply a chopped up paratha which you dip into a bowl of dahl. This is a very popular and filling breakfast throughout the region. Or perhaps a samosa – roughly an Indian equivalent of a Chinese spring roll.

A favourite north Indian dish, and one that is easy to find at low cost and of excellent standard, is biriyani. Served with a chicken or mutton curry the dish takes its name from the saffron coloured rice it is served with. Another particular favourite in the north is tandoori food which takes its name from the clay tandoor oven in which meat is cooked after an over-night marinade in a complex yoghurt and spice mixture. Tandoori chicken is the best known tandoori dish. Although rice is also eaten in the north it is not so much the ever present staple it is in the south. North Indian food makes wide use of the delicious Indian breads like chappatis, parathas or rotis.

Indonesian, Malay & Nonya Food

Surprisingly Malay food is not all that easily found in Malaysia or Singapore although many Malay dishes, like satay, are essentially the same as Indonesian. Malay dishes you may have a chance to try include tahu goreng – fried soy bean curd and bean curd sprouts in a peanut sauce; ikan bilis – tiny fish fried whole; ikan assam – fried fish in a sour tamarind curry; sambal udang – fiery curry prawns.

Indonesian, or rather Javanese, food includes dishes like nasi goreng – nasi is rice and goreng is fried and nasi goreng is a close cousin to Chinese fried rice. Gado gado is an Indonesian salad dressed with a peanut sauce. Peanut sauce again finds its way on to satay – tiny kebabs of chicken, mutton or beef. Ayam goreng is fried chicken, soto ayam is a thin chicken soup, rendang is a sort of spiced and curried beef.

In Sumatra the Indonesian food bends much more towards curries and chillies. The popular Sumatran dish is nasi padang – rice from the town of Padang. In a nasi padang restaurant all the different dishes are on display in the window and you select as many as you want to share amongst your group. The Dutch developed a variation on nasi padang called rijstaffel or 'rice table'. You can find rijstaffel at many major hotels.

Nonya cooking is a local variation on Chinese and Malay food – it uses Chinese ingredients, but with local spices like chillies and coconut cream. Nonya cooking is essentially a home skill, rather than a restaurant one – there are few places where you can find nonya food.

Other

Western fast food addicts will find Ronald McDonald, the Colonel from Kentucky and A&W have all made inroads into the regional eating scene. At big hotels you can find all the usual western dishes. In Singapore you will also find Japanese, Korean and other regional restaurants. Both countries have modern air-con supermarkets where you can find anything from yoghurt to packaged muesli.

Tropical Fruit

Once you've tried rambutans, mangosteens, jackfruit and durians how can you ever go back to boring old apples and oranges? If you're already addicted to tropical fruit, Singapore and Malaysia are great places to indulge the passion. If you've not yet been initiated then there could hardly be a better place in the world to develop a taste for exotic flavours. In Singapore in particular the places to head for an easy introduction are the fruit stalls which you'll find in food centres or even just on the streets. Slices of a whole variety of fruits (including those dull old apples and oranges) are laid out on ice in a colourful and mouth-watering display which you can make a selection from for just 20c and up. You can also have a fruit salad made up on the spot from as many fruits as you care to choose. Some tastes to sample include:

Rambutan The Malay name means 'spiny' and that's just what they are. Rambutans are the size of a large walnut or small tangerine and they're covered in soft red spines. You peel the skin away to reveal a very close cousin to the lychee with cool and mouth watering flesh around a central stone.

Pineapple Probably the most popular tropical fruit, a slice of pineapple is always a delicious thirst quencher. You've not really tasted pineapple until you're handed a whole one, skin sliced away and with the central stem to hold it by while the juice runs down your arm!

Mangosteen One of the finest tropical fruits, the mangosteen is about the size of a small orange or apple. The dark purple outer skin breaks open to reveal pure white segments shaped like orange segments – but with a sweet-sour flavour which has been compared to a combination of strawberries and grapes. Queen Victoria, so the story goes, offered a considerable prize to anybody able to bring a mangosteen back intact from the east for her to try.

Durians The region's most infamous fruit, the durian is a large oval fruit about 20 to

25 cm long although it may often grow much larger. The durian is renowned for its phenomenal smell, a stink so powerful that first timers are often forced to hold their noses while they taste. In fact durians emanate a stench so redolent of open sewers that in season you'll see signs in hotels all over Malaysia warning that durians are expressly forbidden entry.

When the hardy, spiny shell is cracked open pale white-green segments are revealed with a taste as distinctive as their smell. Durians are so highly esteemed that great care is taken over their selection and you'll see gourmets feeling them carefully, sniffing them reverently and finally demanding a preliminary taste before purchasing. Durians are also expensive and unlike other fruits which are generally ying (or cooling) durians are yang (or heaty). So much so that the durian is said to be a powerful aphrodisiac. It's no wonder that durians are reputed to be the only fruit which a tiger craves!

Jackfruit or Nangka This enormous watermelon-size fruit hangs from trees and when opened breaks up into a large number of bright orange-yellow segments with a slightly rubbery texture. Externally the nangka is covered by a green pimply skin, but it's too big and too messy to clean to make buying a whole one worthwhile. From street fruit stalls you can often buy several nangka segments skewered on a stick.

Papaya The papaya or paw paw originated in Central America but is now quite common throughout South-East Asia and is very popular at breakfast time when, served with a dash of lemon juice, a slice of papaya is the perfect way to start the day. The papaya is about 30 cm or so in length and the bright orange flesh is somewhat similar in texture and appearance to pumpkin but related in taste to a melon. The numerous black seeds in the centre of a papaya are said to have a contraceptive effect if eaten by women.

Starfruit Known in Indonesia as blimbing, the starfruit takes its name from the fruit's cross-sectional star shape. A translucent green-yellow in colour, starfruit has a crisp, cool, watery taste.

Custard Apple or Zirzat Sometimes known as soursop or white mango the custard apple has a warty green outer covering and is ripe and ready to eat when it begins to look slightly off – the fresh green skin begins to look blackish and the feel becomes slightly squishy. Inside the creamy white flesh has a deliciously thirst quenching flavour with a hint of lemon in it. This is another fruit you can often find at fruit stalls.

Other Then there are coconuts, mangoes, lychees, bananas, jambu, buah duku, chiku, jeruks, even strawberries up in the Cameron Highlands. Plus all the temperate climate fruits which are imported from Australia, New Zealand and further afield.

Drinks
Life can be thirsty in Singapore and Malaysia so you'll be relieved to hear that drinks are excellent, economical and readily available. For a start water is drinkable straight from the taps in Singapore and in most larger Malaysian cities – that's an excellent start compared to many Asian countries where drinking water without elaborate preparations is foolhardy. Secondly there are a wide variety of soft drinks from Coca Cola, Pepsi, 7-Up, Fanta to a variety of F&N flavours (including sarsparilla for old fashioned root beer fans) and even Kickapoo Joy Juice (for Lil Abner fans)! Soft drinks are generally around 50 to 70c.

You can also find those fruit juice in a box drinks all over the region with both normal fruit flavours and also oddities like chrysanthemum tea. Beer drinkers will probably find Anchor Beer or Tiger Beer to their taste although the minimum price of a bottle of beer is now nearly M$2.50.

Travelling Irishmen may be surprised to find that Guinness has a considerable following – in part because the Chinese believe it has a strong medicinal value. ABC Stout is a cheaper priced local equivalent for the dark black brew.

Sipping a coffee or tea in a Chinese cafe is a time honoured pursuit at any time of day or night. If you want your tea, which the Chinese and Malays make very well, without the added enticement of condensed milk, then ask for *teh-o*. Shout it – that's another of those words which cannot be said quietly. If you want it without sugar as well you have to ask for *teh-o kosong*, but you're unlikely to get it, they simply cannot believe anyone would drink tea that way! Fruit juices are very popular and very good, particularly in Singapore where, with the aid of a blender and crushed ice, delicious concoctions like watermelon juice can be whipped up in seconds. Old fashioned sugar cane crushers, which look like grandma's washing machine mangle, can still be seen in operation.

Halfway between a drink and a dessert are chendol and ice kachang. An ice kachang is rather like an old fashioned sno-cone but the shaved ice is topped with syrups, condensed milk, and piled on top of a foundation of beans and jellies! The taste is terrific. Chendol is somewhat similar. Other oddities? Well, the milky white drink in clear plastic bins at street drink sellers is soybean milk, also available in soft drink bottles. Medicinal teas are a big deal with the health-minded Chinese.

Desserts

Although desserts are not a really big deal in the region you can find some interesting after dinner snacks like pisang goreng (banana fritters) or even bo-bo cha-cha (another ice kachang or chendol style concoction). Ice cream addicts will be relieved to hear they can find good ice cream all over the region – soft-serve, multi-flavour gelati-style, packaged ice cream on a stick – they're all available.

CONDUCT & CUSTOMS

Like many Muslim countries Malaysia has been going through a period of increasing concentration on religion and religious activity in the past 10 years or so. It's wise to be appropriately discreet in dress and behaviour, particularly on the staunchly Muslim east coast of the peninsula. Unfortunately some people also seem to be taking a staunchly Muslim view of women and a number of women travellers have written to complain of hotel peeping toms and other harassments.

WHAT TO BRING

There's really very little you need to worry about forgetting when you come to Malaysia or Singapore. There are none of those problems of finding your favourite brand of toothpaste or even common medicines. If you want a film for your camera it will be cheaper in Singapore than back home.

Clothes are readily available and very reasonably priced – in fact some people reckon that Singapore is better for off the shelf clothing than Hong Kong. More variety and lower costs. In any case you don't need too much to start with – the weather is perpetually of the shirt sleeve variety although if you're planning to head up for the hill stations you may appreciate a sweater or light jacket in the evenings. Dress is casual throughout the region – budget travellers may find a set of 'dress up' gear sensible for dealing with officialdom but up-market you're highly unlikely to need a coat and tie or equivalent too often.

TAKE THE CHILDREN

Researching the first edition of this book was familiar in one respect and totally unfamiliar in another. It was familiar in that we'd pretty well covered Malaysia in the past. We'd made one trip all over the country on a motorcycle and in subsequent years had returned to Malaysia on a number of occasions, travelling by air, train, bus, long-distance taxi and even by thumb. So we felt pretty well at home in Malaysia and knew our way round fairly well. The trip was totally unfamiliar in that it was the first time out with our daughter, who was seven months old when we arrived in Singapore at the start of our travels.

The end verdict? Harder work than we might have expected but quite possible and in many ways great fun. For starters Malaysia is a very civilised country for travelling with kids. It's clean and hygienic by Asian standards and travel is relatively easy. Equally important the people of Singapore and Malaysia love kids, especially blonde blue-eyed ones, so Tashi was thoroughly spoilt. The pleasant surprises were how well equipped many places were to deal with children. Even the tiniest little coffee-shop restaurants seemed to have a high chair ready to be whisked out when we appeared. And, of course, Chinese food is designed to be messed with – you're bound to end up with prawn shells and fish bones littered all around you, so any additional mess a baby can make hardly seems to matter.

As far as the western necessities of dealing with babies went everything was pretty simple. Milk is, of course, hard to obtain, as in most of Asia, but we did find plenty of fruit juice, soy milk drinks and often did find milk too. Our initial intention to wash nappies (diapers) as we went along soon went out the window. Perhaps if you're travelling slowly you could manage that, but when you're covering a lot of ground (as you have to when researching a guidebook) it simply wasn't possible to get them dried in time to move on. But finding disposable nappies was no trouble in the big cities (Singapore, KL, Penang, etc) and prices were not much more than in the west. They were usually American (higher stick failure) or Japanese (pretty, but not always effective).

As for Tashi, she had a great time, loved Chinese food (especially baby sweet corn), delighted in the water (beach or pool) and generally enjoyed herself. The biggest problem, and this would have been a problem anywhere, not just in Asia, was that she was too big to take along after she'd reached her bedtime but too small to keep up late. At times we had to miss meals or rush out for take-aways because she was asleep and could not be stirred. Plus the constant moving, every second night a new hotel room, did unsettle her a bit and we had rather too many middle-of-the-night wake-ups for comfort. But then Tashi has never been a great sleeper. We've subsequently made several more trips in Asia with Tashi and, when he came along, her younger brother Kieran. For more information on taking the kids see Maureen's forthcoming book *Travel with Children*.

Tony Wheeler

Getting There

AIRLINE TICKETS – A WARNING

Singapore and Malaysia both have a reputation as good centres for buying discounted airline tickets. As in many other places in the world ticket discounting can be a slightly shady activity – it may be under the counter, quietly tolerated or even openly tolerated but it's never totally free and open. Additionally the official attitudes towards it can blow hot and cold – one year it's OK (happy days, the prices drop); the next year it's a no no (disaster, the prices soar). It can also go in and out of official favour depending on where you want to fly to – one year tickets to Europe may be a bargain, tickets around Asia very expensive. The next year the opposite may apply.

So don't expect anything when it comes to cheap tickets – what applies this week certainly may not apply next. Nevertheless Singapore, Kuala Lumpur and Penang are certainly three of the best places around to find bargains on airline tickets. Beware, however, of unscrupulous people in this field. There are many fly by night operators and the agent everybody speaks highly of one year can all too easily do a midnight flit next. As did a ticket agent we recommended in the previous edition of this book. Many travellers have written to us recommending particular agents and where appropriate we've mentioned agents who have been highly and frequently recommended. Curiously enough, however, some agents, in Penang in particular, seem to simultaneously get 'great guy, very reliable' recommendations and 'danger, avoid at all costs' warnings!

The only suggestion we can make from direct experience is that over the years we have bought a number of tickets for Lonely Planet researchers from Airmaster Travel in Singapore. From time to time we've had letters from people saying that other Singapore agents are cheaper, but we've never had a letter from anyone saying they had any trouble with tickets bought from Airmaster.

FROM/TO EUROPE

Tickets are available from travel agents in London to Kuala Lumpur or Singapore from around £200 to £250 or return from around £400 to £450. It's possible to get flights from London to Australia with stop-overs in Singapore or KL from around £360. To Auckland with a Singapore stop-over costs around £425. For more information check the travel ad pages in *Time Out* or the *Australasian Express*. Two good agents for cheap airline tickets are Trailfinders at 46 Earls Court Rd or STA at 74 Old Brompton Rd.

FROM/TO AUSTRALIA

Air Advance purchase one-way fares from the Australian east coast to Singapore vary from A$506 off-peak to A$612 in the peak season. To Kuala Lumpur the variation is A$533 to A$641. There are also advance purchase round-trip fares varying from A$778 to A$940 to Singapore; A$820 to A$986 to Kuala Lumpur. The regular economy fare to Singapore is A$881, to Kuala Lumpur A$968. Shopping around travel agents you can probably find one-way tickets to Singapore at around A$365 (A$730 return) or to KL for about A$400 (A$800 return).

Sea You can still travel between Fremantle in Western Australia and Singapore by ship. From Singapore fares vary from around S$1200 to S$2600. Check with Mansfield Travel (tel 93071), G8 Ocean Building Shopping Centre, Collyer Quay, Singapore for schedules on the Blue Funnel Line *Centaur* and the Palanga Line *Kota Bali*.

FROM/TO NEW ZEALAND

Air New Zealand and Singapore Airlines fly from Auckland to Singapore. The regular economy one-way fare is NZ$1245 while an excursion return fare of NZ$1300 (low season) to NZ$1500 (high season) is also available. Cheaper still is the 30 day advance purchase return fare which varies from NZ$1186 low season to NZ$1300 high season.

FROM/TO THE USA

There is now a lot of ticket discounting with Asian airlines from the US west coast to Asia. Whereas this used to be basically a closed shop operation for Asians only it's now fairly wide open. It's possible, with a little shopping around, to find fares from the US west coast to Singapore for around US$500 one-way or US$850 return. Scan the Sunday travel section of west coast newspapers like the *LA Times* or the *San Francisco Chronicle-Examiner* for agents handling discounted tickets. Some cheap fares include a stop-over in Hong Kong. There are also budget and super Apex fares available out of the west coast. Similar deals from the east coast can be found in the Sunday papers there.

FROM/TO THAILAND

There are a number of ways of getting from Singapore or Malaysia into Thailand. You can fly from Singapore, Kuala Lumpur or Penang. You can cross the border by land at Padang Besar (rail or road), Changlun-Sadao (road) or Keroh-Betong (road) in the west or at Rantau Panjang-Sungai Golok in the east. There's also a rather unusual route by sea from Kuala Perlis on the west coast.

Air Typical air fares to Bangkok include Singapore-Bangkok for around S$300 or Penang-Bangkok for around M$250. You can also fly Penang-Hat Yai for M$51 or Penang-Phuket for M$106. Add on a Phuket-Bangkok flight and it works out no more expensive than flying to Bangkok directly. Flying from Penang to Hat Yai or Phuket can save a lot of time wasted in crossing the border by land.

Road – West Coast Although there are border points at Padang Besar and Keroh the majority of travellers cross by road between Changlun and Sadao for Hat Yai. There's a long stretch of no-man's land between these two points so although you can easily get a bus or taxi up to Changlun on the Malay side and on from Sadao to Hat Yai on the Thai side, crossing the actual border is difficult. There are two easy alternatives – one is a Thai taxi from Georgetown (see Penang) for around M$20 to Hat Yai. The other is to cross at Padang Besar, where the railway also crosses and where the border is an easy walk across. Note that the Sadao-Changlun border is only open to 6 pm. From Hat Yai there are plenty of buses and trains to Phuket, Bangkok or other places.

Road – East Coast From Kota Bahru you can take a 29 bus to Rantau Panjang – the 45 km trip takes 1½ hours and costs about M$2. Once there you've got a half km walk to the Thai train station at Sungai Golok. On Sundays, Tuesdays, Thursdays and Saturdays an express train departs for Bangkok at 8.30 am or there's a regular train every day at 10.40 am. These trains both go through Hat Yai. A number of travellers have pointed out in the past that the Malay immigration post at Rantau Panjang is very slack and it's quite easy to miss them, but it seems to be more efficient now. Local buses would zip straight by, since locals did not need special clearance to go to Sungai Golok. It's your responsibility to make sure your passport is stamped on entry. Failure to do so can mean a stiff fine for 'illegal entry'.

Rail The rail route into Thailand is on the Butterworth-Alor Setar-Hat Yai route which crosses into Thailand at Padang Besar. You can take the International Express from Butterworth all the way to

		Singapore	Kuala Lumpur	Butterworth
Hat Yai	1st class	M$102.90	M$ 60.70	M$ 22.10
	2nd class	M$ 48.70	M$ 28.80	M$ 10.60
Bangkok	1st class	M$163.00	M$120.80	M$ 82.20
	2nd class	M$ 77.40	M$ 57.50	M$ 39.30

schedule:

1	2		2	3
07.55	06.50	Butterworth	17.39	17.53
10.00	09.08	Alor Setar	15.03	15.25
12.32	11.20	Hat Yai	11.40	10.43
06.45	–	Bangkok	–	16.10

1 International Express from Butterworth Monday, Wednesday, Friday
2 daily ordinary train
3 International Express from Bangkok Monday, Wednesday, Saturday

In addition there is a small express surcharge on the International Express. Additional cost for berths ranges from around M$6 to M$25 depending on whether you want a 2nd class upper, 2nd class lower, 1st class ordinary or 1st class air-con.

Bangkok three days a week with connections from Singapore and KL. On Sunday nights there is a special first class coach attached to the night express from KL which is then attached to the Monday International Express from Butterworth. Or there is a daily connection between Butterworth and Hat Yai. Once in Hat Yai there are frequent train and bus connections to other parts of Thailand.

See above table for details.

Sea – West Cost You can often get yachts between Penang and Phuket in Thailand. Look for advertisements in the cheap hotels and restaurants in Georgetown. Encounter Overland used to run a regular yacht trip costing around £200 for a 10 day voyage between Penang and Phuket. Although it appears that operation has stopped now there are other yachts still sailing.

Cheaper and more frequent are the small boats that skip across the border from Kuala Perlis in the north-west corner of Malaysia to Setul in Thailand. There are customs and immigration posts here so you can cross quite legally although it's an unusual and rarely used entry/exit point. The boats will be those open long boats, unique to Thailand, with a car engine mounted on gimbels on the back and a long, solid shaft from the end of the engine driving the prop. The whole engine is swivelled to steer the boat. Fare for the short trip is M$3 and from Setul you can bus to Hat Yai. Make sure you get your passport stamped on entry.

Thai Visas
You can get Thai visas from the embassies in Singapore or Kuala Lumpur or the consulates in Penang or Kota Bahru. The consulates are quick and convenient. There are three types of Thai visa: If you have an onward air ticket and will not be staying in Thailand for more than 14 days then you do not need to pre-arrange a visa and can get a free entry permit on arrival by air or land. For M$15 you can get a one month transit visa or for M$30 a two month tourist visa. Three photos are required.

FROM/TO INDONESIA
Air There are several interesting variations

from Indonesia to Singapore or Malaysia. Simplest is to fly from Jakarta to Singapore with tickets available from around US$110 to 150 depending on the airline. Medan in Sumatra to Penang will cost around US$50. These are the two standard flight possibilities but others also exist – such as Pekanbaru to Singapore or even Pekanbaru to Melaka.

There are also flights between Kuching in Sarawak and Pontianak in Kalimantan, the Indonesian, southern half of the island of Borneo. Similarly at the eastern end of Borneo there are flights between Tawau in Sabah and Tarakan in Kalimantan. Both these routes tend to open and close depending on the attitude of the moment.

Sea Curiously there is no direct shipping service between Indonesia and near neighbour Singapore or between Indonesia and Malaysia. There used to be a ferry service between Medan in Sumatra and Penang in Malaysia but that shut down a few years ago. You can, however, travel by sea between Singapore and Indonesia via Tanjung Pinang – the Indonesian island south of Singapore in the Riau Archipelago.

This service has, however, gone through quite an upheaval recently and is no longer nearly as convenient. Once a week the Pelni ship *KM Tampomas* makes a round trip Jakarta-Tanjung Pinang-Medan-Jakarta. It used to operate through Tanjung Pinang on the Medan-Jakarta leg too but that stop has been cut out. So the only way to travel Singapore-Jakarta now is via Medan – a very long way out of your way. You can, however, still take the *Tampomas* Jakarta-Tanjung Pinang.

Coming from Jakarta you take a hydrofoil from Tanjung Pinang to Singapore for 21,000 rp. There's an additional 1000 rp port charge at Tanjung Pinang (only 100 rp for locals!) and you stop at Batam to clear Indonesian immigration. From Singapore ferries to Tanjung Pinang depart daily from Finger Pier and cost S$45 for the 2½ hour fast ferry or S$26 for the five to six hour slow ferry. Make sure if

you pay the fast fare it really is a fast ferry. Finger Pier is on Prince Edward Rd which is reached by a large number of bus services. The usual ferry departure time is from around 11 am. Beware of pickpockets during the mad stampede at Tanjung Priok port in Jakarta.

Fares between Jakarta and Tanjung Pinang start from around US$20 for deck class then go up to about US$35 for a 3rd class cabin or for US$40 you can get an air-con cabin with private facilities and travel in some comfort. Deck class includes nothing – you have to provide your own sleeping bag, even your own plate and eating utensils if you want to eat the *Tampomas'* infamous rice-and-a-fish-head food. Toilet facilities are nothing to write home about either. Four berth cabins utilise the same facilities too. It's a wise idea to bring some food with you and drinks too, since they tend to be expensive on the *Tampomas*. One advantage the *Tampomas* does have is the 'nightclub' that operates at night, anyone is welcome (not just cabin class passengers) and beers are reasonably priced. Note that cabins tend to be booked out some time ahead, but for deck class you simply turn up and buy your ticket on the boat.

If you want to take the ship to Medan then each Wednesday at 6 am it departs Tanjung Pinang travelling north and arrives at Belawan (the port for Medan) on Thursday afternoon. It is also possible to find ships from Tanjung Pinang to Pekanbaru in Sumatra.

Indonesian Visas

The Indonesian visa situation went through some major changes in 1983. For most western nationalities a visa can be issued on arrival in Indonesia allowing a one month stay. This visa can be extended for a further month at no cost. The only catch to this new situation is that the 'no visa' entry only applies if you both enter and leave Indonesia through certain recognised gateways. These entry and exit points include all the usual airports and seaports, but they do not include Pontianak and Tarakan in Kalimantan or Jayapura in Irian Jaya. They do include Batam in the Riau Archipelago, south of Singapore. If you intend to arrive or leave Indonesia through one of the oddball places then you have to get a visa in advance.

Be very careful about this, numerous travellers have discovered to their expense that Indonesian diplomatic offices are very uncertain about the full story on the new visa plan and happily tell you that entering without a visa at Jakarta is fine, failing to add if you then try to leave from Jayapura you'll be told no. Note also that not only do you have to pay for a pre-arrival visa, but you also get hit for the expensive 'landing fee' if you want to extend for more than a month.

FROM/TO INDIA & OTHER PLACES IN ASIA

Air Although Indonesia and Thailand are the two 'normal' places to travel to or from there are plenty of other possibilities including India, Sri Lanka, Burma, Hong Kong or the Philippines. For details on cheap air fares check the relevant sections in Singapore and Penang – these are the two airline ticket centres.

Sea In Penang R Jumabhoy & Sons, 39 Green Hall, is the agent for the Shipping Corporation of India ship *MV Chidambaram* which goes to Madras about every two weeks. The four-day crossing costs about US$200 in economic class or M$280 in 1st class. There are other cheaper classes available, but these are the only two non-Indians are allowed to take!

The *Chidambaram* has a swimming pool and other de-luxe facilities and also operates Singapore-Penang, although few travellers will opt to make that longer trip. Sometimes the Penang-Madras sailing will include Trincomalee in Sri Lanka and/or Nagapattinam in Tamil Nadu on its route. It is possible to take cars and motorcycles on the *Chidambaram*. A VW Kombi or other vehicle from 14 foot 6 inches to 16 foot long would cost about US$700 plus US$80 in loading charges. A motorcycle would be about US$185 plus US$15 in additional charges.

A recent traveller on this route advised that 'it's wise to ring the agents in Penang to find the departure time then go down just a few hours before and avoid the thousands of Indians and their tons of luggage'. The ship is principally used by Tamils from the south of India who take the ship, rather than fly, simply because of the ability to take lots of baggage. There is little price difference between sea and air. The trip is OK, air-con is cold so have a sleeping bag. Food is not great but Anchor beer is cheap. They only accept M$ and S$ and they offer a lousy exchange rate from other currencies.

AIRPORT TAXES

Both Singapore and Malaysia levy airport taxes on all their flights. From Singapore the tax is S$5 on flights to Malaysia, S$12 on longer international flights. From Malaysia it's M$3 on domestic flights, M$5 to Singapore or Brunei and M$15 on other international flights. There is no airport tax out of Brunei.

Getting Around

BUSES

Malaysia has an excellent bus system throughout the country with public buses on local runs and a whole variety of privately operated buses on the longer trips as well as the big fleet of MARA Express buses. In larger towns there may be a number of bus stops – a main station or two plus some of the private companies may operate directly from their own offices.

Buses are fast, economical, reasonably comfortable and seats are reservable. On many routes there are also air-con buses which usually cost just a few dollars more than the regular buses. They make midday travel a sweat-free activity, but beware – as one traveller put it, 'Malaysian air-con buses are really meat lockers on wheels with just two settings: cold and suspended animation'.

LONG DISTANCE TAXIS

Malaysia's real travel bargain is the long distance taxis. They make Malaysian travel, already easy and convenient even by the best Asian standards, a real breeze. A long distance taxi is usually a diesel Mercedes, Peugeot or, more recently, Japanese car. In almost every town there will be a 'teksi' stand where the cars are lined up and ready to go to their various destinations. As soon as a full complement of four passengers turns up off you go. Between major towns the wait will rarely be long.

You can often get the taxis to pick you up or drop you off at your hotel or for four times the single fare you can 'charter' the whole taxi. You can also take a taxi to other destinations at charter rates. Taxi fares generally work out at about twice the comparable bus fares. Thus from KL to Butterworth it's M$30, KL to Melaka is M$12. Of course there has to be a drawback to all this and that is the frightening driving which the taxi pilots often indulge in. They don't have as many head-on collisions as you might expect, but closing your eyes at times of high stress certainly helps.

CAR RENTAL & DRIVING IN MALAYSIA

Rent-a-car operations in Malaysia and Singapore are still in their infancy, but they're bound to grow. In many Asian countries driving is either a fraught experience (ever seen the rush hour in Bangkok or Jakarta?), full of local dangers (I'd hate to think what would happen if you collided with a cow in India), or the roads are terrible, cars unavailable or for some other reason driving yourself is not really possible. None of these drawbacks apply in Malaysia and Singapore. The roads are generally of an excellent standard, there are plenty of new cars available and driving standards are not too hair raising.

Basically driving in Singapore and Malaysia follows much the same rules as in England or Australia – cars are right-hand drive, you drive on the left side of the road. The only additional precaution one needs to take is to remain constantly aware of the possible additional road hazards of stray animals, larger than usual (in the west) numbers of bicycles and occasionally suicidal motorcycles.

Although most drivers in Malaysia are relatively sane, safe and slow there are also a fair few who specialise in overtaking on blind corners and otherwise trusting in divine intervention. Long distance taxi drivers are particular specialists in these activities. Malaysian drivers also operate a curious signalling system where a left flashing indicator means 'you are safe to overtake' .... or 'I'm about to turn off' .... or 'I've forgotten to turn my indicator off' .... or something.

Petrol is more expensive than in the US, fairly comparable in price to Australia, a bit cheaper than in Europe at around M$4.60 an imperial gallon. Remember that wearing safety belts is now compulsory in both countries. Parking regulations are a little curious in both Singapore and Malaysia. Singapore has its coupon parking system and central business district entry regulations. In Malaysia they have a strange human parking meter system where your car collects a stack of little tickets under its wiper and you then have to find somebody to pay for them at so many cents per ticket.

Major rental operators in Singapore and Malaysia include Sintat, Avis, Hertz and Mayflower Acme although there are numerous others including many local operators only found in one city. Singapore in particular has a simply phenomenal number of local operators. Rates are quoted both for unlimited distance and with an additional mileage charge, cheaper rates are available by the week. Unlimited distance rates with Sintat vary from around M$118 a day for a Toyota Corolla to M$328 for a Mercedes.

AIR

Three airlines operate regional routes in this area – Singapore International Airlines, Malaysian Airlines System and Royal Brunei Airlines. Since every Royal Brunei or Singapore Airlines flight is an international flight it's Malaysian Airlines who have the major regional network. The chart details some of the main regional routes and their fares in M$. MAS have many other regional routes in Sarawak and Sabah. They operate Airbuses, Boeing 737s and Fokker F27 Friendships on their domestic routes plus Britten Norman Islanders on some of their remote Sarawak and Sabah routes. On some sectors the economy F27 fare is somewhat cheaper than the 737 fare.

You can also save quite a few dollars if flying to Sarawak or Sabah by flying from Johore Bahru rather than Singapore. To

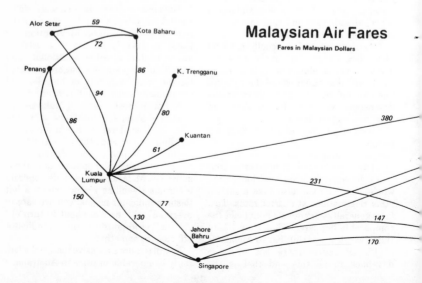

Malaysian Air Fares

Fares in Malaysian Dollars

Kuching the regular economy fare is M$147 from JB against M$170 from Singapore. To KK the respective fares are M$301 against M$346. To persuade travellers to take advantage of these lower fares MAS offer a bus service directly from their Singapore downtown office to the JB airport.

MAS also have a number of special night flights and advance purchase fares. The 14-day advance puchase tickets are available for one way/return flights from JB to Kuching – M$125/250; JB to Kota Kinabalu – M$256/512; Kuala Lumpur to Kuching – M$197/394; and Kuala Lumpur to Kota Kinabalu – M$323/646. There are also economy night flights between Kuala Lumpur and Kota Kinabalu M$266, Kuching M$162 and Penang M$61.

In north Borneo, where air transport is much more important than on the peninsula, there are many local flights which are often cancelled on short notice. Don't count too heavily on flight schedules here.

Don't believe too implicitly that flights are fully booked either. In Sarawak and Sabah you can often go out to the airport and find seats readily available on a supposedly full flight.

RAIL

Malaysia has a modern, comfortable and economical rail service although there are basically only two rail lines. One runs from Singapore to Kuala Lumpur, Butterworth and on into Thailand. The other branches off from this line at Gemas and runs through Kuala Lipis up to the north-east corner of the country near Kota Bahru. A road is now being pushed through paralleling this second 'jungle' line and it's probable that eventually it will be closed down. Other lines are just minor branches off these two routes and are not much used. The line to Port Dickson from Kuala Lumpur is only used for weekend excursions, for example.

Malaysia's first railway line was a 13 km

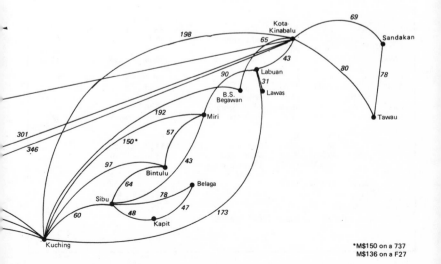

*M$150 on a 737
M$136 on a F27

route from Taiping to Port Weld which was laid in 1884, but is no longer in use. By 1903 you could travel all the way from Johore Bahru to near Butterworth and the extension of the line to the Thai border in 1918 and across the causeway to Singapore in 1923 meant you could travel by train from Singapore right into Thailand. In 1931 the east coast line was completed, effectively bringing the rail system to its present state.

The KTM, Keretapi Tanah Melayu, offers a number of concessions to rail travellers including a Railpass entitling the holder to unlimited travel for 30 days for M$150 or 10 days for M$70. The pass entitles you to travel on any class of train, but does not include sleeping berth charges. Railpasses are only available to foreign tourists and can be purchased at a number of main railway stations.

Malaysia has two types of rail services. First there are the conventional 1st-2nd-3rd class trains with both express and slower ordinary services. On these trains you can reserve seats on 1st and 2nd class up to 90 days in advance and there are day and overnight trains. On the overnight trains sleeping berths are available in 1st and 2nd class. The other trains are known as the Ekspres Rakyat (People's Express) and the Ekspres Sinaran. On these trains there is only a choice of air-con or non air-con carriages, but the trains only stop at main stations and consequently are faster than the regular express trains. In fact in most respects these services are definitely the ones to take. Fares on the Ekspres Rakyat and Ekspres Sinaran are very reasonable, not much more than 3rd class for the non air-con carriages, not much more than 2nd for air-con. Ekspres Rakyat and Ekspres Sinaran services are only operated between Singapore and KL or KL and Butterworth. Timetables for the main express train services are listed below.

There are a number of other ordinary (biasa) train services, particularly on the central route to the east coast where there are numerous local trains. For details on the fares and schedules to Hat Yai and Bangkok in Thailand see the From/To Thailand section in Getting There.

ER	E	ES	E		ES	E	ER	E
08.15	08.45	13.55	22.00	Butterworth	13.25	18.20	21.25	07.10
11.12	12.43	16.39	02.13	Ipoh	10.30	14.02	18.21	02.47
14.35	17.25	19.45	07.00	Kuala Lumpur	07.30	09.15	15.00	22.00

ES	E	ER	E		ER	E	ES	E
07.30	09.00	15.05	22.00	Kualu Lumpur	14.20	17.50	20.35	07.05
–	12.36	–	01.37	Gemas	–	13.52	–	02.57
13.18	17.08	21.16	06.36	Johore Bahru	08.28	09.17	14.56	22.34
13.45	17.55	21.40	07.25	Singapore	08.00	08.45	14.30	22.00

	O	E		E	O
	06.15	09.00	Tumpat	19.00	17.55
	06.43	09.25	Wakaf Bahru	18.18	17.20
	16.13	16.35	Kuala Lipis	09.48	07.30
	–	18.50	Jerantut	08.19	
–	23.45		Gemas	03.30	

- E – Express, ER – Ekspres Rakyat, ES – Ekspres Sinaran, 0 – Ordinary

Fares from Butterworth

	1st	2nd	3rd	ER/ES ac	non ac
Padang Besar	21.30	9.60	5.90	–	-
Alor Setar	12.00	5.65	3.55	–	-
Butterworth	–	–	–	–	-
Ipoh	22.50	10.20	6.30	17.00	10.00
Kuala Lumpur	48.60	21.90	13.50	28.00	17.00
Gemas	69.20	31.30	19.20	–	-
Johore Bahru	93.50	42.20	25.90	49.00	29.00
Singapore	96.00	43.30	26.60	50.00	30.00
Kuala Lipis	97.10	45.20	28.60	–	-
Tumpat	133.60	60.20	37.00	–	-

Fares from Singapore

	1st	2nd	3rd	ER/ES ac	non ac
Padang Besar	114.20	51.50	31.60	–	-
Alor Setar	105.60	49.80	31.10	–	-
Butterworth	96.00	43.30	26.60	50.00	30.00
Ipoh	74.10	43.30	26.60	40.00	24.00
Kuala Lumpur	48.60	21.90	13.50	28.00	17.00
Gemas	27.90	13.20	8.30	–	-
Johore Bahru	3.20	1.50	0.90	8.00	4.00
Singapore	–	–	–	–	-
Kuala Lipis	54.70	25.80	16.10	–	-
Tumpat	91.10	41.10	25.20	–	-

Fares from Kuala Lumpur

	1st	2nd	3rd	ER/ES ac	non ac
Padang Besar	65.60	29.60	18.20	–	-
Alor Setar	58.30	27.50	17.20	–	-
Butterworth	48.60	21.90	13.50	28.00	17.00
Ipoh	25.50	11.50	7.10	18.00	11.00
Kuala Lumpur	–	–	–	–	-
Gemas	22.00	10.30	6.45	–	-
Johore Bahru	46.20	20.80	12.80	27.00	16.00
Singapore	48.60	21.90	13.50	28.00	17.00
Kuala Lipis	50.00	23.50	14.80	–	-
Tumpat	86.20	38.90	23.90	–	-

Supplementary berth charges are M$20 for 1st class air-con, M$10.00 1st class ordinary, M$8 for 2nd class lower berth, M$6 for 2nd class upper berth.
ER/ES – Ekspres Rakyat/Ekspres Sinaran   ac = air conditioned

HITCHING

Malaysia has long had a reputation for being an excellent place for hitch-hiking and it's generally still true. You'll get picked up both by expats and by Malaysians and Singaporeans, but it's strictly an activity for foreigners – a hitch-hiking Malaysian would probably just get left by the roadside! So the first rule of thumb in Malaysia is look foreign. Look neat and tidy too, a world-wide rule for successful hitching, but make sure your backpack is on view and you look like someone on his way around the country.

Apart from the basic point of hitching, getting from A to B cheaply, hitching in Malaysia has the additional benefit that it's a fine way to meet the local people. In our hitching up and down the peninsula Maureen and I have met many interesting people, been shown many things we wouldn't have otherwise seen and even tried many things to eat that we wouldn't have otherwise known about. Foreign hitch-hikers are also looked upon as a neutral ear – you're likely to find out much more about the *bumiputra* situation from disgruntled Chinese when you're in their car. Or hear much more about the Chinese from disgruntled Malaysians!

Don't try hitching in Singapore, it's too small, too built up and the government probably doesn't approve of it. On the west coast of Malaysia, particularly on the busy Johore Bahru-Kuala Lumpur-Butterworth route, hitching is generally quite easy. Much of the traffic is businessmen, the sort of people interested in conversation and likely to pick up hitch-hikers. On the east coast traffic can often be quite light and there may be long waits between rides. Hitching in north Borneo also depends on the traffic although it's quite possible. Hitching into Bandar Seri Begawan from the Sarawak-Brunei border is quite easy.

LOCAL TRANSPORT

Local transport varies widely from place to place. Almost everywhere there will be taxis and in most cases these will be metered. In major cities there will be buses – in Singapore they are all government operated, in Kuala Lumpur the government buses are backed up by private operators. In many towns there are also bicycle-rickshaws – while they are dying out in KL and have become principally a tourist gimmick in most of Singapore they are still a viable form of transport in many Malaysian cities. Indeed in places like Georgetown, with its convoluted and narrow streets, a bicycle rickshaw is probably the best way of getting around. See the relevant city by city sections for more details on local transport.

The universal Malay taxi signal for "can't stop, full up." (usually works)

At a taxi driver's funeral...
(MALAYSIA)

Singapore

Singapore is an island at the tip of the Malay peninsula. It was once just a small fishing kampong on a rather swampy island. It took its improbable name, 'Lion City', from a Sumatran prince who thought he saw a lion where they have probably never been. Singapore would have drifted quietly on if Sir Stamford Raffles had not decided, in 1819, that it was just the port he needed to ensure Britain's pre-eminent position in the east.

His choice proved to be a sound one because today Singapore not only thrives on trade but has become a jet age travel crossroads with one of the busiest airports in Asia. Under its efficient and forward looking government Singapore has become the most affluent country in Asia after Japan and a model for developing nations. Singapore celebrates 20 years of independence in 1985. For the visitor it's promoted as 'instant Asia' – a place offering colourful variety in a small, handy package.

Facts

Population Singapore's polyglot population numbers 2.5 million. It's made up of 76% Chinese, 15% Malay, 7% Indian and Pakistani and the remaining 2% a variety of races. Singapore's population density is high but the government has waged a particularly successful birth control campaign. Great emphasis is placed on the two child family being the ideal (two girls or not) and there are a number of financial disincentives to larger families.

Geography Singapore is a low-lying island of 616 square km, not much over 100 km from the equator. Apart from the main island there are also about 50 smaller islands. Singapore is connected with peninsular Malaysia by a km long causeway. Bukit Timah (Hill of Tin) is the highest point on the island at 166 metres altitude.

Economy Singapore's economy is based on trade, shipping, banking and tourism with a growing programme of light industrialisation. Singapore has a major oil refining business producing much of the petroleum for the South-East Asian region. Other important industries include ship building and maintenance and electronics. Singapore's port is the third busiest in the world.

There are few social programmes in Singapore although medical care is heavily subsidised. As part of the government's 'rugged society' programme there are also no unemployment payments or programmes – but unemployment is negligible and the government insists that anyone who wants to work can find work. In fact Singapore actually has negative unemployment and has to import workers from neighbouring countries, particularly to do the hard, dirty work which Singaporeans no longer want any part of.

Strikes are virtually unknown in Singapore but the government has a policy to actually push wages up in order to drive the inefficient labour intensive industries out and force more capital intensive industries to the fore. At a time when some western countries are trying to protect their inefficient 'twilight' industries it's quite a different policy! All Singaporeans have to save money with the Central Provident Fund, a form of superannuation that is returned to them on retirement. They can, however, invest their CPF savings in the purchase of government housing.

Information

The Singapore Tourist Promotion Board (tel 235 6611) has its office at 131 Tudor Court, Tanglin Rd. The office is open from 8 am to 5 pm Monday to Saturday and can provide a variety of useful leaflets and information. They also have the *Singapore*

Weekly Guide which provides a useful and colourful run down on the entire island.

There is a hotel booking desk at the airport but they will not book rooms in the bottom end hotels. Student Travel have an office in the Ming Court Hotel on the mezzanine level. They can provide advice on student cards, cheap airline tickets and also offer discounts on various hotels.

Although the signs announcing that 'Men with long hair will be served last' are still prominently displayed the famous anti-long-hair campaign has been toned down of late. You're unlikely to be turned away on arrival or given short back and sides on the spot unless you look really outrageous. Singapore remains heavy on a number of other issues, however. The successful anti-littering campaign continues – up to S$500 fine for dropping even a cigarette butt on the street. Actually nobody does get fined that amount but no matter, it works, Singapore is amazingly clean. Similarly you can get hit for a S$500 fine for smoking in a public place – buses, lifts, cinemas and even government offices. Jaywalking is the latest activity to get the Singapore treatment – walk across the road within 50 metres of a designated crossing and it could cost you S$50.

Post & Phone The GPO, with its efficient poste restante service, is on Raffles Quay close to the Singapore River. It's open for stamps 8.30 am – 6 pm daily, till 2 pm Saturday. For poste restante till 5.30 daily, 1.30 pm Saturday. For overseas telephone calls it's open 24 hours and very efficient. To make international phone calls go to a telecom centre like the ones on Hill St or Robinson Rd.

Immigration & Health If you plan to stay in Singapore for longer than your initial two week entry permit the Immigration Office is on Empress Place, just across the river from the GPO. For cheap immunisations go to the Health Centre, 5th floor, Office Tower Block, Tanjung Pagar Complex, 280 Tanjung Pagar Rd, Singapore 0208.

Banks Most of the major banks are in the central business area although there are also a number of banks along Orchard Rd and local banks all over the city. Note that exchange rates tend to vary from bank to bank and that some also make a service charge on each exchange transaction. This usually costs S$2 to 3, ask first.

Money changers usually offer a better rate for cash than banks do. Most of them are found in the shops opposite Raffles Quay or along the Change Alley shopping arcade, although you will also find them scattered in other places in Singapore. Apart from changing other currencies to Singapore dollars they also offer a wide variety of other currencies for sale and will do amazing multiple currency transactions at the blink of an eye.

Airlines Singapore is a major international crossroads and a great number of airlines fly here. Some of the most frequently used airlines include:

Aeroflot
  Sinsov Building, Market St (tel 532 6711)
Air India
  UIC Building, 5 Shenton Way (tel 220 5277)
Air New Zealand
  Ocean Building, Collyer Quay (tel 91 8266)
Air Lanka
  Crosby House, 75 Robinson Rd (tel 223 6026)
Bangladesh Biman
  Fidvi Building, 97-99 Market St (tel 91 2155)
British Airways
  International Building, Orchard Rd (tel 737 1422)
Cathay Pacific
  Ocean Building, Collyer Quay (tel 91 1811)
China Airlines
  Lucky Plaza, 304 ,Orchard Rd (tel 737 2144)
Garuda
  101 Thomson Rd, Goldhill Square (tel 250 5888)

Japan Air Lines
Hong Leong Building, Raffles Quay (tel 220 2211)
KLM
Mandarin Hotel, 333 Orchard Rd (tel 737 7211)
Korean Air Lines
10 Anson Rd, International Plaza (tel 221 1333)
MAS
Singapore Shopping Centre, Clemenceau Ave (tel 336 6777)
Pakistan International
Hilton International, Orchard Rd (tel 737 3233)
Pan Am
Hong Leong Building, Robinson Rd (tel 220 0488)
Philippine Airlines
902-904 Parklane Shopping Mall (tel 336 1611)
Qantas
Mandarin Hotel, 333 Orchard Rd (tel 737 3744)
Royal Brunei Airlines
Orchard Towers, 400 Orchard Rd (tel 235 4672)
Singapore Airlines
77 Robinson Rd (tel 223 8888)
Thai International
Denmark House, Raffles Quay (tel 224 2041)
UTA
Ming Court Hotel, Tanglin Rd (tel 737 7166)

Consulates & Embassies

Australia
25 Napier Rd (tel 737 9311)
Bangladesh
Thomson Rd, Godhill Square (tel 250 6323)
Britain
Tanglin Rd (tel 63 9333)
Burma
15 St Martin's Drive (tel 235 8704)
Canada
Faber House, Orchard Rd (tel 737 1322)
Denmark
Thomson Rd, Goldhill Square (tel 250 3383)
Germany
Far East Shopping Centre, Orchard Rd (tel 737 1355)

India
31 Grange Rd (tel 737 6809)
Indonesia
6-D Orange Grove Rd
Japan
16 Nassim Rd (tel 235 8855)
Malaysia
301 Jervois Rd (tel 235 0111)
Netherlands
Liat Towers, Orchard Rd (tel 737 1155)
New Zealand
13 Nassim Rd (tel 235 9966)
Philippines
Thong Teck Building, Scotts Rd (tel 737 3977)
Sri Lanka
Goldhill Plaza, Newton Rd (tel 254 4595)
Sweden
PUB Building, Somerset Rd (tel 734 2771)
Thailand
370 Orchard Rd (tel 737 2644)
USA
30 Hill St (tel 338 0251)

Orientation

Singapore Island is relatively easy to find your way around. At the top it is joined to Malaysia by the causeway which carries both road and rail traffic. At the bottom centre of the island is Singapore city. Changi Airport is at the extreme eastern tip of the island while the major industrial centre, Jurong, is towards the western tip. If you thought of the island as having a north, south, east and west corner, which in essence it does, those four places (causeway, city, airport and Jurong) would define it.

In the city itself Orchard Rd and Bras Basah Rd make a very useful dividing line. Orchard Rd continues more or less directly on to Bras Basah Rd and they run more or less perpendicularly towards the waterfront. Both are one way so a parallel road carries traffic in the opposite direction away from the waterfront. Bras Basah Rd is the watershed for cheap hotels – backpackers almost always stay in the older hotels to the east of Bras Basah Rd.

On the other hand Orchard Rd is the address of a large percentage of Singapore's

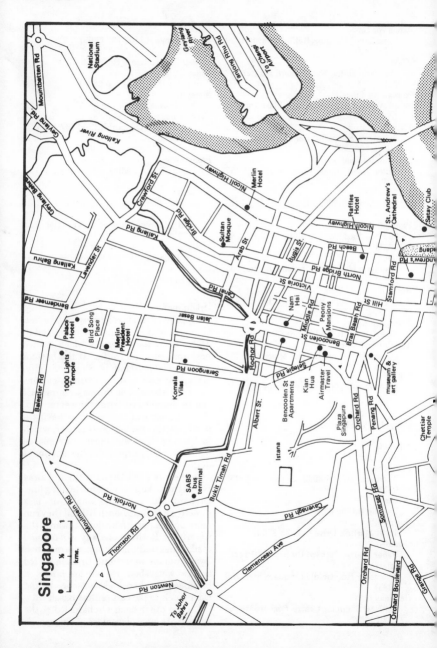

Singapore

kms.

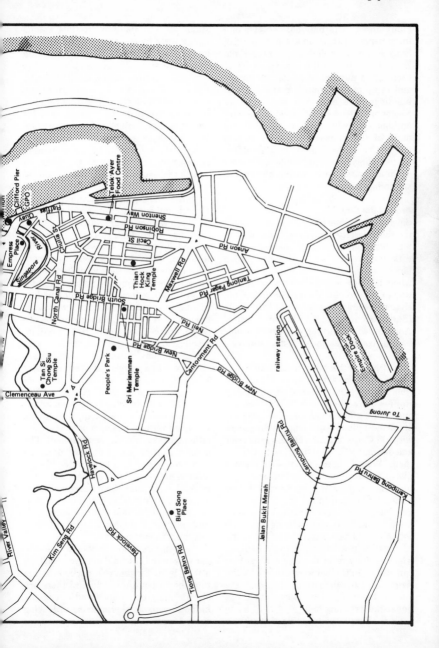

multi-storey international hotels and interspersed with them are a number of Singapore's major shopping centres. From Bras Basah Rd to the Singapore River there are a number of parks and greens and some of Singapore's major colonial buildings. The modern office centre of Singapore is to the south-west of the river and here you will also find the GPO and most of the banks. North-east of this modern centre is Chinatown, the oldest part of Singapore city, while north-east again are many new housing blocks and shopping centres.

Around the City

Singapore's greatest attraction is probably the sheer variety it offers – you can walk in minutes from the modern business centre with its soaring, air-conditioned office blocks into the narrow streets of Chinatown where the bicycle-rickshaw is still the best way to get around. Meanwhile across the river there are areas known as little India (Serangoon Rd) and the Moslem centre of Arab St while further out are the new housing complexes and industrial centres.

City, River & Harbour Singapore's city centre straddles the Singapore River and runs parallel to the waterfront along Raffles Quay, Shenton Way, Robinson Rd and Cecil St. The Singapore River was one of the most picturesque areas of Singapore with old shops and houses along the river and soaring office buildings right behind them. Well, it doesn't look like the old places will be around much longer. All the bustling activity along this stretch of river – the loading and unloading of sampans and bumboats – has ceased. The cranes are gone and the yelling, sweating labourers, too. All boats have been kicked out of the area and relocated to the Pasir Panjang wharves away from the city centre. You can still sit in the hawkers centres by the river, but rather than watch all the activity you can bet on which building will be next under the wrecking ball.

On the Empress Place side of the river a statue of Sir Stamford Raffles stands imperiously by the river, in the approximate place where he first set foot on Singapore island. There is a second statue of Raffles in front of the clock tower by Empress Place. Nearby is the Supreme Court and City Hall, across from which is the open green of the Padang, site for cricket, hockey, football and rugby matches. Here too there are memorials to civilians who died as a result of the Japanese occupation and to Lim Bo Seng, a resistance leader killed by the Japanese.

If you continue up Coleman St from the Padang you pass the Armenian Church and come to Fort Canning Hill, a good viewpoint over Singapore. Once known as 'Forbidden Hill', the hill is now topped by the Old Christian Cemetery with many gravestones with their poignant tales of hopeful settlers who died young. Here too is the tomb of Sultan Iskander Shah, the last ruler of the ancient kingdom of Singapura. At the mouth of the river, or at least what used to be the mouth before the most recent bout of land reclamation, stands Singapore's symbol, the Merlion.

Change Alley, Singapore's most famous spot for bargains has survived or rather adapted to modernisation. It still cuts through from Collyer Quay to Raffles Place, but has become a pedestrian bridge and is known as 'Aerial Change Alley'. It's still lined with shops and money changers although now it's air conditioned! The older alley runs below. Further along the waterfront you'll find large office blocks, airlines offices and more shops. Here too is Telok Ayer Market, an octagonal, open Victorian-style market building now used as a very popular food centre. Singapore's disappearing Chinatown is inland from this modern city centre.

You can hire a boat to go out onto the harbour from Clifford Pier or you can take a tour boat. Singapore's harbour is the third busiest in the world and there are always many boats anchored out in the harbour, with another arriving or leaving every 15 minutes.

Chinatown One of the most fascinating areas of Singapore is also, unfortunately, one of the most rapidly disappearing. Any time you can spare an hour or two it's worth devoting it to wandering the tightly packed streets of Chinatown – in a few years it's probable that there will be very little left to explore. Meanwhile any time of day is a good time, but you'll probably find the early morning hours not only the most interesting but also the coolest. Chinatown is roughly bounded by the Singapore River to the east, New Bridge Rd to the north, Maxwell Rd and Kreta Ayer Rd to the west and Cecil Rd to the south. Roughly, because already urban renewal and new office blocks are nibbling at the edges of Chinatown and wider roads are being ploughed right through the middle of it.

You could start a Chinatown walking tour from Boon Tat St beside the Telok

Ayer food centre. This is still a narrow street lined with typical Chinese shop-fronts and at the junction with Telok Ayer St you'll find the Nagore Durgha Shrine (1), an old mosque built by Moslems from south India in 1829-30. It's not too interesting, but just a little down the street is the Chinese Thian Hock Keng or Temple of Heavenly Happiness (2) – one of the most interesting in Singapore. See Temples, Mosques & Churches for more details.

Continue walking along Telok Ayer St and you'll soon come to the Al-Abrar Mosque (3) which was originally built in 1827 and rebuilt in its present form in 1850-55. A right turn and another right turn will bring you into Amoy St where once again there are rows of typical Chinese shop fronts with their convoluted 'five-foot ways'. Walking on these covered walkways is always a continuous obstacle

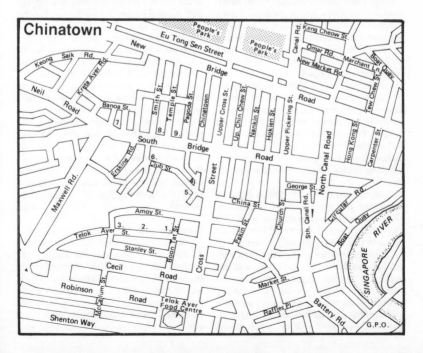

course. Notice how on many of these old Chinese houses bushes and even large trees seem to sprout straight out of the walls – it's a tribute to the amazing fertility which Singapore's steamy climate seems to engender.

Cross Cross St, a wide new road which has been ruthlessly pushed right through the middle of Chinatown, and then turn up Pekin St to China St. This whole street is a fascinating conglomeration of shops and shopfront activity. Old men ride by on bicycle-rickshaws, shops sell provisions and Chinese groceries, you can peer into a darkened Chinese wine shop where old men cluster around equally old marble-topped tables. Further along there are shops making and selling temple equipment and the paraphernalia you burn for good luck. Another shop deals in eggs – brown eggs, white eggs, chicken eggs, duck eggs, even hundred year old eggs.

If you cross back over Cross St the name changes to Club St, a curious street because it seems to go steeply uphill when you would think this part of Singapore was all pancake flat. On the corner with Mohamed Ali Lane a tiny hole in the wall shop (4) makes 'popiah' skins – the outer covering for Chinese spring rolls. Across the road are a couple of places where Chinese religious figures and temple furniture are carved and painted (5). At the top of Club St you meet Ann Siang Hill and on the corner here you'll find a place making paper transport for the after life – anything from a bicycle-rickshaw to a car (6).

Continue up to South Bridge Rd and you enter the real heart of Chinatown although here too urban renewal is cutting its swath. Many of the most interesting sights in this area could only be seen very early in the morning, when the food and produce markets were operating, or in the evening when the night markets would swing into action. Along Trengannu, Smith and Banda Sts you could see fish stalls selling fish, turtles, snails, frogs and even snakes – dead or alive. A fish would

be netted out of a tank and clubbed to death right there in the street so you could be certain it was fresh. Vegetable stalls sold glistening fruit and vegetables. Chickens were carried off in baskets or unceremoniously carted off by the legs. In the evening the daytime produce markets gave way to night markets where you could find anything from general second hand rubbish to fortune tellers, pirated cassettes, old records or Chinese medicines. It's all past tense because on 30 September 1983 the street hawkers were all shut down and moved to an antiseptic new centre just off New Bridge Rd, another nail in the coffin of colourful old Singapore.

All the streets in this area are full of interest but some particular things to look for include the last few old 'Death Houses' (7). Old folk were once packed off here towards the end of their lives, thus avoiding the possible bad luck of a death in the home. This ancient idea is fast dying out! Along Temple St look for the funeral paraphernalia dealers (8) who turn out paper cars, houses, ships, and other equipment just in case you can take it with you. Also in this area is the Sri Mariamman Temple (9) which is described elsewhere.

Other things you may see in the bustling streets of Chinatown include calligraphers who will quickly pen a message in Chinese script for you. Chinese delicacies like shark's fins, abalone, sea slugs or deer horns can be seen in some shops. Across the New Bridge Rd is the huge People's Park Complex – a modern shopping centre, but with much more local appeal than the general run of Orchard Rd centres.

Serangoon Rd Although Singapore is a predominantly Chinese city it does have its minority groups and the Indians are probably the most visible – particularly in the colourful streets of 'little India'. This is another area, like Chinatown, where you simply wander around and take in the flavours. Indeed around Serangoon Rd it can be very much a case of following your nose because the heady aromas of Indian spices and cooking seem to be everywhere.

If you want a new sari, a pair of Indian sandals, a recent issue of *India Today* or the *Illustrated Weekly of India*, a tape of Indian music or a framed portrait of your favourite Hindu god then this is the place to come. It's also, not surprisingly, a good place to eat and you'll see streetside cooks frying up chappatis at all times of the day. Since many of Singapore's Indians are Tamils from the south of India the accent on food is chiefly vegetarian and there are some superb places to eat vegetarian food – number one being the well known *Komala Vilas*.

Arab Street While Chinatown is the centre for Singapore's old-time Chinese flavour and Serangoon Rd is where you head to for the tastes and smells of India, Arab St is the Moslem centre. Along the street you'll find batiks from Indonesia, sarongs, songkok hats, basketware and other rattan goods. The Sultan Mosque, focus for Singapore's Moslem community, is at the junction of Arab St and North Bridge Rd and you'll also find good north Indian food at restaurants along North Bridge Rd.

Other Areas Singapore's international tourists also have an area of Singapore to themselves – Orchard Rd where the international hotels predominate. Beyond Orchard Rd you enter yet another Singapore area – prior to independence the mansions of the colonial rulers were located here and today Singapore's wealthy elite as well as many expatriate personnel live in these fine old houses.

Still another side of Singapore is found in the modern HDB (Housing & Development Board) satellite cities like Toa Payoh. Already 60% of Singaporeans live in these government housing blocks and it is intended to raise the figure to 80% by the end of the decade. Once again it's a programme that Singapore manages to make work. While high rise flats have

become a dirty word in many countries, in Singapore they're almost universally popular. In many cases the occupants actually own their own flats and, Singapore being Singapore once again, with prices escalating it's often possible to sell your flat at a profit before you even move in.

Jurong Town, in the west of the island, is more than just a new housing area. Here a huge industrial complex has been built from the ground up on land that was still a swamp at the end of WW II. Today it's the power house of Singapore's economic success story.

Temples, Mosques & Churches
Singapore's polyglot population has resulted in an equally varied collection of places of worship. There are Chinese, Hindu and Buddhist temples, Moslem mosques and Christian churches. Even here there are further interesting subdivisions. The churches chiefly date from the English colonial period, but Singapore's oldest church is Armenian, since Armenian traders were here at virtually the same time as Raffles. The Hindu temples are basically of the Dravidian style of south India since so many of Singapore's Indian settlers are Tamils from that region.

Thian Hock Keng The temple of Heavenly Happiness on Telok Ayer St in Chinatown is the oldest and also one of the most colourful temples in Singapore – in part due to a restoration in 1979. The temple was originally built in 1840 and dedicated to Ma-Cho-Po, the Queen of Heaven and protector of sailors.

At that time it was on the waterfront and since many Chinese settlers were arriving in Singapore by sea it was inevitable that a joss house be built where they could offer thanks for a safe voyage. As you wander the courtyards of the temple look for the rooftop dragons, the intricately decorated beams, the burning joss sticks, the gold leafed panels and, best of all, the beautifully painted doors. It's open from 5.30 am to 9 pm.

Sri Mariamman Temple On South Bridge Rd, right in the heart of Chinatown, the Sri Mariamman Temple is the oldest Hindu temple in Singapore. It was originally built in 1827, but its present form dates from 1862 when the original wooden temple was rebuilt. With its colourful gopuram or tower over the entrance gate this is clearly a temple in the south Indian Dravidian style. A superb collection of colourfully painted Hindu figures gaze out from the gopuram. In October of each year the temple is the scene for the Thimithi festival in which devotees walk barefoot over burning coals – supposedly feeling no pain although spectators report that quite a few hot-foot it over the final few steps! The Sri Mariamman Temple is open from 6 am to 12 noon and from 4.30 to 8.30 pm.

Temple of 1000 Lights Situated towards the end of Race Course Rd, close to the Serangoon Rd/Lavender St junction, this Buddhist temple is dominated by a brightly painted 15 metre high seated figure of Buddha. The temple was inspired by a Thai monk named Vutthisasara, but although it is said to be similar to the temples of Bangkok in fact it's far more Chinese in its technicolour flavour.

Apart from the huge Buddha image the temple includes oddities like a wax model of Gandhi and a figure of Ganesh, the elephant-headed Hindu god. A huge mother-of-pearl footprint is said to be a replica of the footprint on top of Adam's Peak in Sri Lanka, complete with the 108 auspicious marks which distinguish a Buddha foot from any other two metre long foot. Go round behind the giant statue and inside is a smaller image of the reclining Buddha, in the act of entering nirvana. Right round the base models tell the story of the Buddha's life, and, of course, there are the 1000 lights which give the temple its name.

Directly across the road is a colourful new Chinese temple. Any bus going down Serangoon Rd will get you there.

Sultan Mosque On North Bridge Rd the Sultan Mosque is the biggest mosque in Singapore. It was originally built in 1825 with the aid of a grant from Raffles and the East India Company as a result of his treaty with the Sultan of Johore. A hundred years later the original mosque was replaced by today's more magnificent gold-domed building. The mosque is open to visitors from 5 am to 8.30 pm daily and the best time to visit is during a religious ceremony.

Churches St Andrew's Cathedral on North Bridge Rd is Singapore's Anglican cathedral, built in Gothic style between 1856 and 1863. It's located on Coleman St and Stamford Rd. There's a Catholic Cathedral too, the Cathedral of the Good Shepherd on Queen St. This was built between 1843 and 1846 and is a Singapore historic monument. The oldest church in Singapore, however, is the Armenian Church of St Gregory the Illuminator on Hill St which is no longer used for services.

Other Temples & Mosques Singapore has many other Chinese and Indian temples and mosques. On Tank Rd, near the intersection of Clemenceau Avenue and River Valley Rd, the Chettiar Hindu Temple was built in 1855-60 and is dedicated to six-headed Lord Subramaniam.

The Islamic Durgha Shrine and Al Abrar Mosque are on Telok Ayer St in Chinatown. The Hajjah Fatimah Mosque on Java Rd is near the Crawford St end of Beach Rd. It's a picturesque small mosque built around 1845 and has a leaning minaret. The Jamae or Chulia Mosque on South Bridge Rd is only a short distance from the Sri Mariamman Temple. It was built by Moslem Indians from the Coromandel Coast of Tamil Nadu between 1830 and 1855.

The large new Siong Lim Temple and Garden is on Jalan Toa Payoh, out towards Paya Lebar Airport. On Magazine Rd, near Clemenceau Avenue and the Singapore River, the Tan Si Chong Su

Top: Chinatown, Singapore (TW)
Left: washing still hangs from modern government apartments, Singapore (TW)
Right: unloading boats on Singapore river (TW)

Top: Chinatown, Singapore (TW)
Left: Singapore River & the central business district office blocks (TW)
Right: Raffles statue at his landing place on the Singapore River (TW)

Temple is a temple and ancestral hall built in 1876 for the Tan clan. The Kuan Yin Temple on Waterloo St is one of the most popular Chinese temples – after all she's also one of the most popular goddesses. This temple has just undergone a massive facelift and reconstruction. On top of Mt Faber on Pender Rd stands the One Thousand Buddhas Hilltop Temple.

Places to Go, Things to Do

Apart from parks, islands, gardens, temples and colourful city areas Singapore also has a whole list of conventional attractions from museums and galleries to an aquarium, the Instant Asia show, and the famous Raffles Hotel.

Instant Asia & the Singapore Experience

For jetset tourists who want to see it all in one fast, painless performance the Instant Asia show is just the ticket. In 45 action packed minutes you'll see everything from lion dances to Indian snake charmers and Chinese opera. Some of the costumes and dances you are unlikely to see elsewhere. It's very popular with photographers. The show takes place at 9.45 am daily at the Singapore Cultural Theatre behind the Rasa Singapore food centre and the Singapore Handicraft Centre. Admission is S$5.

The Singapore Experience, a multi-screen story of Singapore also takes place at the theatre. It takes 35 minutes and begins at 11 am, 12.30 pm and 2.30 pm. Admission is S$5 here, too.

National Museum & Art Gallery

Centrally located on Stamford Rd the National Museum traces its ancestry back to Sir Stamford Raffles who first brought up the idea of a museum for Singapore in 1823. The original museum was finally opened in 1849 then moved to another location in 1862 before being rehoused in the present building in 1887. Exhibits include archaeological artifacts from the Asia region, articles relating to Chinese trade and settlement in the region, Malaysian and Indonesian arts and crafts and a wide collection of items relating to Raffles. These include his manuscripts plus maps and paintings of old Singapore.

The art gallery includes contemporary paintings from both Singaporean and other South-East Asian artists. A recent addition to the museum is the superb jade collection from Haw Par House which has now been closed. The Aw brothers, of Tiger Balm fame, amassed not only this priceless collection of jade pieces but also a variety of other valuable pieces of art. The museum is open from 10.30 am to 7 pm daily and admission is free but major renovations began in early '84 and the reopening date has not been set.

Van Kleef Aquarium

On River Valley Rd in Central Park the Van Kleef Aquarium has 71 tanks displaying nearly 5000 fish and other creatures including crocodiles and turtles. The aquarium is open from 9.30 am to 9 pm daily and admission is 60c.

Jurong Science Centre

On Science Centre Rd, off Jurong Town Hall Rd, the Science Centre is great fun. It attempts to make science come alive by providing countless opportunities to try things out yourself. There are handles to crank, buttons to push, levers to pull, microscopes to look through, films to watch. The centre is open from 10 am to 6 pm from Tuesday to Sunday and admission is S$1. You can get there on a 143 or 158 bus.

Raffles Hotel

The Raffles Hotel is far more than just an expensive place to stay or even just the best known hotel in Singapore. It's a Singapore institution, an architectural landmark which has been classified by the government as a part of Singapore's 'cultural heritage' and a place that virtually oozes the old fashioned atmosphere of the east as Somerset Maugham would have known it.

Originally the Raffles started as a tiffin house run by a Captain Dare – tiffin is the colonial era terminology for a curry lunch.

IN A CHINESE CAFE IN SINGAPORE

On a steamy night near the Equator
Chinese men drink Irish beer and watch
the F.A. Cup from Wembly...

Later he expanded it into a hotel which in 1886 was taken over by the Sarkies brothers, three Armenians who built a string of hotels which were to become famous throughout the east. They include the Strand in Rangoon and the E&O in Penang as well as the Raffles.

The Raffles soon became a by word for oriental luxury, featured in novels by Joseph Conrad and Somerset Maugham, was recommended by Rudyard Kipling as the place to 'feed at' when in Singapore (but stay elsewhere he added!) and in its Long Bar one Ngiam Tong Boon created the Singapore Sling in 1915. You can still front the bar and order a Singapore Sling today. More recently the Raffles was threatened by redevelopment, it had lost its waterfront location to land reclamation and more modern hotels could offer better facilities and far lower running costs. Fortunately there are enough discerning visitors to keep the Raffles balance sheet in the black and future developments will be in the form of extensions, not replacement of the existing building.

Meanwhile a visit to the Raffles is well worthwhile even if you're not staying there. You can sip a drink in the bar or order tea on the immaculate lawn. And turn the clock back a century.

Sunday Morning Bird Singing One of the nicest things to do on a Sunday morning in Singapore is to go hear the birds sing. The Chinese love caged birds as their beautifully ornate bird cages indicate. The birds – thrushes, merboks, sharmas, and mata putehs – are treasured for their singing ability. To ensure the quality of their song the doting owner will feed his bird a carefully prepared diet and once a week crowds of bird fanciers get together for a bird song session.

The bird cages are hung up on wires strung between trees or under verandahs. They're not mixed indiscriminately – sharmas sing with sharmas, merboks with merboks – and each type of bird has its own design of cage. Tall pointy ones for tall pointy birds, short and squat ones for short squat birds. Having assembled the birds the proud owners then congregate around tables, sip coffee and listen to their birds go through their paces. It's a delightful scene both musically and visually.

You'll find bird concerts on Sunday mornings from around 8 to 11 am at the junction of Tiong Bahru and Seng Poh Rds and at Sturdee Lane by Petain Rd, just off Jalan Besar near the Lavender St intersection.

Other Places The Thong Chai Medical Institution building on Wayang St was built in 1892 and now houses, among other things, a display of Chinese medicines. On Clemenceau Avenue the House of Tan Yeok Nee is now the headquarters of the Salvation Army, but in 1885 it was built as the townhouse of a prosperous merchant in a style then common in the south of China.

Near the Malaysia Causeway off Woodlands Rd the Kranji War Memorial includes the graves of thousands of Allied servicemen who died in the region in WW II. There are a number of art galleries and displays apart from the major National Museum Art Gallery. On Clemenceau Avenue the National Theatre also has a gallery with paintings and ceramics. The Alpha Gallery at 7 Alexandra Avenue displays work by local and Balinese artists. Sculptures and batik paintings can be seen in the Seah Gallery in the Shangri-La Hotel. The three Centre of Fine Arts displays (see Things to Buy) also have a wide variety of artwork.

After Dark Singapore has plenty of night time activity although it is certainly not of the Bangkok or Manila sex and sin variety. Even Bugis St, Singapore's raucous transvestite parade ground, has been cleaned up. It was never, officially, more than simply another food stall centre, but in practice at the witching hour certain young men turned into something much more exotic than pumpkins.

Today you can still eat and drink to all hours, but you're unlikely to see many strange fantasies mincing between tables. It remains, however, a lively and interesting area to browse around in the evening. Chinese men hawk powerful medicines and smash bricks with their bare hands to show what they will do for your sexual potency. Astrologers and fortune tellers set up their cards, gamblers run shell games that appear so easy to win it's a joke and various novelties are displayed. Good-quality pirated cassettes are offered at booths for just S$2.

Still, if you're worried that Singapore is simply too squeaky clean for belief, you may be relieved to hear that there's a real locals-only low class red light district stretching along a narrow alley from Jalan Besar to Serangoon Rd. Also, there's apparently another street that the transvestites now use, but it's kept fairly quiet these days.

There are many more mundane ways you can spend the night in Singapore. There are plenty of cinemas although Singaporean taste in western films runs very much to the action-packed spectaculars, despairing Singaporean movie fans occasionally pen letters to the *Straits Times* asking why one acclaimed film or another has never (and may never) be shown in Singapore. Or you can kung fu it in Chinese films or see an all-singing all-dancing Indian movie.

The big hotels have cocktail lounges, cabarets, discos and theatre restaurants. At the Mandarin there is a four times weekly ASEAN night featuring activities from all over the region – rather like the Instant Asia show. The Raffles Hotel also puts on a nightly cultural show which you can combine with dinner. Trishaw tours, lasting 1½ to three hours, start at the Raffles Hotel each evening and include a visit to Chinatown before depositing patrons on Orchard Rd. There are also night harbour cruises (two to three hours) including a cheap S$2 cruise from the World Trade Centre ferry terminal.

The impecunious can find free entertainment by simply wandering the streets. In Chinatown or in the older streets around Serangoon Rd and Jalan Besar you may well chance upon a Wayang – the brilliantly costumed Chinese street operas. In these noisy and colourful extravaganzas over-acting is all important; there's nothing subtle about it at all. At the many food centres eating can be combined with entertainment – the food preparation is all out front and it goes on fairly late in many centres.

Parks & Gardens

Singapore has been dubbed the Garden City and with good reason – it's green and lush with parks and gardens scattered everywhere. In part this fertility is a factor of the climate – you only have to stick a twig in the ground for it to become a tree in weeks! The government has backed up this natural advantage with a concentrated programme that has even turned the dividing strip on highways into flourishing gardens – you notice it even as you drive into Singapore from the Malaysia causeway.

Botanic Gardens Singapore's Botanic Gardens are on Cluny and Holland Rds, not far from Tanglin Rd and the Tourist Office. They're a popular peaceful retreat for Singaporeans although they also house the herbarium where much work has been done on breeding orchids, for which Singapore is famous. In an earlier era the gardens pioneered the development of rubber plants that were to be spread all over South-East Asia. The gardens are open from 5 am to 11 pm on weekdays, to midnight on weekends, admission is free.

Tiger Balm Gardens About 10 km out from the city centre on Pasir Panjang Rd the Tiger Balm Gardens are a magnificent tribute to bad taste. An exotic collection of concrete and plaster figures cover six hillside hectares. It's a delight to children of all ages, a gaudy grotesquerie of statues

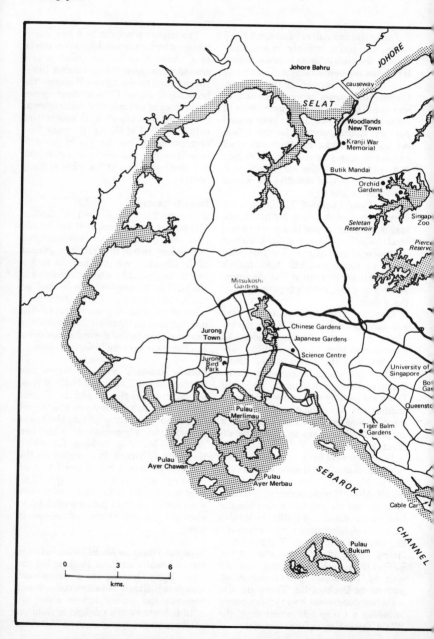

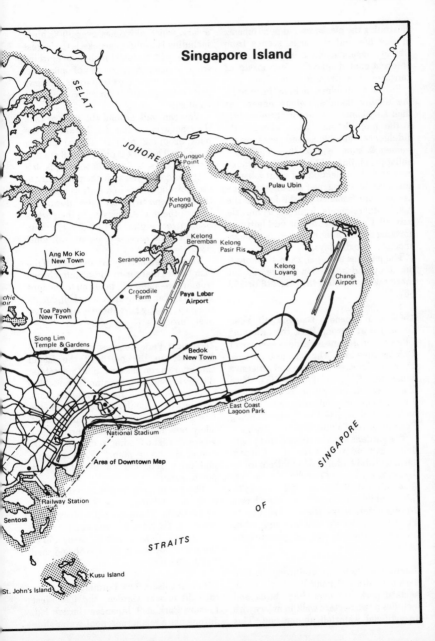

Singapore Island

SELAT

JOHORE

Punggol Point

Pulau Ubin

Kelong Punggol

Kelong Beremban

Kelong Pasir Ris

Ang Mo Kio New Town

Serangoon

Kelong Loyang

Changi Airport

Crocodile Farm

Paya Lebar Airport

Toa Payoh New Town

chie oir

Siong Lim Temple & Gardens

Bedok New Town

East Coast Lagoon Park

National Stadium

Area of Downtown Map

SINGAPORE

Railway Station

Sentosa

OF

STRAITS

Kusu Island

St. John's Island

illustrating the pleasures and punishments of this life and the next, scenes from Chinese legends and a whole series of 'international displays' – ie a group of kangaroos to represent Australia.

Favourite displays include, inevitably, the 'torture chamber', where sinners get their gory come-uppance in the after life, or the 'moral lessons' aisle, where sloth, indulgence, gambling and even wine, women & song lead to their inevitable unhappy endings. More curious groups even include collections of giant lobsters and frogs tumbling over one another. The gardens are financed by the fortune the Aw brothers made from their miracle cure-all Tiger Balm and the odd bottle of amazing Tiger Oil duly makes its appearance in some displays.

The gardens are open from 10 am to 6 pm daily and admission is free. To get there take a 10, 30, 143, 145, 146 or 192 bus.

Chinese & Japanese Gardens Off Yuan Ching Rd at Jurong Park the adjoining Chinese and Japanese gardens each cover 13.5 hectares each. The Japanese gardens, known as Seiwaen, are calm and reflective while the Chinese gardens (Yu Hwa Yuan), which occupy an island by the Jurong Lake, are exuberant and colourful with attractions like the 'Cloud-Piercing Pagoda' or the 'White Rainbow Bridge'.

The gardens are open from 8 am to 7 pm daily and admission to the Chinese gardens is S$2 adults, $1 children; to the Japanese gardens, S$1 adults, 50c children. A combined ticket is S$2.50 adults, S$1.20 children. To get there take a bus to Jurong Interchange then a 242 bus to Yuan Ching Rd. On Sundays and public holidays a 406 bus will take you directly there.

Jurong Bird Park Also at Jurong the bird park is on Jalan Ahmad Ibrahim. The 20 hectare park has over 7000 birds and includes a two hectare walk-in aviary with an artificial waterfall at one end. This aviary, which alone has over 3000 birds including 100-plus peacocks, is the largest in the world. Exhibits include everything from cassowaries, birds of paradise, eagles and cockatoos to parrots, macaws and even penguins in air-conditioned comfort.

You can walk around the park or take the tram service that shuttles around the park dropping people off and picking them up. The park is open from 9 am to 6 pm weekdays, to 7 pm on weekends. It's suggested that you visit the park early in the morning or late in the afternoon since the birds tend to be less active during the heat of the day. Admission to the park is S$3.50 for adults, S$1.50 for children, and the tram service costs an additional S$1.

You can get there by taxi or by any of the many buses that run to Jurong Interchange from where a 250 will take you to the bird park. You can climb up Jurong Hill, beside the park, from where there is a good view over Jurong.

Zoological Park Located at 80 Mandai Lake Rd in the north of the island Singapore's zoo has over 1000 animals on display in conditions as natural as possible – wherever possible moats replace bars. Exhibits of particular interest include the orang utan colony and the tiny mousedeer. They now have a breakfast programme where you get a feeding and are joined by one of the orang utans! There is also a children's zoo and an elephant work performance.

The zoo is open from 8.30 am to 6 pm daily and admission is S$3.50 adults, S$1.50 kids. There are extra charges for cameras. To get there you can take any bus going to Bukit Timah Rd then a 171 to the zoo or any bus to Toa Payoh and then 137 to the zoo.

CN West Leisure Park Formerly known as the Mitsukoshi Garden, the CN West Leisure Park at 9 Japanese Garden Rd, Jurong has a restaurant, pool, water slide and so on. Hours are 10 am to 6 pm on weekdays, 9 am to 8 pm on weekends. Weekdays admission is S$3 (children S$1) and weekends it is S$4 (children S$2). To get there take a bus to Jurong Interchange then a 242 bus from there to Yuan Ching Rd. On Sundays and public holidays a 406 bus runs directly there.

Other Parks Despite Singapore's dense population there are many small parks and gardens and, of course, every traffic island or highway divide is turned into a green plantation. Central Park off Clemenceau Avenue provides 40 hectares of green right in the city – the National Theatre and the Van Kleef Aquarium are both here. A crocodile farm is located at 790 Upper Serangoon Rd.

Off Kampong Bahru Rd the 116 metre-high Mount Faber provides fine views over the harbour and the city. To get there just take the cable car up from the World Trade Centre, it's conveniently visited in conjunction with Sentosa Island. Singapore has a major business in cultivating orchids and the Orchid Gardens, beside the zoo on Mandai Lake Rd, is the best place to see them – four hectares of solid orchids! The gardens are open from 9 am to 6 pm daily and admission is S$1.

Bukit Timah Nature Reserve on the Upper Bukit Timah Rd boasts the highest point in Singapore, 177 metre Bukit Timah. MacRitchie Reservoir provides good walking tracks around the reservoir and is popular with joggers. Close to the centre there's Elizabeth Walk, across from the Padang, and the small Merlion Park at the mouth of Singapore River. There the merlion, symbol of Singapore, spouts a fountain of water out into the river.

The East Coast Park, out of town toward the airport, is built on reclaimed land and has swimming, windsurfing with rentals, bike hire, a food centre and the Singapore Crocodilarium with 1000 of the friendlies.

Islands, Beaches & Watersports
Singapore is, of course, an island, but there are a number of other islands around Singapore. Best known is Sentosa, 'tranquillity' in Malay, which has been developed into a locally popular resort. Other islands include Kusu and St John's, the Sisters' Islands and islands such as Pulau Bukom, which are used as refineries and for other commercial purposes. South of Singapore's Southern Islands are many more islands – the scattered Indonesian islands of the Riau Archipelago.

There are other islands to the north and east, between Singapore and Malaysia. Here you will also find the kelongs, long arrow shaped fences erected to trap fish. The fish swim down the 'shaft' of the arrow into the 'arrowhead' then cannot find their way out. You can clearly see a number of these kelongs if your flight into Singapore approaches Changi Airport from the north. They're another disappearing sight since the Singapore government doesn't want any of these untidy things in the water. Permits for kelongs are not renewed once they expire.

Nor do you have to cross the sea to find beaches and watersport activities. Although the construction of Changi Airport destroyed one of Singapore's favourite stretches of beach there is still the huge East Coast Lagoon on the East Coast Parkway, not to mention the CN West Leisure Park at Jurong. Skin diving enthusiasts will find coral reefs at Sisters' Islands and Pulau Semakan, while if you want to water ski head to Ponggol Point on the north coast.

Sentosa Island Sentosa Island has been through a major development programme to turn it into a tourist attraction. It has been only half successful, Sentosa attracts few overseas tourists (who can find the real thing in the tropical island line when they get to Malaysia), but has proved a big hit with Singaporeans, particularly on weekends when it can get very crowded. Sentosa was once used as a military base and the gun emplacements and underground tunnels of Fort Siloso, from the late 19th century, can be explored. The guns were all pointing in the wrong direction when the Japanese invaded in WW II, but the island was then used by the victorious Japanese as a prisoner of war camp.

Other Sentosa attractions include the Surrender Chamber with 27 wax-work figures recreating the formal surrender by the Japanese forces in 1945. The Maritime Museum has exhibits recording the history of Singapore as a port while the Sentosa Arts Centre displays local art works. In the Coralarium there is, not surprisingly, a display of live corals. These attractions are all open from 10 am to 6 pm, Mondays to Saturdays and from 9 am to 6 pm on Sundays and public holidays.

There are a wide variety of sporting facilities on Sentosa including an 18 hole golf course, a swimming lagoon, a canoeing centre and a roller skating centre. Major improvements are taking shape with plans for a family entertainment park by the middle of 1985. Also work is being done on upgrading the swimming lagoon and wax museum. An oceanarium is being planned.

You can get around Sentosa by bicycle – hire a bike for S$3 per day (9 am to 4.30 pm) from the hire kiosk by the ferry terminal. Or you can take the free bus service which runs around the island roads with departures every 10 minutes. Or you can take the five stop monorail loop service which costs S$3.

To get to Sentosa take a bus or taxi to the World Trade Centre from where ferries operate and where the Jardine Steps Cable Car terminal is also located. There are three types of admission tickets. Ticket 1 is S$6.50 (S$3.50 child) and covers return ferry trip, monorail and all attractions including the Coralarium. Ticket 2 is S$4.50 (S$2.50 child) and covers return ferry trip and all attractions except the Coralarium. Ticket 3 is S$3 (S$2 child) and covers return ferry trip, monorail ride and entry after 5 pm only.

By cable car you can also go to Mt Faber and then make the longer return trip via Jardine Steps to Sentosa Island. There is a complete four sector round trip, a two sector trip (Mt Faber-Jardine Steps-Sentosa or Jardine Steps-Sentosa-Jardine Steps) or a one sector trip (Jardine Steps-Sentosa or Mt Faber). The cost varies from S$2.50 to 5. The cable car ride, with its spectacular views, is the best part of a visit to Sentosa so take it at least one-way. In 1983 a ship managed to run into the cable car line but additional precautions have been taken to ensure such a disaster could not occur again. Accommodation is available on Sentosa either at the *Apollo Sentosa Hotel* or at the camping site.

St John's & Kusu Islands Although Sentosa is Singapore's best known island there are two others which are also locally popular as city escapes. On weekends they can become rather crowded, but during the week St John's and Kusu are fairly quiet – good for a peaceful swim. Both islands have cafeterias, changing rooms, toilet facilities and grassy picnic areas.

St John's is much bigger than Kusu which you can walk around in 10 minutes. Kusu has a Chinese temple and a Malay shrine. To get there take a ferry from the World Trade Centre, the round trip is S$5. It takes 45 minutes to reach Kusu and one hour to St. John's. On weekdays a visit to both islands is an all day trip since there are only three services – if you left at 9 am you wouldn't be able to continue on to St John's until 3 pm, unless you continued straight through. There are far more departures on weekends:

Sundays & Public Holidays

WTC	Kusu	St John's
9.00 am	10.00 am	10.20 am
10.00 am	11.00 am	11.20 am
11.20 am	12.20 pm	12.40 pm
12.20 pm	1.20 pm	1.40 pm
1.40 pm	2.40 pm	3.00 pm
2.40 pm	3.40 pm	4.00 pm
4.00 pm	5.00 pm	5.20 pm
5.00 pm	6.00 pm	6.20 pm
7.20 pm	8.00 pm	8.20 pm

Mondays to Saturdays

WTC	Kusu	St John's
9.00 am	10.30 am	11.00 am
2.30 pm	4.00 pm	4.30 pm

Other Islands There are other islands both to the north and to the south of Singapore. To get to the Northern Islands like Pulau Seletar go to Ponggol Boatel at Ponggol Point or to Sembawang. A five passenger speedboat will cost about S$25. Kusu and St John's are both part of the Southern Islands group. These also include Sisters' Islands, Pulau Hantu, Lazarus Island, Buran Darat, Terumbu Retan Laut and Pulau Renggit.

By special arrangement (tel 271 2211) you can get a ferry to Pulau Hantu or Sisters' Islands for S$5 return. Otherwise you can charter a motorised 'bumboat' (sampan) from Jardine Steps or Clifford Pier for about S$60 per day. These boats are big enough for 12 people, but finding one is simply a matter of going down to the waterfront and asking.

Weekend boat trips around the southern islands on the 43-foot cruiser, *Farah*, can be arranged at 41 8082. One day is S$48 with lunch. Swimming and snorkelling are featured.

Off the eastern end of Singapore Island Pulau Tekong is Singapore's largest 'off shore' island, but tends to be forgotten because it is often cut off the edge of Singapore maps (including the one in this book). To get there take a ferry from Changi Point to the delightfully old-fashioned village of Kampong Salabin. There's great seafood at a dilapidated waterfront restaurant on stilts, close to the dock. The best way to get around the island is on a bicycle brought with you. There are no private cars here, just a few ancient and run down unofficial taxis.

From the east end of the island you can also take the 1½ hour trip to Pengerang in Malaysia where you have to go through customs and immigration. I don't know where you'd go to from there though!

Riau Archipelago South of the Southern Islands are the Indonesian islands of the Riau Archipelago. The largest of these islands, which stretch across to Sumatra, is Pulau Bintang and it covers three times the area of Singapore. The entire island group is lightly populated, many of the islands having no permanent population at all, and there are fine opportunities for scuba diving or simply exploring. The simple, quiet and poor way of life on the islands here is a dramatic contrast to the bustle of downtown Singapore.

Tanjung Pinang is the main town in the Riau Archipelago and is also the port for the weekly shipping service to Indonesia. You can visit Tanjung Pinang either by chartering a bumboat, by taking the regular ferry boats from Singapore or by going on a tour. The ferry boats are inexpensive. German Asian Travels (tel 915116) at room 1303/4, Straits Trading Building, 9 Battery Rd, operate round trip tours which cost about S$150 per person including overnight accommodation and tours from Tanjung Pinang.

There are a number of small hotels at Tanjung Pinang, which also has an interesting market, a Chinese temple and a mosque. Nearby you can see the ruins of ancient Sea Dayak capitals or you can take excursions to other islands like Pulau Mapor or Pulau Terkulai. If you're energetic you can even climb Gunung Bintang Besar, the highest hill on Pulau Bintang. The ferry trip to Tanjung Pinang takes about two hours and you have to obtain an Indonesian visa in order to visit the Riau Archipelago. November to March is the best time to visit as the water is clearest.

Places to Stay

Singapore has a wide variety of accommodation in all price categories – you can get a dorm bed in a 'crash pad' for S$6, a reasonable room in a cheap Chinese hotel for around S$20 or pay over S$200 for a room in an 'international standard' hotel, even over S$1000 for some super de-luxe suites.

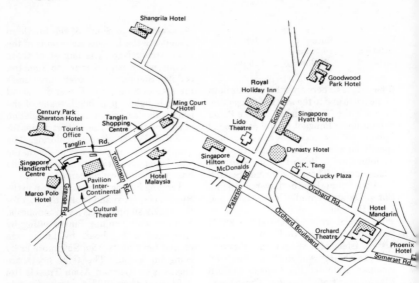

Over the last couple of years Singapore's accommodation squeeze has changed into an accommodation surplus and as a result prices have been fairly static. At the top end it's a result of a great number of new hotels recently built or under construction. At the bottom end, where the cheap Chinese hotels were disappearing to redevelopments, the proliferation of crash pads has taken the strain of the old hotels and provided lots of new accommodation possibilities. There still may be times when accommodation is a little tight and Chinese New Year is a particularly bad time of year, everything tends to be full and the cheaper hotels may push their prices up.

In the major hotels there will be a 3% government tax and a 10% service charge added to your bill. The hotels stipulate that you should not tip. The 3% government tax also applies to the cheaper hotels with a minimum of S\$1 but this is usually added straight into the original quoted price.

Hotels have been approximately categorised into three groups. 'Top end' hotels are roughly from S\$120 for a double and up. The main centre for these large hotels is along Orchard Rd. At the other extreme most 'bottom end' hotels cost under S\$40, often under S\$20. They can chiefly be found to the east of Bras Basah Rd; particularly along Beach Rd, Middle Rd, Bencoolen St and Jalan Besar. 'Middle' range hotels cover the middle ground – some of them are bigger and better cheaper Chinese hotels, some of them are smaller air-con hotels. They tend to be scattered widely over Singapore. For reservations you can call an agency at 542 6955 which coordinates bookings for 62 different middle and upper-class hotels.

Places to Stay – bottom end

Singapore's rapid modernisation is even hitting the cheap places to stay. Many of these small, family-run hotels are in areas destined for eventual redevelopment and already some popular cheapies are gone – to be replaced by ever more air-con shopping centres. You can be certain that there are no new hotels planned without air-con, bars and restaurants, high speed lifts, swimming pools and all the other

Singapore Downtown Area

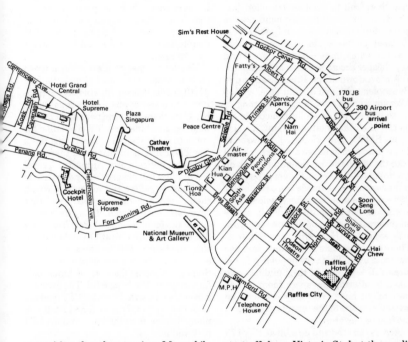

necessities of modern tourism. Meanwhile the Singapore answer for backpackers seems to be crash pads which have sprung up like wildfire. Bencoolen St is the main crash pad centre and it is also the main centre for cheap hotels.

Singapore's cheap accommodation is mainly concentrated in the streets that run off Bras Basah Rd to the north-east. Amongst the buses that run out that way from the city centre are 101, 131 and 146 down Serangoon Rd; 94, 100 and 120 along Victoria St; 125, 161, 172 and 175

start off down Victoria St, but then split across Middle Rd while the 130 and 141 continue further down before turning off across Jalan Besar. Jalan Besar, which becomes Bencoolen St at Rochor Rd, runs one way – the wrong way if you're coming from the city centre, the docks or the railway station.

Coming in from the airport the public bus will drop you at the Queen St terminus, conveniently close to most of the Bencoolen St and Beach Rd hotels.

Crash Pads Singapore's crash pads are all mildly illegal since they're just residential flats which have been broken up into dormitories and cubicle-like rooms. But then this is Singapore and free enterprise is what counts! The trouble with them is that the jam-packed crowds tend to overstretch the limited facilities and the rooms really are small. Plus everybody else there will be another traveller, just like yourself. On the other hand they're good information sources and good places to meet people – since so many other travellers stay there – and you won't find any cheaper accommodation in Singapore.

Almost down at the Bras Basah end of Bencoolen St you'll find the *Peony Mansions* crash pad, longest running of these places. It's at 46-52 Bencoolen St, on top of a Mazda (at last count, it's also been BMWs and Holdens) showroom. There's no sign at all, go around back and take the lift to the 5th floor and knock on the door at 50E. Like all the crash pads it's rather anonymous. Inside you can stay for S$8 a night; simple dormitory-style accommodation, but it's quite OK. As in nearly all the crash pads some private rooms are also available. Here they are S$20-24. There are other flats in the block, but also run from 50E. This very popular place is often full – people in the building have taken to offering any spare room or bed they might have. You may get such an invitation if one of the tenants sees you in the hall or elevator.

Across the road and up a bit at 173/175 is another centre for crash pads. They are in the newish Hong Guan Building nearly opposite the *Nam Hai Hotel*. There are no outside signs here either, again go around back and up the elevator by the parking lot. The *Bencoolen St Service Apartments*, also known as *Goh's Homestay*, has a reception desk at the 5th floor, but also has rooms on the 6th. In their dorm you get a mattress on the floor and a locker for S$6. Shared rooms are S$8 and private rooms go for S$24. They've got a good noticeboard with bus guides.

On the third floor is *Philip Choo's*. Here the foam mattress dorm is S$8, rooms S$22. Again the dorm has lockers and there's a noticeboard. There may be other places in the building as well, they come and go.

Bencoolen House Home Stay (tel 338 1206 or 292 6000) is on the 7th and 8th floors at 27 Bencoolen St near Middle Rd. It's very good, clean and pretty quiet and there's a kitchen you can use. The dorm costs S$7, rooms are S$22 single, S$24 double, three people S$26. A bit extra for air-con rooms.

Nearby another of these central crash pads is *Airmaster Travel Centre* (tel 338 9720) at 36G Prinsep St, a block over from Bencoolen and down towards Bras Basah Rd. Here there are dorm beds at S$7 and a washing machine and TV available for your use. Travellers report this is a friendly, convenient place and there's an excellent noticeboard. Airmaster Travel is a popular travel agent for cheap tickets to almost anywhere and you enter through their office. A last minute letter said that Airmaster have moved, it may be true.

Not too far away is *Sim's Rest House* (tel 336 4957 or 336 0176) at 114A Mackenzie Rd. Mackenzie Rd becomes Albert St across Serangoon. It's a bit of a walk from Serangoon along the sort of industrial/factory-lined Mackenzie Rd. The owner is a friendly guy with dorms for S$7 (lockers available) and real rooms for S$20. If you phone him up from the bus terminus he'll pick you up.

There are a couple of others too, in a different area of town. The *Friendly Rest House* (tel 294 0847) is just that and is found at 357A Serangoon Rd just past Kitchener Rd. The door is actually around the corner from Serangoon on Perumal Rd. Look for Fong Tat Auto – it's below the guest house which is one floor up. It's well run and helpful and has dorm beds for S$6, double room at S$23 with attached bathroom. A bus 390 from the airport gets you in the general area, then a bus 131 or 140 will take you down Serangoon Rd. A bus 146 from the train station will get you practically to the door.

Sandy's Place (tel 292 6720) nearby at 28B Rangoon Rd, has a S$6 mattress on the floor dorm; S$8 with a bed. They also ask a S$10 deposit which you get back when leaving. It's clean and the management are friendly. Rangoon Rd runs off Serangoon Rd by the New World Amusement Park and can be a bit noisy. The stairs for Sandy's Place are beside the Swiss Bar.

Other crash pad possibilities to investigate include *Traveller's Lodge* at 16 Penhaus St off Lavender St at the far end of Jalan Besar. This is a slightly run-down industrial area. Rooms with fan cost S$14 to 17. *Sunseeker's Rest House* is next to the Neptune Building on the 2nd floor of 20 South Quay. Or there's *New Handy Place* right in the heart of Orchard Rd.

Chinese Hotels – Bras Basah Rd to Rochor Canal Rd

Many travellers would prefer to spend a few dollars more for the cheap Chinese hotels. Your money will get you a fairly spartan room with a bare floor, a few pieces of furniture, a sink and a fan. Toilets are usually shared, but you might even get hot water in the showers. Couples should always ask for a single room – a single usually means just one double bed, whereas a double would have two. As for the crash pads Bencoolen St is a good place to start looking.

The *Nam Hai* (tel 337 5395) at 166 is pretty well an institution and usually full every night. The two old Cantonese women who used to run it have retired and gone back to China and the place is now run by a small family. They're friendly, the man in particular can tell a funny story or two and they don't watch the TV late at night! This new owner figures that his place and others on Bencoolen don't have many years left before the ball hits them. Singles/doubles are S$22/24 and there's cold water in the fridge. A bit further up towards Bras Basah Rd at 81 is the *Kian Hua* (tel 338 3492) with rooms from S$20 single, S$28 double.

Other places around Bencoolen St include the rather more expensive *San Wah* (tel 336 2428) at 36 Bencoolen St with singles at S$30 and doubles S$32, S$35 with air-con. Almost at the end at 12 Bencoolen St is the clean *Hotel Ben* with singles from S$24 and doubles from S$30. Rooms with bathroom or air-con cost more. These latter two are both a little up market from the cheapest Chinese hotels. Round on Prinsep St (next one over) is the *Tiong Hoa* (tel 338 4522) at number 4. Rooms in this very pleasantly run air-con hotel are S$20 single, S$30 double, S$36 air-con.

The Park is around the corner from the Nam Hai at 239B Victoria at the corner where Albert becomes Bugis St. It's the freshly painted white place with blue shutters. Inside it's very clean with lots of tilework and has singles for S$27, doubles for S$30 to 34. The *South-East Asia Hotel* (tel 338 2394) at 190 Waterloo St, directly behind the Nam Hai, is a bit more costly, but if you really need a rest it has air-con, and is quiet and modern with singles/doubles at S$34/41. Also on Waterloo St the *Waterloo Hotel* is good value for a middle range hotel at S$45/57.50.

Beach Rd, a few blocks over towards the (ever-receding) waterfront, is another centre for cheap hotels although some of them have already fallen prey to re-development. If you aspire to the Raffles, but can't afford to stay there, at least you can stay close at these places! The *Shang Onn* (tel 338 4153) at 37 Beach Rd, on the corner of Purvis St, has singles at S$26, doubles at S$30 and is clean and friendly. Another one hanging on despite construction all around is the Hai Hin (tel 3363739) at 97. Singles or doubles cost S$30.

If you follow Middle Rd from Beach Rd back towards Bencoolen St you'd find a few more cheapies like the rather inconspicuous *Soon Seng Long* (tel 337 6318) at 26 Middle Rd where rooms are also around S$20. Big rooms, if you can wake the proprietor up from his slumbers, or pry him away from that mah-jong table.

Others on Middle Rd include the *Lido* (tel 337 1872) at 54 with singles/doubles at S$24/28. Nearly back at Bencoolen is the *Tai Loke* (tel 337 6209), at 151. There are big, airy rooms with fine old furniture for S$30 single or double. By that time you're almost back at Bencoolen St. Continuing up Middle Road near the corner of Selegie at number 260 and 262 is the clean and very nice *Sun Sun Hotel* (tel 338 4911). It's a little more expensive with singles/doubles at S$30/35 and there's a bar and restaurant downstairs.

Rochor Rd also runs from Beach Rd to Bencoolen St, parallel to Middle Rd. At 228/229 the *New 7th Storey Hotel* (tel 337 0251-4) is an up market cheapie with singles/doubles at S$49/59 or with bath S$65/75.

Chinese Hotels – Rochor Canal Rd to Lavender St Another batch of cheap hotels is across Rochor Rd down to Lavender St on and around Jalan Besar. Going down Jalan Besar from Bencoolen at 315 Jalan Besar there's the *Singapore Island Hotel* (tel 258 3337) with reasonable rooms S$22/25 or S$30 with air-con. Across the road the *International* (tel 258 3347) at 290 costs S$30 single, S$35 double, S$40 double with bath.

Further down Jalan Besar at 383 is the *Kam Leng* (tel 258 2289). It's upstairs and has good, clean rooms at S$22 single or double and also an excellent restaurant with an English menu and fish tanks where you select your fish while it's still swimming. Right down at the end of the street near Lavender is the *Palace Hotel* (tel 258 3108) where singles/doubles are $22. The Palace is spotlessly clean and a favourite touch here is the free coke you're always presented with when you make your hot and sweaty arrival. The front rooms are very noisy, however, due to the round-the-clock traffic along Jalan Besar. Traffic noise is quite a problem in most of these central hotels though.

There are quite a few other ones in this area, too; many about halfway down Jalan Besar around Kitchener Rd. The *Siong Cheong* (tel 294 7147) is at 18 Verdun, near the big President Merlin Hotel. Verdun runs parallel to Serangoon Rd and Jalan Besar, midway between them. It's a quiet street and pleasant rooms cost S$20 single or double, S$28 with air-con. The owners' brother also runs a small hotel (tel 258 4883), clean but maybe not as nice, nearby at 330A Serangoon Rd. Here rooms are S$18 single, S$20 double with fan, more with air-con.

The *Hong Kong Hotel* (tel 293 1145) at 16 Burmah Rd, on the corner with Race Course Rd, is a pleasantly clean place with rooms at S$30 single or double, S$40 with air-con. It's fairly quiet too since it is not on a busy main road. The *Tai Nam* at 187-189 Serangoon Rd charges S$28 single or double, but is a bit grubby.

Chinese Hotels – Other Places Oddly, there are no hotels to speak of in Chinatown, nearly all are in the areas mentioned above, east of Bras Basah Rd. One exception of note is the *Majestic Hotel* (tel 222 3377) at 31 Bukit Pasoh Rd near Chinatown. Bukit Pasoh runs between New Bridge Rd and Neil Rd. It's a quiet street lined with traditional houses and buildings, but all well maintained, in good condition and brightly painted. There's a pleasant park nearby and in the morning and evening people do tai chee and tai kuan do exercises there. The hotel is immaculate and rooms are pleasant, some with a balcony. Singles/doubles are S$25/32 without bath, S$24/44 with bath.

Not far away is the *New Asia*, once a large colonial place but now with just a portion of the rooms open and it's apparently dying a slow death. Fan-cooled singles/doubles are S$18/24. It's on Maxwell Rd at Peck Seah, a couple of blocks up from Robinson.

Remember that at Chinese New Year it can be very difficult to find a room in Singapore and some places are prone to sudden price increases. Student Travel, who have their office in the Ming Court

Hotel, offer substantial discounts at some of Singapore's 'International Standard' hotels – which means they will still cost something like S$70 for a single and up.

The Ys & Camping Singapore has a number of YMCAs and YWCAs, although the cheap old YMCA Katong has now been redeveloped. The *YMCA* (tel 222 4666) is at 70 Palmer Rd and has rooms from S$25 single without bath up to S$40 double with bath. The Stevens Rd *Metropolitan YMCA* (tel 737 7755) at 60 Stevens Rd is rather more expensive at S$55 single, S$60 double with private bath, TV and air-con. They take men or couples only.

There is a large new YMCA under construction which should be open in 1985. It's located on Bras Basah Rd at Prinsep, opposite the big Cathay movie theatre. The *YWCA Hostel* (tel 336 1212) at 6-8 Fort Canning costs S$42 for a private room or S$50 for a double. Nice dorm rooms are available, for women, at S$13. They take women or couples only and this has been recommended by solo women travellers as a safe and secure place.

Singapore is probably overdue to get a real YHA youth hostel, there's no sign of one yet. You can, however, camp out at *Sentosa Island* where there are pre-erected tents available from S$6 per night. There's also the good *East Coast Campsite* on East Coast Parkway, at the five km marker. Unfortunately there are no buses stopping on this expressway so you have to get off at the bus stop in Upper East Coast Rd and then walk 15 minutes; from the end of Bedok Rd a walking track leads under the expressway right to the camp. The site has a clean, well-lit reading and TV room and there are a few shops and a hawkers' centre nearby. The site is deserted during the week but very busy on weekends and school holidays. A four-person tent costs S$5 a night Monday to Friday, S$6 on weekends and holidays.

Places to Stay – middle
Middle range places to stay include higher-class Chinese cheapies, a few colonial-era hangovers and some smaller or second string modern hotels. The *Mitre Hotel*, on Killiney Rd, just off Orchard Rd, is a pleasantly old-fashioned hotel – a rare reminder of the colonial era. On Upper Wilkie Rd, a steep downhill walk to Orchard Rd or Selegie Rd, the *Savoy Hotel* offers surprisingly good standards at a surprisingly low price. You can say the same about the *Station Hotel* although it is a little inconveniently located for most things in modern Singapore. If, however, you've just arrived after a long train trip and can't face heading straight into the city it might be ideal.

Most of the older Chinese-style hotels are down in the bottom end category, in price at least. Smaller modern hotels include the *Bencoolen Hotel* on Bencoolen St, situated amongst the rock-bottom Chinese hotels, but it's nothing special. The *Broadway* is on Serangoon Rd, where you will also find the *New Serangoon Hotel*. At the harbour end of Anson Rd the *New Ritz* is a delightful place although it's in an area being extensively redeveloped and may not be around for long.

The Student Travel Office in the Ming Court Hotel can arrange discounts at the *Hotel Asia* and the *Negara*. The *Premier Hotel*, on Nassim Hill not far from the Tourist Office, is a small hotel also used as a training centre for hotel and catering staff – the standards of service are therefore usually better than the small size might indicate. The *RELC International Centre* (RELC stands for Regional Language Centre) has a hotel in its complex next to the Shangri-La on Orange Grove Rd. There is no service charge or government tax at this hotel. Both YMCA centres bridge the middle– to bottom-end gap. Finally there's *Charlie Tan's Tourist Apartments* on the 3rd floor at 372 Clemenceau, quite near Orchard Rd and Cuppage Plaza. Air-con doubles with bathroom are S$50. Air-con hotels follow.

Ambassador Hotel (tel 446 3311), 42/46 Meyer Rd, 170 rooms, swimming pool, singles S$85, doubles S$95

Hotel Asia (tel 737 8388), 37 Scotts Rd, 146 rooms, singles S$125-145, doubles S$145-160

Hotel Bencoolen (tel 336 0822), 47 Bencoolen St, 69 rooms, singles S$66, doubles S$77

Broadway Hotel (tel 292 4661), 195 Serangoon Rd, 63 rooms, singles S$75-85, doubles S$85-95

Duke Hotel (tel 345 3311), 42/46 Meyer Rd, 170 rooms, singles S$85-125, doubles S$95-135

Great Eastern Hotel (tel 284 8244), 401 Macpherson Rd, 151 rooms, singles S$45-68, doubles S$50-78

Lion City Hotel (tel 345 8111), 15 Tanjong Katong Rd, 168 rooms, singles S$88, doubles S$98

Lloyd House Hotel (tel 737 7011), 2 Lloyd Rd, 19 rooms, singles S$40-60, doubles S$65-75

Metropole Hotel (tel 336 3611), 41 Seah St, 54 rooms, singles S$95-100, doubles S$110-125

Mitre Hotel (tel 737 3811), 145 Killiney Rd, 19 rooms, singles S$46, doubles S$58

Hotel Negara (tel 737 0811), 15 Claymore Drive, 104 rooms, swimming pool, singles S$95-145, doubles S$115-165

New Mayfair Hotel (tel 337 542), 40-44 Armenian St, 27 rooms, singles S$53, doubles S$63

New Ritz Hotel (tel 221 9533), 15 Bernam St, 33 rooms, singles S$44, doubles S$55

New Serangoon Hotel (tel 293 7411), 305 Serangoon Rd, 66 rooms, singles S$54, doubles S$71

Hotel Premier (tel 235 5111), 22 Nassim Hill, 30 rooms, swimming pool, singles S$90, doubles S$105

Queen's Hotel International (tel 737 6088), 24 Mount Elizabeth Rd, 61 rooms, swimming pool, singles S$95-105, doubles S$105-115

RELC International House (tel 737 9044), 30 Orange Grove Rd, 128 rooms, singles S$100, doubles S$120 (all inclusive)

Savoy Hotel (tel 337 6491), 10A Upper Wilkie Rd, 39 rooms, singles or doubles S$60

Sloane Court Hotel (tel 235 3311), 17 Balmoral Rd, 37 rooms, singles S$75-95, doubles S$85-105

Station Hotel (tel 222 1551), Railway Station, Keppel Rd, 34 rooms, singles S$45, doubles S$55

Hotel Supreme (tel 737 8333), 15 Kramat Rd, 86 rooms, singles S$80, doubles S$90

Tanglin Court Hotel (tel 737 3581), 2/4 Kim Yam Rd, 28 rooms, singles S$60-70, doubles S$70-80

UDMC Holiday Chalets (tel 442 7135), 1110 East Coast Parkway, 167 rooms, singles S$35-45, doubles S$55-75

Hotel VIP (tel 235 4277), 5 Balmoral Crescent, 41 rooms, singles S$100-110, doubles S$115-125

Places to Stay – top end

Singapore has a huge number of 'international standard' hotels and after a lull in building there's a spate of new ones going up at present. In 1984, 27 big, top end hotels were under construction around town. Many of these are intended for expense account travellers and are luxurious and expensive. The project garnering the most attention is the US$475 million *Raffles City* – a complex of offices, a convention centre and two luxury class hotels. One of them at 72 stories will become the world's tallest hotel. Together they will add about 2000 rooms to the local hotel scene. Three atrium-style hotels in the 500-1000 room size are slated for the new Marina Centre at the water end of Bras Basah on reclaimed land. These two major projects will be opening through 1985 and a third one, the Rahardja Centre, will add another 4500 rooms through 1988.

Occupancy rates have been dropping from the 90% range of the late '70s and with all the new hotels it's expected to continue sliding to as low as 50%. Some investors may take a bath, but for visitors the increased competition should mean lower prices, added incentives and of course less difficulty in finding a room. If you're arriving independently at a hotel in this category (ie you're not on a tour, prepaid voucher or something similar) then it's always worth asking if there is any sort of discount available. The 'rack rates' listed below will often drop if you ask.

These hotels have a number of characteristics in common. For a start a great many of them are strung along Singapore's 'hotel alley', known as Orchard Rd. This is very much the tourist centre of Singapore with hotels, airline offices and shopping centres in profusion. Quite a few more hotels are situated in roads off Orchard Rd – like Scott's Rd, Tanglin Rd, Somerset Rd or Orange Grove Rd.

Due to the many new hotels opening the severe price escalation of the late '70s and early '80s has slowed down dramatically. As a rough demarcation line 'top end' refers to hotels where a double is something over S$120 to 140 a night. Singapore's best hotels will generally cost over S$200 a night for a double! Naturally all these hotels will be air-conditioned, all rooms will have attached bathrooms and in almost all cases there will be a swimming pool. These places are further subdivided into 'super-luxury', 'other big hotels' and 'old fashioned'.

Super-Luxury Singapore has a number of hotels that in price and standards esteem themselves a cut above the mere international-standard hotels. They include the twin-towered *Mandarin Hotel* on Orchard Rd – with 1200 rooms it is also (currently) the biggest hotel in Singapore and is topped by a revolving restaurant. The *Shangri-La* is set in five hectares of garden on Orange Grove Rd, just a few minutes-walk from Orchard Rd. The rooms in the Garden Wing each have their own balcony over-flowing with plants.

The *Marco Polo* is at the Grange Rd-Orchard Rd intersection just a short distance from the Tourist Office. The smaller *Singapore Hilton* on Orchard Rd is also edging towards the upper-notch bracket. The new *Dynasty Hotel* on Orchard Rd by the junction with Scotts Rd is a strange skyscraper-topped-by-a-pagoda building. Just off Tanglin Rd the equally new *Pavilion Inter-Continental* also fits in this category.

Other Big Hotels The hotels of the international chains are all in this category, which includes places like the *Hyatt Regency* and the *Royal Holiday Inn* which face each other across Scott's Rd, just off Orchard Rd. The *Century Park Sheraton* is a relatively new hotel on Grange Rd, just off Tanglin Rd. The *Oberoi Imperial* on Jalan Rumbia enjoys a hilltop location near River Valley Rd.

At the intersection of Tanglin Rd-Orange Grove-Orchard Rd the *Ming Court* is one of Singapore's better-known hotels, in part because of their superb doormen. Many Singapore hotels vie with one another to have the most exotic doormen, but the Ming Court's take the blue ribbon. Where else can you be ushered into a taxi by a towering, bearded Sikh dressed as a Ming warrior?

Sandwiched between the Ming Court and the Hilton on Orchard Rd the *Singapura Forum* was one of the first international chain hotels in Singapore, but is now a relatively small hotel compared to the huge new hotels of the '80s. The *York Hotel* on Mount Elizabeth, behind Scott's Rd, is one of a Singapore chain which includes the old-world Goodwood Park and the Boulevard Hotel Singapore. Further down Orchard Rd the *Phoenix Hotel* sits on top of the Specialist's Shopping Centre. On Somerset Rd, parallel to Orchard Rd, the *Cockpit Hotel* was much used by airline crew at one time – hence the name.

On Coleman St, over towards the business centre of Singapore, is the *Peninsula Hotel* while the *Tai Pan Hotel Ramada*, which bridges the middle to top gap, is on Victoria St off Bras Basah Rd. The *President Merlin Hotel* has an unusual, but interesting, location on Kitchener St, across from the New World Amusement Park.

Other hotels include the *Apollo Singapore* at the Havelock-Outram Rds intersection; the *Cairnhill*; the *Equatorial*, further out from Orchard Rd; the circular *King's Hotel* on Havelock Rd; the *Boulevard Hotel*

84 Singapore

Singapore on Orchard Boulevard; the *Miramar*, once again on Havelock Rd; the *Royal* on Newton Rd; the *Novotel Orchid Inn*; the smaller *Garden Hotel* and the *Orchard Hotel*. The *Ladyhill Hotel* has a particularly pleasant garden setting. Out on Sentosa Island there is also the *Apollo Sentosa*, for those who really want to get away from it all.

Old Fashioned Singapore also has a couple of hotels with definite old eastern flavour and style. Close to the waterfront at the junction of Bras Basah Rd and Beach Rd the venerable *Raffles* is as much a superb tourist attraction as simply a fine old hotel. The bars and restaurants conjure up all the mysteries of the Orient and what other hotel can claim that a tiger was once shot in the billiards room? The Raffles is built around a beautiful central courtyard complete with fan-shaped travellers' palms – the only two-dimensional tree.

On Scott's Rd is the larger, but nearly as old, *Goodwood Park*. If anything, its architecture is even more delightful than the Raffles.

Amara SAS Hotel (tel 733 2666), 352 rooms, opening 1985
Apollo Sentosa (tel 63 3377), Sentosa Island, 161 rooms & chalets, singles S$100, doubles S$120
Apollo Singapore (tel 733 2081), Havelock & Outram Rds, 332 rooms, singles S$145, doubles S$170
Boulevard Hotel Singapore (tel 737 2911), Cuscaden Rd, 528 rooms, singles S$160-220, doubles S$190-250
Cairnhill Hotel (tel 734 6622), 19 Cairnhill Circle, 220 rooms, singles S$150-170, doubles S$170-190
Century Park Sheraton (tel 737 9677), Nassim Hill, 461 rooms, singles S$180-220, doubles S$200-240
Cockpit Hotel (tel 737 9111), 6/7 Oxley Rise & Penang Rd, 182 rooms, singles S$135-180, doubles S$155-200
Crown Prince Hotel (tel 732 1111) 270

Orchard Rd, 303 rooms, singles S$185, doubles S$215
Dynasty Hotel (tel 734 9900), 320 Orchard Rd, 400 rooms, singles S$195-225, doubles S$225-255
Hotel Equatorial (tel 732 0431), 429 Bukit Timah Rd, 224 rooms, singles S$145-235, doubles S$155-275
Excelsior (tel 338 9644), Coleman St, 300 rooms, singles S$145-175, doubles S$160-190
Furama Singapore (tel 533 2177), Eu Tong Sen St, 354 rooms, singles S$155-175, doubles S$175-195
Garden Hotel (tel 235 3344), 14 Balmoral Rd, 216 rooms, singles from S$110, doubles from S$120
Goodwood Park Hotel (tel 737 7411), 22 Scotts Rd, 300 rooms, singles S$220-250, doubles $250-280
Hotel Grand Central (tel 737 9944), 22 Orchard Rd & Cavanagh Rd, 365 rooms, singles S$130, doubles S$155
Hilton International Singapore (tel 737 2233), 581 Orchard Rd, 463 rooms, singles S$165-215, doubles S$190-245
Hyatt Regency Singapore (tel 733 1188), 10-12 Scotts Rd, 824 rooms, singles S$185-285, S$215-315
King's Hotel (tel 733 0011), Havelock Rd, 319 rooms, singles S$165-185, doubles S$205-225
Ladyhill Hotel (tel 737 2111), Ladyhill Rd, 175 rooms, singles S$130-170, doubles S$155-195
The Mandarin Singapore (tel 737 4411), 333 Orchard Rd, 1200 rooms, singles S$185-200, doubles S$225-280
The Marco Polo (tel 474 7141), Tanglin Rd, 603 rooms, singles S$205-285, doubles S$235-285
Hotel Meridien Singapore (tel 733 8855), 100 Orchard Rd, 419 rooms, singles S$195-215, doubles S$215-250
Hotel Meridien Changi-Singapore (tel 734 3863), 2 Netheravon Rd, 280 rooms, singles S$170-225, doubles S$190-260
Ming Court Hotel (tel 737 1133), Tanglin Rd, 300 rooms, singles S$180, doubles S$205

Hotel Miramar (tel 733 0222), 401 Havelock Rd, 214 rooms, singles S$120, doubles S$140

Hotel New Otani Singapore (tel 339 2941), 177A River Valley Rd, 408 rooms, singles S$175-215, doubles S$195-245

Hotel Nikko Singapore (tel 733 0188), Outram Rd, 509 rooms, singles S$205, doubles S$235

Novotel Orchid Inn (tel 250 3322), 214 Dunearn Rd, 321 rooms, singles S$125-165, doubles S$145-185

Hotel Oberoi Imperial (tel 737 1666), Jalan Rumbia, 600 rooms, singles S$170-200, doubles S$190-220

Orchard Hotel (tel 734 7766), 442 Orchard Rd, 350 rooms, singles S$175-190, doubles S$195-215

Paramount Hotel (tel 344 5577), 25 Marine Parade Rd, 250 rooms, singles S$125-135, doubles S$140-150

Pavilion Inter-Continental Singapore (tel 733 8888), 1 Cuscaden Rd, 450 rooms, singles S$185-245, doubles S$225-285

Peninsula Hotel (tel 337 8091), Coleman St, 315 rooms, singles S$150, doubles S$165

Hotel Phoenix Singapore (tel 737 8666), Orchard & Somerset Rds, 300 rooms, singles S$135-160, doubles S$160-180

Plaza Hotel (tel 298 0011), Beach Rd, 355 rooms, singles S$135-195, doubles S$155-215

President Merlin Hotel (tel 295 0122), 181 Kitchener Rd, 525 rooms, singles S$145, doubles S$170

Raffles Hotel (tel 337 8041), 1-3 Beach Rd, 127 rooms, singles S$130-170, doubles S$155-200

Royal Holiday Inn (tel 737 7966), 25 Scotts Rd, 543 rooms, singles S$180-230, doubles S$210-260

Hotel Royal (tel 253 4411), Newton Rd, 331 rooms, singles S$100-120, doubles S$120-140

Sea View Hotel (tel 345 2222), Amber Close, 460 rooms, singles S$105-165, doubles S$125-165

Shangri-La Hotel (tel 737 3644), 22 Orange Grove Rd, 700 rooms, singles S$185-275, doubles S$220-310

Hotel Tai-Pan Ramada (tel 336 2526), 101 Victoria St, 269 rooms, singles S$105-145, doubles S$125-165

The York Hotel (tel 737 0511), 21 Mount Elizabeth, 400 rooms, singles S$180-205, doubles S$205-230

Places to Eat

Singapore is far and away the food capital of Asia. When it comes to superb Chinese food Hong Kong may actually be a step ahead but it's Singapore's sheer variety and pleasantly low prices which make it so good. Equally important, Singapore's food is superbly accessible – you haven't got to search out obscure places, you don't face communication problems, you don't even have to have a big bankroll.

On the other hand if you want to make gastronomic discoveries there are lots of out-of-the-way little places where you'll find marvellous food that nobody else knows about. The Singaporeans' enthusiasm for food (and economical food at that) is amply illustrated by the competitions newspapers run every so often to find the best hawker's stall in the city. To get to grips with food in Singapore you first have to know what types of food are available in Singapore, then where to find them. What is available has already been covered in the opening Food section, where to go follows.

Look for *Singapore Feasts* (Apa Productions) for a complete rundown on eating out in Singapore. The various guides, throw-aways and *What's on this Week* – available at the airport, tourist office and better hotels – also list restaurants, advertise them and make recommendations.

Hawker's Food Hawkers are the mobile food stalls, pushcarts which set their tables and stools up around them and sell their food right on the streets. This is the base line for Singapore food, the place where it all starts, where the prices are lowest and the eating quite possibly the most interesting.

Real, mobile, on-the-street hawkers are a disappearing species, but they've been replaced by hawkers' centres where a large number of non-mobile hawkers can all be found under the one roof. Scattered amongst them are tables and stools and you can sit and eat at any one you choose – none of them belong to a specific stall. Indeed a group of you can sit at one table and all eat from different stalls and at the same time have drinks from another.

It's one of the wonders of food centre eating how the various operators keep track of their plates and utensils – and manage to chase you up with the bill. The real joy of food centres is the sheer variety; while you're having Chinese food your companion can be eating a biriyani and across the table somebody else can be trying the satay. As a rough guide meals cost from one-dish meals cost from S$1.20-3. Higher for more elaborate dishes.

There are hawkers' centres all over Singapore and more are being built as areas are redeveloped and the hawkers moved off the streets. In the business centre one of the best is *Telok Ayer*, built in an old Victorian market building between Robinson Rd and Shenton Way. The two other business centre places – *Empress Place* beside the Singapore River and *Boat Quay* directly across the river have recently been demolished. Telok Ayer and others in the business district are very busy at lunch, but tend to be quiet or closed in the evenings, apart from the ones by the river.

The once popular and still well-known *Satay Club* area by the waterfront at the foot of Stamford Rd seems to have fallen on hard times. It's still there, but never busy. There's demolition and construction all over the place at this end of town and with less housing in the area few people bother coming to eat I suppose. Still, it is near the river and Raffles Quay – a pleasant strolling area in the evening.

Right beside the Handicraft Centre on Tanglin Rd is the *Rasa Singapura* centre where the hawkers were all selected in a special competition to find the best stalls for each individual dish. This centre is promoted heavily for tourists although all the food centres are perfectly safe and healthy – you really can eat anywhere in Singapore. As a result prices are a bit higher than at other centres and some people say the food is not really any better – decide for yourself.

Continue down Orchard Rd and there's another popular centre upstairs in the *Cuppage Street* centre. The downstairs section is a vegetable and produce market, but the upstairs food stalls section includes many of the operators relocated from the famous old Orchard Rd car park (Gluttons' Square) when it was redeveloped. The *Newton Circus* centre, at the traffic circle at the end of Scotts Rd, is particularly popular at night as it stays open later than usual. There are other centres on Serangoon Rd, just beyond Rochor Rd, on Jalan Besar; just before Kitchener St; in the Peoples' Park complex near Chinatown; and in the high-rise block on the corner of Waterloo and Rochor Rds. Bugis St still has a number of traditional hawkers' stalls.

Near Bugis St, at the corner of Waterloo or Queen and Albert Sts there is a very busy, very popular and very good centre with all types of food at low prices. It's conveniently close to the Bencoolen area hotels. Also along the alleys off Bugis St there are stalls. Some people now set up a dozen tables or so with white tablecloths, napkins, wine glasses – the whole bit. The prices are a bit higher, of course.

In Chinatown, there's a hawkers' centre alongside the *Tanjong Market* not far from the train station. There's also the *Amory St Food Centre*, where Amory meets Telok Ayer, in Chinatown.

On Kitchener Rd, across from the big President Merlin Hotel near Serangoon Rd is an outdoor food stall area that has steamboats – as does the Satay Club – one of the few that offers it as standard fare. Another centre is at the corner of Serangoon and Bukit Timah Rds.

Some typical hawkers' food you may find with average sorts of prices includes carrot cake or *chye tow kway* (S$1 to 2) – also known as radish cake, it's a fried vegetable dish utterly unlike our western health food idea of carrot cake. Indian *biriyanis* cost S$1.50 to 3 or you can have a *murtabak* from S$1.20 to 3. Naturally chicken rice will always be available in food centres (S$1.80 to 3). Similar to chicken rice is *char siew* or roast pork. All the usual Cantonese dishes are available – like fried rice (S$1.50 to 3), fried vegetables (S$3), beef & vegetables (S$5), sweet & sour pork (S$3 to 5), plus other dishes like fish heads with black beans & chilli for S$3 to 5.

There will often be Malay or Indonesian stalls with *satay* at 25c a stick, *mee rebus* at 80c to S$1, *gado gado* or *mee soto* at similar prices. Omelettes are available at several stalls at Rasa Singapura from around S$1.50. *Wan ton mee*, that substantial soup dish, costs S$2 for shredded chicken or braised beef. You could try a *chee chong fun*, a type of stuffed noodle dish, costing from S$1.50 depending on whether you want the noodles with prawns, mushrooms or chicken & pork. *Hokkien fried prawn mee* is S$1.50 to 3, *prawn mee soup* S$1 to 2, *popiah* (spring rolls) 80c, *laksa* S$1.50 to 2. There's a whole variety of other dishes and soups.

Or you could even opt for western food like sausage, egg & chips for S$2.40, burgers for S$2.50 or fish & chips for S$2.50. To drink you could have a beer for S$2.20, soft drinks for 30 to 50c, ice kachang for 40c or sugar cane juice for 20 to 50c depending on size. Fruit juices range from 50c for melon, papaya or pineapple to 80c for apple, orange or starfruit may cost up to S$1 or even 1.50 at some centres. To finish up you might try a fruit salad for S$1.50 to 2 or just a *pisang goreng* (fried banana) for 20 or 30c.

Chinese Food Singapore has plenty of restaurants serving everything from a south Indian thali to an all-American hamburger, but naturally it's Chinese restaurants that predominate. They range all the way from streetside hawkers' stalls to fancy five-star hotel restaurants with a whole gamut of possibilities in between.

One very popular place that has now fallen on hard times is *Albert St*. A couple of years ago half the street disappeared to make way for a multistorey car park. Now the government has put another nail in the coffin by preventing the restaurants from spilling out into the street. And if you can't eat out on the street in Albert St, why, most people seem to think, eat there at all. So *Fatty's* (Wing Seong) at 184 Albert St may still be turning out great Cantonese food, but the crowds aren't like they used to be. If eating in Albert St, because you certainly can still eat there and the food is still superb, be certain to agree beforehand on a price for the meal.

The *Manhill* at 99 Pasir Panjang Rd and its companion the *Hillman* at 159 Cantonment Rd are two more traditional-style Cantonese restaurants with moderate prices in straightforward surroundings. The *Mayflower Peking* at the International Building on Orchard Rd (beside the Thai Embassy) and the *Mayflower* at the DBS Building on Shenton Way are the opposite end of the scale in size and setting. They're huge Hong Kong-style dim sum specialists, but surprisingly reasonably priced for all the carpeting and air-conditioning. Dim sum starts from around S$1 per plate.

Other dim sum places include the more expensive *Ming Palace Restaurant* in the Ming Court Hotel or the luxurious *Shang Palace* in the Shangri-la. Remember that dim sum is a lunchtime or Sunday breakfast dish – in the evening these restaurants revert to other menus. Other more expensive Cantonese restaurants include the *Fortuna* in the Asia Hotel, and the old-fashioned *Majestic* on Bukit Pasoh Rd near Chinatown.

At 147-153 Kitchener Rd, between Jalan Besar and Serangoon Rd, the *Fut Sai Kai* (which translates as 'monk's world') is another spartan old coffee shop where the speciality is vegetarian cooking. Prices are not low, but it offers a good chance to sample a slightly unusual variation of Chinese cuisine. Ditto for the *Lok Woh Yuen* at Jalan Tanjang Pagar 25.

Chicken rice is a common, but popular,

dish all over town and *Swee Kee* on the 4th floor of the Fortuna Centre at the corner of Middle Rd and Bencoolen St is a long-running specialist with a high reputation. Chicken and rice is S$3.30 served with chili, ginger and thick soya sauce. They also do steamboats; a S$20 version has a stock enriched by various Chinese herbs and Mao Tai wine. The menu includes mostly Cantonese dishes, mainly seafood – S$5 for a basic, S$10 for a varied meal. They used to be at 51 Middle Rd too – without air-con, simpler and a bit cheaper – but that branch seems to be closed now. The *Rasa Singapura* chicken rice stall also does a good job of it – they even offer the chicken as 'regular' or boneless'.

Although Cantonese is the most readily available Chinese cuisine in Singapore you can also find most of the regional variations although they often tend to be more expensive than the common, everyday Cantonese restaurants. If you've got a yen to try Peking duck then the *Eastern Palace* on the 4th floor of Supreme House is one of the best Peking restaurants.

Szechuan restaurants are relatively common. They include the reasonably priced *Omei* in the Hotel Grand Centre at one end of the scale and the decidedly expensive *Golden Phoenix* at the Hotel Equatorial at the other. In the old Mayfair Hotel on Armenian St the *Great Shanghai* is the place to go for Shanghainese food like drunken chicken.

Hokkien food is not all that popular a cuisine despite the large number of Hokkiens in Singapore, but *Beng Hiang* at 20 Murray St is renowned for its Hokkien food. Teochew food is a relatively widely available cuisine – you could try *Guan Hin* at 1 Bendemeer Rd where steamboat is also very popular. Or the traditional *Chui Wah Lin* at 49 Mosque St. At several of these places there may be no menu, but a request for suggestions and prices will be readily answered. Finally there's Taiwanese food – try the *May Garden* at 101 Orchard Towers or the reasonably priced *Goldleaf* at 185 Orchard Rd.

Singapore has another local variation on Chinese food which it's worth making the effort to try. Seafood in Singapore is simply superb, whether it's prawns or abalone, fish head curry or chilli crabs. Most of the better seafood specialists are some distance out from the city centre, but the travelling is worthwhile. Upper East Coast Rd is one of the best areas where you will find places like *Seaview* at 779A. Or try the *Chin Wah Heng* at 785 Upper East Cost Rd, at about the 14½ km marker – moderately priced, but with the usual glass tanks containing crabs, eels, prawns and fish all ready to head for the wok. Others include the *Choon Seng* at 892 Ponggol Rd at Ponggol Point right up at the north of the island or the *Chin Lee* at 18C Jalan Tuas in the small fishing village of Tuas, way out beyond Jurong at the western tip of the island, 30 km from the city. The trip out to Ponggol Point, on an 82 or 83 bus, is quite an experience in itself; you pass miles of cemeteries and then chicken and pig farms, surprisingly rural for Singapore.

Indian Food As with everything else some of the best Indian food can be found in the hawkers' centres, this especially applies to biriyani dishes. In most of the centres, but particularly Telok Ayer, you can have a superb chicken biriyani for just S$2.50.

If you want to sample eat-with-your-fingers south Indian vegetarian food then the place to go is the famous and very popular *Komala Vilas* at 76 Serangoon Rd. Established soon after the war, Komala Vilas has an open downstairs area where you have masala dosa (S$2.25) and other snacks, while upstairs, which is now all air-conditioned, S$3.50 buys you their eat-all-you-can rice meal. Remember to wash your hands before you start, to use only your right hand and to ask for eating utensils only if you really have to! On your way out try an Indian sweet from the showcase at the back of the downstairs section. Another rice plate specialist is *Sri Krishna Vilas* at 229 Selegie Rd.

— Singapore is multi racial in both dinners & diners —

For north Indian food *Jubilee* at 771 North Bridge Rd, near the Sultan Mosque and Arab St, is an even more venerable establishment – it has been in operation since before the war. It's a great place for a biriyani or other north Indian dishes and again the price is quite absurdly cheap. A few doors down at 791-793 the *Islamic* is very similar.

Much pricier, but with a great reputation for high-quality food, is *Omar Khayyam* at 55 Hill St, virtually opposite the American Embassy. Here the food is Kashmiri, a subtle variation on normal north Indian food, but the tandoori dishes are the highlight. There's a small, basic north Indian place called the *Muslim Restaurant* or something similar on Bencoolen St near Middle Rd, across from the Fortuna Centre. They have very good food and specialise in fish dishes, including fish head curry, but have chicken and vegetable items too. Cost is S$3 to 4. There are plenty of modest Indian places in little India along Serangoon Rd.

Malay, Thai, Indonesian & Nonya Food You won't find a great deal of Malay or Nonya food in Singapore although there are one or two Nonya specialists in the food centres – particularly *Telok Ayer*. Satay, of course, is available in many centres – you'll find good satay in the *Rasa Singapura* and, of course, at the *Satay Club* on Elizabeth Walk, where the stalls all specialise in satay.

There are a number of nasi padang specialists, one of the best known being *Rendezvous* at 4-5 Bras Basah Rd, at the junction with Prinsep St. At lunchtime only *Nasi Padang* at 24 Tanglin Rd, across from the Tanglin Centre, is equally good. For Thai food try *Siamese's Chef Snack Bar* on the 3rd floor of the Fortuna Centre, corner of Bencoolen St and Middle Rd. It's open 11 am to 3.30 pm only, closed Sundays. Sliced beef and duck Kway Teow soup costs S$2; most dishes are just S$1.50 to 2. A lunch of curry vegetables and rice is S$2.50. Various cheap desserts

are also offered. Although the restaurant is tucked away in a corner, most of the food is sold out by 2 pm.

Western Food Yes, you can get western food in Singapore too – including *McDonald's* at a string of places such as Orchard Rd near Scotts Rd, Peoples' Park and Changi Airport. There are also *A&W Root Beer* and *Kentucky Fried Chicken* outlets and you can even try eat-all-you-can pizzas, spaghetti or other meals at *Shakey's Pizza* in the City Plaza Shopping Complex in Geylang.

The *Pavilion Steak House*, next door to the Specialists Centre on Orchard Rd, is a curious colonial hangover; a Singapore equivalent to the *Coliseum* in Kuala Lumpur. Unfortunately their prices, drinks in particular, have got very high of late. Or try *The Beefeater* at 417 River Valley Rd where you can sip a pint in the air-conditioned comfort and forget how close you are to the equator.

For upscale western food, but at bargain prices, there is the *Restaurant Shatec* (tel 235 9533), the Singapore Hotel Association's Training and Educational Centre. Now open to the public, the place is really a training centre for hotel dining room food preparation and presentation. They offer set, five-course meals at lunch and dinner as well as an a la carte menu in a fairly elegant setting. Lunch is S$9.50, dinner S$12.50 with items such as escargot, Scottish salmon and duck a l'orange.

Odds & Ends Naturally Singapore has a lot of personal favourites and obscure odds and ends. If you want a light snack at any time of the day there are quite a few Chinese coffee bars selling interesting cakes which go just nicely with a cup of coffee or teh-o. Try the *Dong Log Wee Cake House* at 235 Orchard Rd.

There are several places worth trying for breakfast around the Bencoolen St cheap hotel area. *Bakers Cafeteria*, at the corner of Bras Basah and Victoria, has complete breakfasts for S$3.80. Set western lunches go for S$5.20. The little Chinese coffee shop beside the Nam Hai Hotel where the city buses stop serves two eggs, toast and tea or coffee – watch out for that sweetened milk – for S$2. They're basic, but they try, and might even lend you an English paper to read while you eat. Others in the area can give you toast and jam if you can make yourself understood. A few doors down Middle Rd there's an Indian place that does great breakfast roti chanai.

The *Cafe de Coral*, in the Far East Plaza on Scotts Rd opposite the Holiday Inn, does orange juice, eggs, bacon, toast and coffee for a bargain S$4.

Towards the back of the Empress Place food centre *Neuborne's* is a great place for fish and chips, believe it or not. There are plenty of supermarkets in Singapore with everything from French wine to Australian beer, yoghurt to muesli, cheese to ice cream. A pot of tea on the lawn at the Raffles Hotel is a fine investment and a chance to relive the Singapore of an earlier era.

Getting There

Air Singapore is a major travel crossroads and flights operate in and out of Changi Airport at all hours. See the introductory Getting There section for details on flying to Singapore from all over the world. Singapore Airlines and MAS have flights between Singapore and Kuala Lumpur, Penang, Kuching and Kota Kinabalu in Malaysia. There are also frequent flights between Singapore and Bangkok in Thailand, Jakarta in Indonesia and Hong Kong.

Singapore is also a very good place for looking for cheap airline tickets. Try agents like Airmaster Travel on Selegie Rd or others that advertise in the Straits Times classified columns. Some typical one-way fares being quoted out of Singapore include Bangkok S$240, Denpasar S$400 or S$590 return, Manila S$699 or S$971 return, Colombo S$380, Madras S$555, Bombay S$671, Jakarta S$210 or S$260-

280 return, Hong Kong S$842, Sydney S$780 to S$900, Auckland S$950, London S$680 to S$750 direct or from S$800 with stops, Vancouver S$1270, USA west coast S$950 by the northern (Asian) route with stops or S$1620 by the southern (Pacific) route, Seattle S$1050, Perth or Darwin via Bali and Jakarta S$658. STA (Student Travel Australia) (tel 734 5681) in the Ming Court Hotel is another reliable place for airline tickets.

Rail Singapore is the southern termination point for the Malaysian railway system although Singapore has no rail system of its own. See the introductory Getting Around section for fare details and timetable. Leaving Singapore you clear immigration and customs at the station so there is no further delay at the causeway when crossing into Malaysia.

Road Although there are a great variety of bus services operating from Singapore the choice is much greater in Johore Bahru where there are also a wide variety of taxi services. To get to Johore Bahru you can take the 170 bus from Queen St for 80c. Or for S$1 you can take the direct bus which departs every 10 minutes from the nearby Rochor Road Terminus. It's a red and grey bus and leaves from Albert St across from the food centre. Don't be worried if the bus departs while you're clearing immigration and customs for Malaysia, you can just hop on the next one that comes along. Take it all the way to the Johore Bahru terminus though, don't abandon the bus at Malaysian immigration.

In the same locality in Singapore you will find taxis operating to Johore Bahru at S$4 per person or S$16 for a full car. Foreigners are likely to have to pay slightly more since they take longer to clear the border than Singaporeans or Malaysians.

You can get taxis into Malaysia right from Singapore and don't need to bother getting to Johore Bahru first. Try Malaysia Taxi Service (tel 298 3831) at 290 Jalan

Besar, for all points in Malaysia. Another is Kuala Lumpur Taxi Service (tel 223 1889), 191 New Bridge Rd.

To Melaka buses operate from 579 New Bridge Rd (tel 223 8868), nearly opposite the main bus station. Buses leave at 8 am, 9.30 am, 11 am, 2 pm and 3 pm and the cost is S$11, with air-con it's S$16. Most other buses operate from the New Bridge Rd Fringe Car Park Terminus. Some fares and times:

air-con

Kuala Lumpur	9 am or 9 pm	S$17
Ipoh	7 pm	S$25
Butterworth	7 pm	S$30
Kuantan	9 am or 10 pm	S$11
Kuala Trengganu	8 pm	S$23
Kota Bahru	7.30 pm	S$31

non air-con

Kuantan	10 am	S$8.50
Kuala Trengganu	8 am	S$19
Kota Bahru	7.30 pm	S$26

There is a money changer at the bus depot – if you don't see him ask at the desk and they will point him out to you. Last visit he was giving 8% extra on the Singapore over the Malaysian dollar.

Many of the air-con Kuala Lumpur buses are really spifo – new, immaculate, with radio, TV and toilet. The trip takes about eight hours, mainly because the road is very busy in both directions. Parts of it are now divided with toll booths (!), but this widening project will not be completed for a while yet. There's also a lunch break on the way. If you want to hitch into Malaysia get to Johore Bahru first.

Sea There used to be lots of shipping services out of Singapore, but very few still operate – it's all airlines today. The only passage available today is the five-day service to Tawau in Sabah which costs about S$400. For details, check with Mansfield Travel behind the Ocean Building on Collyer Quay. They are also the people to see for details on ships to Fremantle in Western Australia.

Getting Around

A fairly extensive subway system is being put in, but is not due to start operating for a couple of years. Its construction adds a good deal to the general turmoil and noise of the downtown redevelopment, but should in future ease traffic and the overworked bus system.

Singapore Airport Singapore's ultra-modern new Changi International Airport is another of those miracles that Singapore specialises in. It's vast, efficient, organised and was built in record time. See airport transport for details on getting to or from the airport. At the airport there are banking and money-changing facilities, two post offices, a free hotel reservation service from 7 am to 11 pm, left luggage facilities, a variety of shops in the boarding area, and a supermarket in the basement. The reservation service will not call or book a room to the cheap hotels.

On your way through the arrivals concourse pick up a free copy of the *Singapore Weekly Guide* which is available from stands. This gives you a lot of useful information and good-quality colour maps of Singapore city and Singapore island.

There are plenty of places to eat at the airport (this is Singapore after all, food capital of South-East Asia), including a Swensen's ice cream bar upstairs, a Chinese restaurant, a Japanese restaurant and a cafeteria-style restaurant. If you are one of the millions of air travellers fed up with over-priced and terrible food at airports, then Changi Airport has the answer to that too – there is a McDonald's at one end of the arrival hall and a Church's Texas Fried Chicken at the other end. Both at normal prices. To find even cheaper food just take the elevator beside McDonald's on the arrival level and press the button marked 'staff cafeteria' one floor below. There you'll find a kind of hawkers' centre with Chinese and Malay food.

Airport tax from Singapore is S$5 to Malaysia and Brunei, S$12 further afield.

Airport Transport Singapore's Changi International Airport opened in mid-81. It's at the extreme eastern end of the island, about 20 km from the city, so it is not as conveniently located as the old Paya Lebar Airport. On the other hand, with typical Singaporean efficiency, a new expressway has been built along reclaimed land to the city and with fast bus services it is still no problem getting into the city.

You've got a choice of a very convenient public bus, taxis and more expensive limousine services. For the public buses follow the signs in the airport terminal to the basement bus stop. You can take a 392 bus to Somapah for 50c; Somapah is an interchange for other bus services around Singapore. Or you can take a 394 bus to Batu Interchange for 80c.

For budget travellers heading for the Bencoolen St-Beach Rd-Middle Rd cheap accommodation enclave, by far the best bus service is the 390, which also costs 80c. You must have exact change for this bus so when you first change money on arrival make sure you get some coins. This drops you off at Rochor Rd, only a block from Bencoolen St. The 390 bus departs frequently and takes about half an hour to the city. In the city, near Bencoolen, catch the 390 from the Peace Centre at the corner of Selegie and Middle Rds or from the side of Rochor Centre opposite its arrival point. From Orchard Rd take a 7 bus to Bedok Interchange and from there you can take the 390 or a 347.

Ignore the other bus services from the airport – amusingly numbered 727, 737, 747 and 757 – these are intended for airport workers and run to the major housing areas.

Taxis from the airport are subject to a S$3 supplementary charge on top of the meter fare, which will probably be S$7 to 10 to most places. Note that this only applies from the airport, not from the city. Sintat (tel 235 5855) operate an airport limousine service at S$40 from the airport to your hotel, S$35 hotel to airport. At the airport, pick up a free taxi guide, which lists many fares around town. There are many taxi companies; for radio bookings 24 hours call 293 3111 or 452 5555.

Bus Singapore has an extremely frequent and comprehensive bus network. You rarely have to wait more than a few minutes for a bus and they will get you almost anywhere you want to go. If you intend to do much travelling by bus in Singapore, a copy of the bus guide, which also includes a bus route map, is a vital investment. They cost 70c at bookshops, but shoestring travellers may well find their hotel has a supply left behind by departing visitors.

The buses follow the same route into and out of the city, and fares start from 40c and go up in 10c increments to a maximum of 80c. There are also OMO (One Man Operated) buses which charge a flat fare – you must have the exact change as none is given. There are two types of OMO bus – one charges a flat 80c (like the 390 airport bus) while the other operates a step fare system where you pay 80, 60 or 40c depending on where you board. A sign in the front of the bus indicates the fare to be paid. For information on how to reach a certain point call 284 8866 during business hours.

Taxis Singapore has a good supply of taxis – 12,500 of them – and it's usually not too difficult to find one. The exceptions may include rush hours, trips out to the airport (which taxi drivers are somewhat reluctant to make), or at meal times (Singaporeans are not at all enthusiastic about missing a meal).

It is quite easy to recognise Singapore taxis although they come in several varieties – most common being black with a yellow roof or pale blue. Taxis are all metered and although you should ensure the meter is flagged down it's usually no problem – unlike some Asian countries where meters always seem to be 'broken'. Flag fall is S$1.20 (there are still some non air-con taxis which cost S$1, but they're mainly air-con now) for the first 1.5 km then 10c for each additional 375 metres. A third and fourth passenger adds 10c each to the cost as does each piece of luggage other than hand luggage.

From 1 am to 6 am there is a 50% surcharge over the meter fare. From the airport there is a surcharge of S$3 for each journey – but not to the airport. You can also book taxis by radio by phoning 293 3111 – this costs an additional 40c. Note the information on area licences for the restricted zone.

Restricted Area & Car Parking From 7.30 to 10.15 am each morning the Central Business District is a restricted zone where cars may only enter with a licence or if they carry at least four people. A daily licence costs S$5 – not surprisingly this has dramatically reduced traffic problems in the rush hour! The licence requirement also applies to taxis so if you want to take a taxi into the CBD during the above hours you must pay for the taxi licence which costs S$2 – unless somebody else has already done so of course. The area licences are sold at booths just outside the district boundaries.

And if you should carelessly enter the CBD without a licence? Well, there may well be inspectors standing by the roadside noting down the number plates of unlicenced cars as they enter the CBD. A S$50 fine will soon arrive at the car owner's address.

Parking in many places in Singapore is operated by a coupon system. You can buy a booklet of coupons at parking kiosks and must display one in your car window with holes punched out to indicate the time, day and date your car was parked.

Trishaws Singapore's bicycle rickshaws are fast disappearing although you'll find a surprising number still operating in Chinatown and off Serangoon Rd. Today they are mainly used for local shopping trips or to transport articles too heavy to carry. They rarely venture on to Singapore's heavily trafficked main streets.

There are, however, trishaws at many tourist centres in case you really have to try one out. Always agree the fare beforehand. A recent innovation has been nighttime trishaw tours which are operated from a number of the large hotels. Trishaw Tours (tel 223 8809) offer a nightly ride through Chinatown for S$13. On the street a very short ride is S$2 and the price goes up from there. Trishaws had their peak just after WW II when motorised transport was almost non-existent and trishaw riders could turn a very healthy income.

Rent-a-Car Singapore has branches of the three major regional rent-a-car operators – Sintat, Hertz and Avis. There are also a large number of smaller and local operators. Many of these quote rental rates that undercut the major operators if you want a car just for local use. Rates are lower, however, in Malaysia. Main addresses of some operators include:

Avis
    204-B Boon Liew Building, Bukit Timah Rd (tel 737 9477)
Best Car Rental
    £03-20 Coronation Shopping Plaza, Bukit Timah Rd (tel 468 9777)
Blue Star Car Rental
    £02-19 Balestier Complex, Balestier Rd (tel 253 4661)
Budget
    Orchard Plaza, Orchard Rd (tel 734 5511)
Hertz Rent-a-Car
    33 Tanglin Rd (tel 734 4646)
Sime Darby Services
    475 Tanglin Halt Rd (tel 62 3433)
Sintat Rent-a-Car
    £01-27 OUB Building, Collyer Quay (tel 224 4155)
Sunrise Car Rental
    107 Bukit Timah Rd (tel 336 0626)

Boats & Ferries There are a wide variety of boating possibilities in Singapore. You can charter a bumboat (motorised sampan) to take a tour up the Singapore River or to get out to the islands around Singapore. Speedboats can be hired from Ponggol Boatel to get across to the Northern Islands or for water skiing. There are regular ferry services from Clifford Pier or the World Trade Centre to Sentosa and the other Southern Islands. There are also Port of Singapore Authority ferry tours or you can take more luxurious junk tours around the harbour either by daylight or as an evening dinner cruise with operators like Fairwind or Watertours.

Walking Getting around Singapore on foot has one small problem – apart from the heat and humidity that is. The problem is the 'five foot ways' – what Singapore, and indeed most towns in Malaysia, have instead of sidewalks or pavements. A five foot way, which takes its name from the fact that it is roughly five feet wide, is a walkway at the front of the traditional Chinese shop-houses, but enclosed, verandah-like, in the front of the building.

The problem with them is that every shop's walkway is individual. It may well be higher or lower than the shop next door or closer to or further from the street. Walking thus becomes a constant up and down and side to side, further complicated by the fact that half the shops seem to overflow right across the walkway forcing you to venture into the street. Plus people park their bikes or motorcycles across them and at night you are likely to trip over the odd chowkidar asleep on his charpoy. (A chowkidar is an Indian nightwatchman and a charpoy is the traditional rope-strung bed which chowkidars seem to spend most of their time horizontal upon.) To further add to the joys of walking in Singapore there are open drains waiting to catch the unwary.

Still, if you can drag your eyes away from where your feet are going, there is plenty to see as you stroll the five foot ways.

Tours A wide variety of tours are available in Singapore. They include morning or afternoon tours in the city or to Jurong, Changi on the east coast, or the various parks and gardens. These vary in price from around S\$15 to 20. To Jurong Bird Park is S\$20, a three-hour city tour is S\$16, to Sentosa for 3½ hours is S\$28. Nightly tours of Chinatown by bicycle trishaw cost from S\$25 to 35 including a preliminary gin sling at the Raffles Hotel although there are also cheaper trishaw tours for S\$13.

More unusual tours include a daybreak walking tour of Chinatown for S\$15. Port of Singapore Authority tours include a two-hour harbour cruise (10 am or 2.30 pm from Monday to Saturday, departing from the World Trade Centre). The PSA also have evening harbour cruises and there are a number of private operators with junk trips on the harbour or bumboat trips up the river. These start from around S\$18 for daytime cruises and cost up towards S\$40 for dinner cruises including a buffet meal.

Tour East (tel 220 2200) has one for the drinkers, a tour of Malayan Breweries, makers of Anchor and Tiger Beer. After the tour there's a 30-minute taste session. The same company offers a tour outside of the city with a glimpse at the fast-fading countryside and village life. Gray Line, the international sightseeing tour company, runs trips around town and to local area attractions. They have seven different tours from S\$16 to 147.

Licensed guides are available through the tourist office. They charge S\$9 an hour if using any of the four official languages and S\$17 an hour in any other. Ask at your hotel about other types of tours.

Things to Buy

One of Singapore's major attractions is, of course, shopping. There are plenty of bargains to be had in all sorts of goods, but there are also a number of guidelines to follow if you want to be certain you get your money's worth. First of all don't buy anything unless you really want it and don't buy anything where the hassle of getting it back home will cost you more than the saving you make. Remember that 'duty free' and 'free port' are pretty throwaway terms. Not everything is necessarily loaded down with import duty in your own country, for one thing. For another, Singapore also has some local industries to protect these days so not everything in Singapore is necessarily the cheapest.

Price Before you leap on anything as a great bargain, find out what the price really is. If you're going to Singapore with the intention of buying a camera or a tape recorder, for example, check what they would cost you back home first. Then in Singapore find out what the 'real' price is. It's no triumph to knock a starting price of S$200 down to S$150 if the real price was S$150 to start with. To find what something should cost you can check with the main agent or showroom in Singapore or you can check a big fixed-price department store where the price is unlikely to be rock bottom, but is certainly likely to be in the ball park. Most important, ask around – never buy in the first shop you come to; always check a few places to see what is being asked.

Bargaining You've got to bargain in Singapore in almost any shop. The secret of successful bargaining is to keep it good humoured and try to make them move rather than you. Your first gambit can be 'is that your best price', for their opening offer certainly won't be. Then when you have to offer make it an offer a fair bit lower than you are willing to spend, but not so low that you seem totally uninterested.

Maintain some disinterest, however. You want to always keep the impression that if the price isn't right you can quite happily do without it; or that if his price isn't right the shop next door probably will be. Remember also that when you've made an offer you've committed yourself. If you really don't want something don't offer anything – you might just end up buying it with a totally ludicrous offer.

Guarantees They're one of the most important considerations if you're buying electronic gear, watches, cameras or the like, and the important point is that the guarantee must be an international one. A national guarantee is next to useless – are you going to bring your calculator back to Singapore to be fixed? Usually this is no problem, but always ask before you get down to haggling if the guarantee is international. Make sure it is filled out correctly, that the shop's name and the serial number of the item are all down.

As important as the guarantee is the item's compatibility back home. You don't want a brand or model that has never found its way to your country.

Shops You buy in Singapore on one basis only – price. The goods (high-technology goods this is) are just the same as you'd get back home so quality doesn't enter into it. You're not going to come back for after-sales service, so service doesn't come into the picture either. You're not there to admire the display or get good advice from the assistants. In Singapore it's price, price, price.

As a spin-off from this, Singapore's shops are generally pretty unexciting places – it's simply a case of pack the goods in 99 times out of 100. Nor are the staff always that helpful or friendly – they may be a long way behind Hong Kong shop assistants when it comes to out-and-out rudeness, but a few shopping trips in Singapore will soon indicate why the government runs 'be polite' campaigns so often!

Where to Shop Singapore is almost wall-to-wall shops but there are certain places worth heading to for certain items. People's Park is a large shopping complex, but a little off the regular tourist track.

Top: Singapore city skyline from the harbour (TW)
Left: courtyard of the Raffles Hotel, Singapore (TW)
Right: Laughing Buddha, Tiger Balm Gardens, Singapore (TW)

Top: Sunday morning bird singing session, Singapore (TW)
Left: Buddha Foot, 1000 Lights Temple, Singapore (TW)
Right: seated Buddha figure, 1000 Lights Temple, Singapore (TW)

Therefore prices may be a bit lower so if you want cameras, film, electrical equipment, watches or whatever, but you're not looking for something highly unusual, then this is a good place to try.

Otherwise the major shopping complexes on and around Orchard Rd – like Plaza Singapura, Specialists Centre, Lucky Plaza, Orchard Towers, Shaw Centre on Scott's Rd, Supreme House on Penang Rd, Tanglin Centre on Tanglin Rd – will all have a very wide variety of shops and goods. Recently opened centres are the huge Daimaru Centre on River Valley Rd opposite the National Theatre and the Parkway Parade complex at Marine Parade Centre.

Singapore has a number of Chinese emporiums if you're after something from the People's Republic. Try Overseas in the People's Park, Chinese in the International Building on Orchard Rd, Yu Yi in Orchard Building on Grange Rd. There are also a wide variety of department stores offering both their own branded goods and other items, generally at fixed prices – ideal if you've had enough of bargaining. They include shops like C K Tang, Isetan or Yaohan, all along Orchard Rd.

For oddities you could try Chinatown or the shops along Arab St. High St and North Bridge Rd also provide more traditional shopping possibilities. The famous Change Alley, a narrow tunnel running between Collyer Quay and Raffles Place, is still hanging on in the face of redevelopment, but is now supplemented by a modern, overhead shopping arcade. The Singapore Handicrafts Centre is the place to look for regional handicrafts and to see many of them actually being made.

What to Buy Anything and everything is the easy answer. Cameras are available throughout the city; when buying film bargain for lower prices if you're buying in bulk – 10 films cost less than 10 times one film. For TVs, stereo equipment, radios, tape recorders, calculators and watches the same story applies – compare prices and be certain of the guarantee. And be certain you're paying less than you would back home – duty free is a somewhat over-used term these days. Camera prices are heavily discounted in the west just as much as in Singapore or Hong Kong.

Clothes and shoes are widely available both imported, locally made and made to measure. Some of the best buys include brand name jeans and clothes (Levis, Wranglers, etc). Orchard Rd is again the place for expensive crafts like Persian carpets. Try the Singapore Handicrafts Centre for all types of regional craft work.

Malaysia

Malaysia is a country of beautiful scenery, easy and comfortable travel and friendly people, rather than of deep historical or cultural interest. It's one of the most advanced countries in Asia and offers a wide variety of beaches, mountains and parks for lovers of the outdoors. For convenience this guide divides Malaysia into four sections. First it's split east and west into East Malaysia and Peninsular Malaysia. Then the peninsula is divided into east and west coasts, and East Malaysia into Sabah and Sarawak.

FACTS

Population Malaysia has a population of nearly 14 million. Malays and other indigenous people comprise 54%, Chinese 35%, Indians 10% and others 1%. It's a reasonable approximation to say that the Malays control the government while the Chinese have their fingers on the economic pulse. Approximately 85% of the population lives in Peninsular Malaysia and the remaining 15% (a bit over two million) in the much more lightly populated states of Sabah and Sarawak.

Geography Malaysia covers an area of 330,000 square km, 40% in Peninsular Malaysia and 60% in Sabah and Sarawak. Malaysia is densely forested – about 75% of the land area is covered with jungle – and quite mountainous. All of Malaysia is north of the equator although it runs only a short distance south of the southern tip of the peninsula and just south of the southernmost point of Sarawak.

Economy Malaysia is a prosperous and progressive country and one of the world's major suppliers of tin, natural rubber and palm oil. Indeed, rubber plantations, interspersed with palm oil plantations, seem to cover a large part of the peninsula. In East Malaysia the economy is based on

timber in Sabah while in Sarawak oil and pepper are major exports. Malaysia is self sufficient in oil and also manages to export some. This healthy economic base contributes to Malaysia's position as one of the best-off countries in Asia – only Singapore and Japan have higher per-capita incomes.

STATES

Malaysia is a confederation of 13 states and a capital district of Kuala Lumpur. Nine of the peninsular states have sultans and every five years an election is held to determine which one will become the Yang di-Pertuan Agong or 'King' of Malaysia. The states of Sabah and Sarawak in East Malaysia are rather different from the peninsular Malaysian states since they were separate colonies, not parts of Malaya, prior to independence. They still retain a greater degree of local administration than the peninsular states.

Johore
area: 18,984 square km
population: 1,690,000
capital: Johore Bahru
Forms the southern end of the peninsula, connected to Singapore by the causeway.

Kedah
area: 9,316 square km
population: 1,210,000
capital: Alor Setar
Northern state where much of Malaysia's rice is grown. The island of Langkawi is a popular resort in Kedah.

Kelantan
area: 14,758 square km
population: 860,000
capital: Kota Bahru
Northernmost east coast state, a centre of Malay culture and handicrafts.

The touristically popular island of Penang plus a narrow coastal strip known as Province Wellesley.

Perak
area: 21,005 square km
population: 1,960,000
capital: Ipoh
The name means silver although the mineral which has created the state's wealth is tin. Important towns are Ipoh, Taiping, Telok Anson and Kuala Kangsar. Pangkor Island is also in Perak.

Perlis
area: 795 square km
population: 150,000
capital: Kangar
Northern border state with Thailand, smallest state in Malaysia.

Sabah
area: 72,858 square km
population: 860,000
capital: Kota Kinabalu
Malaysia's frontier state in north Borneo has the highest mountain in South-East Asia.

Sarawak
area: 124,450 square km
population: 1,300,000
capital: Kuching
North Borneo state of rivers, longhouses and colourful tribes.

Melaka
area: 1,650 square km
population: 520,000
A small state centred around the historically important port of Melaka.

Negri Sembilan
area: 6,645 square km
population: 640,000
capital: Seremban
A federation of nine (negri) states in an area of Minangkabau culture.

Selangor
area: 124,450 square km
population: 1,300,000
capital: Shah Alam
State around Kuala Lumpur which includes the satellite town Petaling Jaya.

Pahang
area: 35,960 square km
population: 750,000
capital: Kuantan
Largest state in the peninsula with varied attractions including a stretch of the east coast, most of Malaysia's hill stations and most of Taman Negara, the national park.

Kuala Lumpur
area: 244 square km
population: 1,000,000
Federal capital territory.

Penang
area: 1,021 square km
population: 970,000
capital: Georgetown

Trengganu
area: 12,955 square km
population: 541,250
capital: Kuala Trengganu
Popular beach state of the east coast with many beautiful beaches and interesting fishing villages plus the turtle beach strip.

CULTURE, CRAFTS & GAMES

It's along the east coast, the predominantly Malay part of Malaysia, that you'll find Malay crafts, culture and games at their liveliest and most widely practised.

Top Spinning – Main Gasing

Spinning tops hardly seems to be an activity for grown men to engage in but Malaysian tops (gasing) are not child's play. A top can weigh up to seven kilograms and it takes a good deal of strength to whip the five metre cord back and spin them competitively.

Top spinning contests are held in east coast villages during the slack time of year while the rice is ripening. Contests are usually between teams of fighting tops, where the attackers attempt to dislodge the defenders from a pre-arranged pattern, or there are contests for length of spin. The record spinning time approaches two hours!

Kite Flying

Flying kites is another child's game that takes on man-size proportions on the east coast. Kite flying contests include events for greatest height reached and also competitions between fighting kites. The kites, which can be up to 2½ metres wide, are real works of art. There are cat kites, bird kites and, most popular, the *wau balun* or moon kite. An attachment to the front of the kite makes a humming noise and in favourable conditions a kite may be left flying, humming pleasantly, all night. Kites are popular souvenirs of Malaysia and a stylised Kelantan kite is the symbol of Malaysian Airlines System.

Sepak Raga

One of the most popular kampong games, the equipment needed to play sepak raga is simplicity itself – a lightweight ball made of strips of rotan. Drawn up in a circle the opposing teams must keep the ball continuously in the air, using legs, head and shoulders. Points are scored for each time a team member hits the ball. Sepak takraw is a version of the same game where the players hit the ball back and forth over a net just like in volleyball – but again without using hands. It's a popular sport in a number of South-East Asian countries but the Malays are the champions.

Silat

Also known as bersilat this is the Malay martial art which originated in Melaka in the 15th century. Today it is a highly refined and stylised activity, demonstrations of which are often performed at ceremonies and weddings, accompanied by music from drums and gongs.

Wayang Kulit – Shadow Play

Similar to the shadow puppet performances of other South-East Asian countries, in particular Java in Indonesia, the Wayang Kulit retells tales from the Hindu epic the *Ramayana*. The To'Dalang or 'Father of the Mysteries' sits behind the semi-transparent screen and manipulates the buffalo hide puppets whose images are thrown onto the screen. Characters include heroes, demons, kings, animals and, ever favourites, clowns.

Performances can last for many hours and throughout that time the puppeteer has to move the figures, sing all the voice parts and conduct the orchestra – it's a feat of some endurance. There are two forms of Wayang Kulit – the Wayang Siam and Wayang Melayu. Performances often take place at weddings or after the harvest.

Dances & Other Activities

There are a variety of dances and dance dramas performed in Malaysia. They include Menora, a dance drama of Thai origin performed by an all-male cast dressed in grotesque masks. Ma'yong is a similar traditional form of theatre but the participants are of both sexes. These performances are often made at Puja Keteks, Buddhist festivals held at temples in Kelantan, near the Thai border.

The Ronggeng is one of the oldest and most traditional Malay dance forms. Rebana Kercing is a dance performed by young men to the accompaniment of tambourines. Other dances, not all of which are from the east coast, include the Tari Piring, Hadrah and Zapin. Berdikir Barat is a comparatively recent activity – a sort of poetic debating contest where two teams have to ridicule and argue with each other in instantaneously composed verse!

Musical Instruments

As in other parts of the region Malay music is principally percussion. The large, hollowed-out log drum known as a rebana is one of the most important Malay instruments. Drum-beating contests are sometimes held. The kertok is a small drum which takes its name from the distinctive sound it makes.

Kain Songket & Other Weaving

A speciality of Kelantan, kain songket is a handwoven fabric with gold and silver threads are woven into the material. Clothes made from this beautiful fabric are usually reserved for the most important festivals and occasions. Mengkuang is a far more prosaic form of weaving using pandanus leaves and strips of bamboo to make baskets, bags and mats.

Silver & Brasswork

Kelantan is famed for its silverworkers who work in a variety of ways and specialise in filigree and repousse work. In the latter, designs are hammered into the silver from behind. Kampong Sireh at Kota Bahru is a centre for silverwork. Brasswork is an equally traditional skill in Kuala Trengganu.

Batik

Although originally an Indonesian craft, batik has made itself equally at home in Malaysia. You'll find it in Penang on the west coast but Kelantan is its true home. Batik cloths are produced by drawing out a pattern with wax and then dyeing the material. The wax is then melted away by boiling the cloth, and a second wax design is drawn in. By repeating waxing, dyeing and boiling processes an intricate and beautifully coloured design is produced. Batik can be found as clothes, cushion covers, tablecloths, placemats or simply as works of art. Malay designs are usually less traditional than those found in neighbouring Indonesia. The wax designs can either be drawn out on a one-off basis or printed on with a stencil.

Peninsular Malaysia – West Coast

The east and west coasts of the peninsula are surprisingly different both in population and in geography. The west coast is more heavily populated and connected by more roads and railways. To a large extent this is a factor of geography – the west coast is lower lying and has a larger coastal plain area before the land rises up into the central mountain range. Therefore cities became established here at an earlier time and more roads and communications were built. Also it was on this coast that tin was first discovered and where the rubber plantations were first developed – the two mainstays of the economy. Since far more of the cities are on this side of the peninsula this is also much more the 'Chinese' half of the peninsula.

JOHORE BAHRU

Capital of the state of Johore, which comprises the entire southern tip of the peninsula, Johore Bahru is the southern gateway to Peninsular Malaysia. Connected by the 1038-metre-long causeway to Singapore it inevitably suffers as a poor relation to its more glamorous neighbour. Despite its historical significance and the various points of interest in the city few travellers pause in Johore; it's just the place where you get your passport stamped on arrival or departure in Malaysia.

Johore has had a long and colourful history. When Melaka fell to the Portuguese the sultans fled to the Johore River and re-established their capital there at Johore Lama. In 1536 a Portuguese fleet attacked and sacked the town, but Johore was soon rebuilt another 30 km upriver. Further attempts also failed to destroy the Johore sultanate, but in 1866 Sultan Abu Bakar, who had been educated by the English in Singapore, moved his capital to its present location and renamed it Johore Bahru, New Johore. Abu Bakar was a modern and progressive ruler and to this day Johore is one of Malaysia's most prosperous states.

Information & Orientation

The road and railway across the causeway run straight into the middle of Johore Bahru through the modern shopping centre of the town. The taxi and bus stations are to the left, the railway station to the right. A little beyond the station you turn off to the right towards the east coast, a congested trip as far as Kota Tinggi. If you're heading towards Kuala Lumpur or Melaka on the west coast then you turn off to the left almost as soon as you cross the causeway and for the first few km the road runs right along the waterfront with good views across to Singapore Island.

Istana Besar

Overlooking the straits of Johore the Istana Besar is the main palace of the Johore royal family. It was built in Victorian style by anglophile Sultan Abu Bakar in 1866. The palace houses a collection of royal treasures and is open to the public from 9 am to 12 noon except on Fridays and public holidays. Advance permission to visit the palace must be arranged, however, with the Controller of the Royal Household or the State Tourist Household, or with the State Tourist Office. Phone 073-54750, extension 30 for the latter.

Istana Gardens

The Istana Besar stands within the 53 hectare Istana Gardens which includes a fernery, orchid gardens, children's playground, Japanese gardens and a Japanese tea house. The zoo in the gardens is open from 8 am to 6 pm and admission is M$1.

Other

The Abu Bakar Mosque is on Jalan Abu Bakar and was built between 1892 and 1900. The large mosque can accommodate 2000 people and overlooks the Straits of Johore. With a 32-metre-high tower that serves as a city landmark, Bukit Serene is the actual residence of the Sultan of Johore. The Istana Bukit Serene was built in 1938.

Another city landmark is the 64-metre-high square tower of the imposing Government Offices Building on Bukit Timbalan, overlooking the city centre. The Royal Mausoleum has been the burial site of Johore's sultans since the shift from Johore Lama, but it is not open to the public. On the seafront opposite the court house the Sultan Abu Bakar Monument was erected in 1955.

Places to Stay – bottom end

Few visitors stay in Johore Bahru; it's too close to the greater attractions of Singapore. On the other hand Johore is an important business centre, in part due to the volume of trade carried on between Malaysia and Singapore which goes through Johore, so there are plenty of hotels.

At the bottom of the price scale there are a number of Chinese cheapies along Jalan Meldrum, which runs parallel to the main Jalan Tun Abdul Razak close to the causeway. The *Nam Yang* and the *Suan Fang* both have rooms from less than M$15. On Jalan Station in the Tan Chang Cheng building slightly more expensive rooms are available in the *First Hotel*. The *Fortuna Hotel* is handy to the railway and bus terminals and has air-con rooms at M$30. The *New Asia Hotel* has doubles with fan at M$19, with air-con at M$30. The *Top Hotel* (tel 073-255344) is a middle range place at 12 Jalan Meldrum.

Places to Stay – top end

At the other end of the price scale there's the *Johor Baharu Merlin Inn* (tel 073-227400) at 10 Jalan Bukit Meldrum with 104 rooms at M$105-220 for singles,

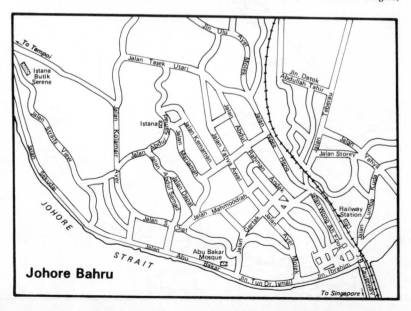

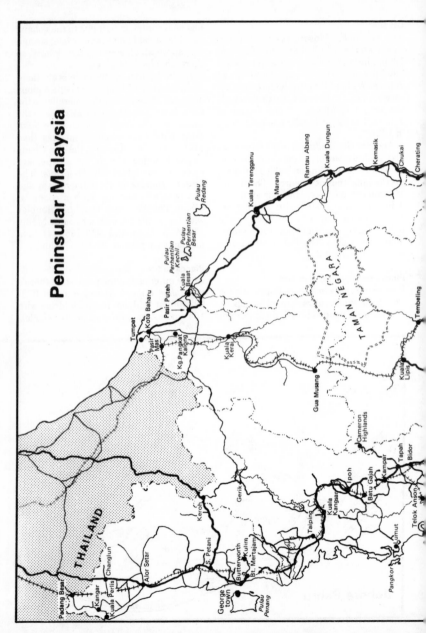

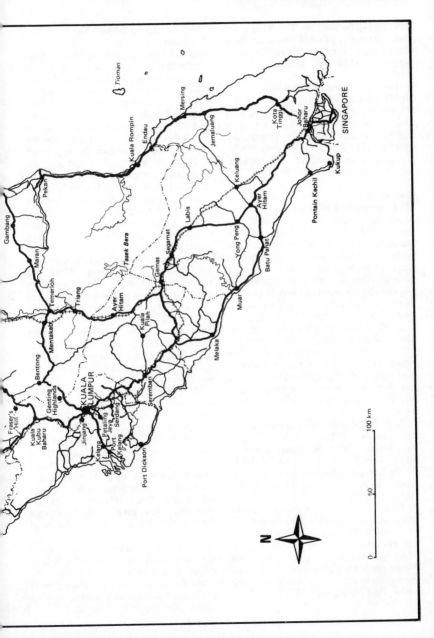

M$125-140 for doubles. The *Holiday Inn Johor Baru* (tel 073-323800) is on Jalan Dato Century Garden and has 200 rooms, singles M$110-130, doubles M$130-150.

The *Straits View Hotel* (tel 073-224133) at 1D Jalan Scudai has singles at M$65-75, doubles M$75-85. In the *Regent Elite* (tel 073-223811) at 1 Jalan Siu Nam rooms cost from M$60. The *Tropical Inn* (tel 073-221888) at Johor Tower No 15, Jalan Greja has 160 rooms with singles at M$110-140, doubles M$130-160.

Getting There

With Singapore so close travel connections there are important. Because of the hassles of crossing the causeway – customs, immigration and so on – there's a much wider selection of buses and long-distance taxis to other towns in Peninsular Malaysia from JB than there are in Singapore. The regular 170 bus operates every 15 minutes between JB and Queen St in Singapore; it costs 90c. The Johore Bahru Express costs M$1 and its Singapore terminus is at Rochor Rd, only a stone's throw from the 170 bus terminus. Or you can make the trip by taxi for M$4 per person. You may end up paying slightly more for a whole taxi than a party of Malays or Singaporeans would because of the extra hassles at the border.

From JB taxis cost M$7 to Ayer Hitam, M$12 to Muar, M$16 to Melaka, M$22 to Seremban, M$28 to Kuala Lumpur. Buses cost M$10 to Melaka, M$18 to Kuala Lumpur, M$26 to Ipoh, M$30 to Butterworth or M$40 all the way to Hat Yai in Thailand.

Johore Bahru's airport is some distance out of JB on the road to Melaka and KL. Air fares to Kuching and Kota Kinabalu are cheaper than from Singapore, and MAS operate an express bus service from Singapore with high-speed immigration clearance to attract you to fly from JB rather than Singapore.

JOHORE BAHRU TO MELAKA

The main road north from Johore Bahru runs to Kuala Lumpur and Melaka. It's a productive region of oil palms, rubber trees and pineapple plantations. At Ayer Hitam, an important crossroads, you can turn left to Batu Pahat, Muar and Melaka, continue straight on for Segamat, Seremban and KL or alternatively for Segamat and Temerloh, or you can turn right for Keluang and Mersing on the east coast. Ayer Hitam is a popular rest stop for buses, taxis and general motorists so there are lots of small restaurants here. Kampong Macap, south of Ayer Hitam, is well known for its Aw Pottery works.

Batu Pahat is a riverine town famed for its Chinese cuisine although it also has a minor reputation as a 'sin city' for jaded Singaporeans. Accommodation can be hard to find on weekends. Muar, the second largest town in Johore, is another riverside town and between here and Melaka there are a number of kampongs with traditional-style Melaka houses. Muar is a centre of traditional Malay culture, including ghazal music and the Kuda Kepang, 'prancing horse', dances. Keluang is really just a crossroads on the way to the east coast.

Mt Ophir (Gunung Legang in Malay) has a series of waterfalls and pools for swimming on one side. There's also a trail that goes a long way up. 'The falls are a lot nicer than those at Kota Tinggi and they stretch along the mountainside for a longer way', reported a visitor. Local kids camp here and leave a lot of trash. To get there take a Muar-Segamat bus and get out at the 25-mile marker or ask the conductor. It's then a km-plus walk through the plantation to the bottom of the falls.

Kukup, as far south as you can get along the west coast, is a delightful fishing village built over the sea on stilts. It's noted for its fine (if sometimes pricey) seafood but avoid it on weekends as it's a popular day trip from Singapore.

Places to Stay

Batu Pahat In Batu Pahat the *Government Rest House* has air-con doubles for M$25 or at the *Fairyland Hotel* (great name!) you can get a good large double with fan for less than M$20. The *Asia Hotel* (tel 072-43344) at 1 Jalan Omar is more expensive with rooms from M$30 to 50.

Keluang In Keluang there's another *Rest House* and the *Merdeka Hotel*.

Muar In Muar there's a very good *Rest House* with a restaurant overlooking the river but it's expensive at M$35 for a single or double. It's a typical Malaysian town with plenty of Chinese restaurants and hotels but no tourists.

Segamat At 26 Jalan Ros there's the expensive *Segamat Merlin Inn* (tel 07-914611) with singles at M$65-70, doubles at M$75-80.

MELAKA (Malacca)

Malaysia's most historically interesting city, Melaka has been through some dramatic events over the years. The complete series of European incursions in Malaysia – Portuguese, Dutch and English – have been played out here. Yet this was an important trading port long before the first Portuguese adventurers set foot in the city. Under the Melaka Sultanates the city was a wealthy centre of trade with China, India, Siam and Indonesia due to its strategic position on the Straits of Melaka.

In 1405 Admiral Cheng Ho, the 'three-jewelled eunuch prince', arrived in Melaka bearing gifts from the Ming Emperor, the promise of protection from arch-enemies (the Siamese) and, surprisingly, the Moslem religion. Chinese settlers from this earliest contact came to be known as the Babas or Straits Chinese; they are the longest-settled Chinese people in Malaysia. Despite internal squabbles and intrigues Melaka grew to be a powerful trading state and successfully repulsed Siamese attacks.

In 1509 the Portuguese, seeking trading opportunities in the east, arrived at Melaka, but after an initially friendly reception the Melakans attacked the Portuguese fleet and took a number of prisoners. This action was the pretext for an outright assault by the Portuguese – in 1511 Alfonso d'Albuquerque took the city and the Sultan fled to Johore where he re-established his kingdom. Under the Portuguese Melaka continued to thrive as a trading post, the fortress of A'Famosa was constructed and missionaries like the famous Francis Xavier strove to implant Christianity.

The period of Portuguese strength in the east was a short one. As Dutch influence in Indonesia grew and Batavia, modern-day Jakarta, developed as the principal European port of the region, Melaka declined. Finally the Dutch attacked the city and in 1641 it passed into their hands after a siege lasting eight months. The Dutch built fine public buildings and churches which today are the most solid reminders of the European presence in the city – but like their Portuguese predecessors they stayed in power only about 150 years.

In 1795 the French occupied Holland, and the British, allies of the Dutch, temporarily took over administration of the Dutch colonies. The British administrators, essentially trading men who were opposed to the Dutch policy of trade monopoly, clearly saw that the Dutch and British would be bitter rivals in Malaysia, when and if Melaka was returned. Accordingly in 1807 they commenced to demolish the fortress to ensure that if Melaka was restored to the Dutch it would be no rival to the British Malayan centres. Fortunately Stamford Raffles, the far-sighted founder of Singapore, stepped in before these destructive policies could go too far and in 1824 Melaka was permanently ceded to the British in exchange for the Sumatran port of Bencoolen (Bengkulu today).

From that time until independence all of Peninsular Malaysia was under British influence or control, except for the period of Japanese occupation during WW II. Under the British, Melaka once more flourished as a trading centre although it was soon superseded by the growing commercial importance of Singapore. Today it's a sleepy backwater of a town and no longer of any major commercial influence. It's a place of intriguing Chinese streets and antique shops, old Chinese temples and cemeteries and nostalgic reminders of the now-departed European colonial powers.

Information & Orientation

Melaka is a small town – easy to find your way around and compact enough to explore on foot or by bicycle-rickshaw. Jalan Munshi Abdullah is the main road through Melaka and on this road you could zip through Melaka thinking it was simply another noisy small Malaysian town. The interesting and older parts of Melaka are mainly closer to the waterfront, particularly around the old Dutch-built Stadthuys (town hall) where you'll also find the GPO, Tourist Office (tel 06-25711) and the Dutch Christ Church. The long-distance taxi stand is by the bus stand, beside Jalan Munshi Abdullah, on the northern edge of the town centre.

Stadthuys

The most imposing relic of the Dutch period is the massive pink town hall which was built between 1641 and 1660. It is believed to be the oldest Dutch building in the east and is used today for government

offices. It displays all the typical features of Dutch colonial architecture, including substantial solid doors and louvred windows. The other buildings around the main square, including the GPO and the old clock tower, also follow the same pink theme.

Christ Church

Between the Stadthuys and the GPO, facing one end of the square, is the bright red Christ Church. The pink bricks were brought out from Zeeland in Holland and faced with local red laterite when the church was constructed in 1753. Under the British the church was converted for Anglican use, but it still has its old Dutch tombstones laid in the floor and its massive 15-metre-long ceiling beams, each cut from a single tree.

St Paul's Church

Residency Hill rises up above the Stadthuys and on top stand the ruins of St Paul's Church. Originally built by the Portuguese in 1571 as the small 'Our Lady of the Hill' chapel, it was regularly visited by Francis Xavier and following his death in China the saint's body was brought back here and buried for nine months before being transferred to Goa in India where it remains today.

In 1556 the church was enlarged to two stories and a tower was added to the front in 1590. The church was renamed following the Dutch takeover, but with the completion of their own Christ Church at the base of the hill it fell into disuse. Under the

1	Majestic Hotel	
2	Rex Cinema	
3	Regal Hotel	
4	Wisma Hotel	
5	Kampong Hulu Mosque	
6	Cheng Hoon Teng Temple	
7	Kampong Kling Mosque	
8	Tourist Office	
9	Sri Pogyatha Vinayagar	
10	GPO	
11	Church of St. Francis
12	Stadthuys
13	St. Paul's Church
14	Porta de Santiago
15	Museum
16	UE Tea House
17	Sultan's Well
18	Po San Teng
19	Palua Hotel
20	St. Peter's Church

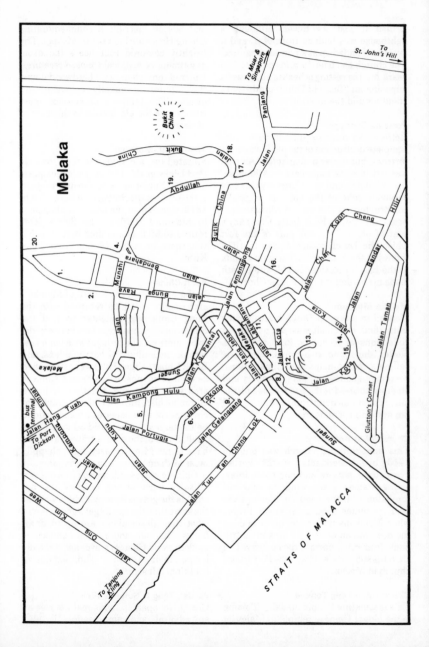

Melaka

To St. John's Hill

To Muar & Singapore

Jalan Panjang

Bukit China

Bukit China

Jalan Abdullah

19.

17.

18.

Jalan Bukit China

20.

4.

Jalan Bendahara

1.

Jalan Munshi

2.

Jalan Bunga Raya

3.

Jalan Temenggong

16.

Jalan Chan

Koon Cheng

Bandar Hilir

Jalan Taman

Sungei Melaka

Jalan Pantai

Jalan Laksamana

Jalan Melaka

11.

7.

Jalan Kota

13.

12.

14.

15.

Jalan Kota

Jalan Kota

8.

Glutton's Corner

Jalan Kampong Hulu

Jalan Tokong

9.

5.

6.

Jalan Gelanggang

Jalan Portugis

bus terminal

Jalan Hang Tuah

To Port Dickson

Jalan Kampong Kuli

Jalan Tun Tan Cheng Lok

Jalan Ong Kim Wee

To Tanjong Kling

Sungei

STRAITS OF MALACCA

British it lost its tower, although a lighthouse was built in front of it, and it eventually ended up as a powder magazine. The church has been in ruins now for 150 years, but the setting is beautiful, the walls imposing and fine old Dutch tombstones stand around the interior.

Porta de Santiago

Raffles may have stepped in before the complete destruction of the old Portuguese fortress, but it was a near thing. All that was left was the main gate to A'Famosa, the Porta de Santiago. Curiously this sole surviving relic of the old fort originally constructed by Alfonso d'Albuquerque bears the Dutch East India Company's coat of arms. This was part of the fort which the Dutch reconstructed in 1670 following their takeover. The gate stands at the base of Residency Hill and a path leads up behind it to St Paul's Church.

Melaka Museum

Housed in a typical Dutch house dating from 1660, the small museum has varied collections of weapons, kris, porcelain, model ships and fish traps, furniture, cabinets, early maps and illustrations, costumes, shadow puppets, jewellery and stamps. Located at the base of the hill, the museum is open daily from 9.30 am to 4.30 pm and admission is free.

Church of St Peter

This unexceptional church was built in 1710 by descendants of the earlier Portuguese settlers and has some interesting stained glass windows and old tombstones. Little used for much of the year, it comes alive each Good Friday when Melakans flock here, many making the occasion an excuse for an annual trip home from other parts of the country. The church is still associated with the Portuguese church in Macau.

Cheng Hoon Teng Temple

This fascinating temple on Jalan Tokong is the oldest Chinese temple in Malaysia and has an inscription commemorating Cheng Ho's epochal visit to Melaka. The brightly coloured roof bears the usual assortment of mythical Chinese creatures. Entered through massive hardwood doors, the interior is equally colourful and ornate. The temple's ceremonial mast rises above the old houses in this part of Melaka.

Tranquerah Mosque

Situated two km along the road towards Port Dickson, this 150-year-old mosque is of typical Sumatran design. In its graveyard is the tomb of the Sultan of Johore who, in 1819, signed over the island of Singapore to Stamford Raffles. The Sultan later retired to Melaka and died here in 1853. Get there on a No 18 bus from Jalan Kubu.

Bukit China

In the mid-1400s the Sultan of Melaka's ambassador to China returned with the Ming Emperor's daughter to wed the Sultan and thus seal relations between the two countries. She brought with her a vast retinue, including 500 handmaidens, and Bukit China ('China Hill') was established as their residence. It has been a Chinese area ever since and, together with two adjoining hills, forms a Chinese graveyard covering over 60 hectares which is said to be the largest in the world outside China itself. Some of the ornate graves date right back to the Ming dynasty, but unhappily most of them are now in a sorry state.

Chinese graveyards are so often built on hillsides because the bulk of the hill shields the graves from evil winds while at the same time the spirits get a good view of what their descendants are up to down below. In our more space-conscious modern world Chinese graves are gradually losing their spacious and expansive traditional design.

Po San Teng & Sultan's Well

Cheng Ho, apart from his real-life role as an admiral and ambassador, is also religiously venerated and this temple is dedicated to him as Po San. Built in 1795, it's at the foot of Bukit China and nearby is the Sultan's Well. The well is said to date back to the founding of Melaka in the 14th century by Raja Iskandar Shah. Cheng Ho drank from the well, legends relate, after which its water became incredibly pure and taking a drink would ensure a visitor's return to the city. Today the water is visibly impure and tossing a coin into the well is the recommended way of ensuring a return trip.

Old Melaka

The old part of Melaka is fascinating to wander around. Although Melaka has long lost its importance as a port, ancient-looking junks still sail up the river and moor at the banks. Today, however, their cargo is not the varied treasures of the east, but simply mundane charcoal for the cooking fires of the city. There's a good view of the river and boats from the bridge beside the tourist office.

You may still find some of the treasures of the east in the antique shops scattered along Jalan Gelanggang, formerly known as Jonkers St. You'll find a whole assortment of interesting shops and the odd Chinese or Hindu temple or mosque squeezed into this intriguing old street. Melaka is famed for its antique shops and there are several along the street which are worth a leisurely browse. The Sri Pogyatha Vinoyagar Moorthi Temple, dating from 1781, and the Sumatran-style Kampong Kling Mosque are both in this area. Jalan Tun Tan Cheng Lock, running parallel to Jalan Gelanggang, is also worth a stroll.

Other

Although the British demolished most of Fort Santiago they left the small Dutch fort of St John untouched. It stands on a hilltop a little to the east of town, but there's not much to be seen. A little beyond the fort is the area known as the Portuguese Eurasian settlement. In this small kampong there are about 500 descendants of intermarriage between the colonial Portuguese and Malays 400 years ago. There's little of interest for the visitor here.

Melaka's beaches offer little attraction either. Tanjong Kling and, a little further out, Tanjong Bidara, are the main beaches, but the Straits of Melaka have become increasingly polluted over the years and it's worst around Melaka itself. There are also occasional plagues of jellyfish. The small island of Pulau Besar, a little south of Melaka, is a popular weekend joyride – there are boats operating across from Umbai near Melaka.

Places to Stay – bottom end

Melaka At the bottom end of the price scale Melaka has a very wide variety of places although many budget travellers will choose to head 15 km north to the places at Tanjong Kling. In the town itself you can start at basic and bare doss houses like *Suan Kee* at 105 Jalan Bunga Raya where rooms cost from just M$10 – 'very basic and noisy, they played mahjong outside our room for most of the night', wrote one sleepless traveller. The *Tong Ah* at 16 Kee Ann Rd is equally bottom-of-the-heap and equally cheap. Rather better standards can be found for a few dollars more at the *Hotel Hong Kong*, 154A Jalan Bunga Raya or a few doors down at the *Hotel Ng Fook* (tel 06-28055) at 154H.

Close by at 100-105 Jalan Munshi Abdullah the *Cathay Hotel* (tel 23744) is quiet and comfortable with singles from M$12. Other cheapies in Melaka include the *Chong Hoe Hotel* (tel 06-226102) at 26 Goldsmith St directly across from Kampong Kling Mosque. it's very clean, friendly and in a good location, plus it's cheap with singles/doubles at just M$8.80/13.20. Or there's the *Federal Hotel* (tel 06-22161) at 60B Jalan Bendahara and the *Valiant Hotel* (tel 06-22323) a few doors down at 41B.

The *Malacca Hotel* (tel 06-22325) is at 27A Jalan Munshi Abdullah and has singles at M$16 – good rooms with fan and attached bathroom. The staff are friendly but the cinema next door and its car park can be noisy at night. Across the road at number 22 the *Hotel Belangi* is fairly quiet and rooms with bath and fan are M$14/18. You can get air-con at either of these hotels if you want it.

Still on Jalan Munshi Abdullah the *Central Hotel* is excellent value with fan, soap and towels provided, or there's the *May Chiang Hotel* with similarly low prices (M$12), equivalent facilities and a friendly proprietor. Several travellers have written to confirm what a pleasant shoestring place this is.

Best of the places bridging the bottom-to-top gap is the *Majestic Hotel* (tel 06-22455) at 188 Jalan Bunga Raya with rooms at around M$15 to 20 or with air-con and attached bathroom at M$30 to 35. This well-kept place is built in true Chinese hotel-style with a central lounge, and it's also well back from the street. Their cheaper rooms are not very good, however. Also bridging the bottom-to-top range is the *Wisma Hotel* (tel 06-28311) at the corner of Jalan Munshi Abdullah and Jalan Bendahara. Finally two more middle range places with air-con are the *Lotus Inn* (tel 06-27011) at 2846 Jalan Semabok and the *Sentosa Hotel* (tel 06-28325) further out of town on the north side at 92 Jalan Bachang.

Tanjong Kling Melaka's travellers' centre is at the ninth milestone Tanjong Kling, where you'll find a string of places opposite the now derelict youth hostel. They're all pretty basic – no electricity, little more than a mattress on bare boards, not that clean. Once again Malaysian beach accommodation proves to be pretty miserable value compared to that of Thailand or Bali. *SHM's Caffee* at the southern end and *Hawaii's Restaurant* at the northern end are the longest established. Between these two are the *Restoren Sun Set* (or Sunset Losmen) and the *Restoren Rasa Sayang*, both more recent estab-

lishments. Standard costs are M$2 for dorm beds or double rooms or chalet huts at M$5 or 6. They also have surprisingly good restaurants with menus featuring all the travellers' favourites, from banana pancakes to fruit salad.

To get to Tanjong Kling take a 51 bus (60c) from Melaka. A word of caution – there have been hints of the old Batu Ferringhi-style immigration hassles here although the place has now become pretty well established. It's also somewhat plagued by Malaysia's peeping toms – 'I had to make a couple of surprise night sorties with a solid stick in hand to deter them from prowling around our hut', wrote one visitor.

Places to Stay – top end
Melaka The relatively new *Malacca Village Resort* (tel 06-313600) is at Ayer Keroh. It has 160 rooms, all air-con, with singles at M$140, doubles at M$160-180. There's a swimming pool and all the other usual mod cons.

The *Malacca Straits Inn* (tel 06-221211) has 45 rooms with singles/doubles from M$75/85 and up. It's situated near the waterfront at 37A Jalan Bandar Hilir. *Hotel Admiral* (tel 06-226822) on Jalan Mata Kuching has singles at M$50, doubles M$60 to 75.

Other more expensive hotels in town include the *Palace Hotel* (tel 06-25115) at 201 Jalan Munshi Abdullah on the Muar side of town. Singles run M$45 to 58, doubles M$55 to 68, all air-con. Even more central at 66 Jalan Munshi Abdullah, the *Regal Hotel* (tel 06-22282) is cheaper at M$38/48 for singles/doubles. It's quite livable although the rooms are a bit drab and the floors below the noisy bar-restaurant should be avoided.

Tanjong Kling Just as with the bottom-end hotels there's also a top-end place at Tanjong Kling. It's the delightful beachfront *Shah's Beach Motel* (tel 06-26222) about 10 km north at the 6-1/2 milestone, Tanjong Kling. There are 50 chalets built

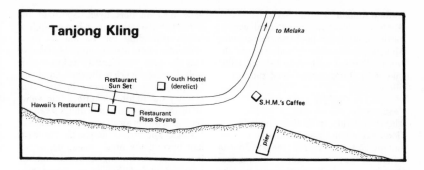

around a central swimming pool with costs of M$85 for the poolside chalets, M$75 for the rest. There's a pleasant open-air bar and restaurant and it's a very relaxing place to stay although the sea here is not clean enough for swimming and you really need a vehicle to get back and forth to the city.

Places to Eat

All the larger hotels (Wisma, Regal, Palace) have air-con restaurants or coffee lounges with a predilection for fixed-price lunches or dinners in 'English style' at M$6-10. Just the thing if you want soup, chicken & chips and dessert. Melaka's real eating centre is along the waterfront on Jalan Taman, across from the museum and Porta de Santiago. At night the assortment of stalls along here are all in action and the area is known locally as *Glutton's Corner*. All the usual food centre specialities can be found here and some of them are also open at lunch time. The *Bunga Raya Restaurant* here has excellent steamed crabs.

There are plenty of other food stalls around Melaka. In particular there are a number, including a good steamboat stall, in Lorong Bendahara, opposite the Rex Cinema on Jalan Bunga Raya. Next to the Capital Theatre the *Capital Restaurant* has excellent Chinese food at M$5 per dish. The *Dondang Sagang Restaurant* on Jalan Laksamana, near the Church of St Francis, has real Malaysian food and a

menu – spicy and very good at about M$5 per dish.

Amongst Melaka's many other restaurants and cafes two worth looking at are the *Tai Chong Hygienic Ice Cafe* at 39/72 Jalan Bunga Raya where a wide variety of ice cream dishes and snacks are available. Or at 20 Lorong Bukit China the *UE Tea House* is a great place for a dim sum breakfast with prices from 50c per plate.

Getting There

Melaka is 149 km from KL, 216 km from Johore Bahru, just 90 km from Port Dickson. You can fly to Melaka from KL or Johore Bahru.

There is no railway line to Melaka, but there are plenty of buses and long-distance taxis. From KL it's M$5.20 by bus, M$10.50 by taxi. There are also air-con buses to KL for M$6.50. If for any reason you can't get a direct bus KL-Melaka it's usually easy to go to Seremban and change there. A Singapore-Melaka bus costs M$9 – from Melaka the buses run from the Central Omnibus Station on Jalan Kilang. Johore Bahru to Melaka taxis cost M$15. Buses cost M$1.70 to Muar, M$1.45 to Tampin, M$3.30 to Port Dickson, M$14.50 to Ipoh, M$22 to Butterworth, M$7.50 to Keluang, M$19 to Kuala Trengganu, M$25 all the way to Kota Bahru. A taxi to Muar is M$3.20, to Batu Pahat M$6.50 or to Seremban M$5.80. The bus and taxi stands are off Jalan Hang Tuah, just across the river.

Getting Around

A bicycle rickshaw is the ideal way of getting around compact and slow-moving Melaka. You can easily walk around the central sights. To get out to Tanjong Kling take a 51 'Long Beach' bus; the fare is 60c.

Festivals

Major festivals in Melaka include the Good Friday and Easter Sunday processions at St Peter's and the feast in June in honour of the patron saint of fishermen at the same church. The nationwide bathing festival known as Mandi Safar is particularly exuberantly celebrated at Tanjong Kling during the Moslem month of Safar – usually April.

AROUND MELAKA

There are many fine old Minangkabau-style houses around Melaka. Note the characteristic 'buffalo horn' roof shape, the verandah and lower-level 'pre-verandah' or *anjong*. The steps which lead up to the sometimes intricately carved wooden houses are often decorated with beautiful tiles.

About 40 km south of Port Dickson is the small town of Pengkalan Kempas. Just a short distance on the Lubok China or Melaka side of town a sign indicates the grave of Sheikh Ahmad Majnun, about a hundred metres off the road. This local hero died in 1467 and beside his grave, which is sheltered by a structure in the final stages of complete collapse, are three two-metre-high stones standing upright in the ground. These mysterious stones, known as the sword, the spoon and the rudder, are thought to be older than the grave itself. Immediately in front of the grave is another stone with a hole through it. The circular opening is said to tighten up on the arm of any liar foolish enough to thrust it through.

PORT DICKSON

There's nothing of great interest in Port Dickson itself although it's a pleasant enough small port town. South of the town, however, there is a fine stretch of beach extending for 17 km to Cape Rachado. There are a number of places to stay along the beach and it's an interesting walk down the beach to the cape. Originally built by the Portuguese in the 16th century the lighthouse offers fine views along the coast – on a clear day you can see Sumatra, 38 km away across the Straits of Melaka. The turn-off to the lighthouse is just beyond the ninth milestone, or it's just a short stroll along the beach from the Pantai Motel. Officially you need permission from the Marine Department at the end of the pier in Melaka if you want to ascend the lighthouse.

Places to Stay

There's no reason to stay in Port Dickson unless you stay on the beach, so the hotels in and close to the town itself can be discounted. The beach stretches south of Port Dickson for 16 km to Cape Rachado, but the best beach starts from around the fifth milestone (eight km). The *Port Dickson Youth Hostel* is on a hill above the road at 3¾ miles. It attracts few visitors although it costs just M$2.50 for the first night, M$2 thereafter and there are a number of food stalls beside the road below it. The *Sunshine Rotary Club* at M$7 is also a nice, basic sort of place.

At the seventh milestone *Si Rusa Inn* (tel 06-795233) is a large establishment right by the beach with 220 doubles plus 120 chalets. Rooms cost M$60/66 for singles/doubles. The *Ming Court Beach Hotel* (tel 06-405244) has 165 rooms with singles at M$110-120, doubles at M$130-140.

At the eighth milestone there are a couple of Chinese hotels. The *Lido Hotel* (tel 06-795273) has rooms at less than M$30, more with air-con. The nearby *Kong Ming Hotel* (tel 06-795239) has some smaller rooms for a few dollars less and some chalets at rather higher prices. This beach is popular with local vacationers and there are food and drink stalls.

Finally there's another clump of places to stay at the ninth milestone. You have to follow a dirt road for several hundred metres off the main road to the *Pantai Motel* (tel 06-795265) where there are a variety of rooms and chalets. They start from around M$25 and go up to M$30 to 60 for the most expensive air-con chalet with bathroom. It's a quiet, grassy place with steps down to the beach below. Nearby is the *Holiday Inn* and the *Halcyon Guest House*. From here it's only a short walk along the beach to Cape Rachado; you can see the top of the lighthouse through the trees.

Getting There

Port Dickson is 94 km south of KL, only 34 km south of Seremban and 90 km north of Melaka. You can get there by taxi or bus from any of these places. By bus it's M$3.30 from Melaka, M$3.70 from KL. A taxi would be about M$6.50 from either town. On Sundays only there is a train-bus excursion available from KL – the train leaves at 7.50 am and returns at 5.20 pm and the trip takes two hours via Seremban. From Port Dickson there's a connecting bus which will drop you off anywhere along the beach.

SEREMBAN

South of Kuala Lumpur, Seremban is the capital of Negri Sembilan or 'Nine States' – a group of small Malay lands united by the British. This is the centre of the Minangkabau area of Malaysia. Originating in Sumatra, the Minangkabau people have a matrilineal system whereby inheritance passes through the female rather than the male line. They take their name from the unique architecture of their buildings where the roof sweeps up at each end like buffalo horns or 'minangkabau'.

The small state museum is a good example of Minangkabau architecture. Originally the home of a Malay prince, it was brought to its present location and reassembled in the lake area which overlooks the commercial part of town.

Traditionally Minangkabau houses are built entirely without nails. The museum, which is open 9.30 am to 12 noon and 2 to 5.30 pm daily (9.30 am to 1 pm on Wednesdays, 9.30 am to 6 pm on holidays), houses a small collection of ceremonial weapons and other regalia.

Lower down towards the town is the new state mosque with its nine pillars symbolising the nine states of Negri Sembilan. Nearby is a huge A&W hamburger drive-in to prove Seremban is really in the 20th century!

Places to Stay

The bustling streets of Seremban have the usual varied assortment of Chinese hotels. The *Ruby Hotel* (tel 06-75201) at 39 Jalan Leman has rooms with and without ai-con from less than M$20. The *Carlton Hotel* (tel 06-75336) at 47 Jalan Tuan Sheikh has singles at around M$15, doubles from M$25. The cheaper *Tong Fong* (tel 06-73022) on Birch Rd has rooms as low as M$12. The *Ria Hotel* (tel 06-287744) at Jalan Tetamu is more expensive with singles/doubles at M$85/95.

There are all sorts of restaurants, including the previously mentioned *A&W* drive-in.

Getting There

Seremban is 62 km south of Kuala Lumpur, connected by the same modern highway that now extends down to Melaka. From KL there are frequent buses (M$2.50) and taxis (M$5). It's a further 34 km south to Port Dickson or 82 km to Melaka.

AROUND SEREMBAN

Kajang, about 20 km south of Kuala Lumpur on the Seremban-Kuala Lumpur route, is said to have the best satay in all Malaysia. If mealtime is approaching it's worth pausing here to sample them. If you want to study more Minangkabau architecture take a bus from Seremban east towards Kuala Pilah. Get down eight to 10 km out where there are many traditional houses on both sides of the road. Pantai and Nilai, a short distance north-east of Seremban, also have Minangkabau houses.

Kuala Pilah, 40 km east of Seremban, has an interesting old Chinese temple on Jalan Lister near the bus station. Seri Menanti, 16 km from Kuala Pilah, has a palace or istana in Minangkabau style and also a royal mosque. The central pillars of the istana are impressively carved.

KUALA LUMPUR

Malaysia's capital city is a curious blend of the old and new. On one hand it's modern and fast moving although the traffic never takes on the nightmare proportions of Bangkok. Gleaming office blocks rise up beside multi-lane highways, but the old colonial architecture still manages to stand out proudly. It's also a blend of cultures – the Malay capital with a vibrant Chinatown, an Indian quarter and a playing field in the middle of the city where the crack of cricket bat on ball can still be heard.

KL, as it's almost always called, came into being in the 1860s when a band of prospectors in search of tin landed at the meeting point of the Kelang and Gombek Rivers, and named the place Kuala Lumpur – 'Muddy Estuary'. More than half of those first arrivals were to die of malaria and other tropical diseases, but the tin they discovered in Ampang attracted more miners and KL quickly became a brawling, noisy, violent boom town. As in other parts of Malaysia the local Sultan appointed a 'Kapitan China' to bring the unruly Chinese fortune seekers into line – a problem which Yap Ah Loy jumped into with such ruthless relish that he became known as the founder of KL.

In the 1880s successful miners and merchants began to build fine homes along Jalan Ampang, the British Resident Frank Swettenham pushed through a far-reaching new town plan and in 1886 a railway line linked KL to Port Kelang. The town has never looked back and today it's not only the business and commercial capital of Malaysia, but also the political capital and, with a population of nearly one million, the largest city.

Information

Kuala Lumpur is a relatively easy city to find your way around. It's large but not too large and it never gets too congested so getting from place to place is rarely arduous. The Tourist Information Centre (tel 03-206742) is in the TDC Duty Free Shop in the Bukit Nanas Complex on Jalan Raja Chulan. The complex is at the edge of the park right in the middle of town. Chairlifts go up the large hill in the park. Nearby is the Tourist Development Corporation (TDC) (tel 03-423033) on the 18th floor of Wisma MPI on Jalan Raja Chulan. It's open Monday to Friday, 8.30 am to 4.45 pm and Saturday 8 am to 12.45 pm.

There is also an information counter at Subang Airport which is open 9.15 am to 10.30 pm daily. There's another tourist information office (tel 03-281832) at the railway station. You can store bags at the railway station for 50c per item per day – safe and very useful if you're just in transit.

The National Map Sales Office is on Jalan Tun Perak, but they won't sell you larger scale maps since they're all 'restricted' – due to fear of communists getting hold of them and finding out where KL is. Visiting scholars may find the library at the University of Malaya useful; buses run there from the Kelang station.

If you're going to the national park, Taman Negara, then visit the Department of Wildlife & National Parks (tel 03-941272) at Block K-20, Jalan Duta. Take a 19 bus which terminates at block K.

Orientation

Just to the south of the confluence of those muddy rivers from which KL takes its name is the modern business centre of KL and the older Chinatown – one simply merges into the other. Across the Kelang River is the railway station and the modern National Mosque.

Starting from the important central junction of Jalan Tuanku Abdul Rahman and Jalan Tun Perak, if you continue along Jalan Tun Perak away from the river you'll soon find yourself on Jalan Pudu where you'll find the huge Pudu Raya bus and taxi station. A left turn will take you into Jalan Bukit Bintang with a number of popular mid-range hotels, another right turn leads to Jalan Sultan Ismail with several of KL's top-line hotels. Yet another right turn brings you into historic Jalan Ampang which leads you back to your starting point of Jalan Tun Perak.

Turn the other way from that central junction and head up Jalan Tuanku Abdul Rahman (still often referred to as Batu Rd and henceforth known as Jalan Tuanku etc). It runs one-way the wrong way, but along here are a number of KL's popular cheaper hotels and more modern buildings. The student travel office is in the South-East Asia Hotel at the far end of the road.

The GPO is just south of that landmark central junction. Across the Kelang River, beyond the mosque and railway station, is KL's green belt – the Lake Gardens, National Museum and Monument and the Malaysian Parliament.

Embassies & Consulates

Some of the diplomatic offices in Kuala Lumpur include:

Australia
6 Jalan Yap Kwan Sweng (tel 03-423122)
Burma
7 Jalan Taman U Thant (tel 03-424085)
Canada
5th floor, AIA Building, Jalan Ampang (tel 03-89722)
Denmark
3rd floor, Denmark House, 86 Jalan Ampang (tel 03-25357)
Germany (West)
3 Jalan U Thant (tel 03-429666)
India
United Asian Bank Building, 19 Jalan Melaka (tel 03-21001)
Indonesia
233 Jalan Pekeliling, Kuala Lumpur (tel 03-421011)
Japan
6th floor, AIA Building, Jalan Ampang (tel 03-22400)
Netherlands
4 Jalan Megra (tel 03-431143, 431341, 485151)
New Zealand
193 Jalan Pekeliling (tel 03-486422)
Philippines
1 Changkat Kia Peng (tel 03-484233)
Singapore
209 Jalan Pekeliling (tel 03-486377)
Sri Lanka
29 Jalan Yap Kwan Seng (tel 03-423094)
Sweden
6th floor, Angkasa Raya Building, Jalan Ampang (tel 03-485981)
Switzerland
16 Persiaran Madge (tel 03-480622)
Thailand
206 Jalan Ampang (tel 03-488222)
UK
13th floor, Wisma Damansara, Jalan Semantan (tel 03-941533)
USA
10th floor, AIA Building, Jalan Ampang (tel 03-26321)

Airlines

Silver Travel Services (tel 03-422181) at 15 Jalan Alor, parallel to Jalan Bukit Bintang, has been recommended as a good agent for cheap airline tickets. They also have a dorm for penniless travellers about to depart Malaysia. MSL (tel 03-984132) in the South-East Asia Hotel is the student travel agent here and usually has some interesting fares on offer. They also handle student cards. Some of the airline offices in Kuala Lumpur include:

Aeroflot
Yayasan Selangor Building, Jalan Bukit Bintang (tel 03-423231)
Bangladesh Biman
Maju Travel & Tours, 32 Jalan Tun Perak
British Airways
Hotel Merlin, Jalan Sultan Ismail (tel 03-426177)

Cathay Pacific
Oriental Plaza Building, Jalan Parry (tel 03-486166)
Garuda
1st floor, Angkasa Raya Building, Jalan Ampang (tel 03-483542)
MAS
UMBC Building, Jalan Sulaiman (tel 03-206633)
Qantas
AIA Building, Jalan Ampang (tel 03-26161)
Singapore Airlines
2 Jalan Campbell (tel 03-987033)
Thai International
Denmark House, 84 Jalan Ampang (tel 03-80361)

Masjid Jame

The 'Friday Mosque' is built at the confluence of the Kelang and Gombek Rivers, the 'muddy rivers' from which KL takes its name. This was the point where KL's founders first set foot in the town and where supplies were landed for the tin mines. In a grove of palm trees the mosque is a picturesque structure with onion domes and minarets striped in red and white. It was built in 1907 and is at its best viewed at sunset and early evening from the Benteng street market across the river. Here too there is a new mirror-glass office building which provides excellent reflections of the mosque.

Federal Secretariat & the Selangor Club

Built between 1894 and 1897, the Secretariat building and the adjoining GPO and City Hall are in a Moorish style similar to that of the railway station. Now known as the Sultan Abdul Samad Building, the Secretariat is topped by a 43-metre-high clock tower.

Across the road is the open field known as the Padang – here in colonial days Malaysia's administrators engaged in that curious British rite known as cricket. Malaysia's independence was proclaimed here in 1957, but the cricket games still go on. Beside the Padang is the Selangor Club which became a social centre for

KL's high society in the tin rush days of the 1890s. It's still a gathering place for KL VIPs.

Chinatown

Just south of the Masjid Jame are the teeming streets of KL's Chinatown. Bounded by Jalan Petaling, Jalan Sultan and Jalan Bandar, this crowded, colourful area is the usual melange of signs, shops, activity and noise. At night the central section of Jalan Petaling is closed to traffic to become a brightly lit and frantically busy night market or pasar malam.

Temples & Pagodas

The typically ornate Chan See Shu Yuen temple stands at the end of Jalan Petaling – a fine Chinese temple marking the boundary of Chinatown, it was built in 1906. Dating from 1873, the Sri Mahamariamman temple is a large and ornate south Indian Hindu temple. It's on Jalan Bandar in Chinatown too.

The modern International Buddhist Pagoda is in the south of KL, off Jalan Brickfields. The small temple of See Yeoh, off Jalan Rodger near Central Market, is one of the oldest in KL. Kapitan China Yap Ah Loy himself organised its construction and there's a photograph of him on an altar in the back of the temple. The Shiva temple of Sri Kandaswamy is on Jalan Scott.

Bukit Nanas

'Pineapple Hill' was once a pineapple plantation, but today it's a rather artificial tourist attraction. A chairlift and bubble car transport tourists to the top of the 225-metre hill from the handicraft centre and duty-free shopping complex on Jalan Ampang. The handicraft centre is open every day as is the duty free. The chairlift is open 9.30 am to 5.30 pm Tuesday through Sunday except Fridays, when it operates 12.30 to 2.30 pm. Price is M$1.50 for the round trip. It's never been much of an attraction and it's possible the chairlift has been shut down. The tourist office is also here in the park now.

Jalan Ampang & the National Museum of Art

Lined with impressive mansions, Jalan Ampang was built up by the early tin millionaires. Today many of the fine buildings have become embassies and consulates so that the street is KL's 'Ambassador's Row'. One of these fine 'stately homes' has been converted into a luxurious restaurant, Le Coq d'Or.

Another is now the National Museum of Art in the Dewan Tuanku Abdul Rahman. The museum houses a collection of works of Malaysian artists and also stages temporary exhibitions. It is open from 10 am to 6 pm daily but closed from 12 noon to 2.30 pm on Fridays. It is sometimes closed for about a week between exhibitions.

Masjid Negara – National Mosque

Sited in 5.2 hectares of landscaped garden, close to the railway station, the modernistic national mosque is one of the largest in South-East Asia. A 73-metre-high minaret stands in the centre of a pool and the main dome of the mosque is in the form of an 18-pointed star to represent the 13 states of Malaysia and the five pillars of Islam. Forty-eight smaller domes cover the courtyard; their design is said to be inspired by the Grand Mosque in Mecca. The mosque can accommodate 8000 people.

Visitors must remove their shoes upon entry and be 'properly' attired – they'll loan you a robe should your own clothing not be suitable. Women must use a separate entrance to the mosque. It's open for non-believers from 8 am to 6 pm daily except on Fridays when the hours are 2 to 6 pm.

Railway Station

If the national mosque is altogether too modern for you then you have only to cross the road to find a building full of eastern promise – Kuala Lumpur's magnificent railway station. Built in 1911, this delightful example of British colonial humour is a Moorish fantasy of spires, minarets, towers, cupolas and arches. It couldn't look any better if it had been built as a set for some whimsical Hollywood extravaganza. It's said that construction of the station was delayed because the original roof design did not meet British railway specifications that it be able to support three feet of snow!

Across from this superb railway station is the equally wonderful Malayan Railway Administration Building. Almost directly across the station stands the shell of the once-gracious colonial Majestic Hotel. It has been taken over by the government and is to become an art gallery.

Lake Gardens

The 60-hectare gardens form the green belt of Kuala Lumpur. They were originally founded in 1888 and you can rent boats on Tasek Perdana, the 'Premier Lake', which was once known as Sydney Lake. They cost M$2 per hour and are available from 10 am to 6 pm Monday through Saturday and 8 am to 6 pm Sundays and holidays. A Sri Jaya bus 22 from the 'Toshiba' terminal on Jalan Sultan Mohamed, or a number 10 minibus, will take you to the gardens.

Muzium Negara – National Museum

At the southern end of the Lake Gardens the museum was built on the site of the old Selangor Museum, which was destroyed during WW II. It was opened in 1963. Its design and construction is a mixture of Malay architecture styles and crafts. It houses a varied collection on Malaysia's history, arts, crafts, cultures and people.

There are interesting sections on the history of Kuala Lumpur, on Chinese traditions, on the Orang Asli and on the country's economy. One unusual exhibit is the skull of an elephant which derailed a train although it's doubtful that it actually charged the ironclad invader of its jungle domain. Another strange sight is an 'amok

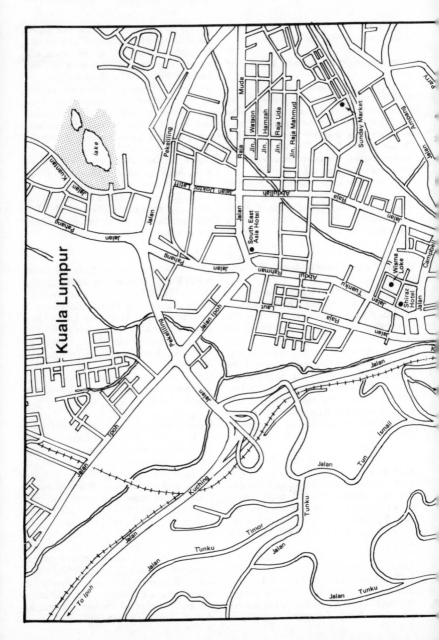

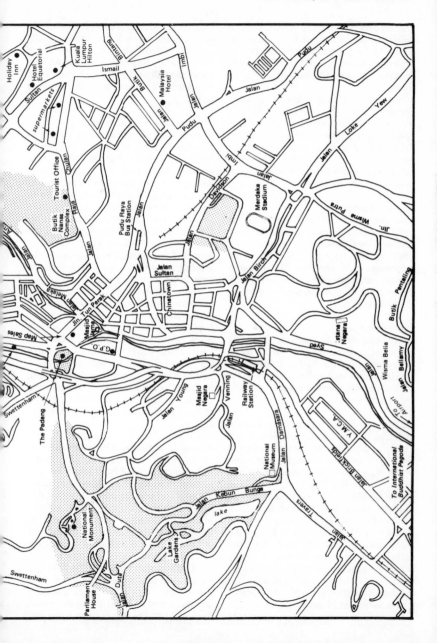

catcher', an ugly barbed device used to catch and hold a man who has run amok. There are frequent art exhibitions held at the museum and outside there are railway engines, an aircraft and other larger items.

Situated less than a km along Jalan Damansara from the railway station, admission to the museum is free and it is open daily from 9 am to 6 pm except on Fridays when it closes between 12 noon and 2.45 pm. A 17, 20, 24, 25, 34 or 37 minibus or most S J Kenderaan buses will take you to the museum.

National Monument

This massive monument overlooks the Lake Gardens from a hillside at their northern end. Sculptured in bronze in 1966 by the creator of the Iwo Jima monument in Washington DC, the monument commemorates the successful defeat of the Communist terrorists during the Emergency.

Parliament House

Overlooking the Lake Gardens, Malaysia's houses of parliament is dominated by an 18-storey office block. There are dress regulations for visitors – no shorts and for women dresses below the knee.

Other

KL has a number of sporting venues, including the indoor Stadium Negara, the Merdeka Stadium, the Royal Selangor Golf Club and the Selangor Turf Club where horse races have been held since 1896. The Istana Negara is the official palace of Malaysia's 'king' or Yang di-Pertuan Agong, a title which is rotated between the various state sultans. Kampong Bahru is a Malay section of KL to the north-east and the site each Saturday night for KL's Sunday Market – possibly because it continues through into Sunday morning. It's a food and produce market, a handicrafts market and a place to sample a wide variety of Malay foods.

Wisma Loke is an antique shop centrally located on Medan Tuanku. One of the oldest buildings in KL, it was originally owned by Cheow Ah Yeok, a compatriot of the legendary Kapitan China Yap Ah Loy. Later the millionaire philanthropist Loke Yew turned it into one of the finest homes in KL.

Places to Stay – bottom end

Bottom-end accommodation in Kuala Lumpur consists of a variety of Chinese hotels and a choice of hostels. Many of the cheap hotels in town are brothels. Some will rent rooms, others don't want straight business at all. None of them seem to be particularly rough and tough, but women should certainly be aware of the situation. It's usually easy to tell in a hurry. Also, the hotels with signs written only in Malaysian, Rumah Tumpangan, are, as a general rule, offering more than rooms. Nearly all the ones listed here are straight.

There are a couple of good hunting areas for cheap hotels. The Jalan Tuanku Abdul Rahman area, with a number of hotels right along the street, is a good place to look, as is the parallel Jalan Raja Laut. These roads run north from Jalan Tun Perak, by the Padang. There are a number of good places around Chinatown, including some excellent traditional old Chinese places. Then there are a number of hostels scattered mainly south of the centre.

Around Jalan Tuanku A popular centre for cheap hotels is Jalan Tuanku Abdul Rahman (also called Batu Road) and the parallel Jalan Raja Laut. Moving up Jalan Tuanku etc from its junction with Jalan Tun Perak there's the *Coliseum* with its famous old-planter's restaurant at 100. Rooms are M$18 to 20. At 132 the *Rex* and at 134 the *Tivoli* offer rock-bottom prices of M$18 for singles or doubles and are good values and popular. The Rex is a little better and more friendly, too. The *Paramount* at 154 is M$25, getting dirty and has a sort of nightclub on the eighth floor. At 142 the *Kowloon* is clean and fairly quiet despite its location – M$39 single or double with air-con and rather more modern than the others. There are other cheap ones nearby.

Continuing on you'll find the *Shiraz Hotel* (tel 03-920159) on the corner of Jalan Tuanku etc and Jalan Medan Tuanku. There are 60 rooms here at M$41/46 for singles/doubles and a good Pakistani restaurant downstairs. Further still the *Lai Ann* at 423 is in the dirt-cheap bracket. Nearby at the corner of Sultan Ishmael is the *Hotel Beautiful* which isn't and is a short-time spot. Ditto the *Reno* further along near Jalan Dewan Sultan Sulaiman.

At 285 Jalan Tuanku is the *Dashrun Hotel*, a modern budget hotel at M$44/50 for singles/doubles. Finally, just off Jalan Tuanku etc at the top end is the *South-East Asia Hotel* – it's in the middle price bracket, rooms cost from M$72/82, but since it houses the student travel office and offers student discounts it attracts some better-off backpackers.

The story is very similar over on Jalan Raja Laut where there's a string of places between 316 and 340 including the *Sentosa* (tel 03-925644) at 316 with rooms from M$25 to 32 with air-con. There's more accommodation across the road although the numbers here are much lower – at 110 the *Cylinman* has rooms at M$20 or M$30 with air-con and hot showers. The *Sun Ya* across the street is similar. The *City Hotel* is more expensive. Nearby, the *Great Wall Hotel* looks a bit dubious for more than an hour's stay. Again this is a short-time area – no real problem but single women travellers should be aware of it.

Chinatown Chinatown also has some cheap Chinese hotels like the very rock-bottom *Sai Woo Juan Kee* on the corner of Jalan Sultan and Jalan Panggang. The *Duni* is for business/pleasure only. The more expensive *Lok Ann* on the corner of Jalan Sultan and Jalan Petaling has rooms running from M$35 single or double with

bath. Opposite the 'Toshiba' bus stand on Jalan Sultan the *Starlight Hotel* has rooms at similar prices. At 83 Jalan Sultan the *Nanyang Hotel* is a good upmarket cheapie at M$30 cold bath, M$35 hot bath and M$40 double.

The popular *Lee Mun Hotel* on Jalan Sultan close to Jalan Petaling and opposite the Mandarin is a good Chinese cheapie. They are friendly and it costs just M$12 single or double. It's a classic old Chinese hotel with wood panelling, soap, towels, free Chinese tea and huge rooms. Although it's noisy it's also safe and central. At 43 Jalan Sultan is the *Colonial* – the bright yellow place. It's also a good one. Walk through the store and upstairs. The place is big, clean and interesting looking and costs M$15.40 single or double. They also have some cheap air-con rooms.

Not actually in Chinatown, the *Lido Hotel*, just across the street from the YMCA, is a big old place with rooms at M$15 or 22 with bath, single or double. See the YMCA below for how to get there. Also near the YMCA, the *Wing Heng Hotel* is good value with quiet rooms in the back with double beds for M$14. The larger rooms at the front are noisy. All rooms are fan-cooled and have attached toilets and showers, but solo women travellers should beware of the 'night life' in the area.

Other Places For medium-price cheapies Jalan Bukit Bintang used to be a good bet but the prices have escalated out of contention. The medium prices places here are interspersed with places to eat and also some more expensive hotels. Jalan Bukit Bintang is a short walk from the Pudu Raya bus station. Starting from the Jalan Pudu end of the street at number 4 you'll find the *Weng Hua* where girls come with the rooms. At 16 the *Mey Wah* has rooms at M$40 to 49, but seems half-hearted about renting them. The *Sungi Wang* is at 76 with singles/doubles at M$79/$89, all air-con. Continue to 78 where the *Tai Ichi* is M$42/48 or at 80 the *Park Hotel* is M$39 single, M$48 double.

Along Jalan Pudu from the Pudu Raya bus station, just beyond Jalan Bukit Bintang, there is a string of about 10 brightly painted Chinese hotels through numbers 172 to 190. They are all clean, all about M$20 for one bed, M$30 for two. And all with painted ladies. Most of the places here will rent rooms and the girls and managers are friendly and not pushy at all.

Hostels Finally there are the hostels. *Wisma Belia* (tel 03-444833 is at 40 Jalan Lornie, (also known as Jalan Syed Putra) a little inconvenient to get to since it's some way out of the centre – take a 52 bus. There are 115 rooms in this government-operated air-con hostel with rooms at M$20/25 without bath, doubles for M$35 with bath. The restaurant is lousy.

Also south of the centre are the YMCA and YWCA. The *YMCA* (tel 03-441439) is at 95 Jalan Kandang Kerbau, just off Jalan Brickfields; get to it on a 12 minibus or a 5, 33, 40, 49, 49A or 243 regular bus and ask for the Lido Cinema. There's a variety of accommodation, from M$7 dorm beds to singles/doubles without private bath at M$15/20; with private bath and air-con costs M$32/40. There's a M$1 temporary membership charge to non-members of the YMCA and women are accepted. The YMCA has a good restaurant with a large menu, not too unreasonable prices and very cheap breakfasts. The small Chinese restaurant across from the YMCA does good cheap meals. Drawbacks of the YMCA are that it is often full and its location is rather depressing but it's clean and staff are very helpful with travel advice. The YWCA (tel 03-283225 or 201623) is at 12 Jalan Davidson and has rooms at M$15/25 for singles/doubles but takes women only.

The Youth Hostel (tel 03-672872) is rather a long way out on Jalan Vethavanam, just off Jalan Ipoh. Ask for a bus that goes down Jalan Ipoh (a 66, 146 or 147 from Pudu Raya or a 71 or 143 from Jalan Ampang) and get off at the 3½ milestone or simply tell the conductr you want the YH. For members it costs M$2.50 for the first night, M$2 thereafter. Non-members pay M$4, then M$3. Catches are its distance from the centre and that there's a touch of the 'lights-out' mentality here. At last report the hostel was being renovated.

Places to Stay – middle
In the middle bracket KL has an equally wide selection of places ranging from the second-string 'international' hotels – like the *Furama*, the *Kuala Lumpur Mandarin*, *the Malaya*, or the *South-East Asia* – down to the more expensive Chinese hotels. The student travel office is located in the *South-East Asia*. The *Ria Hotel* is located on top of the Pudu Raya bus terminal on Jalan Pudu. The *Emerald Hotel* is not very good. Unfortunately the *Station Hotel*, located in Kuala Lumpur's delightfully exotic railway station, seems to have closed down. The venerable old *Majestic*, across the road from the station, has also been closed to become a government-run art gallery. *Shah's Village Motel* is a modern motel located in Petaling Jaya.

City Hotel (tel 03-924466), 366 Jalan Raja Laut, 90 rooms, singles M$38-49, doubles M$46-57

Hotel Emerald (tel 03-429233), 166-168 Jalan Pudu, 45 rooms, singles M$60, doubles M$64

Fortuna Hotel (tel 03-419116), 87 Jalan Berangan off Jalan Bukit Bintang, 100 rooms, doubles M$110

Hotel Furama (tel 03-201777), Kompleks Selangor, Jalan Sultan, 103 rooms, singles M$60-80, doubles M$85-90

Grand Central Hotel (tel 03-923011), 63 Jalan Chow Kit/Jalan Raja Laut, 150 rooms, singles M$72-79, doubles M$99-109

Grand Pacific Hotel (tel 03-982177), 52-56 Jalan Tun Ismail/Jalan Ipoh, 108 rooms, singles M$70-80, doubles M$82-92

Imperial Hotel (tel 03-422377), 76-80 Jalan Hicks, 90 rooms, singles M$78, doubles M$82

Kuala Lumpur Mandarin (tel 03-204533), 2-8 Jalan Sultan, 150 rooms, singles M$72-102, doubles M$78-114

The Lodge (tel 03-420122), Jalan Sultan Ismail, 50 rooms, singles M$95, doubles M$105

Hotel Malaya (tel 03-227722), Jalan Hang Lekir, 250 rooms, singles M$93, doubles M$108

Malaysia Hotel (tel 03-428033), 67-69 Jalan Bukit Bintang, 60 rooms, singles M$75-85, doubles M$85-95

Ria Hotel (tel 03-287744), Hentian Pudra Raya, 147 rooms, singles M$75-90, doubles M$85-100

Shah's Village Motel (tel 03-569322), 3 & 5 Lorong Sultan, Petaling Jaya, 44 rooms, singles & doubles M$80

South-East Asia Hotel (tel 03-926077), Jalan Haji Hussein off Jalan Tuanku Abdul Rahman, 208 rooms, singles M$72-80, doubles M$82-90

Town House (tel 03-420233), 22 Jalan Tong Shin, 64 rooms, singles M$40, doubles M$45-50

Places to Stay – top end

Kuala Lumpur also has number of very expensive hotels, starting at the very top with the 593-room *Kuala Lumpur Hilton* and the 400-room *Regent of Kuala Lumpur*, both on Jalan Sultan Ismail. The *Kuala Lumpur Merlin* and the *Hotel Equatorial* are also on this road and the *Holiday Inn Kuala Lumpur* is close by. The *Federal Hotel* is round the corner on Jalan Bukit Bintang. On Jalan Ampang there's the brand-new *Ming Court Kuala Lumpur*. The *Petaling Jaya Hilton* is out at Petaling Jaya.

Hotel Equatorial (tel 03-422022), Jalan Sultan Ismail, 300 rooms, singles M$175, doubles M$195

Federal Hotel (tel 03-489166), 35 Jalan Bukit Bintang, 450 rooms, singles M$145-175, doubles M$160-195

Holiday Inn Kuala Lumpur (tel 03-481066), Jalan Pinang, 192 rooms, singles M$175, doubles M$195

Kuala Lumpur Hilton (tel 03-422122), Jalan Sultan Ismail, 593 rooms, singles M$180-240, doubles M$210-280

Kuala Lumpur Merlin (tel 03-480033), 2 Jalan Sultan Ismail, 700 rooms, singles M$125-160, doubles M$135-170

Ming Court Kuala Lumpur (tel 03-482608), Jalan Ampang, 447 rooms, M$180-220

Petaling Jaya Hilton (tel 03-553533), 2 Jalan Barat, Petaling Jaya, 398 rooms, singles M$180-220, doubles M$200-240

The Plaza Hotel (tel 03-982255), Jalan Raja Laut, 160 rooms, singles M$120-155, doubles M$135-170

The Regent of Kuala Lumpur (tel 03-425588), Jalan Sultan Ismail, 400 rooms, M$205-255

Subang View Hotel (tel 03-755211), Subang Jaya, 162 rooms, singles M$130-150, doubles M$150-170

Places to Eat

Night Markets KL has some very good nighttime eating places. The tables set up at dusk at the Medan Pasar car park and nearby Benteng, right across the river from the Masjid Jame, are excellent. Nasi ayam is a speciality and the es campur here is simply the best anywhere. The mosque looks romantically eastern across the river and if it should rain you can shelter in the bank frontages. A drink and a meal is about M$4, satay 30c a stick. Unlike in Singapore a lot of sugar is added to fruit drinks here so if you don't want it, say so.

Other night markets with good food include the Sunday market out at Kampong Bahru, and a street off Jalan Tuanku Abdul Rahman close to the South-East Asia Hotel. Both are good places for Malay food. Across the river from the train station is another large food stall area. It's wedged between the river and the edge of Chinatown. There is a big indoor market on Jalan Hang Kasturi near the river between the Masjid Jame and the train station.

Indian Food On Jalan Melayu, near the corner of Jalan Tuanku Abdul Rahman and Jalan Tun Perak, there's the *Ceylon Restaurant* and the *Jai Hind*. Good for Indian snacks and light meals.

Upstairs at 60A Jalan Tuanku etc *Bangles* is an Indian restaurant with a good reputation. Further down the *Shiraz*, on the corner of Jalan Tuanku etc and

Jalan Medan Tuanku, is a good Pakistani restaurant. Right across the road from that is the *Akbar* with excellent north Indian food. There are several others here, too. The *Bilal* restaurants – there are two of them at 40 Jalan Ipoh and 33 Jalan Ampang – are other good Indian restaurants. Roti chanai and murtabaks are good here. The *Omar Khayam* is another.

Chinese Food Chinese restaurants can be found all over the place, but particularly around Chinatown and along Jalan Bukit Bintang near the Pudu Raya bus station. There is interesting Chinese vegetarian food in the crowded *Fook Woh Yuen* at the bottom end of Jalan Petaling. Excellent lunchtime dim sums at the expensive *Merlin Hotel*.

A local speciality in KL is bah kut teh, supposed to have originated in Kelang. It's pork ribs with white rice and Chinese tea and is a very popular breakfast meal.

Western Food KL has a surprising variety of western restaurants including, at the bottom of Jalan Tuanku etc, *Colonel Sanders* and *A&W* take-aways. There are several American-style hamburger joints around the bus station including Wendy's and, over towards Chinatown, McDonald's. There's also an interesting, if expensive, Malay answer to American fast foods here – a take-away satay place. Over on Jalan Bukit Bintang there's also an *Orange Julius* fast food joint. *Uncle Bill's*, in the Tivoli Hotel on Jalan Tuanku etc, is 'plastic but good' reports one traveller.

Not to be missed on the same street is the restaurant in the *Coliseum Hotel* where they have excellent steaks. When they say it's served on a sizzle plate they really mean it; the waiters zip up behind you and whip a bib around your neck to protect your clothes from the sizzle. M$12 buys you a great steak and salad and the place is quite a colonial experience which has scarcely changed over the years.

Down the street the *KK Cafeteria* by the Paramount Hotel has set lunches for M$5.50, soup to tea. The *Ship* near the Regent Hotel is also a splash out steak place. Prior to being closed for extensive renovations the *Station Hotel* did an excellent set dinner for just M$6.50 – worth it just to eat in the station's amazing surroundings. While still in the midst of renovations, it will be worth checking when work is completed. It was always good and reasonable. At the *New Yorker* on Jalan Bukit Bintang you can get not only a good steak but also wine by the glass.

In Chinatown don't miss *English Hotbreads* on Jalan Sultan. They offer all kinds of buns and rolls stuffed with chicken curry or cheeses and fresh from the oven. Also available are pizza, macaroni, fruit tarts and chocolate cakes. Prices are good. There is another similar place across the street and down a bit called the *Angel Cake House*, downstairs from the Nanyang Hotel. The *Brass Rail*, just off Jalan Medan Tuanku, is a British-style pub with cheaper drink prices during the 4 to 7 pm 'happy hour'. Just across the bridge from the GPO is a Chinese bar known to locals as *The Vatican* – it's a popular expat hangout.

Finally *Le Coq d'Or*, a restaurant in a fine turn-of-the-century mansion on Jalan Ampang, is expensive but not quite as expensive as the elegant surroundings might indicate.

Getting There

Kuala Lumpur is Malaysia's principal international arrival gateway and a central travel crossroads for train, bus or taxi travel. Trains all come in to the magnificent Kuala Lumpur railway station. Most long-distance taxis and buses operate from the multi-storey Pudu Raya terminus on Jalan Pudu. The local 'Toshiba' or Kelang bus station is beside Jalan Sultan Mohamed in Chinatown and the Jalan Ampang station is opposite the AIA Building.

Air KL is the central hub for MAS's

domestic air network – see the introductory Getting Around section for fare details.

Rail It's also the midway point for train services between Singapore and Butterworth, again see the introductory Getting Around section.

Bus There are a wide variety of bus services, the majority of which operate from the Pudu Raya terminal. As usual there are regular buses and very often slightly more expensive air-con services. Fares include Port Kelang M$1.50 (from the Kelang or 'Toshiba' terminal), Port Dickson M$3.60, Melaka M$6-8, Johore Bahru M$13-15, Singapore M$15-17, Muar M$9, Ipoh M$7-10, Butterworth M$13-15, Genting Highlands M$5, Cameron Highlands M$7-8, Padang Besar M$23.

Taxi While the buses go from downstairs the taxis are upstairs in the Pudu Raya terminal although there are also long-distance taxi offices along Pudu Rd near the bus station. There are lots of taxis, and fares include Seremban M$5, Melaka M$12, Johore Bahru M$30, Ipoh M$15, Kuala Kangsar M$18, Taiping M$20, Butterworth M$30, Alor Setar M$33, Genting Highlands M$7, Kuala Lipis M$12, Kuantan M$20, Kuala Trengganu M$34, Kota Bahru M$40.

Getting Around
Airport Transport Taxis from Kuala Lumpur's international airport operate on a coupon system. You purchase a coupon from a booth at the airport and use this to pay the driver – it's designed to eliminate fare cheating from the airport. Going to the airport is not so simple because the taxi drivers are uncertain about getting a return trip – count on about M$16 to 18. Beware of taxi touts at the airport, they'll cost you more.

Or you can go by bus – a 47 bus operates every hour from the Toshiba terminal on Jalan Sultan Mohamed and costs M$1.05. The trip takes 45 minutes though it's a good idea to leave more time since traffic can be bad. The first departure is at 6 am. There's also a non-direct 61 bus.

Bus There are two bus systems operating in KL. Fare stage buses start from 15c for the first km and go up 5c each two km. City bus companies include Sri Jaya, Len Seng, Len, Ampang, Kee Hup and Toong Foong. There are a number of bus stands around the city including the huge Pudu Raya terminal on Jalan Pudu and the 'Toshiba' terminal on Jalan Sultan Mohamed (so named from the Toshiba sign on top of the multi-storey car park). The faster minibuses operate on a fixed fare of 50c anywhere along their route. Whenever possible have correct change ready when boarding the bus, particularly during rush hours.

Taxis Trishaws have virtually disappeared from KL's heavily trafficked streets but there are plenty of taxis and fares are quite reasonable. They start from 70c for the first km, then an additional 30c for each 0.8 km. Air-con taxis are about 25% more than this. By time, rates are about M$7 per hour, M$14 air-con. There's an additional charge of 10c for a third and fourth passenger and from 1 to 6 am there's an additional 50% supplement on top of the meter fare.

KL's taxi drivers are not keen on going to the airport or from the station on the meter – in those cases you'll have to bargain your fare. It shouldn't be more than a couple of dollars from the railway station to most places in KL. Because KL seems to be suffering from something of a taxi shortage there's a shadow 'pirate taxi' service springing up; you have to bargain with these operators but they're more open to negotiation than the regular ones.

Rent-a-Car There are a number of local car rental organisations in KL with typical rates around M$100 a day. For example, a Datsun 1300 is M$123 a day unlimited mileage or M$49 plus 49c per km. The major nationwide rental organisations' addresses in KL are:

Avis Rent-a-Car
 Kuala Lumpur Hilton, Jalan Sultan Ismail (tel 03-443188)
Hertz Rent-a-Car
 Kuala Lumpur Hilton, Jalan Sultan Ismail (tel 03-433014)
Mayflower-Acme Tours
 Angkasa Raya Buildings, 123 Jalan Ampang (tel 03-667011)
National Car Rental
 Hotel Equatorial, Jalan Sultan Ismail (tel 03-489188)
Sintat Rent-a-Car
 Holiday Inn, Jalan Pinang (tel 03-482388)
Toyota Rent-a-Car
 Federal Hotel, 35 Jalan Bukit Bintang (tel 03-438142)

Tours MSL Travel in the South-East Asia Hotel have day tours for M$27 or morning tours for M$16.

Shopping

At Bukit Nanas the handicraft centre displays a wide variety of local craftwork. There's also a duty-free shop here, but the prices are not competitive with Singapore. Jalan Tuanku Abdul Rahman has a variety of shops including local crafts along the arcade known as Aked Ibu Kota. Jalan Melayu has Indonesian religious goods and also local batik and other art. Pewterware, made from high-quality Malaysian tin, is an important local craft. You can see batik and silver or copperwork being done near the Batu Caves. Purchases can also be made there.

The large Weld Supermarket and Fitzpatricks's Supermarket, with a number of other shops in the same complex, are on Jalan Raja Chulan. Two other modern shopping centres are the Bukit Bintang Plaza and the Sungai Wang Plaza, both on Jalan Bukit Bintang. Jalan Petaling is, of course, one of the most colourful shopping streets in KL, particularly at night

AROUND KUALA LUMPUR
Batu Caves

The huge Batu Caves are the best-known attraction in the vicinity of KL. They are just 13 km north of the capital, a short distance off the Ipoh road. The caves are in a towering limestone formation and were little known until about a hundred years ago. Later a small Hindu shrine was built in the major cave and it became a pilgrimage centre during the annual Thaipusam festival.

The major cave, a vast open space known as the Cathedral Cave, is reached by a straight flight of 272 steps. For those not feeling up to a steep climb in the tropical heat there's a small railcar which runs beside the steps – at a cost of 50c return. Also reached by the same flight of steps is the long and winding Dark Cave, but this has been closed for the past couple of years because quarrying in the limestone outcrop has made the caves unsafe. There are a number of other caves in the same formation, including a small cave at the base of the outcrop which has been made into a small museum with figures of the various Hindu gods; admission is 50c.

There's good Indian vegetarian food at the restaurant closest to the caves themselves.

Getting There To get to the caves take an 11 minibus (60c) from Jalan Pudu or Jalan Semarang or Len Seng bus number 70 from Jalan Raja Laut/Jalan Ampang. The bus trip takes about 45 minutes and it's wise to tell the driver you're going all the way to the caves; if there aren't many people it sometimes stops earlier. The 11 minibus is more frequent and more convenient.

National Zoo & Aquarium

East of KL on the road to Ulu Kelang, about 13 km out, is the 55-hectare site of the National Zoo and Aquarium. Laid out around a central lake, the zoo collection emphasises the wildlife found in Malaysia.

Top: Porta Santiago, Melaka (TW)
Left: Christ Church, Melaka (TW)
Right: tombstone in St Paul's Church, Melaka (TW)

Top: Foster's Smokehouse, Cameron Highlands (TW)
Left: Jalan Petaling, Kuala Lumpur (TW)
Right: cave temples, Ipoh (TW)

There are also elephant and camel rides and other amusements for children.

The zoo is open daily from 9 am to 6 pm and student admission is 30c; M$2.50 for others, plus M$1 for use of your camera. To get there take a Len Seng bus number 170 or a Lenchee bus 180 from Jalan Leboh Ampang. Or you can take a 17 or 23 minibus.

Mimaland

On the road to the Genting Highlands, 18 km from KL, Mimaland is a 120-hectare amusement park – mainly intended for children. It's intended to be a 'Malaysia in Miniature' and amongst the attractions are a fishing and boating lake, a huge natural swimming pool, a small zoo and a collection of full-size dinosaur models.

You can get there on a Len Seng Bus 168, marked 'Mimaland', from Jalan Ampang. A 17 minibus will also take you there en route to the zoo. Admission is M$1.40.

Places to Stay You can stay at Mimaland in the lodge (M$12.50 per person), in motel rooms (M$89 for doubles) or in Malaysian cottages known as *bagans* (M$150). Phone 03-632133 for details.

Templer Park

Beside the Ipoh road, 22 km north of KL, Templer Park was established during the colonial period by the British High Commissioner Sir Gerald Templer. The 1200-hectare park is intended to be a tract of jungle, preserved within easy reach of the city. There are a number of marked jungle paths, swimming lagoons and several waterfalls within the park boundaries.

To get there take a 66, 72, 78 or 83 bus from the Pudu Raya terminal. Bus fare is 95c and the trip takes 35 minutes. Just north of the park is a 350-metre-high limestone formation known as Bukit Takun and close by the smaller Anak Takun which has many caves.

Petaling Jaya

PJ is a modern suburb of KL. Originally intended as a dormitory town to the capital, it has grown so rapidly and successfully that it has become a major industrial centre in its own right. PJ has a population approaching 250,000. The University of Malaya is en route to PJ.

Port Kelang

Situated 30 km south-west of the capital, Port Kelang is the major seaport for KL. Port Kelang is famed for its excellent seafood, particularly chilli crabs. There are good seafood places only a couple of minutes' walk from the bus terminus. Public ferries leave for offshore islands and passengers are taken out in curious-looking rowing boats. Only eight km before Port Kelang you pass through Kelang, the royal capital of Selangor with a royal mosque and istana. Morib, south of Port Kelang and 64 km from KL, is a popular weekend escape and beach resort. The bus from the 'Toshiba' terminal in KL to Port Kelang costs M$1.50.

Shah Alam

The capital of Selangor State is undergoing a major construction and development plan due for completion in 1986 with the intention of making it a worthy state centre. A new museum, cultural centre, theatre and huge library are included in the scheme being built on a hill over-looking the city's man-made lakes and close to the state mosque. As of yet this area of the country has little to attract visitors.

Other

On the north-eastern outskirts of the city, on Jalan Pahang, you can visit the Selangor Pewter Factory between 8.30 am and 4.45 pm daily and see Malaysia's famous pewter products being made. On the Ipoh road, just north of the turn-off to the Batu Caves, is the Batik Factory Selayang where you can see batik-making demonstrations 8.30 am to 1 pm and 2 to 5 pm Monday through Sunday. There are also numerous rubber plantations and tin mines around KL; visits can be arranged.

GENTING HIGHLANDS

Where the style of other Malaysian hill stations is old English, here it's modern skyscrapers; where the entertainment at the older stations is jungle walks here it's a casino; instead of waterfalls and mountain views Genting has an artificial lake and a cable car. If that does not sound to your taste then drive straight by, for the Genting Highlands are a thoroughly modern hill station designed to cater to the affluent citizens of Kuala Lumpur, just an hour to the south.

The first stage of the Genting Highlands was opened in the early '70s and there are now five hotels and associated developments. These include Malaysia's only casino in the 18-storey Genting Hotel, with all the usual western games of chance and eastern favourites like keno and tai sai, too. Men must wear a tie to enter the casino – or pay M\$3 to hire 'Malaysian national dress'.

Then there's the four-hectare artificial lake with boating facilities and encircled by a miniature railway for children. Naturally there's a golf course 700 metres down from the hotels, reached by a cable car (M\$2 one-way). Forgetting nothing, the resort also has a bowling alley and a brand new cave temple, the Chin Swee Temple, on the road up to the resort. Of course Genting has cooler weather like any other hill station; the main part of the resort is at a little over 1700 metres altitude.

Places to Stay

Although the emphasis here is on international standards, there are several places offering if not cheap at least economy accommodation. There are rooms from M\$40 in the *Genting Palangi* (tel 03-353200) and from M\$35 in the *Hotel Genting Ria* (tel 03-353244) and the *Genting Sri Layang* (tel 03-88393).

At the top there's the 1100-room *Genting Hotel* (tel 03-88393) with rooms at M\$160 and every mod con imaginable from saunas and swimming pool to tennis courts and a 'revolving disco restaurant'! The *Highlands Hotel* (tel 03-205722) has 200 rooms from around M\$80. There are often two– or three-day packages offered at the Genting Highlands, including accommodation and some meals.

Getting There

The jet-set way to the Gentings is by helicopter. A service operates between KL's Subang Airport or the Segambut Helipad in KL to the highlands. Or you can get there by share taxi for M\$7 in around an hour; it's about 50 km from KL. There is also a regular M\$4.50 bus service between the Pudu Raya bus station in KL and the Sri Layang Hotel in Genting. There are about nine services daily on weekdays, more on weekends. The Genting Highlands promotion board run day tours to the highlands – M\$25 gets you transport there and back, a good lunch and M\$9 of gambling chips.

FRASER'S HILL

Fraser's Hill takes its name from Louis James Fraser, a reclusive mule-trader who lived here around the turn of the century. It's said he ran a remote and illegal gambling and opium den up here, but he was long gone when the area's potential as a hill station was recognised in 1910. The station, set at a cool 1524 metres altitude, is quiet and relatively undeveloped – possibly because it's not the easiest hill station to get to.

As in the Cameron Highlands there are many beautiful gardens around the town and also many wildflowers carpeting the hills. The jungle walks here are much more jungle strolls than real walks. The golf course forms the real 'centre' of Fraser's Hill and there are other sporting facilities which include tennis and squash courts. About five km from the information centre is the Jerlau Waterfall with a swimming pool fed from the falls. You have to walk the last km to the falls. A short walk up from the information centre there's a small zoo – open 9 am to 5 pm, admission M$1. Its pleasant setting is probably more interesting than the animals, but beware of the monkeys. While the ones in the cages distract you, their wild cousins will make a dash for anything edible you're carrying!

Information & Orientation

The information centre (tel 095-60201) is between the Puncak Inn and Golf Club on one side and the Merlin Hotel on the other. They can supply maps and information brochures and also will book accommodation in Fraser's Hill – but not at the rest house which is in Selangor rather than Pahang; the state boundary runs through the town. There are films on Saturdays and Sundays at the Merlin Hotel which also has a bank branch which opens when most are closed – at weekends and on holidays. You can hire bicycles for M$1.50 per hour from the Merlin Hotel.

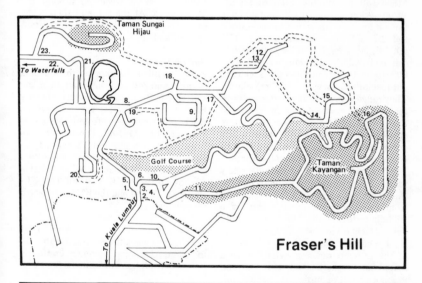

Fraser's Hill

1. Puncak Inn	12 Kuantan Bungalow
2 GPO	13 Station Punai
3 Tourist Information Office	14 Station Tiong
4 Fraser's Hill Merlin	15 Station Serindek
5 Tavern	16 Station Merbok
6 Sports & Golf Complex	17 Station Merpati
7 Mini Zoo & Park	18 Station Murai
8 Temerloh Bungalow	19 Station Kenari
(Steak House)	20 Station Muri
9 Lipis Bungalow	21 Rompin Bungalow
10 Pekan Bungalow	22 Semantan Bungalow
11 Raub Bungalow	23 Station Layang-Layang

Places to Stay

There's nothing really low priced at Fraser's Hill. The *Seri Berkat Rest House* has rooms at M$25 or there's the *Puncak Inn* (tel 071-60201) with rooms at M$20-50. The cheaper rooms are very small – just enough space to swing a kitten – while the more expensive rooms are simply larger, no extra facilities. At peak seasons the costs jump by M$5.

At the other end of the scale there's the *Fraser's Hill Merlin Hotel* (tel 071-60279) with 109 rooms at M$80-120 for singles, M$95-130 for doubles. It's pleasantly situated overlooking the golf course. Then there's Fraser's Hill's bungalows – *Raub* (tel 071-60241), *Semantan* (tel 071-60226), *Temerloh* (tel 071-60242), *Pekan* (tel 071-60213) and *Rompin* (tel 071-60216). In these you often get excellent, old-fashioned service and standards. They range in price from as little as M$30 for an off-season double at the Temerloh to around M$60 for a high-season double at some of the others. All Fraser's Hill accommodation can be booked at the helpful and informative information centre.

If you're in need of something really reasonably priced try the *Corona Nursery*, the flower nursery about a 25-minute walk from the tourist office. It's run by a friendly Indian family. Doubles at M$12 have attached bathroom and you can use the kitchen and fridge. Beware, however, of the ill-tempered dog belonging to a neighbour – it guards the access road and if you arrive at night pick up a stick with which to warn it off.

If you're stuck at the bottom of the hill there's the pleasantly relaxed *Gap Rest House* right at the Gap with rooms at M$12 and up. In fact this wonderfully old-fashioned place is so much better value than anything up the hill that it's worth staying down there and just visiting Fraser's Hill for the day. It's in a pretty setting, has a comfortable lounge, a good restaurant and bathtubs with real hot water! There's a Chinese and an Indian restaurant close by the rest house, but

really nothing else. The electricity goes at 11.30 pm each night.

Places to Eat

There's a reasonable selection of places eat. At one end of Puncak Inn is t Chinese *Hill View Restaurant* which h quite good food and snacks, while at other end is the friendly Malay *Ara Restaurant*. Then there's a snack bar the Golf Club and the straightforward (name says it all) *Kheng Yuen Lee Eat Shop*. Up a notch there's the *Temer Steakhouse* with steaks at around M$10 mark. At the top end there's expensive Merlin Hotel with restaur and coffee bars.

Getting There

Fraser's Hill is 103 km north of Ku Lumpur and 240 km from Kuantan on east coast. By public transport Frase Hill is a little difficult to get to. There twice-daily bus service from Kuala Ku Bahru costing M$1.80. The bus depa from KKB at 8 am and 12 noon, fr Fraser's Hill at 10 am and 2 pm. A t from KKB would be about M$40. KKB 62 km north of KL, just off the K Butterworth road and the KL-Butterwo railway line.

The last five miles up to Fraser's Hil on a steep, winding, one-way section. the Gap you leave the KKB to Raub rc to make this final ascent. Traffic permitted uphill and down at the follow times:

Up from The Gap

7.00 am-7.40 am
9.00 am-9.40 am
11.00 am-11.40 am
1.00 pm-1.40 pm
3.00 pm-3.40 pm
5.00 pm-5.40 pm

Down from Fraser's Hill

8.00 am-8.40 am
10.00 am-10.40 am
12 noon-12.40 pm

2.00 pm-2.40 pm
4.00 pm-4.40 pm
6.00 pm-6.40 pm

From 7 pm to 6.40 am the road is open both ways and you take your chances!

KUALA LUMPUR TO IPOH

It's 219 km from KL to Ipoh and a further 173 km on from there to Butterworth. Heading north, Kuala Kubu Bahru is the first larger town, but it is just off the main road. This is the place from where buses run to Fraser's Hill. Continuing north you pass through Tanjong Malim and Selim River. During WW II the British forces made a last-ditch attempt to halt the Japanese advance at Selim River, but failed.

Continuing north you reach Bidor, from where you can turn off for Telok Anson, then Tapah, the gateway to the Cameron Highlands. At Kampar you can, if you have your own transport, turn off for Lumut and Pangkor Island, but there are a number of routes to this port. Finally you reach Ipoh, heralded by a number of dramatic limestone outcrops.

Places to Stay

There are rest houses in Tapah, Telok Anson and Selim River. The Selim River *Rumah Rekat Rest House* is, according to one traveller, 'fantastic value – singles/doubles for M$4/6 includes fan, sheets, towel, soap, mosquito coils, bathroom with bathtub, WC, toilet paper, plus it's clean and quiet. The only catch is there's really no reason for anybody to stop in Selim River!' There is a cinema, however.

In addition to the Rest House's popular restaurant, there are many stalls with good, cheap food, including Indian food, in the vicinity.

CAMERON HIGHLANDS

Malaysia's most extensive hill station is about 60 km off the main Kuala Lumpur-Ipoh-Butterworth road at Tapah and at an altitude of 1500 to 1800 metres. It's a little difficult to pinpoint exactly where the Cameron Highlands are and at what altitude because they consist of a series of villages strung along the main road.

The Highlands take their name from William Cameron, the surveyor who mapped the area in 1885. He was soon

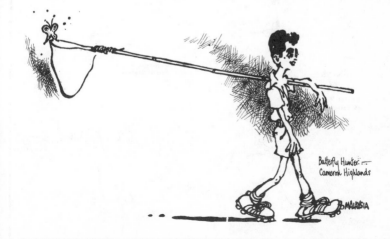

Butterfly Hunter —
Cameron Highlands

MALAYSIA

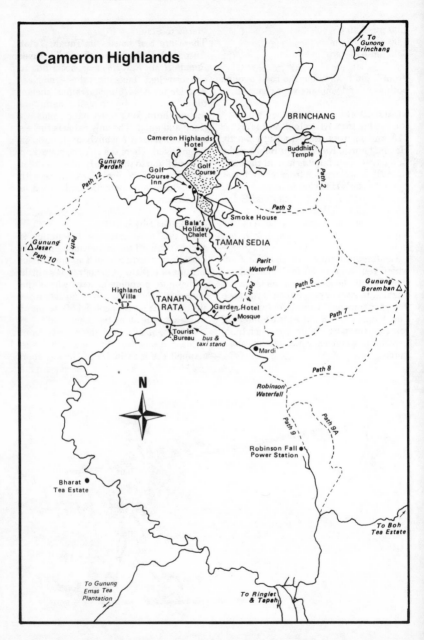

Cameron Highlands

followed by tea planters, Chinese vegetable farmers and finally by those seeking a cool escape from the heat of the lowlands. The temperature rarely drops below 8° C or climbs above 24° C and the area is riotously fertile. Vegetables grow here in profusion, flowers are cultivated for sale all over Malaysia, Malaysian tea production is centred here and wildflowers bloom everywhere.

The cool weather tempts visitors to exertions normally forgotten at sea level – there's an excellent golf course, a network of jungle tracks, waterfalls and mountains and less exercising points of interest such as a colourful Buddhist temple and a number of tea plantations where visitors are welcome.

Information & Orientation

There's a small information centre run by the Cameron Highlands Tourist Promotion Association situated at the bottom end of Tanah Rata. It's open 9 am to 11.45 pm and 1 to 4.30 pm except on Tuesdays when it is closed. From the turn-off at Tapah it's 29 miles (46 km) up to Ringlet, the first village of the Highlands. Ringlet is not particularly interesting and although there are a number of places to stay here most visitors press on higher up. Soon after Ringlet you skirt the lake created by the Sultan Abu Bakar Dam between milestones 30 and 32. Soon after milestone 37 (59 km) you reach Tanah Rata, the main town of the highlands with a variety of mainly lower-priced hotels and a wide choice of restaurants. The post office, banks and taxi station are also here and some buses terminate at Tanah Rata.

Only a few km further brings you up to the golf course around which you'll find most of the Highlands' more expensive accommodation. Continue on beyond the golf course and at around the 49th milestone (65 km) you reach the other main Highland town, Brinchang, where there are more restaurants and cheap hotels. The road continues up beyond Brinchang to smaller villages and the Blue Valley Tea Estate at 56 miles, off to the north-east, or to the top of Gunung Brinchang at 49 miles, to the north-west. The Boh Tea Factory, beyond Brinchang on the road to the radio station, also welcomes visitors. A taxi from Brinchang shouldn't cost more than M$5 if you can't hitch a ride. While you're there visit Mrs Helen Robertson's rose garden and try her delicious rose jam and homemade marmalade.

Walks

There are a variety of walks around the Highlands, leading from place to place or to waterfalls, mountain peaks and other scenic spots. The walks are not all well kept and sometimes can be difficult to follow. Additionally there are no high quality maps available – those supplied by the information centre or available from hotels are generally only sketch maps. You should take care not to get lost and to bring some emergency supplies on the longer or more difficult walks. Walks 4, 9, 11 and 12 (as far as Robinson Falls) are recommended as family strolls taking only about an hour. Walks 3, 5, 7 and 10 are longer walks taking two or more hours while walks 1, 2 and 8 are 'tough going'.

The walks are generally interesting as they pass through relatively unspoilt jungle and the cool weather makes walking a pleasure. Walk 12 is particularly good for wildflowers – the Highlands are famed for their orchids. The deviation from walk 12 up to the summit of 1576-metre Gunung Perdah is a good short walk. Although the walks around the Highlands are all relatively short there is obviously great potential for longer walks from here. A glance at the map will indicate what a short, straight-line distance it is from the Highlands down to Ipoh or the main road. Any walk outside the immediate area has to be notified to the local authorities, however, and once again there are no good maps available.

Waterfalls Walk 9 from Tanah Rata leads

to the Robinson Falls in less than a km. You can also reach them from the road around the golf course in a similar distance. There is a natural swimming pool at the base of the Parit Falls.

You can make an interesting longer walk by taking 9 to the falls, then the steep and 'mildly' challenging 8 to the top of Beremban, then 3 to the golf course or 3 and 2 to the Buddhist temple, finally returning to Tanah Rata on walk 4 past the Smokehouse and the Parit Falls. That makes an interesting round trip walk taking three-plus hours. Another round trip is 10 to Gunung Jasar and back via 12.

Mountains Gunung Brinchang at 2032 metres is the highest point reached by surfaced road on the peninsula. Walk 7 from the Mardi Station will take you to the top of 1841-metre Gunung Beremban in two km. You can also reach the summit in three km on walk 3 from Hopetown near the golf course. Gunung Jasar is 1696 metres high and is reached on path 10 which runs between the golf course and Tanah Rata. From Tanah Rata there are directional signs from near Highland Villa at the 37th milestone. It's two km from there or coming down from the Hilltop Bungalow at the golf course it's about 2½ km along walk 12 and then walk 10.

The Cameron Highlands' most famous jungle walker was the man who never came back from his walk. American Jim Thompson is credited with founding the Thai silk industry after WW II. He made a personal fortune and his beautiful, antique-packed house beside a khlong (canal) in Bangkok is a major tourist attraction today. On 26 March 1967 he was holidaying in the Highlands and left his villa for a pre-dinner stroll – never to be seen again. Despite extensive searches the mystery of Jim Thompson's disappearance has never been explained. Kidnapped? Taken by a tiger? Or simply a planned disappearance or suicide? Nobody knows.

Tea Plantations

A visit to a tea plantation is a popular highlands activity. The first tea was planted in 1926. The main plantations include the Blue Valley Tea Estate (tel 9847 for a visit appointment) about 29 km above Tanah Rata. The Boh Tea Estate (tel 8634) is about 10 km below Tanah Rata. The plantations are all happy to show visitors around the estates although you should ring for an appointment. They're closed on Sundays.

Tea bushes are plucked every seven to eight days. A plucker can gather about 40 kilograms in a day and it takes five kg of leaves to make a kg of tea. The collected leaves are weighed and 'withered' – a drying process in which air is blown across troughs by fans in order to reduce the moisture content by about 50%. The dried leaves are then rolled to twist, break and rupture the leaf cells and release the juices for fermentation. The finer leaves are then separated out and the larger ones are rolled once again.

Fermentation, which is really oxidization of the leaf enzymes, has to be critically controlled to develop the characteristic flavour and aroma of the tea. The fermented leaves are then 'fired', a process in which excess moisture is driven off in a drying machine. It is at this time that the leaves become black. Finally the tea is sorted into grades and stalks and fibres are removed before it is stored in bins to mature.

Other

The new Sam Poh Temple, just below Brinchang and about a km off the road, is a typically Chinese kaleidoscope of colours with Buddha statues, stone lions and incense burners. Mardi is an agricultural research station in Tanah Rata – visits must be arranged in advance.

There are a number of flower nurseries and vegetable farms in the Highlands. There is an Orang Asli settlement near Brinchang and you occasionally see Orang Asli, complete with their hunting blow-pipes, while out walking. The Malaysian authorities are not at all happy about western visitors treating the Orang Asli as something to sightsee. Their culture is frail and treating them as snapshot subjects is going to do it no good at all.

The Highlands are famed for their butterflies and there are many colourful species to be seen. They're particularly prevalent around the waterfalls.

Places to Stay

The Highlands can be very busy in April, August and December when many families come here for vacations. It can be a good idea to book accommodation at those times. Prices in the cheaper places can be very variable with demand – if it's a peak time and few rooms are available you can expect prices to soar. If it's quiet they will often be negotiable. The four main accommodation areas are:

Ringlet Not many people choose to stay down at Ringlet, around 300 metres below Tanah Rata. If you do you could try the base priced *Cathay* or *Hock Sin* or the more expensive *Lake View Bungalows* (tel 05-941630) with chalets and bungalows from M$50. Right beside the lake, *Foster's Lakehouse* (tel 05-941680) is magnificently 'olde worlde' in style and has singles and doubles from M$100 to 180 plus more expensive suites.

Tanah Rata There are a number of popular cheap Chinese hotels in the main Highlands town. At 39 Tanah Rata the popular and amazingly clean *Seah Meng* has rooms from M$16. Next door the *Town House Hotel* (tel 05-941666) at number 41 has doubles at M$18 or M$32 with attached bathroom and there's even hot water. The owner of this clean and well-kept place is very helpful. At 25 there's the *Tanah Rata Hotel*, which gets mixed reactions from people staying there although it's generally agreed that the rooms are big and the prices are low. Or in this same category there's the *Hollywood Hotel*, rooms from M$14. At all these main street hotels try to avoid the noisy rooms at the front. You can get cheaper and quieter shared-bathroom rooms if you're persistent.

Up a price notch there's the *Garden Hotel* (tel 05-941911) which is a little further up the road and off to the right. Rooms here cost from M$45 and there are also more expensive chalets. Yes, it does have a beautiful garden, and also its own little cinema. Apart from on weekends, when the hotel is often packed out, the prices are negotiable.

The *Rest House* in Tanah Rata is expensive by rest house standards, but pleasant and quiet. Even the ordinary doubles have little sitting rooms as well as attached baths for M$28. For M$40 you can have a suite. The Rest House is usually booked out on weekends and holidays.

Brinchang – Golf Course One of the Highlands' most popular places for shoe-stringers is actually between Tanah Rata and the golf course. *Bala's Holiday Chalets* (tel 05-941660) has rooms from around M$5 per person in basic share rooms and go up from there. Prices vary to some extent with the season and demand. Doubles cost from M$10 or so, but you may find yourself being steered towards rooms at M$30 and if Bala can convince you to spend M$40 for a 'luxury room', he will! There's a restaurant and cooking facilities so you can prepare your own food if you wish. There's also a washing machine, a fridge, general travel information available and they'll do bus bookings. Bala is a bit of businessman, which puts some people off, but for all that it's a popular place, a good meeting point, has a pleasant communal feel to it and most people find it a fine place to stay.

In Brinchang *Ye Olde Smokehouse* (tel 05-941214) looks so perfectly like an old English pub that you'd be excused for thinking it was time-warped there by Dr Who himself. Rooms in Foster's Smokehouse range from around M$80 to M$200 and everything inside is as perfectly in step as the exterior would indicate. This is a rather nose-in-the-air establishment; 'we once arrived in jeans and T-shirts

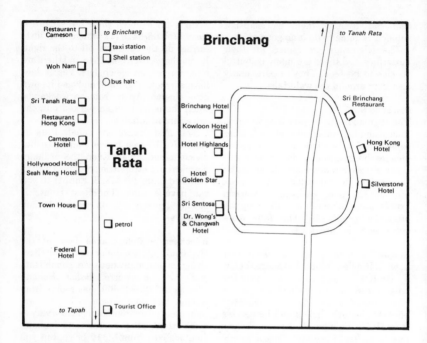

(with a reservation)', wrote a traveller, 'and the arrogant desk personnel started wondering among themselves (but loud enough for us to hear) whether we could afford it. After that, they made our stay as unpleasant as possible; too bad, the place is so beautiful!'

Across the road and about a hundred metres further on is the *Golf Course Inn* (tel 05-941411), a modern motel-style place with modern motel-style rooms from M$75 for a single at the back to M$100 for a double at the front, looking out over the golf course.

Continue around the golf course and you come to the modern *Cameron Highlands Merlin* (tel 05-941211) with singles at M$80-125 and doubles at M$90-135. Other places around the golf course include the *Golf View Villa* (tel 05-941624) where whole bungalows can be rented.

Brinchang The final accommodation centre is the compact town of Brinchang. There are quite a few straightforward Chinese hotels here, mainly a little more expensive than those down in Tanah Rata – here prices start from M$20 although some hunting around will often turn up cheaper places. They include the *Highlands Hotel* (tel 05-941588) at 29-32 Brinchang, the *Kowloon Hotel* (tel 05-941366) at 34-35, and the *Brinchang Hotel* (tel 05-941744) at 36.

Also up at Brinchang *Wong Villa* and *Jolly Villa* are cheap, clean and friendly and will fix meals for you. You can get rooms here for M$10 or less, but they're sometimes packed out with noisy parties of Chinese salesmen.

Places to Eat
There is excellent Indian food available in the Cameron Highlands, perhaps a result

of the tea plantation influence since the majority of the plantation workers are Indians. In fact this is one of the best places for cheap Indian food in Malaysia. Some places to try include the *Restoran Kumar* next to the Sri Tanah Rata supermarket in Tanah Rata where the murtabaks and roti chanai are simply 'fantastic'. Nearby is the small *Bunga Raya*, near the taxi stand, which does good murtabaks and tandoori chicken. Up at Brinchang there's the low-priced, and excellent, *Sri Sentosa* and the newer *Sri Brinchang*.

Of course there's also a good selection of Chinese restaurants although they've not got the same pleasantly low prices as the Indian places. The *Kowloon* in Brinchang has very good food although you can count on around M$8 a head for food and drinks. Down in Tanah Rata the *Hong Kong* is similarly priced and has really good food. The Highlands' real taste treat is steamboat, that Chinese equivalent of a Swiss fondue where you get plates of meat, shrimp, vegetables and eggs and brew your soup up over a burner on the table. You need at least two people (count on around M$6 a head), but the more the better. The *Garden Hotel* in Tanah Rata has a very good steamboat in beautiful settings and at prices only marginally higher than the regular restaurants; a worthwhile investment.

The *Smokehouse* is 'ideal for homesick Brits' where you can get expensive tea and scones (M$6), sandwiches with the crusts cut off and fairly pricey meals. The *Golf Course Inn* has a restaurant with good and not too expensive Chinese food. Up at the *Merlin* you can get a good hamburger or other lunchtime meals in the open-air area overlooking the golf course. The Highlands are famous for their luscious strawberries although a strawberry fancier from Georgia wrote to us in outrage to report he was served frozen strawberries once!

If you're preparing your own food, it's reported that vegetables and other food are fresher and cheaper up at Brinchang

than in Tanah Rata. They're grown up beyond Brinchang at Kampong Raja where there are also a couple of excellent and bargain price restaurants. You can get fresh milk from the dairy on the road beside the playground in Tanah Rata. There's also a bakery on Jalan Sultan which does good scones and the food stalls in Tanah Rata have various snacks including delicious dessert pancakes called *apam balek*. The *Rest House* in Tanah Rata has a good restaurant and its bar is a local social centre.

Getting There

It's a long and gradual climb from Tapah to the Highlands with plenty of corners on the way. From the Golf Course Inn down to the main road junction one visitor reported counting 653! Bus 153 runs approximately hourly from Tapah to Tanah Rata; the trip takes about two hours. The fare is M$2.75 and cheaper return tickets are available. A taxi costs M$5.50.

From the taxi stand in Tanah Rata it's M$5 down to Tapah, M$10 to Ipoh, M$18 to KL, M$22 to Butterworth or just 60c per person to Brinchang. There's a daily MARA bus between Tanah Rata and KL for M$8. It departs KL at 8.30 am and arrives in Tanah Rata around 1 pm. The bus departs for KL at 2.30 pm and arrives at 7 pm. Other direct buses also run between KL and the Highlands.

There is no longer a direct bus between Tanah Rata and Butterworth, but the Town House Hotel will book tickets for the Tapah-Butterworth bus service which costs M$10 to 13 depending on the bus. You must leave Tanah Rata by 8 am in order to catch the bus which then gets you to Butterworth around 2.30 pm. Tapah is on the KL-Butterworth road and there is a railway station at Tapah Road, 20 minutes away by bus.

IPOH

The 'city of millionaires' made its fortune from the rich tin mines of the Kinta Valley.

The elegant mansions of Ipoh testify to the many successful Chinese miners. It's an ongoing process since many of the mines around Ipoh are still producing today. For the visitor Ipoh's mainly a transit town, a place where you change buses if you're heading for Pangkor Island, or where you pause to sample what is reputed to be some of the finest Chinese food in Malaysia. It's worth a longer stop to explore the Buddhist temples cut into the limestone outcrops north and south of the town. To local visitors Ipoh has another side – this is Malaysia's sin city! Ipoh is renowned for its massage parlours and strip clubs and is a frequent target of ribald comments and jokes.

Cave Temples
There are a number of cave temples both south and north of the town – several of them close to the main road so it's no problem to pause for a look. Sam Poh Tong is just six km south of Ipoh and is reputed to be one of the largest of the cave temples. There's even a restaurant in the upper part of the front facade of this ornate temple. Inside you can wander back through the caves and climb a long series of steps to a lookout over the surrounding countryside.

At Perak Tong there's a 12-metre-high seated Buddha figure and painting of Kuan Yin, the Goddess of Mercy, high on the face of the limestone cliff. Wat Thai or Meh Prasit Sumaki Temple has a 24-metre figure of the reclining Buddha, one of the largest in Malaysia.

Places to Stay – bottom end
There are plenty of hotels in all price categories in Ipoh. At the bottom end of the price scale the *Beauty Hotel* on Jalan Yang Kalsom is clean but noisy and has rooms at M$12. At number 92 on the same road the *Kowloon* is similarly priced, as is the *New Nayang* at 22. Or there's the *Embassy* at 37 Jalan Chamberlain.

Moving into the middle price bracket the *New International Hotel* (tel 05-512699) at 23-25 Jalan Toh Puah Chan has rooms from M$25-60. A very clean aircon room at the *Hotel Diamond* (tel 05-513644) at 3-9 Jalan Ali Pitchay costs M$27.50. The *Hotel Fairmont* (tel 05-511100) at 10-12 Kampar Rd is similarly priced. Finally the *Merlin Hotel* (tel 05-71351) at 92-98 Clare St has singles/doubles at M$29/39.

Places to Stay – top end
The *Hotel Excelsior Ipoh* (tel 05-536666) is on Clark St and has 133 rooms with singles/doubles at M$98/118. Other top-end hotels include the *Eastern Hotel* (tel 05-543936) at 118 Jalan Sultan Idris Shah with singles at M$69-85, doubles at M$79-95. The *Hotel Mikado* (tel 05-515855) on Jalan Yang Kalsom has rooms at very similar prices. The larger *Tambun Hotel* (tel 05-552211) at 91 Tambun Rd has singles/doubles at M$70/85 plus more expensive deluxe rooms and suites.

The town's intriguing old railway station was built in 1917 and the *Station Hotel* (tel 05-512588) is at the station on Club Rd. Rooms cost from M$40 up to M$90.

Places to Eat
Ipoh has plenty of restaurants – as well as plenty of strip clubs and massage parlours. The noodle dish known as kway teow is reputed to be better in Ipoh than anywhere else in Malaysia. Good Chinese food is found along Jalan Clare, good Malay food on Osbourne St. Ipoh-ites take their food seriously and are always ready to give an opinion on which restaurant is particularly worth trying. The *Station Hotel* does a great breakfast for M$6.

Getting There
Ipoh is on the main KL-Butterworth road – 219 km north of KL, 173 km south of Butterworth. It's M$8 to 11 by bus from KL, M$14.50 by taxi. It's marginally cheaper from Butterworth. There are buses from Ipoh to Lumut, 101 km away. The bus station is near the railway station; the taxi station is in the town centre.

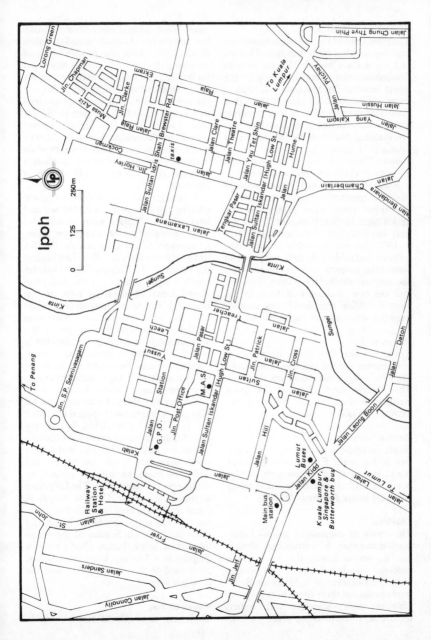

KUALA KANGSAR

The royal town of Perak state is beside the highway, north of Ipoh. A couple of km out of town is the Ubadiah Mosque with its fine golden onion-dome. It's probably the finest mosque in Malaysia although it looks almost as if it's viewed through a distorting mirror since its four minarets are squeezed up tightly against the dome. Overlooking the river is the palace or Istana Iskandariah, but it's not open to visitors. There is also an earlier istana and an intricately carved ceremonial hall.

Kuala Kangsar was the birthplace of Malaysia's great rubber industry. A number of rubber trees were planted at the agricultural station here, but it was not until the invention of the pneumatic tyre in 1888 that rubber suddenly came into demand and rubber plantations sprang up across the country – all descended from the original rubber trees here. You can still see one of those first trees in the District Office compound and another near the agriculture department office.

Places to Stay

There is a fine *Rest House* between the town centre and the mosque. It overlooks the Perak River and rooms are M$17.60. The *Double Lion Hotel* at 74 Jalan Kangsar is cheap at just M$7 but also extremely basic.

Getting There

Kuala Kangsar is 50 km north of Ipoh, beside the main KL-Butterworth road. It's 123 km south of Butterworth, 269 km north of KL. A bus from Butterworth takes 2½ hours and costs M$3.80.

TAIPING

The 'town of everlasting peace' hardly started out that. A century ago, when it was known as Larut, the town was a raucous, rough-and-tumble tin mining centre, the oldest one in Malaysia. Bitter feuds broke out three times between rival Chinese secret societies with injury, torture and death taking place on both sides. When colonial administrators finally brought the bloody mayhem under control in 1874 they took the prudent step of renaming the town. Taiping is renowned for its beautiful Lake Garden, built on the site of an abandoned tin mine right beside the town in 1890. The well-kept gardens owe some of their lush greenery to the fact that Taiping has the highest annual rainfall in Peninsular Malaysia. There's also a small zoo in the Lake Gardens while in the hills which rise above the gardens is Maxwell Hill, the oldest hill station in Malaysia.

At the far end of the gardens is a prison used by the Japanese during the war and later as a rehabilitation centre for captured Communists during the Emergency. Today it houses political detainees under the ISA (Internal Security Act) ruling. Just beyond the prison is the Taiping State Museum which is open 9 am to 5 pm daily, but closed from 12 noon to 2.30 pm on Fridays. It's the oldest museum in Malaysia and its contents include interesting exhibits on the aboriginal people of this area although its fairytale architecture is probably its most interesting aspect. Taiping actually has quite a number of well-preserved old Anglo-Malay buildings apart from misty, Chinese-looking views.

Taiping was also the starting point for Malaysia's first railway; opened in 1885 it ran 13.5 km to Port Weld, but is now closed. Taiping has an Allied war cemetery beside the Lake Garden and in the town itself there are some interesting old buildings from the colonial period, including the old town office. The Ling Nam temple is the oldest Chinese temple in Perak and has a boat figure dedicated to the Chinese emperor who built the first canal in China. On Station St there's an interesting south Indian Hindu temple. Taiping is a low-key town, no tourists, good food in the night market and the museum is great.

Places to Stay

There are a couple of rest houses in

Taiping. The *Rest House* in town is around M$10 for a double including your own bath/toilet, although it is outside the room. Breakfast is served on the verandah and the people who run it are very pleasant. The other *Rest House* is a curious mixture of Sumatran and classical Roman styles and overlooks the Lake Gardens. It's clean, secure and very cheap.

The *Lake View Hotel* (tel 06-822911) has rooms from M$15. The *Wee Bah Hotel* costs from M$10 and is, according to one traveller, 'a perfect copy of the Tye Ann in Georgetown'. There are other cheap Chinese hotels, like the *Towne Hotel* along the main street or the clean and friendly, but rather noisy, *Kwah Sheong Hotel* opposite the Lido Cinema. Taiping's large night market has many open-air eating stalls.

Getting There

Taiping is several km off the main KL-Butterworth road. It's 88 km south of Butterworth, 304 km north of KL. If you're heading south from Butterworth to Lumut for Pangkor Island and miss the direct bus it's straightforward to take a Butterworth-Taiping bus and another bus on from Taiping to Lumut.

MAXWELL HILL

The oldest hill station in Malaysia is 12 km from Taiping at an altitude of 1019 metres. It was formerly a tea estate but has now been closed and the quiet little station is simply a cool and peaceful place to be. There are no golf courses, fancy restaurants and other hill station trappings – let alone casinos. Getting up to Maxwell Hill is half the fun and once there you've got fine views down over Taiping and the Lake Gardens far below. From Cottage, the summit you can walk to from Maxwell Hill, you can see the coast all the way from Penang to Pangkor on a clear day.

Places to Stay

There are quite a number of bungalows up at Maxwell Hill and you can book them by ringing 05-886241 or by writing to the Superintendent, Tempat Peranginan, Taiping. If you've not booked earlier you can ring from the Land-Rover station at the bottom of the hill.

There are two Rest House Bungalows – *Bukit Larut (Maxwell)* and *Gunong Hijau (Speedy)* with rooms from M$18. Other bungalows are *Cempaka (Hugh Low)*, *Beringin (Watson)* and the more expensive *Cendana (Hut)* and *Tempinis (Treacher)*. They're all between the 6th and 7th milestone from the base of the hill. *Watson Rest House* is very cheap although the food is a little expensive. Meals are available at Speedy and Maxwell Rest Houses if you're day-tripping.

Getting There

Prior to WW II you had a choice of walking, pony-back or being carried up in a sedan chair for there was no road up to the station. Japanese prisoners of war were put to work building a road up at the close of the war and it was opened in 1948.

Private cars are not allowed on the road so if you want to go up it has to be in the government Land-Rovers that run a regular service from the station at the foot of the hill, just above the Taiping Lake Gardens. They operate every hour on the hour from 7 am to 6 pm and the trip takes about 40 minutes. The winding road negotiates 72 hairpin bends on the steep ascent and traffic is strictly one-way. You glimpse superb views through the trees on the way up. The up and down Land-Rovers meet at Tea Gardens, the midway point. Fares from the bottom vary from about 70c to Tea Gardens up to just over M$2 all the way to Cottage. Alternatively you can walk to the top in about three hours.

LUMUT

The Malaysian Navy will eventually have its principal base here – a replacement for the old base in Singapore. When the process is complete Lumut will be quite a different place, but meanwhile the small river port is little more than a jumping-off point for nearby Pangkor Island.

The rest house, a stone's throw from the ferry pier, used to have a small museum, but its contents were transferred to the museum in Taiping some years ago. All that's left are a group of cannons from the Dutch fort on Pangkor and a group of Malay cannons cast in Aceh in north Sumatra about 200 years ago. Lumut is the site for the 'Pesta Lumut' sea carnival in July-August each year.

At Teluk Rubiah, Manjong near Lumut, Sam Khoo of mini camp fame in Pangkor has set up a Marine Farmhouse where he intends to try to raise tiger prawns, crabs and other seafood creatures. Visitors are welcome to come and have a look at how he's doing. He may also be setting up a lodging house here.

Places to Stay & Eat

If you get marooned in Lumut because you missed the last ferry to Pangkor or something, there is a fair choice of Chinese hotels and plenty of restaurants. The *Singa Hotel* with rooms around M$10 is typical; there's good Indian food next door. The *Phi Lum Hooi Hotel*, about a half km from the bus stand, costs M$7 for a single and is very good, clean and friendly. The restaurant downstairs is decorated with a collection of shark fins! The fine old waterfront *Rest House* is M$14 a double.

Getting There

Lumut is 206 km south of Butterworth or 101 km from Ipoh, the usual place for Lumut buses if you're travelling north on the KL-Butterworth road. There are daily buses Butterworth-Lumut for M$8 or you can get a bus to Taiping about every half hour and another bus on from there. Ipoh-Lumut is probably the best way to go, however. There are buses hourly for M$3. There are also direct buses from KL to Lumut several times per day. The trip takes about six hours and costs M$11 by air-con bus. There's also a daily bus from Tapah in the Cameron Highlands to Lumut for M$8.

Long-distance taxis would be about M$15 for Butterworth-Lumut or M$7 for Ipoh-Lumut.

PANGKOR ISLAND

The island of Pangkor is close to the coast off Lumut – easily accessible via Ipoh. It's a popular resort island for its fine and often quite isolated beaches, many of which can be walked to along an interesting 'around the island' track. Taking the regular ferry service from Lumut you go out the Dindings River by the Malaysian Navy base. On the mainland coast the huge, almost Singapore-like, apartment complex has been built as naval quarters. When the base is completed and in full operation it will undoubtedly make quite a difference to Pangkor. A visit to the island is principally a 'laze on the beach' operation, but there are also a number of interesting things to do.

Information & Orientation

Finding things on Pangkor is very simple. On the east coast of the island, facing the mainland, there's a continuous village strip comprising Sungei Pinang Kechil (SPK), Sungei Pinang Besar (SPB) and Pangkor village. The ferry from Lumut stops at SPK before Pangkor village. Here you'll find restaurants and shops. The road which runs along the coast on this side turns west at Pangkor village and runs directly across the island, only a km or two wide at this point, to Pasir Bogak where you find almost all the accommodation. From here a track, suitable for motorcycles for part of its distance, runs right around the northern end of the island, reaching Pangkor's other hotel at Telok Belanga in the north-west.

Pangkor is a fairly conservative place – it's wise to behave and dress discreetly. It's also a very friendly place and travellers have written of being invited to weddings, festivals and other events.

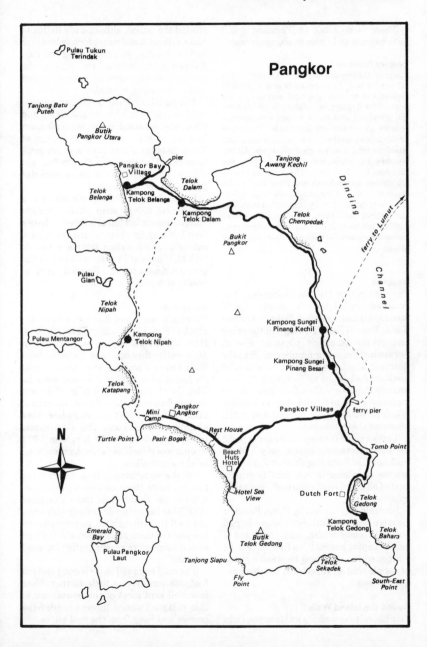

There is no bank on Pangkor; you'll have to cross to Lumut to change money.

Pangkor Problems

Pangkor has two drawbacks. For a start it can get very crowded on weekends and, to a much greater extent, during school holidays. It's a popular local resort, only a short ferry ride from the mainland and close to large population centres so crowds are inevitable. The other problem is an aesthetic one – most of the island could do with a damn good clean up. All the beaches are unpleasantly littered where the tide does not clean them. The paths and roads are strewn with rubbish and Pasir Bogak, the beach with most of the island's accommodation, is a combination of tacky, unplanned buildings and shacks and more of Pangkor's messy garbage problem. It's a shame the island is so uncared for, because basically it's a very pretty place.

Beaches

Pasir Bogak is OK for swimming, but crowded (by Malaysia's 'empty beach' standards) and, as noted, littered. Golden Sands Beach (Telok Belanga) at the other end of the island is pleasant and in between them are a number of virtually deserted beaches which you can reach by boat, on foot or on motorcycles. Unfortunately Pangkor suffers from local young men who come to sit and stare at visitors. Western women may not get too much peace on these beaches.

Turtles come in to lay their eggs at night on Telok Ketapang beach, only a short walk north of Pasir Bogak. May-June-July are the main months and June is usually best of all if you want to go midnight turtle spotting.

Emerald Bay on nearby Pulau Pangkor Laut is a beautiful little horseshoe-shaped bay with clear water, fine coral and a gently sloping beach. It's a fine place to be marooned for a day and between a group of people boat arrangements out there are quite cheap.

Round the Island Walk

Five hours' easy walking will take you right around the island, although it's better to make a day of it and pause for a swim at the various beaches you pass along the way. As you walk, admire the jungle, the monkeys and the prolific butterflies and birds – including hornbills.

The path from Pasir Bogak commences right beside Sam Khoo's Mini Camp and it's a two-hour stroll by a string of pleasant beaches to the Pangkor Bay Village at Telok Belanga. From here you can get a ferry to Lumut or, once a day, to Pangkor village. The path is used by motorcycles the rest of the way around.

From Sungei Pinang Kechil it's a continuous village strip on to Pangkor village – messy but full of interest. There's boat building, fish being dried or frozen, a colourful south Indian temple – lots to look at. Finally at Pangkor village you can grab a taxi back to Pasir Bogak if your feet won't carry you any further.

Dutch Fort

Pangkor's one bit of history is three km south of Pangkor village at Telok Gedong. Here the Dutch built a wooden fort in 1670 – after they had been given the boot from Lower Perak. In 1690 they rebuilt the fort in brick, but lost it soon afterwards. The Dutch retook the fort in 1693 but despite frequent visits did not reoccupy it until 1745 and only three years later they abandoned it for good. The old fort was totally swallowed by the jungle in 1973 when it was rebuilt as far as the remaining bricks would allow.

On the waterfront a little beyond the fort is a huge stone on which the coat of arms of the Dutch East India Company (VOC) has been inscribed along with some old graffiti. A 'thoughtful' conservationist has painted them all in green and red and added some more recent graffiti for good measure!

The road ends at Telok Gedong and the footpath continues a little further. Note how well kept most of the houses are in this village. Tubs of flowers border the houses and hang from the roof edges.

Places to Stay

Almost all Pangkor's accommodation possibilities are strung out along the beach at Pasir Bogak. On the opposite side of the island from Pangkor village, this quite pleasant stretch of beach would be a whole lot more pleasant if it were not spoilt by the tacky development taking place along it and the grubby way rubbish is allowed to collect above the high tide mark.

At the bottom end of the price scale and the far end of the beach is *Sam Khoo's Mini Camp*. It's a collection of thatched-roof huts around a central, open rest-aurant area. In the huts you've just got a bare board to sleep on and the lights all go on at dusk and off at 11 pm – no choice. There are singles, doubles and 'dorm' huts and the cost is M\$5 for singles cabins, M\$8-10 for double cabins. This is Pangkor's backpackers' centre and here you'll meet travellers from all over the world. On weekends and school holidays the mini camp can become very crowded with local students; it's much quieter on weekdays.

Moving back along the beach there's the *Pangkor Anchor* (tel 05-939363). It has 30 neatly laid-out A-frame huts with simple, mattress-on-the-floor accommodation at a cost of M\$10 per night per person. Mrs Wong, who runs the place, 'is a terrific lady – really interesting stories to tell if you can really get her stopped long enough'. The place is spotlessly clean and peaceful. Although it's often fairly busy on weekends it's sometimes more-or-less closed up on weekdays if you haven't booked ahead.

Continuing up the beach you come to the rather run-down *Rest House*. There's one room up above the restaurant for M\$10 or three 'bungalows' at M\$20 each. They're quite a bargain since they have a kitchen, lounge, bathroom and two double rooms, so between four or five people they're cheap accommodation. But they're dismal and drab in appearance and very poorly kept.

Finally at the southern end of the beach there's Pasir Bogak's more expensive establishments. Both offer perfectly adequate and fairly reasonably priced accommodation although neither take much advantage of their excellent water-front positions. A little more imagination is called for. The newer *Beach Huts Hotel* (tel 05-939359) has rooms from M\$40, more with air-con, more again with colour TV. There are also air-con chalets with TV and a fridge. The older *Sea View Hotel* (tel 05-939056) has very friendly staff and offers similar standards at very similar prices – air-con rooms or chalets with and without air-con. Prices range from M\$45-65. Both places have restaurants and bars and there are boating facilities including windsurfers at the Sea View.

Apart from Pasir Bogak there is also a place at Telok Belanga (Golden Sands Beach) at the other end of the island. The *Pangkor Bay Village* (tel 05-939091) has rooms at M\$44/50 or at M\$60/80 with air-con plus chalets at M\$130 or M\$170 with air-con. There is a variety of sporting and recreational facilities and the hotel is sited on a very pleasant stretch of beach, nicely isolated from the local development which mars Pasir Bogak. You can walk from Pasir Bogak to Telok Belanga in about two hours. The beach at the hotel is private – it's an attempt to cut down littering and to stop the local cowboys riding their motor-cycles along the beach.

Places to Eat

All the hotels offer restaurants while at Sam Khoo's you can get a reasonably filling meal at a rock bottom price. Travellers report that the food at the Rest House can be excellent – sweet & sour fish, mee hoon, even fish & chips are on offer, but be sure to fix the price first. There are a number of Chinese and Indian food stalls at the corner opposite the Beach Huts Hotel. They have good food including travellers' specials like fruit salad or pancakes.

There's a real crowd of restaurants, predominantly Chinese, at Pangkor village,

Sungei Pinang Besar and Kechil. Locals report that each place has a 'best' Chinese restaurant. In Pangkor village it's the *Yong Fon*, in SPK the *Hock Kee* and in SPB the *Wah Moi* – the latter is particularly good. If you're trekking around the island and pause for a drink at Pangkor Bay village beware of the prices – a coke will set you back a couple of dollars.

Getting There
From Lumut boats run every half hour or so from 8 am to 7.30 pm. From Pangkor to Lumut they operate 5.50 am to 6.30 pm. The trip takes 30 to 40 minutes and they also stop at Sungei Pinang Kechil (SPK), the fishing village just north of Pangkor village. Min Lian are the ferry operators and the fare is around M$1, slightly more in the newer boats.

There are also four boats a day between Lumut and Golden Sands Beach at the north-west end of the island. They cost M$1 and operate from Lumut at 8.30, 10.30 am, 1.30, 4.15 pm; to Lumut at 9.30 am, 12.30, 3.30, 5 pm. Every morning there is a Pangkor village-to-Telok Belanga service and each evening a service in the opposite direction; fare is M$1.30.

Getting Around
A taxi – they're almost all old Austin Cambridges – for the 10-minute trip from the ferry pier at Pangkor village to the accommodation at Pasir Bogak on the opposite side of the island costs about M$2.50. Direct fare to the mini camp is M$3-4, more on weekends. There are also occasional buses or you can walk it in 20 minutes. You can hire bicycles from the stalls opposite the Beach Huts Hotel. The road runs right around the eastern side of the island to Telok Belanga (Golden Sands Beach), but most of the way it's suitable for motorcycles only. From Telok Belanga a good walking track continues on to Pasir Bogak

It's quite easy to hire a boat to get out to other places – particularly Emerald Bay on Pulau Pangkor Laut. Between a group the cost is fairly reasonable. From the Sea View Hotel costs range from around M$25-40 for trips to Emerald Bay (return), South Point, Nipah Bay or Telok Belanga. You can bargain for lower prices with other boats.

PENANG
The oldest British settlement in Malaysia, predating both Singapore and Melaka, is also one of Malaysia's major tourist attractions. This is hardly surprising, for the 285-square-km island of Penang combines popular beach resorts with an intriguing and historically interesting town also noted for its superb food.

Penang's major town, Georgetown, is often referred to as 'Penang' although correctly that is the name of the island. It's a real Chinatown with far more Chinese flavour than Singapore or Hong Kong can muster today. Those larger cities have had their Chinese flavour submerged under a gleaming concrete, glass and chrome confusion, but in the older parts of Georgetown the clock seems to have stopped 50 years ago. It's an easygoing, colourful city where the bicycle-rickshaw is still the most sensible means of transport.

In 1786 Captain Francis Light acquired possession of Penang (Betelnut) Island from the local sultan on behalf of the East India Company. It's said that Light loaded his ship's cannons with silver dollars and fired them into the jungle to encourage his labourers to hack back the undergrowth. Whatever the truth of the tale he soon established the small town of Georgetown, named after King George III, with Leboh Light, Chulia, Pitt and Bishop as its boundaries. Founding towns must have been a Light family tradition because his son is credited with the founding of Adelaide in Australia; today it's a sister city to Georgetown.

Information & Orientation
Georgetown has a population of about 400,000 while that of the whole island of

Penang is 475,000. Georgetown is in the north-east of the island, where the straits between the island and the mainland are at their narrowest. A vehicle and passenger ferry service operates 24 hours a day across the three-km-wide channel between Georgetown and Butterworth on the mainland. A bridge to link the island with the mainland is on the drawing boards.

The Penang Tourist Association (tel 04-366665) is on Jalan Tun Syed Shed Barakbah, close to Fort Cornwallis in the centre of Georgetown. They are a useful information source and also produce a 50c booklet entitled *Penang for the Visitor* which is a worthwhile investment for your stay in Penang. The office is open 8.30 am to 4.30 pm Monday to Friday and 8.30 am to 1 pm on Saturdays. The immigration office is right across the roundabout from the tourist office and in this same area you'll also find a number of banks and the GPO on Leboh Downing.

Georgetown is a compact city and most places can easily be reached on foot or by bicycle-rickshaw. Two important streets to remember are Leboh Chulia and Leboh Campbell. Both run away from the ferry waterfront and terminate on Jalan Penang. You'll find most of Georgetown's popular cheap hotels along Leboh Chulia or close to it, while Leboh Campbell is one of the town's main shopping streets. Jalan Penang is another popular shopping street and in this area you'll find a number of the more expensive hotels including, at the waterfront end of Jalan Penang, the venerable Eastern & Oriental Hotel.

If you follow Jalan Penang south you'll pass the modern Kompleks Tun Abdul Razak, where the MAS office is located, and eventually leave town and continue towards the Bayan Lepas Airport. If you turned west at the waterfront end of Jalan Penang you'd run round the coastline to the popular northern beaches, including Batu Ferringhi. This road runs right round the island and would eventually bring you back into town, via the airport.

Finding your way around Georgetown is slightly complicated by the street names. Jalan Penang may also be referred to as Jalan Pinang or as Penang Rd – but there's also a Penang St, which may also be referred to as Leboh Pinang! Similarly Pitt St is sometimes called Leboh Pitt, but Leboh Chulia is always Leboh Chulia, never Chulia St.

The Penang Library is on the first floor of the Dewan Sri Pinang on Leboh Duke. It has a large collection of books of local interest and is open from 9 am to 7 pm, Mondays to Fridays and from 9 am to 4.30 pm on Saturdays. There is a good British Council library on Leboh Pinang, near the Hotel Rio. There are several fairly good bookshops along Leboh Pantai and a good one in the E&O Hotel.

Georgetown still has traces of its old duty-free image but the shops offering duty-free goods are not competitive with Singapore prices. There are also traces of Georgetown's seamier past and intrepid travellers can still find opium dens in operation. There are a lot of drugs in Georgetown, but Malaysia's penalties for drug usage are severe so beware of those trishaw riders offering a supermarket variety of illegal drugs.

Consulates Medan, the entry point from Penang to the Indonesian island of Sumatra, is counted as one of the 'usual' entry points where visitors can be issued a visa on arrival. Which is just as well, because the Indonesian Consulate in Penang has long had a reputation for being much less than helpful. The Thai Consulate, on the other hand, is a good place for obtaining Thai visas.

Indonesia
    37 Northam Rd (tel 04-25162)
Thailand
    1 Ayer Rajah Rd (tel 04-63377)
UK
    Bernam Agencies, Hong Kong Bank Chambers (3rd floor), Downing St (tel 04-21457)

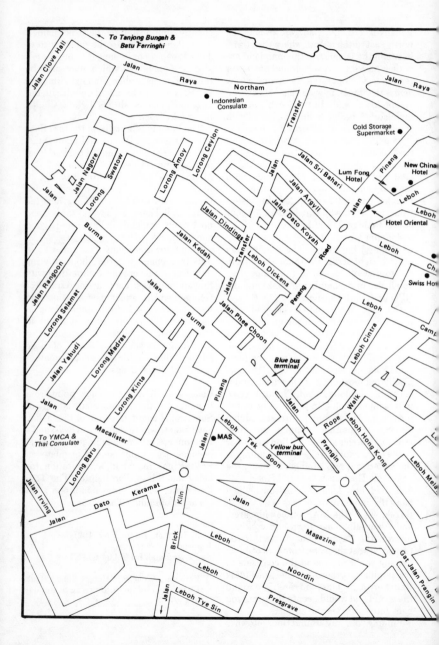

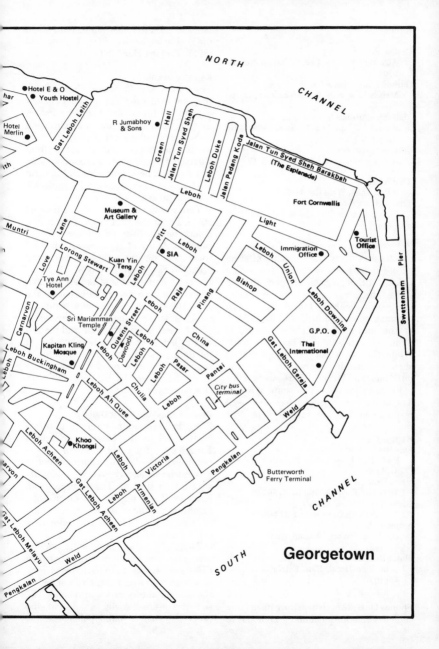

Airlines

Cathay Pacific
    AIA Building, 88 Leboh Bishop (tel 04-370411)
Garuda Indonesian Airways
    Mandarin Arcade 202 Macalister Rd (tel 04-36527)
Malaysian Airlines System
    Kompleks Tun Abdul Razak, Penang Rd (tel 04-21403)
Singapore Airlines
    AIA Building, 88 Leboh Bishop (tel 04-363201)
Thai Airways
    9 Pengkalan Weld (tel 04-67622)
Thai Airways International
    Wisma Central, 202 Macalister Rd (tel 04-64848)

Penang has many travel agents offering excellent bargains in discounted airline tickets. Although most of them are fine there are some who are not totally trustworthy. Silver Travel have been recommended, and MSL (tel 04-24748), in the lobby of the Hotel Merlin, is affiliated with Student Travel Australia. While they may not be cheapest they should certainly be reliable. See the introductory Getting There section for more on airline ticket discounters. King's Travel on Leboh Chulia has also been recommended by several travellers.

Rent-a-Cars

Avis Rent-a-Car
    E&O Hotel, 10 Leboh Farquhar (tel 04-373964)
Hertz Rent-a-Car
    38 Leboh Farquhar (tel 04-375914)
Island Taxi & Tour Agency
    40 Leboh Ah Quee (tel 04-372481)
National Car Rental
    26 Jalan Sultan Ahmad Shah (tel 04-374152)
Sintat Rent-a-Car
    Lone Pine Hotel, Batu Ferringhi (tel 04-811101)

Phones Outside of Georgetown itself (area code 04) an additional phone code has to

be used – Balik Pulau (898), Batu Uban (883), Bayan Lepas (831), Penang Hill (892), Tanjong Bungah (894).

Fort Cornwallis

The timeworn walls of Fort Cornwallis in the centre of town are one of Penang's oldest sites. It was here that Light first set foot on the virtually uninhabited island and established the free port where trade would, he hoped, be attracted from England's Dutch rivals. At first a wooden fort was built here, but between 1808 and 1810 convict labour was used to replace it with the present stone structure.

Today only the outer walls of the fort stand. The area within has been made into a park, but it's liberally studded with old cannons. Many of these were retrieved from local pirates although they were originally cast by the Dutch. Seri Rambai, the most important and largest cannon, faces the north coast and dates back to the early 1600s. It has a chequered history of being passed from the Dutch to the Sultan of Johore to the Portuguese and then to pirates before ending up here. It's famed for its procreative powers and childless women are recommended to place flowers in the barrel of 'the big one' and offer special prayers.

Penang Museum & Art Gallery

From the town's foundation site it's only a short stroll to the museum on Leboh Farquhar. In front is a statue of Light – removed by the Japanese during WW II it was retrieved and re-erected, minus its sword, after the war. The small museum has lots of old photos and documents, furniture, costumes, the medal collection of Tun Abdul Rahman and numerous other memorabilia.

There's a small, interesting section recounting the bloody wrangles between Chinese secret societies in 1867. Georgetown, it appears, suffered a near civil war before the administrators took a firm hand. The societies were heavily fined and the proceeds used to build police stations which subsequently kept the peace. The art gallery is upstairs and one of the original Penang Hill funicular railcars is displayed outside the museum.

Opening hours are 9 am to 5 pm daily except Fridays when it is closed from noon to 2.45 pm and Sundays when it is closed. Admission is free.

Kuan Yin Teng

Just round the corner from the museum on Leboh Pitt is the temple of Kuan Yin, the Goddess of Mercy. It's not a terribly impressive or interesting temple in its own right, but it's right in the centre of the old part of Georgetown and is the most popular Chinese temple in the city. Perhaps it's Kuan Yin's own reputation as a goddess on the lookout for everyone's well-being or possibly it's the presence of other well-known gods, like the God of Prosperity, that accounts for this popularity.

Whatever the reasons there's often something going on, whether it's worshippers burning paper money at the furnaces out front, a nighttime puppet or Chinese theatre performance, or simply offerings of joss sticks inside the temple. The temple was built in the 1800s by the first Chinese settlers in Penang.

Kapitan Kling Mosque

At the same time Kuan Yin's temple was being constructed, Penang's first Indian Moslem settlers set to and built this mosque at the junction of Leboh Pitt and Leboh Buckingham. In a typically Indian-influenced Islamic style the single-minareted mosque is yellow in colour.

Khoo Kongsi

The 'Dragon Mountain Hall' is situated in Cannon Square close to the end of Leboh Pitt. A kongsi is a clan house, a building part-temple and part-meeting hall for Chinese of the same clan or surname. Penang has many kongsis but this one, the clan house of the Khoos, is easily the finest. Its construction was first considered around 1853, but it was not built until

1898. The completed building was so magnificent and elaborate that nobody was surprised when the roof caught fire on the very night it was completed! That misfortune was simply interpreted as a message from above that they'd really been overdoing things, so the Khoos rebuilt it in a marginally less grandiose style. The present kongsi, dating from 1906 and extensively renovated in the 1950s, is a rainbow of dragons, statues, paintings, lamps, coloured tiles and carvings – it's one part of colourful Penang which definitely should not be missed.

Although the Khoo Kongsi is far and away the best known kongsi in Georgetown, there are a number of others, including the modern Lee Kongsi on Burma Rd, the combined kongsi of the Chuah, Sin and Quah clans at the corner of Burma Rd and Codrington Avenue, the Khaw Kongsi on Burma Rd and the Yap Kongsi on Armenian St.

Sri Mariamman Temple

Queen St runs parallel to Leboh Pitt, and about midway between the Kuan Yin Temple and the Kapitan Kling Mosque you'll find another example of Penang's religious diversity. The Sri Mariamman Temple is a typical south Indian temple with its elaborately sculptured and painted gopuram towering over the entrance. Built in 1883, it's the oldest Hindu temple in Georgetown and testifies to the strong Indian influence you'll also find in this most Chinese of towns.

Wat Chayamangkalaram

At Burma Lane, just off the road to Batu Ferringhi, is this major Thai temple, the Temple of the Reclining Buddha. It's a brightly coloured and painted temple and houses a 32-metre-long reclining Buddha, loudly proclaimed in Penang as the third longest in the world – you can take that claim with a pinch of salt since there's at least one larger in Malaysia plus at least one in Thailand and two in Burma. Nevertheless, it's a colourful and picturesque temple and there's a Burmese Buddhist temple directly across the road from it, with two large stone elephants flanking the gates.

Penang Buddhist Association

Completed in 1929 this is a most unusual Chinese Buddhist temple. Instead of the usual gaudy and colourful design of most Chinese temples it is quiet, tasteful and refined. The Buddha statues are carved from Italian marble, and glass chandeliers, made in Penang, hang from above. It's on Anson Rd.

Other Temples, Mosques & Churches

Close to the Kapitan Kling Mosque, the Malay mosque on Acheen St is unusual for its Egyptian-style minaret – most Malay mosques have Moorish minarets. Also in the centre, St George's Church on Leboh Farquhar was built in 1818 and is the oldest Anglican church in South-East Asia. The gracefully proportioned church with its marble floor and towering spire was built by convict labour. Also on Leboh Farquhar is the double-spired Cathedral of the Assumption. The cemetery nearby tells the usual wistful story of the early deaths of English administrators and their families.

The Shiva temple on Jalan Dato Keramat is hidden behind a high wall, but the Nattukotai temple on Waterfall Rd is the largest Hindu temple in Penang and is dedicated to Bala Subramaniam. On Perak Rd, Wat Buppharam is the oldest Thai temple in Penang and has a pagoda and two 30-metre-long dragons. Out at Tanjong Tokong the Tua Pek Kong Temple is dedicated to the God of Prosperity and dates from 1837. Finally the Penang State Mosque at Ayer Itam is glossy and new and there are good views from the 50-metre-high minaret.

Kek Lok Si Temple

On a hilltop at Ayer Itam, close to the funicular station for Penang Hill, stands the largest Buddhist temple in Malaysia.

Construction commenced in 1890 and took more than 20 years to complete. It's really more of a tourist attraction than a temple and you climb up through arcades of souvenir stalls, past a tightly packed turtle pond and murky fish ponds until you reach the Ban Hood or 'Ten Thousand Buddhas' Pagoda. A 'voluntary' contribution is the price to climb to the top of the seven-tier, 30-metre-high tower which is said to be Burmese at the top, Chinese at the bottom and Thai in between.

Around Georgetown

Georgetown is a delight to simply wander around at any time of day. Set off in any direction and you're certain to find plenty of interest, whether it's the beautiful old Chinese houses, an early morning vegetable market, a temple ceremony, the crowded shops or a late pasar malam or night market.

Jalan Penang and Jalan Campbell are the main shopping streets with modern air-conditioned shops, but it's along the more old-fashioned streets like Leboh Chulia or Rope Walk that you'll find the unusual bargains – like a 'Beware of the Dog' sign that adds the warning in Malay (Awas – Ada Anjing) and in Chinese ideograms. At the Leboh Farquhar end of Jalan Penang there are a string of handicraft and antiques shops.

Trishaws are the ideal way of getting around Georgetown, particularly at night when trishaw travel takes on an almost magical property. All the usual Chinese events are likely to be taking place at any time – a funeral procession with what looks like a run-down Dixieland jazz band leading the mourners, colourful parades at festival times, trishaws wobbling by with whole families aboard, ancient grandmas pushing out their stalls to set up for a day's business. All around you'll hear those distinctively Chinese noises – the clatter of mahjong tiles from inside houses, the trilling of caged songbirds, loud arguments and conversations, for Chinese is no quiet language.

Nor can you miss Georgetown's other inhabitants. Dark-skinned Tamils from the south of India cool boiled milk by nonchalantly hurling it through the air from one cup to another. Money changing is almost exclusively an Indian enterprise and a stocky Sikh with an antique-looking gun can be seen guarding many banks or jewellery shops. Altogether Georgetown is a place where there's always something of interest.

Penang Hill

Rising 830 metres above Georgetown, the top of Penang Hill provides a cool retreat from the sticky heat below – it's generally about 5°C cooler than at sea level. From the summit you've got a spectacular view over the island and across to the mainland.

There are pleasant gardens, a small cafe and a hotel as well as a choice of a Hindu temple or a Moslem mosque on the top. Penang Hill is particularly pleasant at dusk as Georgetown starts to light up, far below.

The idea of a hill resort here was first mooted towards the end of the last century, but the first attempt at a mountain railway was a dismal failure. In 1923 a Swiss-built funicular railway system was completed and the tiny cable-pulled cars have trundled up and down ever since. The trip takes half an hour with a change of train at the halfway point. A few years ago the original funicular cars were changed for more modern ones, but the queues on weekends and public holidays can be as long as ever.

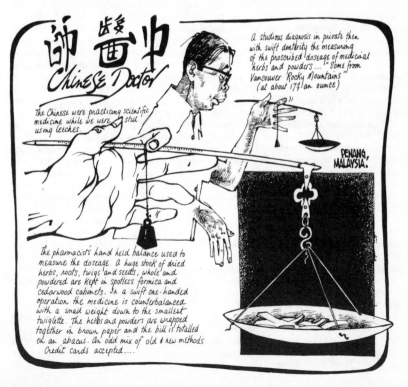

帥 醫 中

Chinese Doctor

The Chinese were practicing scientific medicine while we were still using leeches.

A studious diagnosis in private then with swift dexterity the measuring of the proscribed doseage of medicinal herbs and powders.... "Some from Vancouver Rocky Mountains" (at about 17$ an ounce)

PENANG, MALAYSIA.

The pharmacist's hand held balance used to measure the doseage. A huge stock of dried herbs, roots, twigs and seeds, whole and powdered are kept in spotless formica and cedarwood cabinets. In a swift one-handed operation the medicine is counterbalanced with a small weight down to the smallest twiglette. The herbs and powders are wrapped together in brown paper and the bill is totalled on an abacus. An odd mix of old & new methods Credit cards accepted....

Getting There Take a number 1 bus from Pengkalan Weld to Ayer Itam (every five minutes, 55c), then a number 8 to the funicular station (30c). The ascent of the hill costs M$3 for the round trip. There are departures every 15 minutes from 6.30 to 8.30 am and then every 30 minutes to 9.30 pm from the bottom, 9.15 pm from the top. There are later departures until midnight on Wednesdays and Saturdays. The energetic can get to the top by an interesting eight-km hike starting from the Moon Gate at the Botanical Gardens.

Around Ayer Itam

Ayer Itam Dam, three km from Kek Lok Si, has an 18-hectare lake. It's one of several reservoirs on the island. Penang's largest Hindu temple, the Nattukotai Chettiar, is on top of a hill beyond the dam. There's a good view from the top, 233 metres above sea level. This is the most important site in Penang for ceremonies during the Thaipusam festival.

Botanical Gardens

Penang's 30-hectare botanical gardens are situated off Waterfall Rd and are also known as the Waterfall Gardens after the stream that cascades through them down from Penang Hill. They've also been dubbed the Monkey Gardens due to the many monkeys that appear on the lawn for a feed early each morning and late each afternoon. The gardens also have a small zoo and from them a path leads up Penang Hill.

Festivals

All the usual festivals are celebrated in Penang, but some with special energy. In December the annual Pesta Pulau Penang or Penang Islands Festival is highlighted by colourful dragon boat races. There are also parades, carnivals and all the fun of the fair. The masochistic Hindu festival of Thaipusam is celebrated in Penang with a fervour to rival Singapore and Kuala Lumpur but without quite the same crowds. The Nattukotai temple on

Waterfall Rd is the main centre in Penang for the activities.

At Chinese New Year a wayang or Chinese opera takes place at the snake temple near Bayan Lepas. The number of snakes in residence is also said to be highest at that time of year. The tourist office can tell you what festivals are approaching, where events occur and can also offer information about their origins and significance.

Places to Stay – bottom end

Hotels There are a great number of cheap hotels around Georgetown, some of them very pleasant. Stroll down Leboh Chulia, Leith St or Love Lane and you'll trip over them. Some of the most popular include the long-running *New China Hotel* on Leith St where singles cost M$9-10.50, doubles M$11.50-15. There's also a somewhat airless dorm at M$5.50. The whole place is very clean, particularly the toilets, but the bar in the back can be a bit noisy at times. There is also a restaurant serving western food and breakfasts – the food is OK although the prices are a little high. The New China is 'kept almost rat free by an impressive legion of cats'.

Two other popular places with similar standards to the New China are the *Swiss Hotel* on Leboh Chulia and the *Eng Aun*, directly across the road from it. The Swiss Hotel has rooms at M$11.50 single, M$15 double; upstairs there are rooms at M$19.60. The Eng Aun charges M$10.35 single or double and now also has a travel agency downstairs. Both of these spacious hotels attract a steady stream of travellers and have large car parks in front (as does the New China) – which also insulates them from street noise.

There are also a couple of places close to the New China with similar standards. The *Lum Fong*, right next door, has an excellent restaurant downstairs and singles/doubles at M$10.50/16.50. Facing it across Leboh Muntri you'll find the *Modern Hotel* with single or double rooms at M$16.50, two beds. It's 'excellent, roomy, cheap and clean' reported one traveller, but another added that it was 'friendly but noisy'. Also nearby, at the corner of Penang Rd and Jalan Argyll is the *Hock Beng*, kitty corner from the Oriental, with rooms at M$14 to 15.

Back on Chulia at 509 is the *Eastern Hotel*, a good, clean place and they speak English. Singles or doubles are M$16. Next door is the more basic *Han Chow* run by Indians. Prices are M$14/16 and there is a restaurant downstairs.

Further down Leboh Chulia at 381 is the *Nam Wah*. It's big, old and funky but OK. Rooms are M$10, those at the back are quiet. At the next corner detour round the *Sky*, where the manager is unhelpful. At 362 there's the *Yeng Keng Hotel* with big, cool rooms. They're quiet because it's off the street. Singles/doubles are M$10.35/11.50.

Still further down Leboh Chulia from the Swiss and Eng Aun there are other places, some even cheaper. The *Yee Hing Hotel* at 302 was 'the best value of my entire trip', according to one traveller; adding that the popular restaurant downstairs had a menu which featured a 'baked bean on toast'. They're friendly and it's certainly cheap at M$6.80 single, M$8 double, although not the best-kept place around. At 282 the *Tye Ann* is very popular, particularly for its breakfasts downstairs in the restaurant section. Rooms cost M$10.50 single or double and there are also M$4.50 dorm beds.

Round the corner on Lorong Pasar, behind the Goddess of Mercy Temple, the very friendly *Noble Hotel* has a novel approach. They charge M$12 for a room – for as many people as you want to cram in. The *Hotel Chung King* is at 398 Chulia directly opposite Leboh Cintra – you can only see the sign from across the street. It's cheap but noisy.

Love Lane is another popular hotel street, right off Leboh Chulia. The *Pin Seng* at 82 is OK although the rooms in the new wing tend to be noisy and hot. It's all good and clean though, and the old section

is quiet. Rooms are M$11.50. At 35 Love Lane the *Wan Hai* (tel 61421) costs just M$9.50.

On nearby Rope Walk there are a number of places, usually a bit dingy and/or short-time centres. The *Choong Thean* is OK. The *Kim Sun* at 86 Leboh Campbell near Leboh Cintra is an average sort of place at M$11.50. Burma Road also has a few hotels like the *Hotel Kim Wah* at 114 where a room with bath and fan costs M$19.80 and it is 'central, clean, has a restaurant and the short-time ladies are well in evidence'. Another is the *Tong Lok* which is owned by the New China Hotel and sometimes used by them as an overflow place. There are many, many other hotels around Georgetown. Over on Leboh Light at the corner of King is *Hotel Pathe*, a large place with rooms at M$27 with bath. The *Wen Hai*, between Chulia and Leboh Light, is just M$8.50/11.50 and there's a dorm for M$4.50. It's a quiet place with a travel agency downstairs and small, interesting industrial-type shops next door. Western breakfasts are available across the street. Look around and you'll discover many others.

The Ys Penang has a conveniently situated, but extremely anonymous, *Youth Hostel* right next door to the gracious old E&O Hotel on Leboh Farquhar. The only clue to its existence is a sign proclaiming 'no visitors'. Periodically it's reported to have closed down completely, but it always seems to reappear. First night cost for a dorm bed is M$2.50, subsequent nights are M$2.20.

The *YMCA* (tel 04-362211) is a little inconveniently situated at 211 Jalan Macalister – get there on a number 7 bus. It is, however, conveniently close to the Thai Embassy; an important Penang address for many travellers. Singles/doubles cost M$17/22 or M$20/26 with air-con. All rooms have attached showers and there are also dorms at M$7 per person. Unfortunately they tend to fill up the noisy dorm rooms in the front before starting on the quieter ones at the back. There's a M$1 temporary membership charge for non-members of the YMCA, but this can be waived if you're a YHA member or have a student card. The YMCA also has a TV lounge and cafeteria. Finally the *YWCA* is much further out at 8A Green Lane and, unlike the YMCA, it's single sex only.

Places to Stay – middle

For a bit of a splurge you can stay at the wonderful-looking *Cathay Hotel*, halfway between the Oriental and the Merlin near the New China Hotel. The lobby nearly equals the exterior. Prices are M$31.20 doubles, M$36 with air-con, M$26.40 singles with attached bath. Also a bit pricier is the *Prince* at 456 Chulia. It's modern, all air-con and the M$40 rooms feature piped-in music. The guy at the desk told me they could find me 'some company to share my room'. Other middle-bracket air-con hotels include the *Federal* on Penang Rd at M$34.50 and the *Hotel Fortuna*, also on Penang Rd, at M$34/38.

In this same price bracket you could try the *Peking Hotel* (tel 04-22455) at 50A Penang Rd or the slightly more expensive *United Hotel* (tel 04-21361) at 101 Macalister Rd. More expensive again, the *Hotel Waterfall* (tel 04-27221) is at 160 Western Rd. At 48F Northam Rd the *Paramount Hotel* (tel 04-63773) has singles at M$20-35, doubles M$25-45. The *Singapore Hotel* at 495H Penang Rd has large and well-furnished air-con rooms with a shower from around M$20.

Places to Stay – top end

Penang's biggest hotels are out at Batu Ferringhi. In Georgetown itself you mainly find the older hotels or the second-string places. Grandest (and oldest?) is the fine old *Eastern & Oriental*, one of those superb old establishments in the Raffles manner – indeed it was built by the Sarkies brothers who also constructed the Raffles and the Strand in Rangoon. The

E&O was built in 1885. Located right on the waterfront, it has beautiful gardens down to the water and has featured in several Somerset Maugham stories.

While Leboh Chulia is the main street in Georgetown for cheap hotels, Penang Rd is where you find most of the more expensive places. Virtually across the road from the E&O and at the top of Penang Rd is the much more modern *Merlin*, topped by a revolving restaurant – great views over Georgetown. Other central hotels include the *Ming Court Penang*, the *Central* and the pleasant and very reasonably priced *Oriental*. On top of Penang Hill there's the small *Bellevue Hotel*, formerly known as the Penang Hill Hotel, which is not only small and quiet with a delightful garden but also very tastefully decorated – due to its owner being one of Malaysia's foremost architects.

Hotel Ambassador (tel 04-24101), 55 Penang Rd, 78 rooms, singles from M$65, doubles from M$75

Bellevue Hotel (tel 04-892256), Penang Hill, 12 rooms, singles M$60, doubles M$80

Hotel Central (tel 04-21432), 404 Penang Rd, 140 rooms, singles M$60, doubles M$70

Hotel Continental (tel 04-26381), 5 Penang Rd, 120 rooms, singles M$66, doubles M$76

Eastern & Oriental Hotel (tel 04-63543), 10 Farquhar St, 100 rooms, singles M$120-160, doubles M$140-180, also cheaper rooms not facing the sea

Hotel Malaysia (tel 04-363311), 7 Penang Rd, 126 rooms, singles M$66-76, doubles M$76-86

Ming Court Penang (tel 04-26131), 202A Macalister Rd, 98 rooms, singles M$110-120, doubles M$120-30

Oriental Hotel (tel 04-24211), 105 Penang Rd, 100 rooms, singles M$54-59, doubles M$61-66

Penang Merlin Hotel (tel 04-23301), 25A Farquhar St, 144 rooms, singles M$115-135, doubles M$140-150

Towne House Hotel (tel 04-65133), 70 Penang Rd, 50 rooms, singles M$70, doubles M$85

Places to Eat

Penang is another of the region's delightful food trips with a wide variety of restaurants and many local specialities to tempt you. There are two types of soup particularly associated with Penang which are known as laksa. Laksa assam is a fish soup with a sour taste from the tamarind or assam paste. The soup is served with special white laksa noodles. Laksa lemak was originally a Thai dish, but has been adopted by Penang. It's basically similar to laksa assam except coconut milk is substituted for the tamarind. Seafood is, of course, very popular in Penang and there are many restaurants that specialise in fresh fish, crabs and prawns – particularly along the northern beach fringe.

Despite its Chinese character Penang also has a strong Indian presence and there are some popular specialities to savour. Curry kapitan is a Penang chicken curry which supposedly takes its name from a Dutch sea captain asking his Indonesian mess boy what was on that night. The answer was 'curry kapitan' and it's been on the menu ever since. Murtabak, a thin roti chanai pastry stuffed with egg, vegetables and meat, is not a Penang speciality, but it's a dish done with particular flair here.

Indian Food Amongst the most popular Indian restaurants is *Dawood's* at 63 Queen St, opposite the Sri Mariamman Temple. Curry kapitan is just one of the many curry dishes at this popular and reasonably priced restaurant, and is priced at M$2.60. Beer is not available, but the lime juice is excellent and so is the ice cream. Recently, however, Dawood's standards seem to have been sliding downhill. At 166 Campbell St the *Meerah* and at 164A the *Hameediyah* both have good curries and delicious murtabak.

On the corner of King and Bishop Sts you can get a whole selection of curry dishes plus rice and chappatis at *Rio*. The *Taj Mahal Restaurant* on the corner of Jalan Penang and Leboh Chulia is another

place for murtabak, but this is also an excellent place for a quick snack of roti chanai with a dahl dip – a cheap and nourishing meal at any time of the day. Near the corner of Leboh Chulia and Jalan Pinang the *Islamik Restaurant* has delicious food, particularly the murtabaks and biriyanis.

At *Poshni's*, on the corner of Leboh Light and Leboh Penang, you can get traditional Malay food. There's a wide selection and it's reasonably cheap. This is one of the few real Malay restaurants in Georgetown. The outdoor restaurants at 62 and 38 Macalister Rd also do good Malaysian food

Chinese Food There are so many Chinese restaurants in Penang that making any specific recommendations is really rather redundant. On Syed Sheh, behind the library and cultural centre, the *Seaview Restaurant* has good breakfast dim sum. On Leboh Cintra the *Hong Kong Restaurant* is good, cheap and varied and has a menu in English. At the corner of Leboh Cintra and Campbell St the *Restoran Chup Seng* has excellent chicken rice – as do many of Georgetown's 'excellent Hainanese chicken rice' purveyors. The *Sin Kuan Hiwa Cafe*, on the corner of Chulia and Leboh Cintra, is one that specialises in this.

More good Chinese food can be found at *Dragon King* on the corner of Leboh Bishop and Leboh Pitt which specialises in the not-so-easily-found Nonya cuisine. Or try *Sun Hoe Peng* at 25 Leboh Light. The *Wing Lok*, 300 Penang Rd, is more costly but good. They offer a steamboat for four people at M$20. Give them a day's notice.

Breakfasts & Western Food At breakfast time the popular travellers' hangout is the *Tye Ann Hotel* on Leboh Chulia. Every day crowds of people visit this friendly little establishment for its excellent porridge, toast & marmalade and other breakfast favourites. The manager at the front desk is permanently wreathed with that rarest of Chinese sights – a smile. Western breakfasts are also available at the New China, Eng Aun, Swiss and across from the Wan Hai.

At the *Cold Storage Supermarket* on Jalan Penang you can find all the usual supermarket goodies. The *Super Emporium* on Burma Rd also stocks them. The *Magnolia Snack Bar*, a little further up Jalan Penang, is an excellent place for a hamburger or some other reminder of home. They've also got a wide selection of ice cream flavours. *Diner's Bakery*, across from the Meerah restaurant on Campbell St, has great baked goods ranging from cheesecake to wholemeal bread.

There's more good seafood at *Maple Gardens* on Penang Rd. It's a little high priced if economy is on your mind, but the food is good, the servings large and you select your fish straight from the tank. *Kwikie Fast Food* at 276 Penang Rd has also been recommended. Burma Rd has a number of places and quite a few western fast food joints including an Italian fried chicken place.

Night Markets Georgetown has a wide selection of street stalls with nightly gatherings at places like Gurney Drive or along the Esplanade. The latter is particularly good for trying local Penang specialities. The big night market, 7-11 pm, changes venue every two weeks; check at the tourist office as to current location. Cold fruit, cakes, pancakes, noodles, laksa, are all on sale. Medicated tea is a popular item and one Georgetown tea stall has a sign announcing that it will cure everything from 'headache, stomach ache and kidney trouble' to 'malaria, cholera and' (wait for it) 'fartulence'.

Getting There

Air Penang is connected by MAS to Kota Bahru, Kuala Lumpur and other cities within Malaysia – see the introductory Getting Around section for details of airfares. Internationally MAS and Garuda fly to Medan in Sumatra – a very popular route for travellers. MAS and SIA have regular flights to Singapore. MAS and Thai Airways or Thai International fly between Penang and Hat Yai, Phuket and Bangkok. Other international connections include direct flights to Hong Kong with Cathay Pacific or to Madras in India with MAS. See the introductory Getting There section for fare details.

Penang is a major centre for cheap airline tickets, but there have also been numerous cut-and-run merchants at work. You'll hear lots of stories of rip-offs. The western agents operating in Georgetown seem to be as much to blame as anybody else so relying on your own is no insurance. Ask around and be careful although Penang is, overall, a good place for buying tickets. Fares tend to vary with the airline; the cheapest tickets to London, for example, will be with Aeroflot or Bangladesh Biman, but some typical prices from Penang include:

Medan	M$ 96
Madras	M$ 570
Hat Yai	M$ 51
Phuket	M$ 106
Bangkok	M$ 257
Hong Kong	M$ 595
London	M$ 750-1000
USA West	M$1150
Australia East	M$ 975

Other quoted fares include Singapore-Jakarta M$230 one-way or M$375 return, Bangkok-Kathmandu M$476, Kuala Lumpur-Perth M$700. Interesting multi-stop or return fares can also be found. If you want to visit Australia from Malaysia then M$1650 will take you Penang-Perth-Melbourne-Penang. You could take the southern Pacific route Singapore-Jakarta-Noumea-Sydney-Noumea-Auckland-Papeete-Los Angeles for M$1750. Multi-stop fares to Europe or through Asia are not so easy, but you could do Penang-Bangkok-Delhi for M$625 with extensions on to Europe. A Bangkok-Rangoon-Dacca-Kathmandu ticket would cost

Top: Cheng Hoon Teng Temple, Melaka (TW)
Bottom: children on the beach, Pangkor Island (TW)

Top: Wat Chayamangkalaram, Georgetown, Penang (TW)
Left: Kuan Yin Teng, Georgetown, Penang (TW)
Right: Leboh Campbell at night, Georgetown, Penang (TW)

M$455. A two-night stopover in beautiful Dacca costs extra.

Rail The introductory Getting There and Getting Around sections have full details on fares and schedules for Butterworth-Kuala Lumpur-Singapore services and the international train services to Hat Yai and Bangkok in Thailand. The station is by the Butterworth ferry terminal and you can make reservations there (tel 04-347962) or at the Railway Booking Station (tel 04-360290) at the Ferry Terminal, Weld Quay, Georgetown. There are good left luggage facilities at Butterworth station.

Bus The bus terminal is also beside the ferry terminal in Butterworth. For long distance bus information contact MARA – phone 04-345021 or 04-349865. Some travel agents in Georgetown (the one in the Eng Aun hotel for example) offer good bargains on bus tickets. Typical fares are Ipoh M$12, Kuala Lumpur M$13-15, Singapore M$25-27, Kota Bahru M$17-20, Tapoh M$12.50, Kuantan M$23. The fairly new route connecting Kota Bahru on the east coast takes about seven hours by bus. There are also bus services out of Malaysia to Hat Yai for M$20 (and about another M$30 to Bangkok), to Phuket M$42, to Ko Samui M$48.

To Kuala Perlis, for the Langkawi ferry, the bus is M$5. To Lumut, for Pangkor Island, it is M$7.

Taxis Yes, the long-distance taxis also operate from a depot beside the Butterworth ferry terminal. It's also possible to book them at some of the hot spot backpacker hotels or directly with drivers. Typical fares include Alor Setar M$7, Ipoh M$14, Kuala Lumpur M$30, Cameron Highlands M$30. Kota Bahru doesn't yet seem to be a main taxi run; fare should be about M$30. There are Thai taxis operating to Hat Yai too – a convenient way of getting across the border. They're usually big old Chevies and you'll find them at the

popular cheap hotels –fare is around M$25.

Sea There are two interesting possibilities for arriving or departing from Penang (and Malaysia) by sea. See the introductory Getting There section for details on the regular scheduled service between Penang and Madras in India. The Shipping Corporation of India agents in Georgetown are R Jumabhoy & Sons, 39 Green Hall, just off Leboh Light.

Yacht departures are less regular although they're fairly easy to find. There are often yachts passing through Penang looking for paying passengers, most often to Phuket in Thailand but also further afield to places like Sri Lanka. Some run almost regular services between Penang and Phuket, only a few days north. You'll find ads and notices pinned to the wall in the cheap hotels and restaurants along Leboh Chulia. One worth looking for is the *Szygie* which may still be operating between Penang and Phuket on six-day trips departing on the 7th and 21st of each month.

Getting Around
Airport Transport Penang's Bayan Lepas Airport with its new, but plain and simple, Minangkabau-style terminal is 18 km south of Georgetown. A coupon system operates for taxis from the airport. The fare to Georgetown should be M$15, to Batu Ferringhi M$20. You can get a yellow 66 bus to the airport for M$1.50. Taxis take about 30 minutes from the centre of town, the bus an hour.

Ferry There's a 24-hour ferry service between Georgetown and Butterworth on the mainland. Passenger ferries and ferries for cars and trucks operate from adjacent terminals. Ferries operate as frequently as every seven minutes for most of the day, but slow down to once each 30 minutes from 2 to 5.30 am. The vehicular ferries operate only slightly less frequently, but do not operate at all between 10 pm (10.20 pm from Penang) and 6.30 am, except on Saturdays, Sundays and public holidays when they continue to 1.30 am.

Fares are only charged between Penang and Butterworth; the other direction is free. Adults cost 40c, cars with driver cost from M$4 to M$6 depending on the engine capacity. A Butterworth-Georgetown bridge is on the drawing board.

Buses There are three main bus departure points in Georgetown and five types of buses. The city buses (MPPP Buses) all depart from the terminal at Leboh Victoria which is directly in front of the ferry terminal. Fares range from 25 to 55c and the main routes are:

1	Ayer Itam – every 5 minutes, 55c
2	Bagan Jermal –every 10 minutes, 45c
3	Jelutong – every 5 minutes, 45c
4	Jalan Yeap Chor Ee via Jalan Perak – every 10 minutes, 55c
5	Green Lane via Dhoby Ghaut – every 30 minutes, 55c
6	Green Lane via Jalan Patani – every 15 minutes, 55c
7	Botanical Gardens – every 30 minutes, 50c
8	Penang Hill Railway from Ayer Itam – 30c
9	Green Lane via Caunter Hall Rd – every 15 minutes, 55c
10	Kampung Melayu – every 15 minutes, 55c
11	Bukit Glogor – every 60 minutes, 55c
12	Ayer Itam from Jelutong – every 20 minutes, 30c
13	Bagan Jermal from Jelutong – every 30 minutes, 40c

From Pengkalan Weld, the waterfront road by the ferry terminal, you can take Sri Negara Buses around Georgetown. The other main stand is at Jalan Maxwell where you can take green, blue or yellow buses. These are the buses you take if you want to do a circuit of the island or get out to Batu Ferringhi and the other northern beaches. The green buses run to Ayer Itam like the number 1 MPPP bus. Blue buses run to the northern beaches although a change of bus is required at Tanjong Bungah. Yellow buses run to the south and west of the island including the aquarium, snake temple, airport and right round to Telok Bahang.

Taxis Penang's taxis officially cost 70c for the first mile and 30c for each additional half mile, but in practice they are none too keen on operating on the meter and you may have to bargain fares, particularly for longer trips. Meter fares can be loaded by 50% from 1 to 6 am. Some sample fares from Georgetown are Batu Ferringhi M$12, Botanical Gardens M$6, Penang Hill/Kek Lok Si M$8, Snake Temple M$12, airport M$15.

Trishaws Bicycle-rickshaws are ideal on Georgetown's relatively uncrowded streets and cost around 40 or 50c per half mile. The fare table displayed on each trishaw doesn't have too much connection to reality – you must agree on the fare before departure. If you come across from Butterworth on the ferry, grab a trishaw to the Leboh Chulia cheap hotels area for M$2 although you can walk there in five or 10 minutes. The riders will know plenty of other hotels if your selected one should be full. For touring, the rate is M$8 an hour.

Bicycles If you want to pedal yourself you can hire bicycles from various places. The Eng Aun Hotel in Georgetown has them for M$5 per day or there are various places at Batu Ferringhi where you can hire them at rather more expensive rates. The New China has a couple of bikes, or try Hire a Bicycle at 206 Prangin Rd, just off Penang Rd. You can also try renting from any repair shops you see around town. They sometimes have the big, heavy-duty grocery bikes at a good rate. Motorcycles can also be hired for around M$30 per day.

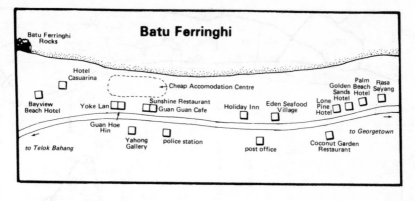

Batu Ferringhi

Batu Ferringhi Rocks

Hotel Casuarina

Cheap Accomodation Centre

Golden Palm Rasa
Sands Beach Sayang
Hotel Hotel

Bayview Beach Hotel

Yoke Lan

Sunshine Restaurant
Guan Guan Cafe

Holiday Inn

Eden Seafood Village

Lone Pine Hotel

Guan Hoe Hin

Yahong Gallery

police station

post office

Coconut Garden Restaurant

to Georgetown

to Telok Bahang

Tours Many companies offer local tours; you'll see sandwich boards along the sidewalks. MSL Travel in the lobby of the Merlin Hotel is reliable and has a 3½-hour tour for M$18. A Penang Hill trip, including the train up, takes four hours and costs M$27. The tourist office also has official guides for personal tours.

PENANG – BEACHES
Penang's beautiful beaches are really somewhat over-rated. They're not as beautiful, as clean or as spectacular as the tourist literature would make out. Beaches close to the city also suffer to some extent from pollution. The beaches along the north coast are the most visited and the most accessible.

They start at the small village of Tanjong Tokong and extend along the north coast to Telok Bahang. Tanjong Bungah (Cape of Flowers) is the first real beach, but it's not attractive for swimming. A little further along the coast Batu Ferringhi (Foreigner's Rock) is the resort strip with a number of large hotels. The beach itself is somewhat of a disappointment compared to other beaches in Malaysia and the water is not of the tropically-clear variety you might expect. At the western end the beach slopes off more gradually and the swimming is better.

At the end of this northern beach strip is

Telok Bahang (Glowing Bay) where there is little development and it's still principally a small fishing village. There are other beaches around the south of the island, but these are not easily accessible without your own transport.

Places to Stay – Tanjong Bungah
There are a number of small Chinese hotels and restaurants along the coast from Georgetown, but Tanjong Bungah is the first real beach you come to. It's not really swim-able, despite which there's the new *Orchard Penang* hotel (tel 04-891111) recently constructed at the Georgetown end of the beach. It has 323 rooms with singles at M$145-175, doubles at M$170-200.

Closer to the village and bus stop is the small *Loke Thean Hotel* with rooms at M$18. Directly opposite the bus stand is the *Eden Hotel* with rooms from around M$10.

Places to Eat – Tanjong Bungah
The beachfront *Eden Hotel* is renowned for its excellent, though a little expensive, seafood. There's also the *Hollywood*, with a variety of dishes including European and Chinese, while on the hillside above the road is the *Seri Batik* restaurant which serves Malay food.

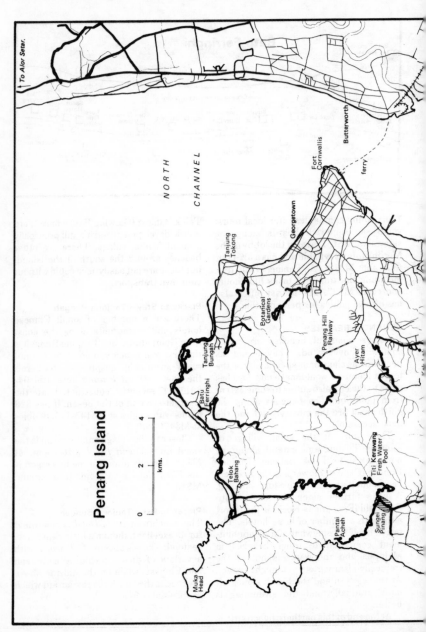

Penang Island

To Alor Setar

NORTH CHANNEL

Butterworth

ferry

Fort Cornwallis

Georgetown

Tanjung Tokong

Botanical Gardens

Penang Hill Railway

Ayer Hitam

Tanjung Bungah

Batu Ferringhi

Telok Bahang

Pantai Acheh

Titi Kerawang Fresh Water Pool

Sungei Pinang

Muka Head

kms.

0   2   4

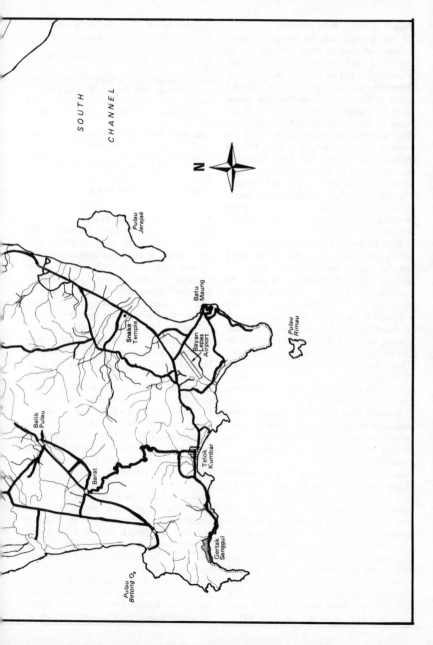

Places to Stay – Batu Ferringhi

At the bottom end of the price scale, accommodation at Batu Ferringhi is all unofficial and all found in the Batu Ferringhi village, at the end of the international hotel strip. If you wander along to the group of restaurants across from the Yahong Gallery you'll soon find a room in the village for M$2-5 per night. The immigration raids of the mid-70s seem to have halted these days, but it's curious that a place like Batu Ferringhi has developed no low-key accommodation facilities to parallel the big hotels. Perhaps it's official policy to discourage grass-roots enterprise like you find at Kuta Beach in Bali, Hikkaduwa in Sri Lanka or Ko Samui in Thailand.

Batu Ferringhi's 'international standard' hotels are strung along the beach over a km. All of them are right on the beach and although Batu Ferringhi is far from the best beach in Malaysia they're pleasantly relaxed places for a family vacation. There are facilities along the beach for a variety of water sport activities, including wind-surfing and para-flying, offered either by the hotels or by independent operators. These hotels have air-con and all except the Lone Pine Hotel have swimming pools. Prices vary depending on whether you're facing the beach or not.

Starting from the eastern, Georgetown end of the beach there's the *Rasa Sayang* – largest and most expensive of them all. Its design is an exotic interpretation of traditional Malay styles – the one place at Batu Ferringhi with real local character. Right beside it is the smaller, older and quite reasonably priced *Palm Beach*. The large and new *Golden Sands* is next to that and next again is the older and much lower-key *Lone Pine Hotel*. This is the cheapest of these hotels. There's quite a gap before the *Holiday Inn*, another gap before the *Casuarina Beach Hotel* (both new places), and finally there's the smaller *Bayview Hotel* at the far end of the beach. The beach slopes into the water more gradually here so swimming is better.

Bayview Beach Hotel (tel 04-811311), 74 rooms, singles M$80-90, doubles M$90-100
Casuarina Beach Hotel (tel 04-811711), 175 rooms, singles M$119-145, doubles M$145-165
Golden Sands (tel 04-811911), 310 rooms, singles M$140-165, doubles M$165-195
Holiday Inn Penang (tel 04-811601), 159 rooms, singles M$125-180, doubles M$145-200
Lone Pine Hotel (tel 04-811511), 54 rooms, singles M$60-70, doubles M$65-75
Palm Beach Hotel (tel 04-811621), 145 rooms, singles M$80-110, doubles M$100-130
Rasa Sayang Hotel (tel 04-811811), 320 rooms, singles M$130-170, doubles M$155-200

Places to Eat – Batu Ferringhi

All the big hotels have restaurants. The Rasa Sayang has a positive plethora of them, from a Japanese restaurant to a 'British grill room'. There's also the *Coconut Garden Restaurant* – typical Chinese food with the accent on seafood – and the more expensive *Eden Seafood Village* with nighttime entertainment.

Further along the road is the travellers' centre with a small group of shops and restaurants. Here you can get a good meal for just a couple of dollars – including all those travellers' favourites like banana-honey pancakes or fruit salad. Most popular is the *Guan Hoe Hin*, others include the *Yoke Lan*, the *Sunshine Restoran* and the *Guan Guan Cafe*. There's also *Pak Din's Bamboo Restaurant* which is run by an interesting and friendly old gentleman and produces excellent, economically priced Malaysian food.

Places to Stay – Telok Bahang

Take the beachward road from the roundabout, follow it round to where it parallels the beach and at 130 there's *Madam Lee* – dorm beds for M$3, rooms for M$6. It backs onto the beach and you can also hire bicycles here. *Miss Loew* can be contacted at the store behind the Shell station, but she has a good house just along from Madam Lee's. There's a fridge, showers, cooking facilities and you can get all your accumulated washing done. A single room starts at M$5; there are larger rooms up towards M$10.

Food in the shopping area of Telok Bahang is good and you can get 'fantastic' murtabaks for M$1.50 at the *Kassim Restoran* at 48 Main Rd.

Getting There
From the Jalan Maxwell bus stand take a blue bus 93 (60c) to Tanjong Bungah and change there for another blue bus (40c) on to Batu Ferringhi or Telok Bahang.

PENANG – AROUND THE ISLAND
You can make an interesting circuit of the island either in your own car, on a tour or by public transport. It's 70 km all the way round, but it's only along the north coast that the road runs right on the coast so you're not beside the beaches all the way. Starting from Georgetown and travelling clockwise you come to:

Snake Temple
At milestone 9, a couple of miles before the airport, you reach Penang's famous

snake temple, the Temple of the Azure Cloud. Dedicated to Chor Soo Kong, the temple was built in 1850 and if you want live snakes are draped over you. The snakes are venomous Wagler's Pit Vipers and are said to be slightly 'doped' by the incense smoke which drifts around the temple. There is no admission fee to the temple although 'donations' are requested. The number of snakes tends to vary through the year.

On Round the Island
After the snake temple you soon reach Bayan Lepas, Penang's international airport. A turn-off at the village of Bayan Lepas leads to the small fishing village of Batu Maung, about three km away. Just beyond the village a small shrine dedicated to the legendary Admiral Cheng Ho (see Melaka) marks a huge 'footprint' on the rock which is said to belong to the famous eunuch. Batu Maung is good for seafood and there is a small children's playground with concrete animal figures.

Back on the main road you climb up, then drop down to Telok Kumbar, from

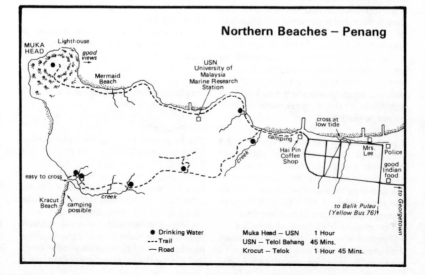

Northern Beaches – Penang

MUKA HEAD
Lighthouse
good views
Mermaid Beach

USN University of Malaysia Marine Research Station

cross at low tide

camping
Hai Pin Coffee Shop

Mrs. Lee
Police
good Indian food

Creek

easy to cross

Kracut Beach
camping possible
creek

to Balik Pulau
(Yellow Bus 76)

to Georgetown

● Drinking Water
--- Trail
— Road

Muka Head – USN   1 Hour
USN – Telol Bahang   45 Mins.
Krocut – Telok   1 Hour 45 Mins.

where you can diverge to the fishing village of Gertak Sanggul. You'll pass some good beaches, including Pantai Asam, on the way. A little further on you reach Balik Pulau, the main town you pass through on the island circuit. There are a number of restaurants and cafes here, but no accommodation – going round the island has to be a one-day operation. Further on another road turns off to Pantai Acheh, another small fishing village. From here the road starts to climb and twist, offering glimpses of the coast and the sea far below. The jungle becomes denser and at around the 20th milestone you reach Titi Kerawang, a waterfall just off the road with a natural swimming pool.

Finally you get back to the coast at Telok Bahang, the village which marks the western end of the northern beach strip. There are a number of batik factories where you're welcome to drop in and see the processes involved in making batik. They also have showrooms where you can buy a wide variety of batik articles.

From here you can also visit the 101-hectare Forest Recreation Park. It's open 8 am to 6 pm and admission is free. The park is intended to preserve a wide variety of local trees and to conduct forest research, but there are also a number of recreation opportunities, including walking tracks. From Telok Bahang you can also trek down the beach to Muka Head, the isolated rocky promontory marked by a lighthouse at the extreme north-western corner of the island.

Transport Round Penang Getting around the island is easiest with your own transport, particularly since the road does not actually run along the coast except on the northern side and you have to leave the main road to get out to the small fishing villages and isolated beaches.

For around M$3 to 4, depending on where and when you stop, you can make the circuit by public transport. Start with a yellow 66 bus for the Bayan Lepas

Airport and hop on and off at the snake temple. This bus will take you all the way to Balik Pulau from where you have to change to another bus, a 76 for Telok Bahang. There are only half a dozen of these each day and the last one leaves around mid-afternoon so it's wise to leave Georgetown early and check the departure times when you reach Balik Pulau. At Telok Bahang you're on the northern beach strip and you simply need a blue bus to Tanjong Bungah and another blue bus for the short trip into Georgetown.

BUTTERWORTH

There's no reason to pause in Butterworth; it's just a jumping-off point for Penang Island and the site of a large Australian air force base.

Places to Stay

If for some reason you want to stop here there are a number of hotels, including the cheap *Ruby Hotel* at M$12 a double with a bar downstairs. Or at the other extreme there's the *Merlin Inn Butterworth* (tel 04-343322) with singles/doubles at M$96/110.

ALOR SETAR

The capital of Kedah state is north of Penang on the main road to the Thai border and it's also the turn-off point for Kuala Perlis, from where ferries run to Langkawi Island. Few people pause very long in Alor Setar although it does have a few places of interest.

The Padang

The large open town square has a number of interesting buildings around its perimeter. The Balai Besar or 'Big Hall' was built in 1898 and is still used by the Sultan of Kedah for ceremonial functions. On the other side of the square is the Zahir Mosque; it's the state mosque and one of the largest in Malaysia, and was completed in 1912. The Balai Nobat is an octagonal building topped by an onion-shaped dome and houses the royal orchestra or nobat. A

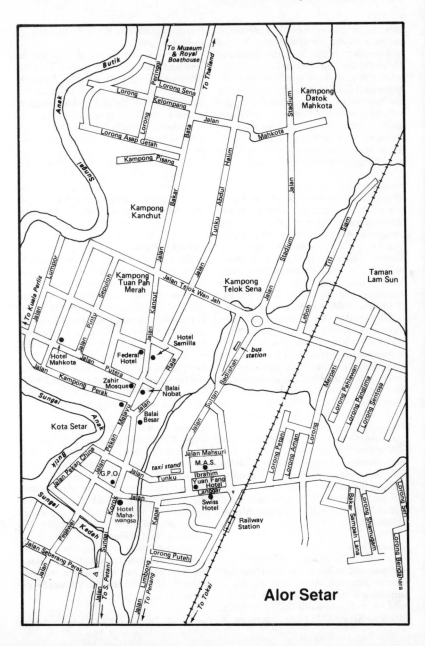

Alor Setar

nobat is principally composed of percussion instruments and the drums here are said to have been a gift from the Sultan of Melaka in the 15th century.

On the main road north is the State Museum, built in a style similar to that of the Balai Besar. The museum has a good collection of early Chinese porcelain and artifacts from the archaeological excavations made at the Bujang Valley. Next to the museum is the royal boathouse where royal barges and boats are housed.

Places to Stay

There are a number of cheap hotels around the bus and taxi stations in the centre of town. The *Swiss Hotel* on Jalan Langgar is basic and, from M$8, cheap. There's a good restaurant downstairs. Across the road on the corner with Lorong Selamat is the equally cheap *Yuan Fang Hotel*. Head north up Jalan Sultan Badlishah and the *Regent Hotel* (tel 04-721900) at 1536 has rooms from M$35.

A little north of the Padang at 42A Jalan Kancut, the *Federal Hotel* has rooms from M$25, more with air-con. Alor Setar has a *Government Rest House* at 75 Pumpong with rooms from M$20. More expensive hotels include the *Hotel Mahawangsa* (tel 04-721433) at 449 Jalan Raja and the *Hotel Mahkota* (tel 04-721344) and *Hotel Putra Jaya* (tel 04-721344) both on Jalan Putera.

Across the road from the Federal is one of Alor Setar's more expensive hotels. The *Hotel Samila* (tel 04-722344) at 27 Jalan Kancut has singles/doubles at M$58/66. Right at the top there's the *Kedah Merlin Inn* (tel 04-726633 at 134-141 Jalan Sultan Badlishah with singles/doubles at M$95/105.

Getting There

Alor Setar is 91 km north of Butterworth and is served by MAS. The road between Butterworth and Alor Setar carries a surprising density of traffic. By bus it's M$2.80 to Butterworth, M$10 to Ipoh, M$16 to KL and M$31 to Singapore. A taxi costs M$2.80 to Kuala Perlis, M$5.50 to Butterworth.

There are also buses to Hat Yai in Thailand for M$9 – go to the Tunjang Ekspress office at the bus station. Although you can easily get to Changlun, the Malay border post for Thailand, by bus or taxi, it is then very difficult to cross the long strip of no man's land to Sadao, the Thai border post, as there is no regular transport just across the border. If, however, you go to Padang Besar, where the railway line crosses the border, you can simply walk across and take a bus from there into Hat Yai. Padang Besar can be reached by road although the main road to Thailand crosses the border at Changlun-Sadao.

KEDAH & PERLIS

In the north-west corner of the peninsula the states of Kedah and Perlis are the rice bowl of Malaysia. A green sea of rice paddies stretches away from the road for much of the distance through the state. Perlis is also the smallest state in Malaysia and both states are important gateways into Thailand. For overseas visitors the most important towns in the state are likely to be the large town of Alor Setar and the small fishing port of Kuala Perlis, from where ferries operate to Langkawi. Other places of interest include:

Gunung Jerai & the Bujang Valley

Kedah Peak or Gunung Jerai is the highest peak in the north-west at 1206 metres. It's between the main road and the coast north of Sungai Petani and is topped by a 6th-century Hindu shrine. The area around the Bujang River which flows off the mountain is the location of important archaeological sites where statues, inscriptions and ancient tombs have been discovered. There is a museum at Bukit Batu Pahat where the Candi Bukit Batu Pahat temple has been reconstructed. Other finds are displayed in the Alor Setar State Museum.

Kangar & Around

Situated 56 km north-west of Alor Setar, this is the main town in Perlis – a low-lying town surrounded by rice paddies. North of here is Padang Besar, a border town to Thailand with both a road and rail crossing. It's a popular place to visit because of the duty free market that operates here, in the no-man's land between the two countries. It's at its most active on weekends.

Arau, near Kangar, is the royal capital of Perlis and has an istana and a royal mosque. Kaki Bukit in the extreme north-west corner of the state has some interesting limestone caverns from which tin is mined.

Places to Stay Kangar has number of hotels including the *Hotel Malaysia* (tel 04-751366) at 65-67 Jalan Jubli Perak where rooms range from M$18. The cheaper *Federal Hotel* (tel 04-751288) at 104 Jalan Besar has rooms from as little as M$10, as does the *Hotel Ban Cheong* (tel 04-751074) at 79A on the same street. There is also a *Rest House* on Jalan Kangar (tel 04-751183).

KUALA PERLIS

This small port town in the extreme north-west of the peninsula is visited mainly as the departure point for Langkawi. You can also use Kuala Perlis as an unusual gateway into Thailand. The main part of Kuala Perlis is just a couple of streets – plenty of restaurants and shops, one hotel and no banks. Kangar is only 10 km away if you need more facilities.

If you've got to kill some time waiting for a boat there's plenty to see. Beside the dock there's an ice works and fish are packed into ice-filled crates on the quay. You can cross the river by a foot bridge to the other part of town where the houses and mosques are built on stilts over the water around the mangrove swamps.

Places to Stay

Kuala Perlis's one and only hotel is the *Soon Hin* opposite the taxi stand where a room will cost you M$10.

Getting There

There are direct buses from Butterworth at 8.30 and 11 am for M$5. They connect, more or less, with ferry departures. A taxi between Butterworth and Kuala Perlis costs M$9. From Alor Setar there are buses at M$1.70 or taxis at M$2.80. Buses also depart from Kuala Perlis to Padang Besar (for Thailand) for M$1.90 (taxi M$3.30) and to Kuala Lumpur for M$18. The short taxi ride into Kangar costs 60c.

LANGKAWI

The 99 islands of the Langkawi group are 30 km off the coast from Kuala Perlis, at the northern end of peninsular Malaysia. They're accessible by boat from Kuala Perlis or Penang or by air from Penang, 112 km south. The islands, strategically situated where the Indian Ocean narrows down into the Straits of Melaka, were once a haven for pirates and could easily have become the site for the first British foothold in Malaya instead of Penang. Earlier they were charted by Admiral Cheng Ho on his visit to Melaka in 1405.

Today they're a quiet and relatively unspoilt place with a population of around 30,000. Attempts to promote Langkawi as a tourist destination have not been very successful, perhaps due to the island's relative remoteness. Whatever the reason, this does mean that visitors have the beaches pretty much to themselves. The islands of the group often rise sheer from the water and only narrow channels separate one island from another.

Information & Orientation

Kuah, with a population of about 2000, is the main town and the arrival point for the ferries from Kuala Perlis. Almost all the accommodation is also centred here, but the best beaches are scattered around the island, which can make transport logistics

Langkawi

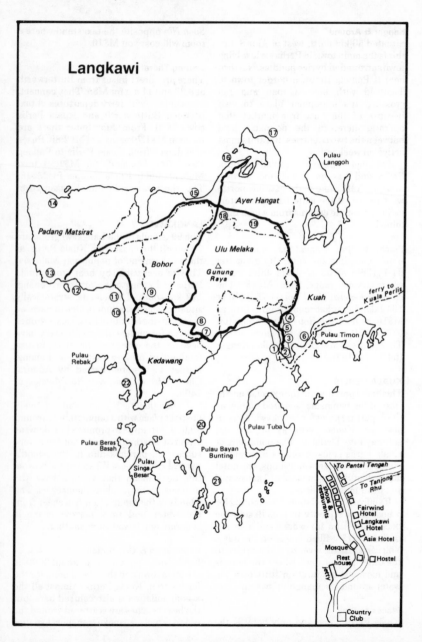

a little difficult. Apart from building their money-losing hotel, the TDC has confined other work on tourist development on the island to erecting a fairly comprehensive, but often rather misleading, collection of signposts.

Kuah (Pekan Kuah)

The island's main town is a one street affair along the waterfront. The bay is dotted with sunken fishing boats – the remains of confiscated Thai poachers or unlicensed local boats, which have sunk while the government got slowly around to prosecuting the fishermen. Kuah's only 'sight' is the picturesque waterside mosque with its golden dome and Moorish arches and minarets rising prettily above the palm trees.

Durian Perangin

From Kuah you pass through a long series of rubber plantations before the turnoff to this waterfall at the 9th milestone. There's a small sign by the shop there and a larger sign by a second turnoff a bit further on. The falls are three km off the road – the first part of the path is passable by motorcycle.

Telaga Air Panas

These hot springs are towards the north of the island, 13 km from Kuah. Like so many places in Malaysia there's an intriguing legend to go with them. The island's two most powerful families, so the story goes,

became involved in a bitter argument over a marriage proposal. A fight broke out and all the kitchen utensils were used as missiles. The gravy (kuah) was spilt at (yes!) Kuah and seeped into the ground at Kisap (seep). A pot landed at Belanga Perak (broken pot) and finally the saucepan of hot water (air panas) came to land here. The fathers of these two families got their come-uppance for causing all this mayhem – they're now the island's two major mountain peaks. The hot springs themselves are no tourist attraction – just an ugly little clump of green buildings by the roadside.

Pantai Rhu

On the north coast of the island, 23 km from Kuah, this is one of Langkawi's better known beaches. The water here is shallow and at low tide you can walk across the sand bank to the neighbouring island. The water swirls across the bank as the tide comes in. Around the promontory, accessible by boat, is the Gua Cherita cave. Along the coast for a couple of km before the beach the tiny fish known as ikan bilis are spread out on mats to dry in the sun. There's a group of new chalets and a restaurant at Pantai Rhu.

Pasir Hitam

A couple of km west of Pantai Rhu this beach is noted for its black sand although it's not a real black sand beach – simply streaks of black through the sand. The

1 Jetty	12 Pantai Kok
2 Langkawi Country Club	13 Telaga Tujuh
3 Rest House	14 Datai
4 Kuah Town	15 Pasir Hitam
5 Hotel Langkawi	16 Pantai Rhu
6 Pantai Dato'Syed Omar	17 Gua Cherita
7 Golf Course	18 Telaga Air Panas
8 Mahsuri's Grave	19 Durian Perangin
9 Burnt Rice Area	20 Gua Langsir
10 Airstrip	21 Tasek Dayang Bunting
11 Kuala Teriang Village	22 Pantai Tengak

waters off Pasir Hitam are dotted with huge boulders.

Telaga Tujuh

Water cascades nearly 100 metres down a hillside through a series of seven (tujuh) wells. You can slide down from one of these shallow pools to another. To get there you can hire a fishing boat at the fishing village of Kuala Teriang or at Pantai Chenang, which can be reached by bus after a three-km walk, The boats go to the beach – Pantai Kok – from where there is short walk to the foot of the falls. By motorcycle it's a long trip along an unsurfaced road from Ayer Hangat in the north of the island. The effort's worthwhile – 'I had a fun that I haven't had since I was a child' wrote a Danish visitor.

Mahsuri's Tomb & Padang Masirat

Mahsuri was a legendary 10th-century Malay princess unjustly accused of adultery and sentenced to death. All attempts to execute her failed until the indignant Mahsuri agreed to die. But not before issuing the curse that 'there shall be no peace or prosperity on this island for a period of seven generations'. A result of that curse can still sometimes be seen at nearby Padang Masirat, the 'field of burnt rice'. Here villagers burnt their rice fields rather than allow them to fall into the hands of Siamese invaders. Heavy rain, it is said, still sometimes brings traces of burnt rice to the surface.

Pantai Tengah

A beautiful km-long strip of beach lies at the south-west corner of Langkawi. Temoyong is the village at the end of the road from where you have to walk about a km to the beach.

Tasek Dayang Bunting & Gua Langsir

The 'Lake of the Pregnant Maiden' is a freshwater lake with good swimming on Pulau Dayang Bunting, the large island south of Langkawi itself. A legend states that a childless couple, after 19 years of unsuccessful efforts, had a baby girl after drinking from this lake. Since then it has been a popular pilgrimage centre for those in search of children! Nearby is Gua Langsir, the 'Cave of the Banshee', which is inhabited by thousands of bats. Marble is quarried on the island and shipped to the mainland for processing.

Pulau Bumbon

Only 15 minutes offshore from Langkawi, this island has three bungalows which you can rent for M$10; food is an additional M$10 per day per person. There's a pleasant beach nearby and another about 15 minutes' walk over the hill. Look for Pa Wan or Omar to get out there – the yellow boat with Bumbon written on it is a clue!

Places to Stay – bottom end

A short ride by share taxi will take you from the pier to any of Kuah's cheaper accommodation, all of which is strung out along the waterfront around the bay. Kuah is strictly a one-street town and that street follows the bay all the way. It's only a few hundred metres to the pleasantly spacious although not very well kept *Rest House* (tel 04-749234) where huge doubles cost M$18 and there's a pleasant open grassy area down to the water. The government *Youth Chalet* (tel 04-749206) is directly across the road, but is strictly for groups and must be pre-arranged – M$1 per person and it's all 15 beds or nothing.

On past the mosque, about a km from the pier, and you come to Kuah's other places. First the *Asia Hotel* (tel 04-749216) has fan-cooled rooms for M$14, air-con rooms for M$26. Same prices a few doors down at the *Langkawi Hotel* (tel 04-749209) while a couple of doors down again there's the slightly cheaper *Fairwind Hotel*. These Chinese hotels – all fairly similar and all neat, clean and tidy – are very close together.

Places to Stay – top end

You pass the *Langkawi Country Club* (tel

04-749209) just before docking as you arrive at Langkawi. The TDC-operated hotel has been a sad white elephant ever since its opening in 1973 – people simply don't come to Langkawi in large enough numbers. It's got a fine waterfront position, swimming pool, bars, restaurants, 100 rooms with all the usual mod-cons, but not enough customers to even come close to making money. Singles cost M$80-90, doubles M$90-100.

Nevertheless Langkawi must be getting more popular because there is now also the *Tanjung Rhu Merlin* (tel 04-749488) in Kuah. It only has 20 rooms, singles from M$70 to 100, doubles M$80 to 120.

Places to Eat

Chinese food is available in the restaurants at the *Asia* and *Langkawi Hotels* and also at the *Rose Restaurant* under the Fairwind Hotel. There are a number of other Chinese and Indian restaurants and stalls along the road through Kuah – excellent roti chanai in the various Indian places. The *Rest House* also does excellent food. As in so many other Malaysian towns Kuah has a far greater number and variety of eating places than its size would indicate.

Getting There

Sea Commencing in mid-84 the *Gadis Langkasuka* operates a daily service between Penang and Langkawi. The boat departs the Swettenham Pier in Georgetown at 11 pm and arrives in Langkawi at around 7 am the next morning. It departs Langkawi at noon the same day and arrives in Penang about 6 pm the same evening. One-way fare is M$35.

Officially there are ferries from Kuala Perlis to Langkawi at 10.30 am and 3 pm, but in actual fact there are several boats operating and departures are pretty much controlled by the tides. Although there may be as many as six departures in a day

you can't count on any specific departure time. Fares depend on the boat and the class – some are air-con, some not; some have economy and first-class sections, some are one class. Generally fares will be in the M$3.50-6 bracket for the two – to 2½-hour crossing although there is an air-con express boat which costs M$10. For returns from Langkawi the official departure times are 8 am and 1 pm, but there will probably be boats going until 2 or 3 pm.

A recent innovation is supposed to be a 10-times-daily hovercraft operating 9 am to 5 pm from Kuala Perlis to the Langkawi resort for M$12 one-way.

Between the jetty and Kuah town itself a share taxi is 60c.

Air Malaysia Air Charters have regular flights between Penang and Langkawi.

Getting Around

You've got to get out and about on Langkawi since there's little of interest in Kuah itself. This can be a bit of a problem since although the buses are cheap enough (M$1 will take you almost anywhere on the island), departure times and, an important, return times, are very uncertain. You can also get out to the beaches by taxi (say M$2 to Pantai Tengah), but once again you have to get back.

Easiest is to hire a motorcycle (usually Honda 50 step-thrus) for the day. They usually cost about M$20 including unlimited km and the hirers prefer you to have an international license. The fit can also hire bicycles and, it is said, you can ride around the island in a day. You can hire a boat to get across to Pulau Dayang Bunting for around M$70-90 per day – get a group together. There are tours operated from Langkawi Country Club to the various island attractions, but the Asia Hotel also organises boat trips at much lower prices.

Where the western side of the peninsula is the more crowded, enterprising, strongly Chinese-influenced part of the country, the east coast is open, relaxed and very Malay in character. It's a long series of gleaming beaches, backed by dense jungle and interspersed with colourful and easygoing fishing villages or kampongs. It's along this coast that you have the opportunity to witness Malay handicrafts and cultures or even stay in a small kampong and watch the scarcely changing rituals of village life.

To some extent the east coast's slower development is a result of its relative isolation. There were few roads along the coast until WW II and it was well into the '70s before the last of the ferries across the many east coast rivers was replaced by a bridge. Today you can follow an excellent 730 km road all the way from Johore Bahru, across the causeway from Singapore in the south, to Kota Bahru, close to the Thai border in the north. The recently completed east-west road in the north has also brought the two coasts much closer together and made possible, at long last, a Malaysian round trip. You can also take the railway line down through the dense central jungle, disembarking at the National Park if you wish. Cars can also be transported on this route.

The east coast is affected by the monsoon and November through January, particularly in December, is not a good time to visit since the heavy rainfall sometimes floods rivers and makes road travel a difficult proposition. From May through September is a peak time on the east coast since this is the season when the giant leatherback turtles, and their smaller relations, come ashore to lay their eggs. Remember that the east coast is predominantly Malay and Muslim and therefore Friday will be the day of rest. Solo women

travellers should exercise a little caution in some cheaper hotels and rest houses – a number of travellers have reported a surprising number of peeping toms and other such unwanted attention along the east coast.

KOTA TINGGI

The small town of Kota Tinggi is 42 km from Johore Bahru on the road to Mersing. The town itself is of little interest but the Kota Tinggi waterfalls, 15 km north-east of the town, are a very popular weekend retreat. The falls, at the base of 624-metre-high Gunung Muntahak, leap down 36 metres and then flow through a series of pools which are ideal for a cooling dip. The smaller pools are shallow enough for safe use by children. Kampong Makam, where the Sultans of Johore have their mausoleums, is only a couple of km from Kota Tinggi town.

Places to Stay

There are self-contained chalets at the falls which cost about M$40 per night, complete with cooking facilities and fridges. To book them ring 073-891146. Day chalets are also available at a cost of M$18 per day. Weekend bookings are heavy. There is a restaurant on the hillside facing the falls.

Getting There

There are regular buses (number 44) and taxis from Johore Bahru to the town. From there you can take another bus (number 43) or taxi to the waterfalls. From Johore Bahru the taxi fare to Kota Tinggi is M$4, the bus fare is M$2.20.

JOHORE LAMA

Following the fall of Melaka to the Portuguese the Malay kingdom was transferred here, about 30 km down the Johore River from Kota Tinggi. The town was built as a fortified capital between 1547 and 1587 but later abandoned as Johore Bahru rose in prominence. There were a number of skirmishes between Malay and Portuguese fleets along the Sungei Johore and on two occasions the town was sacked and burnt. Today the old fort of Kota Batu, overlooking the river, has been restored but getting to Johore Lama entails arranging a boat for the downriver trip.

JASON'S BAY (Telok Mahkota)

A turn-off 13 km north of Kota Tinggi leads down 24 km of rather rough road to the sheltered waters of Jason's Bay. There are 10 km of sandy beach but few facilities at this relatively isolated spot.

DESARU

On a 20 km stretch of beach at Tanjong Penawar, 88 km north-east of Johore Bahru and also reached via Kota Tinggi, this is a new beach resort area which is being heavily promoted and developed. It's already becoming popular as a weekend escape for Singaporeans but is unlikely to be a major attraction for international visitors to Malaysia.

Places to Stay

The *Desaru Merlin Inn* (tel 073-838101) on the beach has 100 rooms with singles at M$95-105, doubles at M$110-120. At the *Desaru View Hotel* (tel 073-838221) there are 134 rooms with singles at M$140-170, doubles M$160-190.

There are also chalets at the *Desaru Holiday Resort* with rooms from M$50-100. You can camp with your own or rented equipment for M$5 per person, there's a dormitory (for groups of at least 15) for M$10 per person and there's a day visit charge of 50c.

Getting There

Buses and taxis operate from Kota Tinggi.

MERSING

The east coast port of Mersing serves as a departure point for boats out to the islands that sprinkle the seas off the east coast at this point. The river here is bustling with fishing boats and there's plenty to look at. Mersing has an impressive-looking mosque on a hill above the town, and some good beaches such as Sri Pantai six km south, Tanjong Sekakap 13 km south, Ayer Papan 10 km north and Panyabong 50 km north. Mersing is a very small town and easy to find your way around.

Places to Stay

There are a lot of places to stay in Mersing while you arrange to get out to Tioman or the other islands offshore. Mersing's most pleasant place to stay is the 18-room *Mersing Rest House* (tel 072-791103) situated on a slight rise overlooking the six-hole (yes, six) golf course. Rooms cost from around M$35 but the Rest House tends to be booked out so you may have to fall back on the many Chinese hotels clustered in the town centre.

Several travellers have written to praise the *Mandarin Hotel* in front of the bus station. It's convenient and clean with doubles with shower for M$12, as well as smaller and cheaper rooms and more expensive rooms with air-con. The manager is helpful too and they'll arrange boats to Tioman.

The excellent *Hotel Embassy* (tel 072-791301) at 2 Jalan Ismail, close to the roundabout, has rooms from M$20, or with air-con M$30. Other Chinese hotels include the *Hotel Golden City*, the *East Coast Hotel* and the *Merdeka Hotel*. *Hotel Mersing* on Jalan Dato Timor has rooms from just M$10.50 and it's clean and roomy and the staff are friendly. Other similarly cheap rooms are available at the *Syuan Koong* on Jalan Abu Bakar. *Tong Ah Lodgings*, with doubles at $M6 and on-off water, is even cheaper. The *Tioman Safari* people (see Tioman) have a hostel at their office for people going out to the island with them. Nightly cost is M$6 per person in rooms or dorm-style.

Apart from the rest house the other 'top end' place is the *Mersing Merlin Inn* (tel 072-791312/3) at 1½ miles on the Kuantan road. The 34 rooms are all air-con and cost M$65/75 for singles/doubles.

Places to Eat

The *Long Fong Restaurant*, downstairs in the Hotel Embassy, has excellent seafood and western-style breakfasts. There's good Chinese food at several other places around town while the *Taj Mahal Restaurant* on Jalan Abu Bakar has excellent roti chanai for breakfast. The small restaurant, to the right just beyond the Tioman jetty, has superb mee goreng.

Getting There

Mersing is 133 km north of Johore Bahru, 189 km south of Kuantan. Taxi fares are M$9.20 to Johore Bahru, M$2.60 to Endau, M$4.50 to Kuala Rompin, M$7.30 to Keluang (for the west coast), M$28 to Kuala Lumpur, M$14 to Kuantan, M$29 to Kuala Trengganu and M$40 all the way north to Kota Bahru.

The express bus to Johore Bahru is M$5.50, the regular bus only M$4.50. There are also buses to and from Singapore for S$8 or a pricey M$15 with air-con. An air-con bus from Rompin, further north, to Singapore is only M$10! The bus and taxi stands are side by side close to the waterfront at the town centre.

TIOMAN

The largest of the east coast islands, Tioman is large (19 km by 12 km) and mountainous (Gunung Kajang is 1049 metres high). It's densely wooded, ringed with beautiful beaches and fine coral, and relatively unspoilt. Tioman is lightly populated – there are just a handful of small kampongs dotted around the coast and the hilly inland area is virgin forest with no settlements at all. Tioman's only road runs from the telecommunications tower a km south of the Merlin Hotel to

the airstrip at Tekek, about two km north. The hotel has a couple of vehicles and there are also a handful of motorcycles on the island – they can continue a couple of km north of the airstrip on the walking track before being stopped by a headland.

Tioman has beautiful beaches, clear water and coral for snorkelling or diving enthusiasts, but its major attraction has to be the contrasts and diversity it offers – high mountains and dense jungle are only a short walk away from the coast. As evidence of the island's abundant natural beauty it's generally quoted that this was the setting for the mythical Bali Hai in the film *South Pacific*.

Two thousand years ago Arab traders noted Tioman on their charts as a place with good anchorages and fresh water. It's an island that would be hard to miss with spectacular peaks like Batu Sirau and Nenek Si-muka at the southern end of the island. To this day the streams run rapid and clear from the high peaks of the island. Tioman has also been blessed with some delightful names. The highest peak, Gunung Kajang is 'Palm-Frond Hill'. Gunung Chula Naga is 'Dragon-Horn Hill' and the villages are equally imaginatively named. There's Kampong Tekek (Lizard Village), Kampong Lalang (Elephant Village), Kampong Juara (Catfish Village) and even Kampong Merkut (Village of Doubt).

Information & Orientation

The island is wilder and more mountainous at the southern end. The single strip of road, the one big hotel and most of the smaller, cheaper places are along the west coast. At the waist of the island a good trail crosses the island to the other larger settlement on the east coast – where there is also cheap accommodation. If you want to read more about the wildlife and plant life of the island get a copy of *The Natural History of Pulau Tioman*, a University of Malaya research project published by the Merlin Hotel and available at the hotel.

The Merlin Hotel has the only phone on

the island, a radiophone. They will make calls for outsiders, to reconfirm flights for example, but you'll probably have to leave the message and a MS$30 deposit and come back later to see if they got through and what it cost.

Walks

Using Tekek as a base you can walk south to the Merlin Hotel at Lalang in about half an hour either by the road (it's steep) or by rock-hopping around the headland. From there you can continue another half hour south to the deserted beach beyond the telecom tower. It's a bit further south to Kampong Paya from where the climb up Gunung Kajang commences.

Heading north from Tekek you follow the coast round a series of beaches and headlands to Monkey Bay. Or you can head inland on the easiest of the cross-island tracks which starts right beside the mosque in the main part of the village. It's a relatively steep climb through dense jungle following the course of the Sungei Besar river to the highest point. Then it slopes down much more gradually and soon leaves the damp, dark jungle for the cooler and brighter area of a rubber plantation and eventually coconut palms at the coast. The walk across the island to Juara takes about two hours.

Wildlife

Tioman is of great interest to biologists because of its relative isolation from similarly forested terrain of the peninsula. Some common animals are completely missing from the island while others are present in unexpectedly large numbers. Tioman has a very large mouse deer population, for example, and also has a wide variety of lizards which are also present in larger than usual numbers. You've got a good chance of seeing at least some wildlife while you are on Tioman, particularly bats which come out in force each evening.

The waters around Tioman shelter the usual technicolour assembly of fish and a surprising number of turtles. At Kampong Nipah, Juara and Pulau Tulai you have a good chance of seeing turtles come ashore to lay their eggs.

Places to Stay

It's an all or nothing situation on Tioman – top or bottom end with nothing in between. There are many cheap accommodation places going up and the island is so delightful that it's likely more 'big' hotels will also be built in the future. At present you've got a choice of the top-end Merlin or a host of little local places with rock-bottom prices and facilities to match. They're generally found at Tekek village and along the beach north of there although if you really want to get-away-from-it-all you could try Juara on the east coast.

Lalang The *Merlin Samudra Tioman* (tel 095-65444/445) is the only 'international class' hotel on the island. It has 74 rooms from around M$90 to nearly M$200. The rooms are air-con but relatively simple – which is just fine since the hotel's number one attraction is nothing to do with the hotel itself, it's the delightful location that counts. The superb beach is just a few steps from the hotel, the water is clear and ideal for snorkelling, there are plenty of opportunities for water-sports and there's a small island within swimming distance of the shore. Note that the Merlin can be heavily booked, particularly during school holidays. The restaurant here is very good and the prices not too extravagant.

Tekek Strung along the beach at Tekek and to the north are a whole series of places to stay and there are a lot more under construction. Most of them are in the M$4-7 per person bracket although there are a few at higher prices. For what is offered, Tioman's prices are definitely higher than on the mainland and a little bargaining is often in order. The basic places are just that – basic. You certainly won't get a fan, toilets will be outhouse

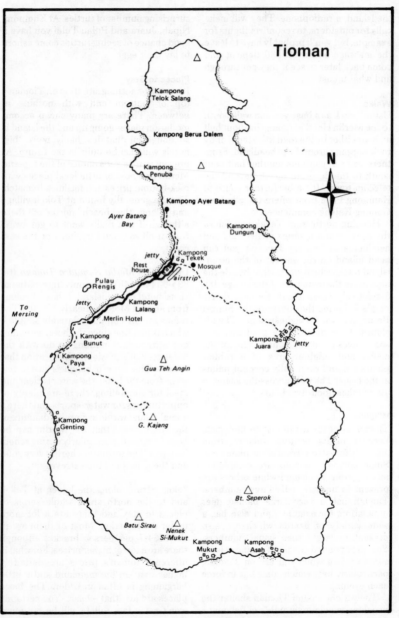

Tioman

N

To
Mersing

Kampong
Telok Salang

Kampong Berus Dalem

Kampong
Penuba

Kampong Ayer Batang

*Ayer Batang
Bay*

Kampong
Dungun

jetty

Kampong
Tekek

Rest
house

Mosque

Pulau
Rengis

airstrip

jetty

Kampong
Lalang

Merlin Hotel

Kampong
Bunut

Kampong
Juara

jetty

Kampong
Paya

Gua Teh Angin

G. Kajang

Kampong
Genting

Bt. Seperok

Batu Sirau

Nenek
Si-Mukut

Kampong
Mukut

Kampong
Asah

style and ditto the washing facilities. Tioman could do with more places a notch up from these 'basic' standards yet still well below the Merlin's level.

Even more important, Tioman badly needs places to eat. Most of the small places will fix meals, but there are few other places to fall back on and it's easy to be left high and dry. If there's a wedding or something on you may find yourself reduced to coconuts and crackers. A few entrepreneurs from Ko Samui or Phuket in Thailand or, even better, Bali could show them how it's done! Tioman does seem to be in the process of becoming another travellers' centre; meanwhile it's worth bringing some fruit juice cartons, some fruit and other food from the mainland. Although food is more readily available than a few years ago the prices are, not surprisingly, somewhat higher. In season, however, there is much fruit grown right on the island.

Finding accommodation is fairly simple – you'll probably get some offers at the wharf in Mersing. The boatmen will undoubtedly have some contacts to pass you on to. Secondly, when you arrive at the island people with rooms to spare will be down at the wharf looking for customers. Thirdly you can simply wander around and ask – either other travellers or likely-looking places. There are virtually no signs out saying 'This is a Hotel'.

Starting from the south (Merlin) end of Tekek, *Roger's Place* is M$12 per person and is one of the better places. Rooms have their own shower and toilet, but not fans, and the walls are just flimsy ply. Good, if slightly pricey, food is available. Back from the beach on the road to the Merlin is *Nazri's*, which is very basic and costs M$4 per person. He seems to be working on developing some sort of monopoly on Tekek accommodation! It's also a popular place to eat at night.

On the beach at Tekek is the *Rest House* which in some ways is Tioman's best value. A double with fan and attached bathroom is only around M$10. The catches are that it is terribly run down and decrepit, the furniture is all falling apart, it's surrounded by ugly and rusting barbed wire, it's desperately in need of a coat of paint and the water supply is erratic. During a three-day stay the taps ran one day. Still it's cheap and rooms do have a fan. Check with the last of the small kedais to the left of the jetty to see if there's space (it's often booked out).

There are a number of other places along the beach and more under construction. In Tekek there's electricity from 6 am to 6 pm; further along there's no power unless places have their own generator. Several of the kedais in Tekek have coldish drinks and you can sometimes get meals at the kedai nearest the jetty. *Nazri's* has food around 8 pm most evenings (meals for M$3) and sometimes has cold drinks.

Ayer Batang If you keep right on walking north from Tekek, at the far end of Kampong Ayer Batang (an hour and a half walk from the Merlin, an hour from Tekek) you'll come to a group of A-frame huts. They're fairly comfortable and roomy, but toilets and washing facilities are all outside. Cost is about M$12 per person. As well as his place in Tekek, *Nazri* has huts at Ayer Batang. The beach there is good, the huts are M$5 per person and there's a cafe next door.

The *Tioman Safari* people have a three-room guest house at Ayer Batang which can accommodate up to 10 people and costs M$60 a day. They also have other, simpler accommodation here at M$5-8 per person.

Salang Kampong Salang is the settlement at the north-west end of the island and there's more cheap accommodation available there – try *Bidim's*. Chalet-type accommodation costs M$6 a night.

Juara If you really want to get away from it all you can stay at this small kampong on the other side of the island. The *Happy*

Cafe, with its delightfully cheerful proprietor, is right by the jetty. It's a spotlessly clean and tidy little establishment with one small room with a mosquito-netted double bed available at M$5 per person. If the room should be in use he'll arrange for you to stay in his own house nearby.

Other places are starting to appear here. You can also stay at *Atans* and eat at the *Turtle Cafe*. Boat trips to other beaches on this coast can be arranged.

Getting There

It's about 50 km from Mersing to Tioman and the trip takes 2½ (on the Merlin Hotel's speedy launch) to four hours (on most other boats). Departures are dependent upon the tides at Mersing's shallow river so everything goes at much the same time and the easiest way to get out there is to find what time the Merlin launch leaves and go down to their jetty then. The jetty is a couple of hundred metres downriver from the town centre and the Merlin and the Rawa Chalet companies both have their offices here. There'll probably be a number of boats leaving and M$15 is the usual price for the one-way trip. Tioman Safari, opposite the post office at 1D Jalan Abu Bakar, have boats at that regular M$15 price. There are often local fishing boats willing to take passengers too.

On the Merlin launch the fare is M$25 and space permitting (which there usually is) you do not have to be a hotel guest to use it. You can also charter a boat – around M$150 is the usual going price. The trip out tends to get a bit choppier when you get beyond the line of island at around one-third distance. At the island it's often possible to charter boats for excursions around Tioman or to nearby islands – M$80 a day for the Tioman Safari boat.

Friday to Monday there are usually one or more Malaysian Air Charter flights at a one-way cost of about M$75. The flight takes about 20 minutes.

RAWA, BESAR & OTHER ISLANDS

Although Tioman is the biggest and best known of the islands off Mersing there are many others, most of them uninhabited and often too rocky and precipitous to land on. Pulau Rawa is the second most touristically developed of the 64 islands. It's a tiny island, privately owned with simple chalets and bungalows costing from M$32 a day. Phone number for *Rawa Island Chalets* is 072-791204. The island is only 12 km offshore and the trip out costs M$12 and takes 1¼ hours. Day-visitors to the island are charged M$3 and the island operators stipulate that there is to be no camping or picnicking and that you cannot bring your own food and drink to the island!

Even closer to the mainland is the larger island of Babi Besar. It's only an hour from Mersing and a boat across should cost about M$10 per person. There are some pleasant huts on the island at M$6 per person and meals can also be supplied at around M$10 per day. If you bring your own food out to this quiet and idyllic little spot there are cooking facilities available.

Other islands have good reefs and diving opportunities if you want to charter a boat. They include Pulau Pemanggil, Pulau Aur, Pulau Tulai near Tioman and Pulau Sibu, the 'island of perilous passage'. Tioman Safari, see the Tioman section above, operate to numerous islands from Mersing.

MERSING TO KUANTAN

The 133 km from Johore Bahru to Mersing are surprisingly uninhabited, but you pass through rather more settlements on the 189 km from Mersing to Kuantan. This was the last stretch of the east coast road to replace river ferries with bridges and there were still a number of ferry crossings even into the early '70s. Even the wide Pahang River has now been bridged, with a 50c toll to cross the river. At a number of places the road touches the coast, there are good beaches and you can bus or taxi from town to town.

Endau

There's nothing of interest in Endau itself, but you can hire boats here to make trips up the remote Endau River to the Orang Asli settlements in the interior. You can get about 110 km upriver in fair size boats, almost to Kampong Patah which is the last village up the river. From here smaller boats are required to negotiate the rapids into Orang Asli country. Smaller boats can be hired at Kampong Punan, about 100 km from Endau.

Kuala Rompin & Nenasi

Again there is nothing to see or do in the town, but with four-wheel drive you can drive inland to Iban, 10 km, and a further 25 km to Kampong Aur where there are Orang Asli settlements. At Nenasi boats can be hired and you can go upriver to the Orang Asli village of Kampong Ulu Serai.

Places to Stay Near Kuala Rompin at the 122½ milestone the small *Government Rest House* (tel 095-65245) has rooms at M\$14, more with air-con. The *Mee Chew Hotel* in Kuala Rompin costs M\$10.

Pekan

The royal town of Pahang has a couple of well-built white-marble mosques and the sultan's palace, the modern Istana Abu Bakar. The istana is on the Kuantan edge of town. The Pahang River, crossed here by a lengthy bridge, is the longest river in Malaysia and was the last east coast river to be bridged. At the river mouth on the other side there's the small fishing village of Kuala Pahang.

A road follows the Pahang River to Kampong Melayu or Mempelas, 60 km upriver. From here you can take boats out onto the Tasek Chini lake – see the Around Kuantan section. Buses run along this road. Silk weaving can be seen at Kampong Pulau Keladi, only about five km out of Pekan.

Places to Stay The *Pekan Hotel* (tel 095-71378) at 60 Jalan Clifford and the *Ching Hiang Hotel* (tel 095-71378) have rooms for around M\$10. There's also the equally cheap *Pekan Rest House* (tel 095-71240).

KUANTAN

Situated about midway up the east coast from Singapore to Kota Bahru, Kuantan is the capital of the state of Pahang and the start of the east coast beach strip which extends from here all the way to Kota Bahru. In itself Kuantan has not got much of interest, but it's a useful travel crossroads whether you're bound north or south or across the peninsula. It also has a good supply of hotels and restaurants and there are a number of places of interest close to Kuantan.

Information & Orientation

The tourist office in Kuantan is on Jalan Mahkota, almost next door to the MAS office and the GPO. Kuantan is essentially a two-street town. Jalan Besar runs close to the river and changes name to Telok Sisek partway along. You'll find the long-distance bus station on Jalan Besar, along with most of the cheaper hotels. The other road is Jalan Mahkota, which runs parallel to Jalan Besar/Telok Sisek – these two streets are both one-way, in opposite directions. As well as the offices mentioned above, most of the banks are up at that end of Jalan Mahkota. There's also a bookshop with English language books on this street and further down is the local bus station. The taxi station is between Jalan Mahkota and Jalan Besar.

Around Kuantan

Although the town of Kuantan does not offer a great deal of interest in itself, you'll find a few things to pass the time. The Kuantan area is noted for its handicrafts, including batikwork, and there are a number of shops selling local craftwork along Jalan Besar near the bus stand. Across the road from the bus stand you'll find a string of colourful shops selling

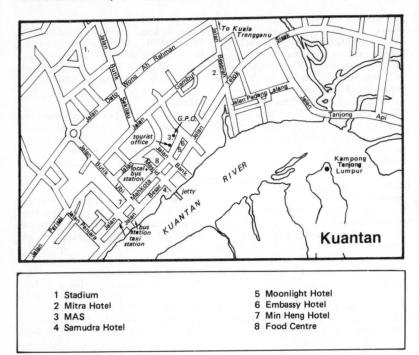

1 Stadium	5 Moonlight Hotel
2 Mitra Hotel	6 Embassy Hotel
3 MAS	7 Min Heng Hotel
4 Samudra Hotel	8 Food Centre

dried fish and other seafoods. It's interesting to stroll along the riverbank and watch the activity on the wide Kuantan River. From a jetty a little downstream from the bus stand, near the fish market, you can get a ferry across the river for 40c to the small fishing village of Kampong Tanjong Lumpur.

Telok Chempedak

Kuantan's major attraction is Telok Chempedak beach, about four km from the town. The beach, bounded by rocky headlands at each end, is quite pleasant but the swimming is only reasonable – Malaysia has better beaches. A short track leads from the southern end of the beach over the hill to the Telok Chempedak Rest House on the river side of the promontory. There are a number of walking tracks in the park here.

Telok Chempedak, which was a quiet little place until the early '70s, now has two big hotels and a sleazy row of bars, clubs and restaurants. On the Hyatt's beachfront is a small wooden junk which carried 162 Vietnamese boat-people on their hazardous voyage to the west – it's now the 'Sampan Bar' where you can pay over the odds for a beer or coke!

Places to Stay – Kuantan

Many people don't stay in Kuantan itself but a few km out at the beach. If you do decide to stay in town there's a good selection of cheap Chinese hotels and a few up-market places although both the 'international' hotels are out at the beach. There are a string of cheap hotels along Telok Sisek. At 58-60 the *Embassy Hotel* (tel 095-24884) has rooms from M$11 – it's a bit quieter than in the centre of town.

The *Moonlight* (tel 095-24277) at 52 is about a dollar more expensive and has pleasant balcony rooms. There's also the *Sin Nam Fong* at 44 in the same M$10-12 price bracket. 'These Chinese places are crazy for the different things which keep you awake', reported one traveller; 'This one had house martins nesting in the roof and they kept up a hell of a racket'.

Further down, Telok Sisek changes name to Jalan Besar and the *Tong Nam Ah*, opposite the bus stand, costs M$14. A block back at 22 Jalan Mahkota the *Min Heng Hotel & Bakery* (tel 095-24885) is properly old-fashioned and rooms cost from M$10. The bathrooms are a bit worn out but the rooms are airy, clean and secure. Plus you get those lovely baking smells that waft up. There are plenty more Chinese cheapies around the town. At 63 Jalan Bukit Ubi the *Weng Yuen Hotel* (tel 095-21547) is similarly priced.

In the more expensive bracket there's the not-so-special *Hotel Samudra* (tel 095-22688) on Jalan Besar with air-con rooms at M$60-75 for singles, M$85-100 for doubles. The *Mitra Hotel* (tel 095-23844) is on Jalan Beserah (also known as Jalan Haji Abdul Aziz) and has singles/doubles at M$50/65.

Places to Eat – Kuantan

As well as a good selection of Chinese restaurants there's even a branch of the ever-present *Colonel Sanders* in Kuantan – it's on the KL side of the bus stand on Jalan Besar. There's a good food stall centre right by the river opposite the Colonel's and another on Jalan Mahkota between the local bus stand and the tourist office. Down by the riverfront there are some good,inexpensive places for fish and other seafood.

The *Min Heng Bakery* has, as its name suggests, good bread and cakes, particularly the coconut ones. 'Delicious local sardine and onion puffs', was another traveller's recommendation. A few doors down you can get excellent roti chanai for breakfast at *Chandra Vilas*. The Chinese

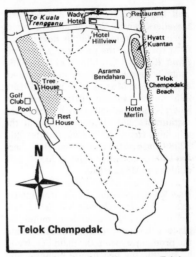

It's about four km from Kuantan to Telok Chempedak, along Jalan Telok Sisek.

hotels over on Telok Sisek have good food – excellent chicken rice and other dishes at the *Moonlight*. The restaurant at the *Hotel Samudra* is 'not cheap, but well worth it'.

Places to Stay – Telok Chempedak

The alternative to staying in Kuantan itself is out at Telok Chempedak beach, only four km from the city. There's a wide variety of accommodation possibilities here. Until the beachfront 'international' hotels were built the popular little *Asrama Bendahara* used to look right on to the beach. It's the lowest-priced place here with rooms at M$12, dorm facilities and a cheap restaurant downstairs. A friendly place report many travellers.

Nearby is the *Kuantan Hotel* (tel 095-24755) with rooms from M$25 or from M$35-60 with air-con. Round on the main road there's the *Hill View Hotel* with fan-cooled and air-con rooms at similar prices. Finally there's a group of 'motels' in the street behind here. Some are very seedy and ill-cared-for but the *Wady Motel* is cheap (small rooms from M$12), reasonably well kept and friendly – a good little travellers' centre. You can also rent good, clean rooms from the family next door.

At the top of the price range here the *Hyatt Kuantan* (tel 095-25211) has 185 centrally air-con rooms (and more planned) at prices from M$130-175 single, M$150-225 double – even more in the high season. There's the usual selection of bars, pools, restaurants and discos here and at the adjoining *Hotel Merlin Kuantan* (tel 095-22388), also on the beachfront. Here there are 106 rooms with singles at M$90-135, doubles at M$110-150.

There's one other Telok Chempedak place which isn't really at Telok Chempedak at all. The *Telok Chempedak Rest House* (tel 095-21711) is a modern, motel-like place with rooms at M$25, but it's round the promontory from the main beach and at low tide the beach here is messy and covered in garbage, and the water is rather shallow. There is a public pool nearby though; entry is M$1.

Places to Eat – Telok Chempedak

The big hotels here have the usual selection of restaurants and there is also a collection of Chinese open-air restaurants further up the beach – good seafood at the *Sea View Restaurant*. The flashy-looking Chinese restaurants along the road to the beach are actually much cheaper than they look. The *Asrama Bendahara* has a restaurant with low prices for food and drinks – filling meals for M$2.

Getting There

Kuantan is on MAS's flight network. By bus from Kuantan it costs M$4.40 to Temerloh, M$10 to KL, M$16 to Ipoh, M$11.80-16 (air-con) to Johore Bahru, M$13-17 to Singapore. Along the east coast it's M$5-7.50 south to Kuala

KAMPONG HOUSE

Rompin, M$7.50 north to Kuala Trengganu or M$14 to Kota Bahru.

Taxis cost M$3.50 to Pekan, M$9 to Kuala Rompin, M$14 to Mersing. Heading north it's M$4.20 to Kemaman, M$9 to Kuala Dungun, M$14.50 to Kuala Trengganu or M$28 to Kota Bahru. Across the peninsula it's M$8 to Temerloh, M$12.50 to Jerantut, M$17 to Raub and M$18 to KL.

Getting Around

Bus 39 will take you to Telok Chempedak beach for just 50c. You want a Kemaman bus for Cherating which will cost you M$1.95. For Beserah take a Beserah bus from the local bus station for 50c. To Panching, near the Charah Caves, the fare is M$1.25; take a Sungei Lembing bus from the main bus stand.

AROUND KUANTAN
Beserah

The fishing village of Beserah is only 10 km north of Kuantan and is a centre for local handicrafts including batik, carvings and shell items from the village of Sungai Karang Darat, a little further north. Kite-flying, top-spinning and other east coast activities can also be seen here. Batu Hitam is a good beach just north of Beserah.

Places to Stay There used to be a delightful little 'halting bungalow' at this small, interesting fishing village. Unfortunately it closed down, but there's now a popular shoestring traveller's place here known as *Jaafar's Place*. It's a kampong house about a half km off the road on the inland side. A small sign points it out and bus drivers know it. Accommodation here costs M$7 a night including bananas, bread and tea for breakfast and a substantial evening meal. Facilities are rudimentary – it's strictly sleeping bag-on-the-floor style, hole-in-the-ground toilets, the river to wash in. Reactions to this are very varied – some travellers feel it's restful, easygoing and friendly. Others claim it's a 'pack-them-in rip-off' with 'bad food and zero facilities'. If you want to stay kampong style you obviously have to make some adjustments, but there's no denying that the places at Cherating, 40 km north, offer a lot more for not much more.

Plus points for a stay here include the interesting kampong life and the local activities you can join in. There are a number of local batik and other handicraft activities. You may well see top-spinning contests and coconut-collecting monkeys, and it's very easy to arrange to go out on fishing trips in the morning – bring back some fish to cook.

Getting There Although any bus travelling north from Kuantan towards Kuala Trengganu will pass through Beserah, it's easiest on a Beserah bus from the main bus stand. Fare is 50c.

Charah Caves

Head out on the Panching road towards Sungei Lembing and take the dirt track turn-off at the 24-km mark. It leads to a limestone outcrop with caves similar to the Batu Caves near Kuala Lumpur, except these are Buddhist, not Hindu. It's a steep climb up an external stairway to the caves' entrance. In the more enclosed cave there's a nine-metre-long reclining Buddha and other Buddhist statuary. There's a M$1 admission charge to the caves, which should include a small boy with a torch (flashlight) to show you around.

Further on at Sungei Lembing there's Malaysia's deepest tin mine, but a visit requires advance arrangements.

Getting There A bus from Kuantan to Panching, halfway to Sungei Lembing, costs M$1.25. From the bus stop in town it's a 3-1/2 km walk each way, but someone *always* stops and offers you a lift. The caves are just OK but the trip to and from Kuantan is very interesting.

Lake Chini

Turn south from the Temerloh road 56 km west of Kuantan, and a rough road will take you to Kampong Tasek Chini. From here you can hire a boat to cross the Pahang River and get out onto the often lotus-covered expanse of Tasek Chini. The lake, which is renowned for its superb fishing, is said to contain a Malaysian monster of the Loch Ness variety. You can also reach the lake via Kampong Melayu which is connected by road with Pekan. A taxi from Kuantan would cost a hefty M$100 plus the boat ride.

Other

The Berkelah Falls are about 50 km from Kuantan; the final six km is a jungle trek from the main road. The falls come down a hillside in a series of eight cascades. The Marathandhavar Temple is the site for a major Hindu festival in March or April each year. It's on the Maran-Jerantut road taken by visitors to the Taman Negara.

KUANTAN TO KUALA TRENGGANU

The 218 km between Kuantan and Kuala Trengganu is probably the most interesting stretch of road along the east coast although it now embraces miles of new petro-chemical developments. The road runs close to the coast most of the way, and there are many good beaches and a number of interesting offshore islands. There are also many places to stay along the coast, and several interesting small towns and fishing villages. This is the turtle beach area of Malaysia, see the separate Rantau Abang section below for more details.

Kuantan to Kuala Dungun

Soon after leaving Kuantan you pass through the village of Beserah. Further north the small island of Pulau Ular, 'Snake Island', is only a short distance offshore and easily reached by a local fishing boat. It's only a couple of km north of here to the kampong of Cherating, a very popular backpackers' accommodation

centre. Just round the promontory from Cherating is accommodation at the other end of the scale – here you'll find Malaysia's Club Mediterranee at Chendor.

Chendor is the start of the turtle beach stretch, although the species that come in here to lay their eggs are not the giant leatherback variety you find further north at Rantau Abang. Kemaman is the first town of any size north of Kuantan and also the first town you reach in Trengganu. It's about 25 km north of Chendor and has a very glossy new mosque on the north side of town.

From here there are more stretches of beach, more small kampongs and fishing villages at river mouths, before you reach Kuala Dungun which is actually a couple of km off the main road. The beaches where the giant leatherbacks come in to lay their eggs stretch north of here, particularly at Rantau Abang. From Kuala Dungun you can make a 2½-hour boat trip out to Pulau Tenggol, 29 km offshore.

Places to Stay – Beserah to Chendor

There are a wide variety of places to stay along the coast from Kuantan. At the 9¼ mile marker the *Hotel Simjifa* (tel 095-23254) is a beachfront Chinese motel with 51 air-con rooms at M$40/50 for singles/doubles. North from here there's quite a gap before you reach the next accommodation area around Chendor and Cherating.

At the 23-mile marker (37 km) the *Twin Islands Motel* has recently been totally rebuilt and has good, clean, modern doubles for around M$30. It's in Kampong Sungei Ular, and the small island of Pulau Ular is only a small distance offshore. Only four km further north is the *Titik Inn* (tel 095-31329), a pleasant beachfront place with chalets at M$45 or two bedroom chalets at M$90. All the chalets have bathrooms, small verandahs and fans, but they're rather expensive for what you get.

At the 45-km marker you come to the small kampong of Cherating where there are a number of places to stay – see below. Just beyond Cherating there's a headland, then the turn-off to the Chendor Motel and the Club Mediterranee at the 29th mile (46 km). The *Chendor Motel* (tel 095-31369) is quite large – it has 58 rooms costing around M$30-100, it's certainly not special value and the restaurant is very expensive.

Nearby is the large (325 room) and securely guarded *Club Mediterranee* complex. This is the first Club Mediterranee holiday resort in Asia and the majority of people staying here will be coming to Malaysia from Europe or Australia on all-inclusive package deals. However, if you've always wanted to try a Club Mediterranee there are often short stay packages offered in Malaysia. Regular cost? Over M$1000 a week!

Places to Stay – Cherating
This small village was virtually abandoned a few years ago but now has become a centre for kampong-style accommodation. There are a half dozen places to stay here with a steady stream of young travellers passing through. Accommodation in all of them is pretty similar – usually separate little 'chalets', each with a mosquito-netted double bed and a verandah to sit out on. Facilities are also similarly basic – no electricity, hole-in-the-ground outhouses and washing from the compound well.

At most places this will cost you M$9-14 per night per person inclusive of two or three meals – lunch or dinner will usually be fish and rice or, alternatively, rice and fish. It can get pretty monotonous after a few meals, but despite this many people settle down and stay for weeks. At easygoing Cherating it's no trouble to let days just drift by. You can watch the kampong life, stroll the beach or swim either off the long stretch of beach in front of the kampong or from the secluded bays just to the north towards the Club Mediterranee.

The guest houses are either close to the main road (convenient but noisier) or by the sea. The former include *Mak Long Tek's* (friendly people and reputed to have the best food), *Ali's*, *Mah De's* and *Semak binti Awang's* (lovely, shy people). The latter include *Hussaien's Bungalows* (pleasant but beware of mosquitoes) which cost M$9; there's also a M$2.50 dormitory. Next door to Hussaien's is the *Sea Breeze Restaurant* which he also runs – breakfast M$1.50, dinner M$3, a beer M$2.60. Nearby, and nearly on the beach, the *Cherating Beach Village* has A-frame huts at M$7.50. The location's good and there's a cafe and facilities.

A bus from Kuantan to Cherating costs M$2.

Places to Stay – Kemaman
Motel Kemaman (tel 095-31205) is about eight km north of the town and right beside a huge construction site for a port. There are rooms and chalets from around M$40. The more expensive rooms and chalets are air-conditioned. There are some cheap Chinese hotels in Kemaman itself.

Places to Stay – Kuala Dungun
There are some cheap Chinese hotels in Kuala Dungun or there's the *Molek Inn* (tel 096-841270) and the *Surra Resort* (tel 096-841280) on the main road with rooms from around M$25 per night. *Hotel Kasanya* (tel 096-841211) at 225-227 Jalan Tambun has large, clean and cheaper rooms from M$15.

RANTAU ABANG
This is the principal turtle beach and the prime area for spotting the great leatherback turtles during the laying season. It's also a fine stretch of beach in its own right – and would be finer still if it were not liberally coated with a varied assortment of old tin cans, plastic bottles and other rubbish. Closer to the water line it's OK for lazing around during the daytime while you wait for the turtles to make their nightly appearance.

A little north of the village itself is the

Rantau Abang Visitors' Centre – part hotel-restaurant-bar and part handicraft centre and turtle museum. It's not all that interesting and the museum has had much more effort put into flashy appearance than worthwhile contents; apart from which all descriptions are only in Malay, considerably reducing its worth to non-Malay speakers. Note that the nearest bank is at Kuala Dungun, 22 km south.

Turtles

Turtle watching is one of the big attractions of the east coast; in fact it's one of Malaysia's biggest attractions. There are seven species of turtles and all seven pay annual visits to the coast from 35 to 150 km north of Kuantan. The area around Rantau Abang, just north of Kuala Dungun, is prime turtle watching territory for here the giant leatherback turtles make their annual excursion onto dry land. At other times of the year the leatherbacks can wander as far away as the Atlantic Ocean, but each year from May to September they return to this one Malaysian beach to lay their eggs. Late August is the peak laying season, but in June and July you can count on seeing turtles on the beach almost every night. Full moon and high tide nights are said to be best.

The egg-laying process is a pretty awesome one, for the female leatherbacks can weigh up to 750 kilos (three quarters of a ton!) and reach over three metres in length. They crawl laboriously up the beach and, well above the high-tide line, dig a deep hole in the sand for their eggs. Usually they dig a false decoy hole first and fill it in again before digging the real hole. Into this cavity the turtle lays, with much huffing and puffing, about 100 eggs which look rather like large ping pong balls. Having covered the eggs she then heads back towards the water, leaving tracks as if a tank had just driven down the beach. It all seems to take an enormous effort and several times the turtle will pause to catch her breath as 'tears', to keep sand out of her eyes, trickle down. Finally the giant turtle reaches the water and an amazing transformation takes place. The heavy, ungainly, cumbersome creature is suddenly back in its element and glides off silently into the night.

The whole process can take two or more hours from start to finish and in each laying season an individual turtle may make several trips to the beach before disappearing until next year. The eggs take about 55 days to hatch and the baby turtles emerge no larger than the tiny turtles of a home aquarium. It's a fraught process, for many eggs are taken by crabs and other predators. Young turtles are seized by birds on their perilous crawl to the sea and even when they reach the water the baby leatherbacks are easy prey for fish and other larger creatures. It's a long time before they rival their parents in size.

Turtle watching is a simple business – you just wander along the beach looking for an emerging turtle or those tell-tale tracks up the beach. In season local villagers patrol the beach to alert visitors. At the Rantau Abang Visitors' Centre it's strictly regimented and you go out to look only when you're told to. Elsewhere it's open to independent turtle watching – 10 pm to 2 am is the usual turtle hunting time although you'll find it quieter and less touristy after that time.

Western visitors usually come away with mixed impressions. The turtles are an amazing sight, but the behaviour of some local turtle watchers can be pretty gross – pulling the turtles' flippers, shining lights in their eyes, even riding on the turtles' backs is all part of the fun and games. Thursday night, start of the weekend in staunchly Muslim Kuala Trengganu, is the worst time.

Also, while the poor turtle is straining to lay the eggs somebody else will be busy collecting them straight from the hole. Unable to focus its eyes out of water, the turtle cannot see any of the spectators nor does it realise the immediate theft of its eggs. Fortunately this is not the conservationist's nightmare one might expect. Around 40,000 young turtles must be hatched out and returned to the sea before the eggs can be collected for consumption or sale in the local markets. Eggs to be hatched are collected and incubated in enclosed hatching areas along the beach. Although you have less chance of seeing turtles early or late in the season you do get far fewer crowds at that time.

Places to Stay & Eat

There are expensive and cheap places to stay here. Situated 13 km north of Kuala Dungun the elegant *Tanjong Jara Beach Hotel* (tel 096-841801/5) is a 100-room beach resort built entirely of wood to a design claimed to be copied from an ancient istana. There's a pool, bar and restaurant and singles/doubles cost M$130/160. There are also some more expensive bungalows. Rantau Abang's other upper-notch establishment is the *Rantau Abang Visitors' Centre* (tel 096-841533), built on stilts over the lagoon behind the beach. It's just a km north of Rantau Abang itself and the 10 chalets cost M$85 per night.

At the other end of the scale there are the travellers' places. They're *Awang's, Sany's* and *Ismail's* – where M$10 will get you a basic little wooden shack right on the beach. Awang's has some simple double huts for M$5 and also some rooms on stilts with a little verandah for M$20. Bigger but not much better. There's reasonable food and cold drinks available from the restaurants – some travellers report that Sany's has the best food. He certainly has good music!

Washing facilities consist of showers with water pumped from the well and a basin with which to carry water from the shower. In other words it's rock bottom, but for on-the-beach convenience these places can't be beat. Compared to beach places in Phuket or Ko Samui in Thailand, however, they're absolutely miserable value. During the turtle season a string of

food stores operate along the beach in the evenings.

There's a new place which falls between the top and bottom stratas here. The *Merantau Inn* (tel 096-841131) is midway between the Tanjong Jara and the Visitors' Centre and has clean two-bed bungalows with bathrooms and fan for M$35. There's also a restaurant.

Getting There

Rantau Abang is only about 22 km north of Kuala Dungun, which in turn is 80 km south of Kuala Trengganu and 138 km north of Kuantan. Any Kuantan-Kuala Trengganu or Kuala Dungun-Kuala Trengganu bus will go right through the village and there's a bus halt right where the cheap accommodation places are. By taxi it's M$9 from Kuantan to Kuala Dungun, M$7 from Kuala Trengganu.

MARANG & PULAU KAPAS

From Rantau Abang the road continues to skirt the coast. Many of the small fishing kampongs along the east coast are found at river mouths, and at Marang the road runs across a long bridge over a wide river. The kampong of Marang, on this river mouth, is quite absurdly picturesque. The river is dotted with brightly painted boats, the water is crystal clear and thick with fish, and over on the beach the kampong huts are interspersed with swaying coconut palms.

Offshore from Marang is the island of Kapas with good swimming and snorkelling, fine coral and good seashell collecting. There's nothing on the island apart from fresh water, so bring camping gear and food if you plan to stay. You can sleep on the beach. You can get a boat out to Pulau Kapas from Marang. The final stretch into Kuala Trengganu has many handicraft centres and shops.

Places to Stay

At *Ibi's Guest House*, 150 metres from the beach and by a small river, rooms are M$10, dorm beds M$4. It's at the northern end of Marang in Kampong Paya, Bandar Marang. A bus costs 80c from Kuala Trengganu. The *Sri Marang Motel* is just south of Marang and there are a number of other accommodation places planned or under construction up the coast to Kuala Trengganu.

KUALA TRENGGANU

Halfway between Kuantan and Kota Bahru on the east coast, the town of Kuala Trengganu is delightfully easygoing. You can almost feel how slow-moving the pace of life is here; it's hardly surprising that there are no local taxis and that trishaws are the usual means of transport around town. Like the other east coast towns, Kuala Trengganu has little of great touristic interest or historical importance, but there's plenty to keep you amused during a short stay.

Information & Orientation

The town stands on a promontory formed by the sea on one side and the wide Trengganu River on the other. There are two main streets in the town centre which together form a complete loop. Coming in from the south you find yourself on the wide, modern Jalan Paya Bunga. Along this street there are a number of hotels, the MAS office, the bus station and banks. Jalan Paya Bunga ends at the river where you will also find the taxi station.

Turn left here if you want to continue north towards Kota Bahru. Or turn right and you'll find yourself on a street as narrow and old-fashioned as Jalan Paya Bunga is modern. Now known as Jalan Bandar, but still often referred to as Jalan Kampong China, this street changes name at the market to Jalan Pantai and continues around the waterfront by the GPO to the roundabout where it meets Jalan Paya Bunga.

Around Town

Most of Kuala Trengganu's colourful atmosphere can be appreciated along Jalan Bandar. Wander along the street from the taxi station end and you'll find interesting little Chinese shops, a bustling Chinese temple and narrow alleys leading to jetties on the waterfront. The clock tower marks the change point from Jalan Bandar to Jalan Pantai.

The municipal market here is one of the most colourful and active in Malaysia with fruit and foods of all types on sale and hordes of trishaws outside waiting to take marketers and their purchases home. When they say the fish at KT's market is fresh, they really mean it – the fishing boats dock right outside! The best time to visit the market is early in the morning when it's at its most active and colourful. There are general shops upstairs in the market building.

Continuing along Jalan Pantai you pass the Istana Mazia on your right. Parts of this old palace are still utilised by the Trengganu royal family. There are some beautiful examples of traditional wood-carving in the old palace buildings. Behind the istana is the gleaming new Zainal Abidin Mosque. The steep road up Bukit Besar on the southern outskirts of town takes you to a viewpoint offering excellent views of the town and the South China Sea.

River Trips

There are a series of jetties behind the taxi station and beside the market from which small ferries shuttle across the river or to the many islands in the river mouth. The jetty behind the taxi station is the place for a 20c ferry ride to Pulau Duyong Besar, the largest island in the estuary. Here fishing boats are built using age-old techniques and tools; it's always worth a wander around.

A boat from beside the market will take you across to Kampong Seberang Takir on the other side of the river mouth. In this fishing village you can see fish being dried and processed. Five km upriver is Kampong Pulau Rusa, with a number of interesting old traditional houses; again ferries run there although you can also

Top: Marang, a small fishing village on the east coast (TW)
Left: Tioman Island (TW)
Right: Mersing fishing boats (TW)

Top: market in Kuala Trengganu (TW)
Bottom: rickshaw riders, Kuala Trengganu (TW)

travel by bus. You can hire a boat on an hourly or daily basis to explore further upriver. Kuala Berang is a good starting point for trips much further up into the interior. If you just want to get away from city life you can cross the river for 40c from the ferry jetty behind the taxi stand to Kampong Dijong on the other side of the river.

Islands & Beaches

There are a number of pleasant islands and beaches accessible from Kuala Trengganu. Boats can be arranged to Pulau Kapas although that beautiful island is more easily reached from Marang, a few km south. Pulau Redang, also with good swimming, snorkelling and jungle walks, is about 50 km offshore from Kuala Trengganu, only about 30 km from Kampong Merang further north. There's a good chance of finding a boat going across to this inhabited island on Thursdays or Fridays. Pulau Bidong is 34 km off KT but only about 16 from Kampong Merang although it can be difficult to get boats out there. Do not confuse Merang, north of KT, with Marang, to the south.

Swimming at Pantai Batu Burok, the beach immediately south of the town, is not so good and there are often fierce undertows. There's a three-day beach festival held here each year in May. It's better at Chenering Head, 10 km south. There are also reasonably good beaches and swimming north of KT at Batu Rakit (rather dirty beach) and Kampong Merang. Both places are off the main road; Batu Rakit is 25 km north and Kampong Merang, with a good beach and swimming in the bay, is a further 15 km north. There's a pleasant guest house at Batu Rakit.

Other

The Sekayu Waterfalls are 56 km west of Kuala Trengganu. You have to walk three km from Kampong Ipoh, a little beyond Kuala Berang, to the falls where there are pleasant natural swimming pools. In Kuala Berang you can stay at the *Selasi Hotel* for M$14.

Kuala Trengganu has a wide variety of handicrafts made in and around the town. At Rusila, 13 km south, you can see palm leaves woven into mats, baskets or bags in the process known as mengkuang weaving. Traditional brocade songket weaving is done at Kampong Pulau Rusa, upriver from KT, and at Kampong Tanjong, on the north bank of the Trengganu River. Brasswork and batik are other popular local crafts.

Places to Stay – bottom end

Cheaper hotels are found along Jalan Paya Bunga or close to it. At number 12 the *Trengganu Hotel* (tel 096-22900) has rooms from M$18 up to M$35 with air-con. Next door to the pricier Warisan Hotel is the *Meriah Hotel* (tel 096-22655) at 67 Jalan Paya Bunga where rooms range from M$24.20 with air-con, plus there are larger rooms for four or more people.

Directly opposite the bus station the *Rex Hotel* has doubles with bathroom and fan for M$15 and it's fairly quiet despite its location. It's clean and well kept, and you even get soap, towels and mosquito coils. There's a good open-air restaurant next door.

Right at the bottom of the heap there's the *Hotel Tong Nam* (tel 096-21540) at 29B Jalan Paya Bunga with rooms at M$18; the *Hotel Lido* (tel 096-21752) at number 62 with rooms at M$12 and on Jalan Masjid the *Seaview Hotel* (tel 096-21911) with rooms at M$12, more with air-con. On Jalan Banggol there's the *Hotel Bunga Raya* (tel 096-21166) at 105 and the *Golden City Hotel* (tel 096-21777) at 101.

Mid-range hotels include the *Hotel Warisan* (tel 096-22688/22713) at 65 Jalan Paya Bunga with air-con singles/ doubles at M$40/60. Or the *Hoover Hotel* at 49 Jalan Paya Bunga with doubles with bath for M$28 or M$40 with air-con. In an island in the river the 'yellow house', *Awi*

House, is a sort of unofficial guest house which may take guests for M$5 – a good opportunity to experience kampong life although mosquitoes can be a nuisance on windless nights.

Places to Stay – top end

The *Pantai Motel* (tel 096-22100) on Jalan Persinggahan is Kuala Trengganu's number one hotel. It's on the beachfront about a km from the centre on the Kuantan side of town. The Pantai Motel has 74 air-con rooms with a major extension on the drawing board. Singles/doubles cost M$90/105. There's a swimming pool, yet another of those Vietnamese boat peoples' boats-become-bars and, a neat little touch, an arrow on the ceiling of every room pointing devoutly towards Mecca! Before you contemplate swimming from the beach in front of the motel, walk a hundred metres or so towards the town and see what the villagers use the beach for every morning.

Alternatively there's the *Motel Desa* (tel 096-22100) on top of Bukit Pak Apil, a hill close to the town. It's a steep climb to the top where singles/doubles cost M$85/95. The motel is air-con and there's a swimming pool.

Places to Eat

There are plenty of Chinese restaurants along Jalan Bunga Raya and Jalan Bandar. If you feel like a minor extravagance the *Pantai Motel's* restaurant sometimes puts on an excellent smorgasbord of Malay food. It's an excellent opportunity to try all sorts of unusual local specialities and the cost is around M$16 for a complete meal including desserts and coffee.

Getting There

The taxi stand is at the bottom of Jalan Paya Bunga, right at the waterfront. Fares include M$7 to Jerteh (for Kuala Besut), M$5.50 to Kuala Dungun, M$11 to Kota Bahru, M$15 to Kuantan, M$27 to Mersing and M$33 to Kuala Lumpur.

By bus it's M$5.30 to Rantau Abang, M$7.50 to Kuantan, M$6 to Kota Bahru, M$14 to 20 to Kuala Lumpur, M$24 to Johore Bahru and M$25 to Singapore. KT's bus station is very grubby.

Small ferries cross the river mouth from wharfs right behind the taxi stand (40c to cross) or from along the waterfront behind Jalan Bandar. The best way to KT's airport is probably to take the ferry across the river and then take a taxi for about M$2.

KUALA TRENGGANU TO KOTA BAHRU

At Kuala Trengganu the road leaves the coast and runs inland to Kota Bahru, 165 km north. There are, however, a number of minor roads branching off to the coast with several good places for swimming. Batu Rakit and Kampong Merang have already been mentioned. Further north there is Kuala Besut, the jumping-off point for trips to Pulau Perhentian. Kuala Keluang, about 10 km south of Kuala Besut, also has good beaches.

The final stretch into Kota Bahru runs through fertile rice-growing areas, mirroring

1	Tourist Information Office	9	Chinese Temple
2	Pantai Motel	10	Central Market
3	Hotel Warisan	11	Mosque
4	Hoover Hotel	12	Istana Mazia
5	Hotel Tong Nam	13	GPO
6	Hotel Lido	14	Seaview Hotel
7	MAS	15	Dot's Motel
8	Trengganu Hotel	16	Sri Trengganu Hotel

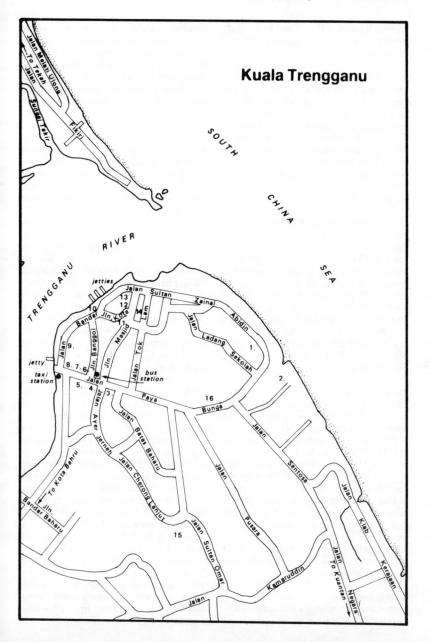

Kuala Trengganu

the similar area in Kedah and Perlis at the northern end of the peninsula on the other, western, side.

KUALA BESUT

On the coast south of Kota Bahru there's a reasonably pleasant beach here and an interesting, though amazingly grubby, little fishing village. A visit to Kampong Kuala Besut is usually just a preliminary to a trip to Perhentian Island though. Since fishing boats out to Perhentian all leave in the morning you're pretty well committed to spending a night at the rest house.

Note that Kuala Besut is in two parts, separated by a river. The northern part (the turn-off is at Pasir Puteh) is the fishing village and has the small shops and market. The southern part, for which the main road turn-off is at Jerteh, has the rest house and various government offices. The small ferries which used to shuttle back and forth across the river have now been replaced by a big bridge. There's a new fisheries centre on the south side of the river and you can catch fishing boats out to Pulau Perhentian from the large dock there.

Places to Stay

The *Rest House* is quite close to the beach on the south side of the river. It's fairly spacious and in a reasonably new building with double rooms with bathroom and fan at M$15. There are also some small, basic rooms at M$7. It's a friendly place and has recently had a long-overdue clean up and coat of paint so it's now a pretty good place to stay. The restaurant food is somewhat pricey (M$1.80 for mee soup) and not all that good although they make excellent tea.

About a km north of the rest house, right by the bridge, the *Banana Leaf Restaurant* has pretty good food.

Getting There

From Kota Bahru take a bus number 3 to Jerteh (M$2.80); from where you can get another bus through Kampong Raja to Kuala Besut. There are also out-station taxis which cost M$1 from Jerteh to Kuala Besut. They'll stop in Kampong Raja for you to check on the rest house bookings for Pulau Perhentian. Heading north a share-taxi Jerteh-Kota Bahru costs M$4.50.

PULAU PERHENTIAN

A two-hour boat trip off the coast from Kuala Besut, south of Kota Bahru, are the beautiful islands of Pulau Perhentian Besar and Pulau Perhentian Kechil, 21 km out from the coast. They're a delightful escape from whatever hustle and bustle the mainland can offer. Although you can day-trip out there it's better to stay a few days. On uninhabited Pulau Perhentian Besar there is a *Rest House* with four double rooms which can be booked through the District Office in Kampong Raja, just a couple of km from Kuala Besut. The booking system is a little haphazard. Nightly cost is M$12 per room and they have flush toilets and a generator which operates from 6.30 to 11 pm each night. A narrow strait separates the besar (big) island from the kechil (small) island, where there is a fishing village.

You must come to the island ready to be self-sufficient, for although you can buy fish and some limited supplies from the village on the other island there's not much available. Nor is there much in the way of equipment at the rest house so cups, utensils and knives and forks are all worth bringing. It's recommended that you boil all drinking water. If the rest house should be full there are four furnished cottages on the beach at M$5 – the beach is better than the rest house but the shower is a well and you have to use a convenient bush for a toilet. The rest house and cottage caretaker is a real character and takes good care of you. You can also camp although by all reports a tent is preferable to sleeping out on the beach – unless you don't mind being trampled on at night by metre-plus iguanas, flying foxes or monkeys!

On the island it's a case of lazing around and watching the coconuts fall. There are beautiful beaches, though rather littered around the rest house, and excellent snorkelling. There are also some walking trails although they don't go too far since most of the island is covered with impenetrable jungle. Bring plenty of books and suntan lotion.

Getting There
Getting out to the island is fairly simple. In Kuala Besut there are plenty of fishing boats which will be going out to the island and will take passengers. The usual price is M$5 to 10 per person although bargaining will probably start from a higher level. If you have to charter a boat it could cost around M$50 to 80 for a day-trip charter. Getting back can be a little difficult – you've just got to wait for a boat to come by. There are plenty of worse places to be stranded.

KOTA BAHRU
In the north-east corner of the peninsula, Kota Bahru is the capital of the state of Kelantan, the termination of the east coast road and an alternative, and much less frequently used, gateway into Thailand. It's also Malaysia at its most Malayan – Kota Bahru is a centre for Malayan culture, crafts and religion. It's the place to see kite-flying contests, study batik, admire traditional woodcarving, photograph the colourful marketplace and marvel at the skills of songket weavers and silversmiths.

Information & Orientation
The Kota Bahru tourist office (tel 097-25533) is open Saturday to Wednesday from 8 to 11.45 am and 2 to 4 pm, Thursday from 8 am to 12.45 pm, closed Friday. It's on Jalan Ibrahim, just a stone's throw south of the clock tower and a little north of the GPO. The tourist office has some useful information sheets which you may be able to pick up even if the office is shut. In Kelantan state public offices and banks are all closed Thursday afternoons and Fridays, but open on Saturdays and Sundays.

The Royal Thai Consulate (tel 097-22545) is on Jalan Pengkalan Chepa and is open from 9 am to 4 pm from Sundays to Thursdays, but may be closed for lunch between 12.30 and 2.30 pm.

Like Kuantan and Kuala Trengganu, the town is beside a wide river, in this case the Kelantan River, but unlike Kuala Trengganu, Kota Bahru is not on the coast but about 10 km inland. The centre of town is a fairly compact, crowded area just north of the clock tower. It centres around the large market place, and the taxi and local bus stations and most of the hotels are also in this central area. The long-distance bus station is in the south of the town while the Kota Bahru railway station is several km away at Wakaf Bahru, across the river. The railway line continues on to terminate at Tumpat.

A little north of the city centre is Merdeka Square, around which a number of the town's points of interest cluster.

Around Merdeka Square
The central Merdeka Square was built as a memorial following WW I. There are several points of interest around it and at night the car park at the end of the square becomes a popular open-air eating place. On one side of the square is the State Mosque, completed in 1926. Next to it is the Hong Kong and Shanghai Bank which is the town's oldest brick building. Built in 1913, it was used by the Japanese army as their headquarters during World War 11.

Beyond the car park at the end of the square is the entrance to the Istana Balai Besar or 'Palace of the Large Audience Hall', which dates from 1844. Constructed largely of timber, the palace contains an opulent royal barge that was used only once for a cruise on the Kelantan River in 1900. The adjacent Istana Jahar was constructed in 1889.

The riverfront in Kota Bahru is sadly neglected and messy.

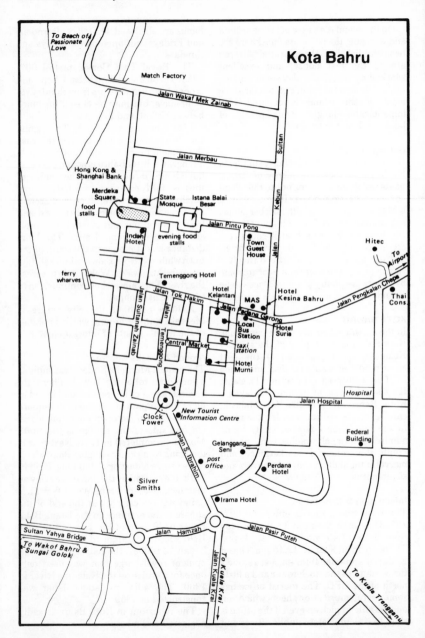

Kota Bahru

To Beach of Passionate Love
Match Factory
Jalan Wakaf Mek Zainab
Jalan Merbau
Sultan
Kebun
Hong Kong & Shanghai Bank
Merdeka Square
food stalls
State Mosque
Istana Balai Besar
Jalan Pintu Pong
Indah Hotel
evening food stalls
Town Guest House
Hitec
To Airport
ferry wharves
Temenggong Hotel
Jalan Tok Hakim
Hotel Kelantan
MAS
Hotel Kesina Bahru
Jalan Pengkalan Chepa
Thai Cons.
Jalan Sultanah Zainab
Jalan Temenggong
Jalan Padana Garong
Local Bus Station
Hotel Suria
Central Market
taxi station
Hotel Murni
Hospital
Jalan Hospital
Clock Tower
New Tourist Information Centre
Federal Building
Jalan S. Ibrahim
Gelanggang Seni
post office
Perdana Hotel
Silver Smiths
Irama Hotel
Sultan Yahya Bridge
To Wakof Bahru & Sungai Golok
Jalan Hamzah
Jalan Pasir Puteh
Jalan Kuala Krai
Jalan Kuala Krai
To Kuala Trengganu

Handicrafts

Kota Bahru is a centre for Malay crafts and there are many you can see in and around the town. Batik is said to be better in Kota Bahru than anywhere else in Malaysia. Amongst the items you can buy are batik sarongs (M$6-8), cloths (M$4-6), tablecloths (M$6-9) and shirts either long-sleeved (M$12-16) or short-sleeved (M$10-14). There's an interesting batik factory at Samasa, down the road beside Lee's Garage which you reach on a bus number 5.

Silverwork is another local speciality and you can see silversmiths at work at Kampong Sireh near KB. Songket weaving can be seen in a number of places along the road to Pantai Cinta Berahi, take a 10 or 28 bus. Along the same road there are a number of places making and selling those fantastic Malaysian kites. Look for the sign Wau Bulan or 'moon kites'. They cost from M$9 or 10 but can be difficult to pack and mail. Traditional woodcarving can be seen out on the airport road; take a bus 4, 9 or 13.

Activities

Every Saturday, except during the fasting months of Ramadan, there are performances of top spinning, traditional dance dramas, wayang kulits, and other east coast activities from 3 to 5.30 pm and from 8 to 11.30 pm. They're held at Gelanggang Seni, across the road from the Hotel Perdana on Jalan Mahmud. Check with the tourist office for more details. The performances are usually free but the hours seem to vary with the season.

Each year in June, Kota Bahru has a bird-singing contest when you can see the prized Merbok or Burong Ketitir birds perform. There are also contests every week in a village about seven km downriver from Kota Bahru. It starts around 8 am with numerous categories of competition. Ask in pet shops.

Places to Stay

There's a varied selection of accom-modation in Kota Bahru although there's not too much of the very upper-notch places. Finding places in KB is somewhat complicated by the curious street-naming and numbering procedures. Jalan Tok Hakim changes name to Jalan Padang Garong and then becomes Jalan Pengkalan Chepa all within the space of a couple of hundred metres for example. The numbering process is even worse; you've only gone down Pengkalan Chepa a few doors and you find yourself into the thousands and one side of the street seems to bear no relationship to the other.

Places to Stay – bottom end

At the bottom end of the price scale there is a popular hostel-style place although it has moved since the previous edition. *Hitec* is at 4398 Jalan Pengkalan Chepa, but it's easier to find if you note that it's right across the road from the Thai Consulate. That's about a km out of town towards the airport; take a number 4 or 9 bus (25c), or it's about M$1 by trishaw. Dorm beds are M$4, rooms about M$10 and there are cooking facilities. There's an excellent travellers' notebook here where visitors write all sorts of useful tips from their trips. 'Mummy', who runs Hitec, is a great talker! A word of caution: Some fast thinker has taken over the old place where Hitec used to be, and opened a guest house called 'Hitect'!

Recently opened, the *Town Guest House* (tel 097-22127) is a clean and friendly place at 2921 Jalan Pintu Pong. There's dorm-style accommodation at M$5 (just a mattress on the floor) or doubles from M$10 and up. It's a few minutes' walk from the bus station in a pleasantly quiet area, close to the night market. Tea and coffee here are free and travel information is available.

Rock-bottom-price Chinese hotels include the clean, pleasant and convenient *Kelantan Hotel*, right by the bus station on Jalan Tok Hakim, with rooms at M$10-14. Unfortunately it's also rather noisy. A little further up Tok Hakim you come to the similarly priced *Mee Ching*. Walk right by the decrepit *Ah Chew* – even if it is, as one traveller put it, 'nothing to be sneezed at'! Another added that it 'hasn't been cleaned since the Japanese left in '45'. Also 'basic with a capital B' is the *Tyhe Ann Hotel*, opposite the bus stand, where rooms cost M$10. *Hotel Maryland* (tel 097-22811) on Jalan Tok Hakim costs from M$16 and is very noisy although otherwise OK. Close to the river at 3655 Jalan Tok Hakim, the *New Bali Hotel* is pleasant, clean and quiet and has rooms from M$10 to 16.

Up a notch in price the *Hotel Aman* (tel 097-43049) is next to the Indah Hotel on Jalan Tengku Besar and has big doubles with bathroom for only M$24 – good value. *Hotel Suria* (tel 097-22188) is on Jalan Padang Garong overlooking the bus station and has rooms from M$20-46; the more expensive rooms have air-con. On the same street the *Hotel Irama* (tel 097-22722) has rooms for around M$24-40, some with air-con.

At 3945 Jalan Tok Hakim, next to the big Hotel Temenggong, the *Hotel Tokyo* has nice fan-cooled doubles with bathroom for M$20. Other central place in the M$15-30 range include the *Bahru Hotel* (tel 097-21164) on Jalan Dato Pati, directly across from the flashy Murni Hotel, and the *Intan Hotel* (tel 097-21277) on the same street. The *Meriah Hotel* (tel 097-21388) is on Jalan Ismail, *Hotel Milton* is on Jalan Pengkalan Chepa and *Hotel Berling* is on Jalan Tengku Petra.

Places to Stay – top end

At the top end, the 136-room *Hotel Perdana* (tel 097-25000) on Jalan Mahmud has singles at M$90-100, doubles at M$100-110. It's the biggest and most expensive hotel in Kota Bahru and is all air-con and has a swimming pool, tennis courts and so on. Right in the centre on Jalan Datuk Pati, the architecturally eccentric *Hotel Murni* (tel 097-22399) has singles/doubles for M$52-90/M$458-100.

On Jalan Padang Garong the slightly run-down *Hotel Kesina Bahru* (tel 097-21455) has singles at M$35-40, doubles at M$40-50. The new *Hotel Temenggong* (tel 077-23844) is at 3988 Jalan Tok Hakim and has singles/doubles at M$45/70. Overlooking Merdeka Square from Jalan Tengku Besar, the *Hotel Indah* (tel 077-25633) is in the same price range.

Finally in this more expensive bracket, but out at the Beach of Passionate Love, the *Resort Pantai Cinta Berahi* (tel 097-21307) has beachfront chalets with air-con and rooms with and without air-con. Prices start from around M$35 and go up to M$100 or more. Recent reports indicate that it has become run down and dilapidated, it's expensive for what you get and the beach is nothing special anyway. You can, however, negotiate on the prices, which for the cheaper rooms may well prove flexible.

Places to Eat

Despite the town's overwhelmingly Malay character there are plenty of Chinese restaurants around, particularly near the bus stop and along Jalan Padang Garong. The *Tyhe Ann Hotel* has a restaurant downstairs 'which must be good, it's always full and noisy'. Some of Kota Bahru's food stalls, however, look decidedly unhygienic.

The food centres in the car park by Merdeka Square and at Taman Sekebun Bunga (the 'floating house') are good places for satay and other Malay dishes. The *Rosliza Restaurant*, next door to the Kesina Bahru Hotel on Jalan Padang Garong, is reputed to have the best Malay food in Kota Bahru although the prices have recently taken a skyward leap.

Western-style bread in Malaysia tends to be an over-sweet disaster area, but KB has a surprising number of bakeries producing surprisingly good bread and other treats like chicken pies. The *Maju Bakery*, opposite the bus stand and the *Choo Chin Hin Bakery* round the corner behind the taxi stand, are just two of them.

Finally for an unforgettable name, if nothing else, beside the clock tower there's the *Kent Turkey Fried Chicken Restaurant*.

Getting There

Bus The opening of the long-awaited east-west highway has brought Kota Bahru and Penang much closer together. Previously you had to make a 1000 km detour south through KL, a slightly less circuitous trip north through Thailand, or fly. Now it's a straightforward day trip. Air-con buses depart from the Butterworth bus terminal by the ferry between 9 and 9.30 am and cost around M\$17 to 20, depending on the company. Departures from Kota Bahru are at about the same time. With a couple of meal stops the trip takes seven or more hours. See the Coast to Coast section at the end of this chapter for details on places along the road.

Buses from Kota Bahru cost M\$6 to Kuala Trengganu, M\$14 to Kuantan, M\$20-28 to Kuala Lumpur, M\$24 to Melaka and M\$24-30 to Johore Bahru. Taxis cost M\$14 to Kuala Trengganu, M\$26 to Kuantan, M\$45 to Kuala Lumpur and M\$50 to Johore Bahru. It takes 19 hours for a bus all the way to Singapore.

Rail See the introductory Getting Around section for train timetable and fare details. Note that the Kota Bahru station is at Wakaf Bahru, a 40c trip on a 19 or 27 bus. It's possible to transport cars in the train between Kuala Lipis and Kuala Krai. Travelling to Kota Bahru by train, get off at Pasir Mas and take a taxi into town – it's the same price as from Tumpat (M\$1.50) and saves an hour of train travel. Buses go from Wakaf Bahru but the saving (M\$1) is hardly worth the effort.

If you're simply heading through to Thailand then you can travel straight from Pasir Mas to the border at Rantau Panjang; taxi fare is around M\$2. Malaysian currency can be spent at Sungei Golok in Thailand (in Hat Yai too, for that matter).

Getting Around

There are a wide variety of local bus services from Kota Bahru. To the coastal village of Bachok take a 2 bus, M\$1.60. For Kuala Besut take a 3 bus to Jerteh, M\$2.70. Kuala Krai is reached by bus 5 for M\$3. This is the last point on the railway line south which you can reach by road. To Pantai Cinta Berahi, the Beach of Passionate Love, take a bus 10 for 60c. Tumpat to the north is reached by bus 19 or 27 for M\$1.

Local taxis run to the airport (whole taxi) for M\$8, to Kuala Krai for M\$4.50, Tanjong Merah for M\$3.50 and Machang for M\$2.80 on a share taxi basis.

AROUND KOTA BAHRU
Beaches

Kota Bahru's best-known beach has a name that's hard to forget. Pantai Cinta Berahi, the 'Beach of Passionate Love', is 10 km north of the town. Actually it's just a normal enough beach with a few casuarinas and palm trees; it hardly lives up to its exotic name. Furthermore any overt passion is likely to be looked on with extreme displeasure in this staunchly Muslim area. Foreigners are generally ignored but local Malaysians have to behave themselves here!

Pantai Dasar Sabak is 13 km from KB, three km's beyond the Pengkalan Chepa Airport. It's a beach with a history; on 7 December 1941 the Pacific Theatre of WW II commenced here, when Japanese troops stormed ashore, a full hour and a half before the rising sun rose over Pearl Harbor.

Other beaches close to Kota Bahru include Pantai Dalam Rhu near the fishing village of Semerak, 19 km from Pasir Puteh, near Kuala Besut. It's sometimes known as Pantai Bisikan Bayu, the 'Beach of Whispering Breeze'. Pantai Irama, the 'Beach of Melody', is 25 km south of KB. North of KB there's Pantai Kuda, 'Horse Beach', 25 km away in the Tumpat area.

Waterfalls

There are a number of popular waterfalls in the Pasir Puteh area. Jeram Pasu is the most popular; to reach it you have to follow an eight-km path from Kampong Padang Pak Amat, about 35 km south of KB en route to Pasir Puteh. Other falls in this same area include Jeram Tapeh, Cherang Tuli and Jeram Lenang.

Kuala Krai

Kuala Krai, 65 km south of Kota Bahru, used to be the end of the road but now it continues on Gua Musang. On the way to Kuala Krai you can stop at Labok, a natural hot springs two km off the road. Kuala Krai has a zoo specialising in local wildlife. It's open from 8 am to 6 pm and admission is 50c.

Places to Stay The *Kiew Shi Hotel*, next to the prominently advertised Bata Shoe Shop, is two minutes' walk from the railway station. It's quiet for a Chinese hotel, and very clean. Rooms cost M$9.

River Trips

You can make a number of river trips from Kota Bahru. A short trip takes you downriver to Kuala Besar at 12 noon. You can then return on a bus No 28. Longer trips can be made from Kuala Krai. Take a number 5 bus there at 8 am for M$3; then between 11 am and 12.15 pm (except Fridays) get a boat to Kuala Balah for M$4. It's a two-hour trip through dense jungle. From Kuala Balah you can hitch or pay for a ride (around M$4) to Jeli, near the Thai border, then bus to Tanah Merah (M$2) and from there back to Kota Bahru (M$1.95). Buses on the new east-west highway also pass through Tanah Merah.

Alternatively you can get the boat back to Kuala Krai next morning around 6.45 am. A third alternative is to get off the boat at Dabong, before you reach Kuala Balah. Dabong is on the railway line and you can get a train back to Kota Bahru in the afternoon. From Dabong you can walk to a cave in about an hour, or a six-km walk on

the road towards Jeli brings you to a small village; turn off the road and another km or two takes you to an impressive 50-metre-high waterfall. You can also get a motorcycle ride there for about M$2.

Places to Stay Kuala Balah has recently been rebuilt a km or so away from its previous flood-prone site. For accommodation contact the headman whose official residence is temporarily the community centre next to the new school buildings.

Wildlife

There are a number of salt-licks in Kelantan where you may see deer, goats and even elephants in search of salt. There's one in the Jenut Sira area, about 1½ hours' walk from Lubok Bongor which is between Kampong Balah and Jeli. The salt-lick near Jenut Ibu is close to the banks of the Sungai Ibu river and can only be reached by boat.

Tumpat

Around Tumpat, in the region bordering with Thailand, there are a number of interesting Buddhist temples. Kampong Berok, about 12 km north of Kota Bahru, has Wat Phothivihan, a Buddhist temple with a 41-metre-long reclining Buddha statue, claimed to be one of the largest in South-East Asia. It was built in 1973. There is a rest house here available for use by sincere devotees for a donation. The abbot is a soccer fan, 'which he watches on his splendid colour TV'!

Other Thai-influenced temple or 'wats' include Wat Mai Suwan Kiri.

Masjid Kampong Laut

Reputed to be the oldest mosque in Peninsular Malaysia, this mosque is not, however, at Kampong Laut as its name would indicate. The mosque is said to have been built about 300 years ago by a group of Javanese Muslims as thanks for a narrow escape from pirates. It originally stood at Kampong Laut, just across the

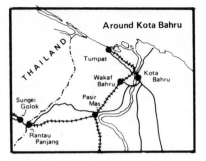

Around Kota Bahru

river from Kota Bahru, but each year the November-to-January monsoon floods caused considerable damage to the wooden mosque and in 1968 the decision was made to shift it to a safer location.

It now stands at Kampong Nilam Puri, about 10 km inland. Nilam Puri is a local centre for religious study, and adjacent to the mosque is the State Religious Council building, a fine example of Kelantan craftsmanship. It was originally established in 1914.

TAMAN NEGARA
Peninsular Malaysia's great national park covers 4343 square km and sprawls across the states of Pahang, Kelantan and Trengganu. The part of the park usually visited is all in Pahang, however, and virtually all visitors will enter the park in Pahang. Reactions to the park depend totally on the individual's experience. Some people see lots of wildlife and come away happy, others see little more than leeches and find the park hardly worth the effort. It's always that way with undependable living things!

The park headquarters are at Kuala Tahan and from here there are a number of jungle walks to hides and salt licks where you may see animals. Getting well away from it all requires long trips upriver by boat and a visit to the park can then become quite expensive.

Information & Orientation
If you want to book accommodation and be met by the park boat and so on, then you should write as far ahead as possible to the Chief Game Warden, Block K20, Government Offices Building, Jalan Duta, Kuala Lumpur (tel 03-941056 or 941272). On arrival at Kuala Tahan you must pay M$5 park entrance and camera fees.

The best time to visit the park is between March and September. It's usually closed from mid-November until mid-January (or later) due to the rainy season.

Although everyday clothes are quite suitable around Kuala Tahan, you'll need heavier-duty gear if you're heading further afield. Jungle attire is a good idea both as protection and to make you less conspicuous to the wildlife you want to see. Although they can be a real nuisance after heavy rain, leeches are generally not a major problem although they're often there. River travel in the early morning hours can be surprisingly cold. Mosquitoes can be a nuisance but you can buy repellent at the park shop, which also seems to work on leeches.

Camping equipment can be provided if you're exploring further into the wilds. If you're overnighting in a hide you'll need a torch (flashlight). The camp office have a couple they'll hire out.

Hides & Salt Licks
There are seven salt-licks in the park which are readily accessible. A number of them are close to Kuala Tahan and Kuala Terenggan. Jenut Tabing and Jenut Belau are both close to Kuala Tahan and at these salt-licks you may see tapir, wild pigs, barking deer and sambar. You can watch the wildlife from hides at four of the salt-licks, including Jenut Kumbang and Jenut Belau. Of course there's no guarantee that you'll see anything from these hides, even with an overnight stay. Bird-watching enthusiasts are generally more impressed with the park wildlife than those who definitely want to see animal life.

It costs M$2.50 to overnight in the high game-viewing hides. A boat to Kumbang hide would cost around M$35. It's a nice five or six hour walk back to the park headquarters.

Rivers & Fishing

Although the rivers are a primary means of transport in the park, some of them are an experience in themselves. From Kuala Tahan to Kuala Terenggan, for example, there are seven rapids to be negotiated and that trip is quite an experience up or downriver. Lubok Simpon, only 10 minutes on foot from the park headquarters, has a good natural bathing pool. Anglers may find the park a real paradise. Fish found in the park rivers include the superb fighting fish known in India as the Mahseer but here as the Kelasa. Popular fishing rivers include the Sungei Tahan, which falls 152 metres from Kuala Teku to Kuala Tahan. The Sungei Kenyam, above Kuala Terenggan, is also popular while the Sungei Sepia is very remote. February through March and July through August are the best fishing months.

Mountains & Walks

Gunung Tahang at 2187 metres is the highest mountain in Peninsular Malaysia, but to climb to the summit requires a 2½ day trek from Kuala Tahang to Kuala Teku at the foot of the mountain and another 2½ days to the summit. A guide is also required.

On the other hand you can climb 590-metre Gunung Gendang in a day-trip from Kuala Tahang. There are also a series of limestone caves in the park but these are 2½ days by boat and on foot from the park headquarters.

Places to Stay

There's a fairly comprehensive choice of accommodation at the park although you're pretty much limited to the basic dormitories unless you've booked ahead. At Kuala Tahan there's a *Rest House* and four chalets with rooms with attached bathrooms at M$15 or dorm beds at M$4. If accommodation is really tight the rangers will rent you a tent.

Elsewhere there are *Visitors' Lodges* at Kuala Atok, Kuala Terenggan and Kuala Kenyam and *Fishing Lodges* at Kuala Perkai and Lata Berkoh. At these lodges bedding, cooking and eating utensils, water and firewood are all provided. You must, however, provide your own food, but supplies can be bought at Kuala Tahan. There's also a restaurant there where you can get a set meal for around M$6, fried rice for M$3. The food is indifferent and the service poor. There's also a cheaper restaurant for the staff which others can use.

Getting There

The entry point into the park is Kuala Tembeling, near Tembeling Halt on the central railway line. To get there you can take the train north or south and a stop at Tembeling Halt will be arranged if you make a request to the stationmaster upon boarding. If you leave Singapore on the night train you get to Gemas at 3 am and change to the Tumpat train which departs at 3.30 am. It arrives at Jerantut at 8.19 am or a little later at Tembeling Halt. Very early for the 2 pm park boat!

Travelling south, the day train from Kota Bahru doesn't get to Tembeling Halt until after 6 pm so you might as well continue to Jerantut, arriving at 6.50 pm and spend the night and morning there before getting to Kuala Tembeling in time for the 2 pm boat.

It's either a short bus trip or a half-hour walk from Tembeling Halt to Kuala Tembeling. Alternatively you can go by bus to Kuala Lipis, then catch the train to Tembeling Halt or go by road direct to Kuala Tembeling. Buses run Jerantut-Tembeling about every 1½ hours. A taxi will be about M$3 per person or M$12 for the whole taxi. Temerloh-Tembeling takes about two hours by bus.

From Tembeling to the park head-quarters at Kuala Tahan is a 2½ to 3½-

hour river trip depending on the river conditions. The park boat starts at M$10 per person provided you have enough people – the trip can cost more if not enough people are going. The boat doesn't run every day, so it really pays to check by phone or in person with the KL parks office. The boat departs from the park compound a couple of hundred metres beyond the village at around 2 pm. Alternatively, a private boat will cost M$15 to 20 per person, depending on bargaining. The river trip is a high point of a park visit. When leaving the park you can sometimes get a boat right down to Jerantut Ferry, beyond Jerantut.

Leaving the park, if you wanted to continue north you'd have to leave the park and overnight in Jerantut, then either catch the early morning train coming north from Gemas or the 12 noon local to Kuala Lipis, and overnight there. Travelling south you can catch the train at Tembeling Halt or Jerantut in the evening. It gets to Gemas at 11.45 pm to connect with the midnight train to Singapore, arriving at 5.55 am.

Getting Around

Around Kuala Tahan there are jungle tracks, and a shoestring visitor to the park can stick to walking. If you want to go further it entails hiring a boat – M$30 to 50 for a six-person boat for the interesting upstream trip from Kuala Tahan to Kuala Terenggan.

COAST TO COAST

With the completion of the northern east-west highway there are now three routes from coast to coast, apart from the crossing in the south between Ayer Hitam and Jemaluang, a little south of Mersing. You can also choose east or west right at the beginning in Johore Bahru.

East-West Highway

The new east-west road starts near Kota Bahru and runs roughly parallel to the Thai border, eventually meeting the little-used road north from Kuala Kangsar to Keroh on the Thai border at Gerik. The views from the highway are often superb. The road runs through jungle which was the last area of the peninsula to be controlled by Communist guerrilla forces so they're rather touchy about it. There are, supposedly, 62 army posts on one 117-km stretch! Furthermore the road is only open from 6 am to 6 pm daily and you must start out by 4 pm. If you're travelling with your own transport you have to fill out two forms that you surrender at the end. Transport along this road is still somewhat sporadic so hitching is unlikely to be easy. Furthermore the road may be subject to closure during the monsoon.

Gerik Also known as Grik, this was once just a logging 'cowboy town' but the east-west highway and the huge Temenggor Dam hydro power scheme has really put it on the map. For WW II buffs there are many associations with the exploits of Force 136.

The Jungle Railway

The central railway line goes largely through aboriginal territory – dense jungle offering magnificent views. Commencing near Kota Bahru, it runs to Kuala Krai, Gua Musang, Kuala Lipis, Jerantut (jumping-off point for the Taman Negara), and eventually meets the Singapore-Kuala Lumpur railway line at Gemas. Unless you have managed to book a sleeping berth right through you'll probably find yourself sharing a seat with vast quantities of agricultural produce, babies and peasants moving their entire homes. Allow for at least a couple of hours' delay, even on the expresses.

The line's days are probably numbered as roads are rapidly being pushed through. Already there is a highway from Kuala Krai to Gua Musang and this cuts the four-hour train trip to a little over an hour by car or taxis. The road from Gua Musang to Kuala Lipis is under construction and should be open by 1986. The trains are not being kept in good repair and most of the rolling stock looks as old as the line – about 50 years.

Gua Musang This former logging camp is now rapidly on its way up. Planners see it as eventually becoming the second largest town in Kelantan, centre of a huge new agricultural area. Early British jungle explorers came out here when they made their way across the main range by river-rafting and jungle tracks.

Kuala Lumpur-Kuantan

This busy road runs 275 km from KL past Bentong and through Temerloh. A bustling Chinese town, Temerloh has hotels and a good rest house. There's an active and colourful market in Temerloh each Saturday afternoon. The town is situated on the Pahang River and you can sometimes find boats going downriver to Pekan on the coast. You can also use Temerloh as a jumping-off point for trips south to Lake Tasek Bera. It's normally approached through Bahau and Ladang Geddes, which can also be reached from Seremban through Kuala Pilah.

As an alternative to the direct KL-Kuantan route you can start north from KL on the Ipoh road and turn off to Fraser's Hill. Continuing from The Gap you reach Raub, a busy gold mining area where the hunt for gold continued right up to 1955, and eventually Kuala Lipis. You can turn off the road just before Raub and rejoin the main KL-Kuantan road at Bentong or turn off at Benta Seberang for Jerantut, en route to the National Park. At Jerantut you can turn south to Temerloh or continue on to rejoin the KL-Kuantan road midway between Temerloh and Kuantan.

Tasek Bera Tasek Bera is the largest lake in Malaysia and around its shores are many Orang Asli kampongs. It's worth visiting if you can get there. You have to get police permission to visit the area in Temerloh. From there you travel Triang-

Bahav-Ladang Geddes and from there either hitch a ride with an Orang Asli (probably on a motorcycle) or walk 30 km. You can stay at the *Government Rest House* at Pos Iskandar or Tasek Bera.

Places to Stay

Gerik The *Rest House* has ancient but spacious doubles with attached bath for M$12 and is probably the best place to stay. The much more central *Sin Wah Hotel* has basic but big rooms for M$8.

Gua Musang The *Rest House* was once the police station and looks like it. It's now very decrepit and overpriced at M$14 for a double with shared bathroom, but it's friendly and from the verandah you can watch the whole life of swinging Gua Musang – you are, in fact, right opposite the volleyball court. Singles are M$8. Other Chinese hotels in the main street are a little cheaper but equally basic and less colourful. A pointer for the future is the newly built *Kesada Inn* just outside town with rooms in the M$30 range and all mod cons. Their van will fetch you from the station.

Jerantut If you're stopping here en route to the national park there are several places to stay. Like the *Jerantut Hotel* (tel 094-208) at 36 Jalan Besar with rooms from M$12. The *Sri Damak Hotel* (tel 094-463) is a little more expensive. There's also a cheap, but run down and unfriendly, *Rest House* with mosquito nets and an erratic water supply. Single rooms are M$12 and it's reasonably quiet once the traffic on the road stops at night.

Kuala Lipis The road from Fraser's Hill through Raub meets the railway line at this town. The *Rest House* has the best rooms around, but they tend to up the prices when they spot an orang putih, especially if it's late at night too. Don't pay more than M$16 and watch out for extra charges.

Cheap hotels here are again very cheap

and since they often provide more than just a bed, to avoid middle-of-the-night disturbances you have to insist 'no girls'. Try the *Central Hotel* (tel 093-21207) at 100 Jalan Besar; the *Southern Park* is probably better although also very basic indeed. The anonymous-looking place next to the Hotel Paris is just M$6 a night. If in trouble the personnel at the railway station will help out.

Beware of over-friendly locals in Kuala Lipis report some solo women travellers. Trains through Kuala Lipis arrive and depart at horrible hours of the night but at least the town is so small and compact you'll have no trouble finding everything.

Mentakab The railway station town where the jungle railway crosses the KL-Kuantan road just before Temerloh has a horde of cheap Chinese hotels. There's the *Cosy-Inn* (tel 094-41977), the *Yien Wah Hotel* (tel 094-41260), the *Walto Hotel* (tel 094-41262), the *London Hotel* (tel 094-41119), the *Mentakab Hotel* (tel 094-41275) and the *Supreme Hotel* (tel 094-41749). Singles down to M$10 or less, doubles for less then M$20.

Raub Between Fraser's Hill and Kuala Lipis, cheapies here include the very basic *Raub Hotel* (tel RB 286) and the *Dragon Hotel* (tel RB 321). Both have singles at around M$10. There may also be a rest house.

Temerloh There are a number of cheap Chinese hotels in Temerloh on the KL-Kuantan road with a variety of rooms under M$20. They include the very cheap *Swiss Hotel* (tel 094-51282), which has rooms with attached bathroom for M$10. It's good value although noisy from the downstairs foodstalls. Others are the *Temerloh Hotel* (tel 094-51499) at 29 Jalan Kuantan, the *Hotel Tropicana* (tel 094-51095) on Jalan Sultan Ahmed and the *Hotel Isis* (tel 094-51234) on Jalan Tengku Bakar.

There is also a *Rest House*, pleasantly situated overlooking the Pahang River. It's clean, quiet, spacious and comfortable with fan-cooled rooms at M$12 or air-con ones for M$25. Temerloh has a large number and variety of food shops.

Getting There

East-West Highway There are buses from Ipoh or Kuala Kangsar to Gerik about every two hours. Taxis to or from Kota Bahru are M$16 but be certain the driver doesn't plan to try and charge you for the whole cab if he hasn't got a full load. See the Kota Bahru section for Butterworth-Kota Bahru transport.

Jungle Railway Route See the introductory Getting Around section for timetable and fares on the jungle railway. Taxis from Kota Bahru to Gua Musang cost M$12, from Kuala Krai M$10. It's three hours by train on from here to Kuala Lipis and costs about M$5 in 2nd, M$3 in 3rd. You've got a better chance of a seat in second.

Kuala Lumpur-Kuantan There are a variety of buses and taxis on this route; see the Getting There sections of Kuala Lumpur and Kuantan for details. A share taxi Temerloh-KL is M$8.50.

Sarawak

Sarawak's period as the personal kingdom of the Brooke family of 'White Rajahs' ended with the arrival of the Japanese in WW II. Following the war the Brooke family handed Sarawak over to the British government, thus putting Britain in the curious position of acquiring a new colony at the same time they were shedding others. Sarawak remained under British control when Malaya gained its independence in 1957, but then joined Malaysia when it was formed in 1963.

Today, with its oil production plus timber, pepper and some rubber, Sarawak is of great economic importance to the nation. Although Sarawak suffered even more than Peninsular Malaysia from the Emergency and then the Confrontation, today things are quite peaceful. For the visitor Sarawak's interest is in its diversity of tribes and the many areas of still untouched jungle. Many of the tribes up the great rivers of Sarawak live in longhouses – 'villages' where the entire population live under one roof with separate rooms leading on to one long communal verandah. Hospitality to visitors is a way of life in these longhouses and many travellers in Sarawak stay overnight at one during their travels.

Visas & Permits

Even though Sarawak is a part of Malaysia it has its own immigration controls which are designed, in theory, to protect the indigenous tribal people from being swamped by migrants from the peninsula and elsewhere. This means that if you're flying into Kuching, Miri, Bintulu or Sibu from the peninsula or from Sabah you will have to go through immigration again even though the flight is officially an internal one.

On arrival you will probably be given a month's stay permit if you ask. If you want more time it's easy to get the permit extended at immigration. You may well be asked to show how much money you have and whether you want to go into the interior. If the answer to the latter question is affirmative they'll put another stamp in your passport which says you're not allowed to go there without permission.

Extensions are easily obtained from the Immigration Department in Kuching. You're required to fill in two forms and these days it usually takes less than half an hour. No photographs are required and there's no fee though they may well want to see all your money down to the last cent and any onward tickets you might have. If you haven't got the latter it's acceptable to say you'll be flying out of Kota Kinabalu, Sabah, and will buy a ticket when you get there. The Sarawak state government is very, very touchy about unannounced researchers, journalists, photographers and the like so remember, you're a tourist, nothing more.

If you plan to visit any of the longhouses above Kapit on the Rajang River or to trek overland between Belaga and Bintulu then you'll need special permits. Both of these are obtainable in Kapit without fuss or fee, but the trekking permit to Bintulu is not available in the wet season. Officially, you need an international cholera vaccination certificate for these permits but no one checks this.

You also need a special permit if you intend to visit the 'Painted Cave' (but not the main cave) in Niah National Park. Get these from the Curator's Office at the Kuching Museum. They're free and take about 10 minutes, but you have to tell them the approximate date you intend to be there. There's a large notice in the office which says, 'We are allergic to long hair'. The woman who typed out the permit had long hair. So did I. If you're coming west from Sabah or Brunei you can get these permits in Miri.

A special permit is also required from immigration in Kuching if you want to cross the land border between Sarawak and Kalimantan, Indonesia (eg if heading for Pontianak) and it's unlikely you'll get it. You'll also need an Indonesian visa of course.

General Costs

East Malaysia is not cheap and you should beware of assuming that transport and accommodation costs are on a par with those of peninsular Malaysia. Outside of Kuching and the National Parks, where hostel accommodation is available, you'll be up for at least M$15 per night and often much more. Likewise, transport on buses and launches is relatively expensive. There's often not a great deal of difference between taking an internal flight and taking a bus or launch.

Overland Travel

It is now possible to traverse Sarawak by land but only just. The last part of the road – that which links Sibu to Bintulu – has been completed but 'road' is using the term loosely. It is often a real muddy mess and getting out and pushing is part of the trip. Expect to get a lot more than your feet muddy. Usually when one vehicle gets stuck those behind will have to stop and help push it out.

Parts of the road between Bintulu and Miri are much the same. There are a couple of rivers to cross and at places the beach is used rather than the rough or muddy road. The roads between Kuching and Lundu, Kuching and Simanggang and Miri to the Brunei border are sealed and in good condition but elsewhere they're atrocious or simply non-existent. Most travel in the interior is by river launch, longboat or internal flight.

KUCHING

Kuching is without doubt the most pleasant and interesting city you'll come across in East Malaysia. Built principally on the south bank of the Sungai Sarawak

(River Sarawak), it was the centre of the White Rajah dynasty which ruled Sarawak until 1945, when the state became a British Crown Colony. It contains many beautifully landscaped parks and gardens, historic buildings, an interesting waterfront, colourful markets, one of Asia's best museums and a collection of Chinese temples, Christian churches and the relatively new mosque.

Orientation

By comparison with the state capitals of peninsular Malaysia, Kuching is small and compact and almost all the places of interest or importance to travellers are within easy walking distance of each other. The only occasions on which you'll need to use either public buses or taxis are to and from the airport (about 12 km), the Chin San Wharf at Pending for boats to Sibu (about six km) and if you need to go to the State Government Complex to buy maps for trekking purposes.

Information

There are several tourist offices. Most convenient is the helpful one on the corner of Temple St and Main Bazaar (tel 20620). They have some maps as well as pamphlets and folders on hotels, sites, shops and parks. The Tourist Development Corporation (TDC) office (tel 56775) over on Song Thian Cheok Rd, not far from Ban Hock Rd, is also good and has maps and other printed material. They are very friendly and will try to answer all your questions. Of course, the same old problem arises. If you're asking about things off the customary tourist route often the people just don't know. At the airport there is an information kiosk, but the staff here isn't as knowledgeable as those in the city.

For information on the National Parks, including advance booking of accommodation and transport, go to the Section Forest Office (tel 24474), Jalan Gertak, near Electra House. Accommodation in Bako National Park must be booked and paid for at least three days in advance.

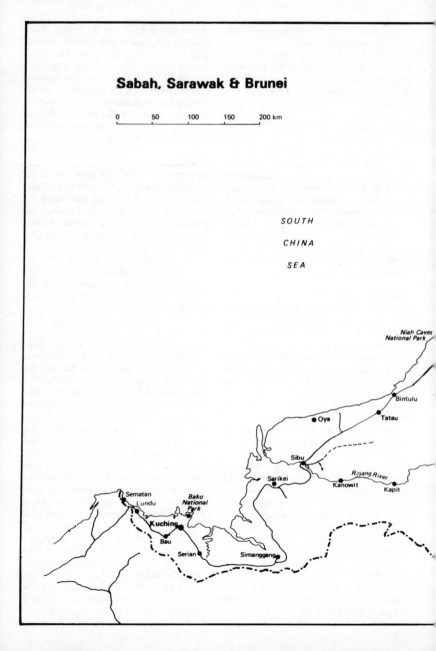

Sabah, Sarawak & Brunei

0   50   100   150   200 km

SOUTH

CHINA

SEA

Niah Caves
National Park

Bintulu

Oya   Tatau

Sibu

Sarikei   Rejang River

Kanowit   Kapit

Sematan   Bako
Lundu   National
Park

Kuching

Bau

Serian   Simanggang

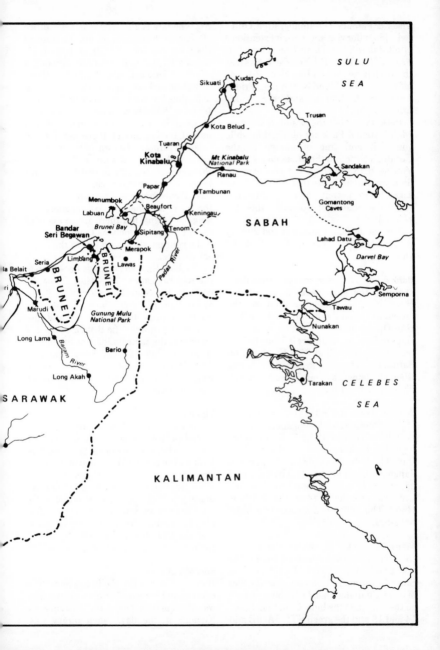

Visas & Permits The Immigration Office (tel 25661) (for visa/stay permit extensions) is off Jalan Song Thian Cheok which is itself off Ban Hock Rd. You can't miss it as there's a large sign on Ban Hock Rd. The office is open Monday through Friday from 9 am to 4.30 pm and on Saturday from 9 am to 12 noon.

Permits to visit the 'Painted Cave' at Niah National Park are obtainable while you wait and free of charge at the Curator's Office on the Museum grounds. You need to tell them the approximate date you intend to be there (I was never asked for my permit when I got there but you'd be wise not to take this for granted).

The Indonesian Consulate (tel 20551) is on Deshun Rd near the Ban Hock Rd end.

Banks For changing money (travellers' cheques) the best places to go are the Hong Kong & Shanghai Bank or the Overseas Union Bank, both on Jalan Tun Haji Openg near the junction with Main Bazaar. Banking hours are 9.30 am to 2.30 pm on weekdays and 9.30 to 11 am on Saturdays. Have your passport handy when changing travellers' cheques; you'll likely be asked for it.

Airlines MAS (tel 55122) is at Electra House, Power St while Singapore Airlines is at Jalan Tengku Abdul Rahman (in the high-rise building next to the Holiday Inn). The Indonesian airline Merpati and Japan Air Lines are handled by the travel agent on Temple St opposite the Rex Cinema, two doors from the Kuching Hotel. This office can also handle MAS bookings.

Maps & Books If you're thinking of trekking in Sarawak and need good maps take a taxi (M$2.50-3) or a local bus to the State Government Complex near the end of Jalan Simpang Tiga. Local buses which go there include the blue 'Chin Lian Long' 14 and 18 and the green STC 8A, 8B and

8C. The fare is 20c. The map sales office (Bahagian Katografi) is on the second floor on the left. Excellent large-scale maps – 1:1,000,000 and 1:500,000 of the whole of Sarawak, plus 1:50,000 (Series T735) of various parts of the state – are available, but you need security clearance from the Police headquarters in the centre of town for the sectional maps. If you intend buying any of these ask for the relevant forms and a form of recommendation at the map sales office. The people there are very friendly and will help you fill in the forms. Security clearance takes a day. The complex is strewn with more of the 'You need a hair cut. We are allergic to long hair' signs, but there are so many of them that no one notices them anymore. Take your passport with you to the maps sales office.

The best English language bookshop is the Rex Bookstore, 28 K Hun Yeang St, opposite the central police station. It has an excellent selection of books, particularly on the various tribal cultures and the history of Sarawak. The British Council is located in the same building as Singapore Airlines on Jalan Tengku Abdul Rahman. Anna Photo Syarikat at 16 Carpenter St has excellent postcard size photos of Sarawak longhouses.

The Istana

Sometimes spelt 'Astana', this shingle-roofed palace, set amid rolling lawns on the north bank of the Sungai Sarawak, was built by the second White Rajah, Charles Brooke, in 1870. It's perhaps the most attractive building in Kuching, but unfortunately no longer open to the public as it's the Governor of Sarawak's residence. It's plainly visible from the small park (Pangkalan Batu) on the opposite side of the river.

Fort Margherita

Built by Charles Brooke in the mid-19th century and named after his wife, the fort was designed to guard the entrance to Kuching in the days when piracy was commonplace. It is now a police museum (Muzium Polis) which houses a collection of weapons, uniformed dummies, memorabilia of the Japanese occupation and the Communist insurgency as well as currency-forging equipment seized at various times.

It's well worth a visit and is open every day except Mondays and public holidays from 10 am to 6 pm. There's no entry charge. To get there take one of the small ferry boats (tambangs) which ply back and forth all day until late in the evening from Pangkalan Batu. The fare is 10c each way. Instead of getting off at the landing near the Istana grounds you can get off at the Malay kampong (village) landing site. From around 2 pm to sunset stalls set up along the path from here to the fort sell many different kinds of home made Malay cakes at 10 to 20c. There's also a conveniently situated *es kachang* shop here.

Sarawak Museum

This is one of the best museums in Asia and should not be missed. It consists of two segments, the old and new, connected by a foot bridge over Jalan Tun Haji Openg. The old part was built in 1880 in the style of a Normandy town house and was strongly influenced by the anthropologist Wallace, a contemporary of Darwin, who spent two years here at the invitation of Charles Brooke.

The new section was opened toward the end of 1983 and is large, modern and air-conditioned. Together they house an incredible collection of tribal artifacts, stuffed animals and birds from the Borneo jungles, a shell collection, whale skeletons, a recreation of a longhouse complete with head-hunting skulls, wild photographs of even wilder tribal people from the beginning of the century and a whole section on the exploration and processing of oil.

Also included are ceramics, brassware, Chinese jars and furniture and a great section on some of the tribal peoples –

their arts, tools, clothes and so on. There's a cave replica and an explanation of gathering birds' nests for soup. Through the day various video and slide shows are offered in the new section. Also there is a souvenir and gift shop with some interesting items. In the old section look for the python that was killed in Kuching strung up on the wall, and the gable ends of the upper floor painted with beautiful motifs inspired by similar ones found in a longhouse at Long Nawang.

You can easily spend a few hours here. And to top it all off, it's free. The museum is open Monday through Thursday from 9.15 am to 5.30 pm and on Saturday from 9.15 am to 6 pm except for lunch between 12 noon and 1 pm. It's closed all day Friday.

Religious Buildings

The most interesting of these are the Chinese temples and the best of these is perhaps the Hong San at the junction of Ewi Hai St (Carpenter St) and Wayang St at the back of the Rex Cinema. It was build in 1897 in honour of Kuek Seng On, a native of Hokkien province in mainland China who was deified about 100 years ago.

Others include the Tua Pek Kong at the junction of Temple St and Jalan Tengku Abdul Rahman, which was built in 1876 and is the oldest in Kuching. The Kwan Yin on Jalan Tabuan was built in 1908 in honour of the goddess of mercy. Visitors are welcome at any of these temples.

The Masjid Negara or state mosque, completed in 1968, is visually impressive, particularly from across the river, but otherwise uninteresting. There is no admission for non-Muslims Thursday 3 pm through Friday 3 pm, Saturday 4 to 6 pm and Sunday 2 to 5 pm. Of the Christian churches perhaps the most interesting is the futuristic, single-roofed Roman Catholic Cathedral past the Sarawak Museum on Jalan Tun Haji Openg.

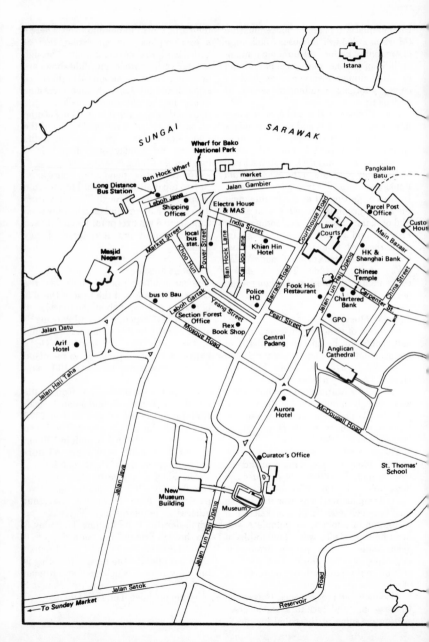

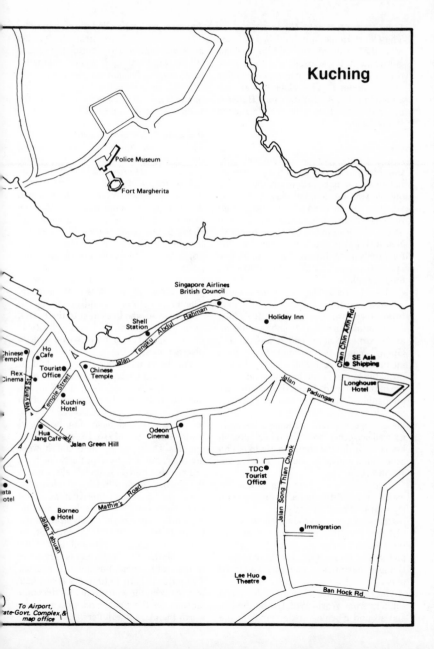

Kuching

Police Museum

Fort Margherita

Singapore Airlines
British Council

Shell
Station

Holiday Inn

Chinese
Temple

Ho
Cafe

Tourist
Office

Chinese
Temple

Rex
Cinema

Kuching
Hotel

Hua
Jang Cafe

Jalan Green Hill

Odeon
Cinema

Chen Chin Ann Rd.

SE Asia
Shipping

Longhouse
Hotel

Jalan Padungan

Jalan Tengku Abdul Rahman

Temple Street

Weyang St.

Mathie's Road

TDC
Tourist
Office

Borneo
Hotel

ata
otel

Jalan Labuan

Immigration

Jalan Song Thian Cheok

Lee Huo
Theatre

Ban Hock Rd.

To Airport,
ate-Govt. Complex &
map office

Court House & Brooke Memorial

The Court House was built in 1871 and was the seat of the White Rajahs' government. It was used until 1973 when the new government complex on Jalan Openg opened. The clock tower was added in 1883. Also at the Court House is a memorial to Charles Brooke, the second White Rajah.

Other

Kuching's open-air market is along Jalan Gambier and Market St by the waterfront. It's small and not particularly interesting unless you hit a good day and some villagers are in town. At the waterfront there is an outdoor area and a clothes and hawkers' centre in the big white building. Nearby is an information bureau, but only for family planning. Along Gambier are open-air food stalls as well as uncooked food for sale.

Much better is the very busy Sunday morning market which is a bit of a walk from downtown, but worth it. It's along Jalan Satok, turn away from the museum at the corner of Satok and Jalan Tun Haji Openg. You'll see all manner of food including some vegetables and herbs you probably haven't seen before. Wild boars are butchered and chopped-up turtles are on display. At the other end are fantastic orchids, live fish hanging in suspended plastic bags of water, cassowaries, monkeys as well as other animals. There are all kinds of birds and then plastic toys and other odds and ends usually reserved for Woolworth's.

Carpenter St is interesting to wander, with its many little shops, businesses and laneways. There are also a couple of restaurants and a bake shop. Sundays are pleasant for strolling as the streets are remarkably quiet – good for taking pictures. It seems a day for those eternal Chinese pastimes – mahjong and card playing.

The Hero's Grave commemorates Allied soldiers from World War II who died in and around Kuching at the hands of the Japanese who controlled the area in 1944. The Supreme Court, near the market area, was built in 1874 during the second White Rajah's time. If you're looking for somewhere pleasant to relax then try either the grounds of the Anglican cathedral or the Sarawak Museum Gardens, at the back of the museum itself.

Places to Stay – bottom end

The *Anglican Cathedral Hostel* is located on the hill at the back of the cathedral itself. A 'donation' of M$15 for a single, M$20 for a double gets you large, spotlessly clean rooms with polished wooden floors, comfortable beds, cane chairs, immaculately clean toilets and showers and good views. There are a couple of cheaper, smaller rooms on the upper level. The number of rooms is not great and if a conference or something is on it could well be booked out. Otherwise, giving rooms to travellers is no problem. The man to see is a friendly chap named Pulin Kantul who lives next to the hostel, down a few steps on the left. The hostel is not registered as a hotel so be a little discreet about using it.

The hotel most popular with budget travellers is the *Kuching Hotel* (tel 57811) on Jalan Temple opposite the Rex Cinema, but they only have 10 rooms so it's often full. The rooms are reasonably clean, provided with washbasin, fan, table and chair and cost M$13/15 for singles/doubles. The common toilets and showers are tatty, but usually kept fairly clean.

The other budget hotel travellers use is the *Khian Hin Hotel* (tel 26981), India St. It's more basic than the Kuching Hotel and charges M$15.40 single or double. Two other very basic hotels are the *Ah Chew Hotel* (tel 56302), 3 Jawa St, at M$18.70 single or double and the *Sun Ah Hotel*, Market St. The former is very noisy in the front rooms, but not bad overall. The latter is hard to find; it's about half way between the waterfront and the main mosque on the right-hand side and not worth the extra few dollars.

Bridging the middle and lower brackets are several lodging houses that have appeared in basically residential and office buildings near the centre of town. Try the *Green Mountain Lodging House* at 1 Jalan Green Hill (tel 59531 or 54952). Rooms, some with air-con, are simple but quite OK and cost M$30. Similar places are the *Kuok Lodging House*, around the corner, and the *Selamat Lodging House*, next door. The area is a little hard to find; it's behind Temple St at the Kuching Hotel and up the small hill. Right at the bottom of the bottom end one traveller suggested the 'grossly undermaintained' M$5 dormitory beds at the *Rumah Dayak* near Radio Malaysia.

Places to Stay – top end

Probably the pleasantest and most convenient of the middle range hotels is the *Fata Hotel* (tel 58111) at the junction of Jalan Tabuan and McDougall Rd, very close to the Borneo Hotel. Rooms here are in the M$65 single, M$75 double range and are at the top end of the middle range.

The *Arif Hotel* (tel 21211), Jalan Haji Taha opposite the Masjid Negara, is more reasonable with air-con rooms at M$55 and non air-con at M$45, cheaper still without bathroom. A third choice is the *Palm Hotel* (tel 20231) at 29 Jalan Palm (tel 20231). This is near the Sunday market and is popular with local business people.

Kuching's most prestigious hotel is the *Holiday Inn* (tel 23111), Jalan Tengku Abdul Rahman which, after recent renovation, has 325 air-conditioned rooms ranging from M$140 single, M$160 double and up. The major rebuilding added additional rooms and two more restaurants. It's beautifully situated on the banks of the Sungai Sarawak and has all the facilities you would associate with a large Holiday Inn.

Other top hotels include the *Country View* (tel 57111) on Jalan Tan Sai Datuk. They have 50 rooms from M$120. The

Liwah Hotel (tel 50222), in the Lee Hua building on Jalan Song Thian Cheok, is smaller still but rooms are about the same price. Slightly more modest, but comfortable and central, is the *Aurora Hotel* (tel 20281), at the junction of Jalan Tun Haji Openg and McDougall Rd, which has 82 air-conditioned rooms, singles at M$85 to 115, doubles at M$105 to 135. The restaurant at this hotel is excellent and popular with monied tourists and local businessmen.

The *Longhouse Hotel* (tel 55333), Abell Rd at the end of Jalan Tengku Abdul Rahman, is also good value but has the disadvantage of being quite a walk from the centre of town. It has 48 air-con rooms which cost M$60 to 70 single, M$90 double and has its own bar and restaurant. The *Borneo Hotel* (tel 24121), on Jalan Tabuan close to the centre, is also in this range. Here singles are M$70 to 80, doubles M$85 to 100. Lastly, the very popular *Mayfair* (tel 56442) at 45 Palm Rd has 42 rooms at M$85/95 for singles/doubles.

Places to Eat

Chinese Food The best place to eat (except in the evenings) is the *Fook Hoi Restaurant*, Jalan Tun Haji Openg, opposite the GPO. The food is usually very good and the helpings should satisfy even the most ravenous traveller. Rice dishes cost around M$2.50, soups M$2, fish, pork and chicken dishes from M$2.50 and prawns M$6. It's very popular with local people and travellers.

In the evenings the liveliest and best place to eat is the *Ho Cafe*, at the back of the Rex Cinema between Temple St and Wayang St. At this extremely popular open-air cafe you can get excellent satay with sweet peanut brittle dip (25c per stick), battered prawn cutlets with sweet and sour chilli sauce and many other dishes as well as cold beers. Because it's a sort of co-operative you'll have to do the rounds of the various stalls to see what's on offer. Not all the stalls are open during the day. Get there early as it fills up rapidly.

On Carpenter St, opposite the Chinese temple, is a huge, inexpensive restaurant popular with locals. Another good place to eat is the *Hua Jang Cafe* at the junction of Temple St and Wayang St opposite the Rex Cinema (there's a large Anchor Beer sign on the gable end which is lit up at night). Good Chinese food, very friendly staff and one of the few places where you can buy refrigerated Anchor beer on draught. Next door is another Chinese restaurant, the *Kwan Fook*.

Indian Food If you're looking for Indian food then try the *Malaya Restaurant*, 53 India St. The food is usually good and cheap and the staff friendly. If you don't see what you want immediately then hang around with a cup of tea and watch what comes out of the kitchen. New dishes appear every 10-15 minutes. The *Jubilee Restaurant*, 49 India St, also serves Indian food. Both these restaurants are of a similar standard, as is the nearby and colourfully painted *Zam Zam Cafe*.

Western Food If you're suffering from fish and chips/T-bone steak/scrambled eggs withdrawal symptoms then try the 4Supersonic Restaurant, Jalan Tun Haji Openg, near the Fook Hoi Restaurant, which is a popular local hangout for young people in the evenings and business people/soldiers at lunchtime. They serve western-style food for M$3 to 8 per dish, but the helpings are quite small so don't come here ravenous. There are telephone books and a public phone here and it's air-con, so it's useful for any business you may have to do.

Also for western food the *Aurora Hotel* is quite good. Sandwiches are M$2, burgers M$2.50, breakfasts M$5. You can get a milk shake or splurge on a steak at M$13. They serve Malaysian food too, but at M$4 to 7 it's not good value. For more expensive western food you could try the *San Francisco Grill House*, up past the

Borneo Hotel and around the corner toward the TDC office. The *Holiday Inn* restaurant is busy, despite asking M$7 for a hamburger! In the Kuching Plaza, across from the cathedral, the *Sugar Bun* is a fast food place offering chicken or chicken or chicken in any of a thousand disguises.

The food in the open stalls around the market area and off Jalan Gambier is pretty wretched: stale, greasy and tough. The food at the Hawkers' Centre on the waterfront is a bit better.

And a Cold Beer The cheapest beer in Kuching is Anchor draught but there are few places which sell it this way. The price of bottled beer depends on whether it's refrigerated or not although it's very unlikely you'll want to settle for anything but a cold beer in this climate. Cold bottles of Anchor cost M$2.90 (small) and M$5 (large); cold Carlsberg is a bit more. Heineken and Tsingtao (an excellent lager beer brewed in mainland China) are usually a little more expensive.

Getting There
Air – To/From Singapore & Peninsular Malaysia The regular MAS fare from KL to Kuching is M$231. There are early morning flights, economy fare, at M$162. From Singapore the fare is S$170.

Skipping over to Johore Bahru from Singapore drops the fare to M$147. To encourage people to fly from Johore Bahru MAS has a direct bus service from their Singapore office to the airport for S$6. Passports are collected at the MAS office and returned to you at the airport where you also go through a security check. There are no customs to clear until you get to Kuching. Fares from Kuching to Singapore and Peninsular Malaysia are similar. MAS also have a 14-day (sometimes more) advance purchase fare which can lower prices even further.

From Kuching flights to Bandar Seri Begawan are M$192 regular fare.

Air – To/From Indonesia Merpati operate one flight per week on Fridays from Kuching to Pontianak (Kalimantan) and Jakarta. They also fly the same route in the opposite direction on the same day. The fare is about M$84 to Pontianak and M$221 to Jakarta. The ticket agent in Kuching is the travel agent opposite the Rex Cinema on Temple St. Pontianak is not a 'no visa' entry point to Indonesia, you must have a visa before you arrive.

Air – Around Sarawak MAS have a fairly extensive provincial network with about 20 regular destinations. Flights are sometimes little more expensive than land transport.

Sea There are no longer any regular passenger shipping services between Singapore and Sarawak but starting in mid-85 there is supposed to be a weekly car ferry service operating from Kuantan on the east coast of the peninsula to Kuching in Sarawak and Kota Kinabalu in Sabah. The planned operator is Pernas National Shipping Line but whether it will actually commence as planned remains to be seen.

Buses Long-distance buses depart from the terminus on Jawa St which is a continuation of Jalan Gambier. Fares include Kuching-Bau M$1.85 (20 buses per day), Kuching-Betong M$12.60 (one bus), Kuching-Kampong Segu M$1.85 (three buses), Kuching-Lundu M$4.80 (three buses), Kuching-Pandawan M$3.90 (two buses), Kuching-Serian M$3.50 (37 buses), Kuching-Simanggang M$11 (two buses).

Connecting buses include Betong-Debak M$3.40 (six buses), Betong-Spaoh M$3 (seven buses), Lundu-Bau M$3.10 (six buses), Lundu-Biawak M$1.80 (eight buses), Lundu-Sematan M$1.90 (10 buses), Serian-Sungai Tenggan M$3.40 (seven buses), Serian-Tebakang M$0.85 (13 buses), Simanggang-Batu Lintang M$2.30 (four buses), Simanggang-Betong M$4.80 (four buses), Simanggang-Engkili M$2.30 (17 buses), Simanggang-Lubok Antu M$5.20 (five buses), Simanggang-Saratok M$8.20 (two buses), Simanggang-Sarikei M$11.20 (two buses).

Note that if you're heading east from Kuching by bus you cannot reach Sibu in one day since you will not arrive in Sarikei until early evening and so will have to stay the night there. As there's precious little of interest in Sarikei itself, and as the road from Simanggang to Sarikei and Sarikei to Sibu is one hell of a bone shaker, most travellers prefer to take a launch or boat from Kuching to Sibu. The alternative is to stop over in Simanggang and to explore the surrounding area since it's possible to reach Sibu from Simanggang in one day. Where there are only a few buses each day to a certain destination it's advisable to book in advance at the ticket office on Jawa St.

Boats – Kuching-Sarikei-Sibu You have a choice on this run of fast launch or cargo/passenger boat. The launch is considerably faster as the cargo boats have to load and unload at the various ports of call (Sarikei and Binatang). If you have the time the cargo/passenger boats are the more interesting way to cover this part of the journey though there's only M$9 difference in the fare.

The fast launch departs Kuching daily at 8 am from the Chin San Wharf at Pending, which is about six km east of the city centre. The fare is M$33 and you must book in advance (one day is sufficient) at the Shell Station on Jalan Tengku Abdul Rahman, just below the Tua Pek Kong temple. The trip takes six hours officially but can take an hour or so more. On the ticket you'll be allocated a seat number, but this is just a figment of the ticket agent's imagination, as you'll discover when you get to the launch. There's generally a change of boat available at Sarikei – something no one tells you when you buy the ticket. The launches dock at Delta Wharf in Sibu. To get to Chin San

Wharf from Kuching take bus number 1 or 17 or a taxi (about M$6). There's a cafe at Chin San Wharf so if you want breakfast, catch it here. The agents at the Shell Station on Jalan Tengku Abdul Rahman may also have a launch to Sarikei, but it doesn't go on to Sibu.

There are a few companies which operate cargo/passenger boats to Sibu and even further along the coast. Finding out about them and when the ships leave can be a real hassle though. It just means asking around a lot. The journey to Sibu takes about 24 hours and the fare is M$24 with the two companies listed below:

Rajah Ramin Shipping Sdn Bhd (tel 57043, 55041, 59472), Lot 164, Chan Chin Ann Rd, Kuching or Thong Hwa Co (tel 5274/5582), Sarikei or Yi Hock Co (tel 93170), Binatang. Their boat, the *MV Hong Lee*, departs Kuching every Wednesday and Saturday at 6 pm and Sibu every Monday and Friday at 11 am, calling en route at Sarikei and Binatang.

Round the corner on Jalan Tengku Abdul Rahman is the South East Asia Shipping Bhd (tel 22966, 20109), Lot 175, Chan Chin Ann Rd, Kuching – it's on the second floor. Or try Lau Hieng Ming (tel 5521), Sarikei or Lian Hing Trading (tel 93170), Binatang. Their boat, the *MV Rajah Mas*, departs Kuching every Monday and Thursday at 6 pm and Sibu every Wednesday and Saturday at 12 noon. If you're heading for Kuching from Sarikei, the boat departs Sarikei at 5.30 pm every Wednesday and Saturday.

The *Soon Bee*, which runs from the docks at the end of Chan Chin Ann Rd, goes to Sibu, leaving at 6 pm Saturday. They charge only M$15. If you don't have any luck at the offices, try the tourist office on Temple St, where the manager is knowledgeable. If that doesn't help, ask around the docks.

Boats – Kuching-Miri Cargo/passenger boats depart twice weekly from Kuching – exact schedule depends on demand – and take about 48 hours to Miri. The fare is M$45 which includes food. Enquire at Miri Sin Ching Shipping Co, 2A Jawa St, Kuching (opposite the long-distance bus terminal).

Boats – Kuching-Santubong & Kuching-Bako National Park For details of these local boats see the Around Kuching section.

Getting Around
Airport Transport A taxi to or from Kuching airport to the centre costs about M$12 though for some reason one drew up to the bus stop where I was waiting and offered me the trip for M$5. Buses are available between the airport and the centre of town for M$1. There are 46 daily, the first at 7 am and the last at 11.50 pm. A number 12 bus will also transport you between the airport and downtown.

Buses Kuching city buses have their terminus in front of Electra House on Market St. There are two types – the blue Chin Lian Long buses (which is a private company) and the green STC buses. You probably won't have much cause to use these buses though one which is useful is the No 1 or 17 which goes to the Chin San Wharf at Pending, east of Kuching, from where the launches to Sibu and Sarikei depart. Local buses are 20 to 30c.

Taxis Taxis collect by the market and at the bus stations. A taxi to Chin San Wharf costs about M$6.

Tours There is an incredible array of travel agents and tour operators in town. Many offer trips to the National Parks, longhouses, short Kayam river trips and excursions around Kuching. Sarawak Travel agencies (tel 23708), 70 Pandungan Rd, is well-established with a variety of tours. Others may be cheaper.

Things to Buy

Kuching is one of the best centres in Sarawak for buying tribal artifacts. Shops selling arts and crafts are scattered around the city, but be warned that prices are high although you can normally bargain. Hog charm sticks go for M$80-100; larger, crudely carved totems for M$400-1000 and intricately patterned baskets for up to M$800 depending on quality, source and age. Another very fine item is the woven textiles. The older ones go for about M$200 and up. Jewellery is likewise expensive. It's best to spend several days browsing before you commit yourself to a purchase.

A couple of shops to try are Sarawak House, 35 Wayang St; Sarawak Batik Art Shop 6, Specialist Centre and the shop in the new section of the museum which probably has the best prices of the lot. For pottery there are a few places along Jalan Penrissen. Also try Loo Pan Arts at 83 Jalan Ban Hock.

Apart from these shops there is a non-profit organisation which has a showroom of new tribal handicrafts on the first floor next to the Tourist Office on the grounds of the Sarawak Museum. Again, it's not particularly cheap, but they do have a good selection of woodcarvings, basketware, weavings and jewellery as well as a selection of books about tribal life and the geography of Sarawak.

Look for the beautiful Borneo pottery with traditional Sarawak designs. They are available from the potters out towards the airport as glazed and unglazed jars, pots and vases.

AROUND KUCHING
Santubong

Situated 32 km north of Kuching on the coast, this is the nearest beach 'resort' to Kuching, other than the beaches in the Bako National Park. It is very popular with locals on the weekends and there is a small village. There are rock carvings at nearby Sungei Jaong, about 1½ km upriver from the coast.

There are government rest houses, but they must be booked in advance at the Kuching District Office (tel 22533). There is no road to the resort and the launches leave early in the morning (around 8.30 am) from the docks behind the market in Kuching for the trip to Santubong. Ask for Pangkalan Panjang, meaning long dock or wharf. It's also here you get launches to Bako National Park. Fare to Santubong is about M$2.

Dyak Longhouses

As you might expect, the most interesting and unspoilt longhouses are to be found furthest from the main urban centres, particularly along the upper reaches of the Rejang River, but if you're not planning on going up there or would like a preview, then the nearest longhouse to Kuching is at Kampong Segu Benuk which is a 35-km bus ride south of the city followed by a short walk. Don't expect too much of this place as all the package tours include it on their itinerary so it's very commercialised. A better choice would be the one on the banks of the Sungei Kayan reached by boat from Lundu.

Lundu & Sematan

Sematan is a tiny coastal village near the extreme western end of Sarawak. It has a very laid-back and relaxing atmosphere with a good deserted beach, warm sea and safe swimming. Many years ago it was a bauxite mining area, but that's all long since gone. A tourist hotel complex is planned, based around the lake left by the bauxite mine, but it will be years before that gets anywhere near completion.

Off-shore are two forest-covered islands, one of which is a turtle sanctuary. Permission is needed to go there and you would have to hire a boat from the village. There's also a crocodile sanctuary near the village which was established by a local group and, further up the coast, a wildlife sanctuary is being set up with the help of VSO volunteers though it is difficult to get to as boats seldom go there.

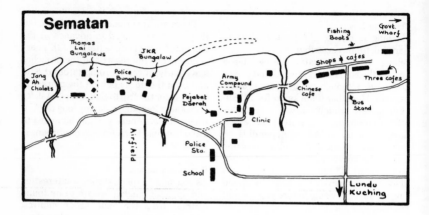

If you're interested in visiting any of these sanctuaries ask for Mr Philip Mejin (or his successor if he has left) at the local administration offices (Pejabat Daerah).

In addition to the sanctuaries there is a longhouse about 15 minutes by car from Sematan. If you want to visit it you'd be wise to ask around to see if anyone is going there as a taxi would be expensive. If you don't mind walking it will take you about three hours round trip.

Places to Stay If you make an effort you may well be offered a free room at Sematan, but if not then you can rent a room at the *Thomas Lai Bungalows*. There are seven of these altogether, set in a coconut palm grove next to the sea. The cheapest unit has two rooms, kitchen and bathroom and costs M$40 a night (maximum of 10 people). The most expensive units have three rooms, kitchen and bathroom and cost M$100 a night (maximum of 15 people). Naturally, at these prices you'd need to get a small group together before setting out from Kuching.

You can either rent them from the caretaker on arrival in Sematan or book in advance through Mrs Doris Lai (tel 21810), 7 Jalan Bidayuh, off Ong Tiang Swee Rd, Kuching or through the Tourist Office. Mrs Lai is very helpful and can offer tips on how to get there and what to do. The best food in Sematan is served at the Muslim restaurant – seafood, omelettes. This cafe also has Sematan T-shirts for sale at M$6.

Getting There Return bus fare from Kuching is about M$14. First take one of three daily express buses from Kuching to Lundu. The two hour journey costs M$5. The road is pretty rough from Bau to Lundu, but sealed up to that point. There are also six ordinary 'milk-run' buses daily, the first at 6.50 am and the last at 3.10 pm. From Lundu there are 10 daily buses to Sematan; it's a one-hour journey over a rough road at a cost of M$2.

If you have to wait around in Lundu and would like to eat, excellent Chinese meals are available at the *Siong Kee Restaurant*, close to the bus stand – look for the large Guinness sign.

There is a longhouse near Lundu Sungei Kayan rarely visited by foreigners. If you'd like to go there ask around on the riverfront for a boat going in that direction. It's located about 40 minutes downriver on the Kuching side. Remember to take a few small gifts of food or whatever with you.

Bako National Park
This is the National Park closest to Kuching and highly recommended. For details see the National Parks section.

SIBU
Sibu is the main port city on the Rejang River – Sarawak's longest and largest river. Situated some 60 km upriver from the ocean, its bustling waterfront sports all manner of craft from motorised dugouts to ocean-going liners. It's here that the raw materials of the interior – lumber, gravel, minerals and agricultural products – are brought for export. Manufactured goods from the outside world also arrive here for distribution along the Rejang and its tributaries.

Sibu is the starting point for a trip up the Rejang to visit the longhouses which are scattered along its entire length, the most interesting, naturally, being those furthest from the urban centres. There's not a lot to do in Sibu unless you like hanging around waterfronts or vegetable markets, and although both of these are quite entertaining most travellers stay only overnight here and head off up the Rejang the next day. A new 36-hectare township near Sibu, to be called Seduan Park, is being worked on and is scheduled to be completed in 1988.

Information
There is no Tourist Office in Sibu. The Information Centre at the junction of Cross Rd and Channel Rd can tell you all about family planning though presumably that's not why you're here. For changing money, the best place to go is the Chartered Bank, Cross Rd. Some of the other banks won't change American Express travellers' cheques.

All the launch and shipping agents are conveniently located either along Jalan Khoo Peng Loong which faces Delta Wharf or along Channel Rd which runs parallel to it. MAS is close by, opposite the huge Premier Hotel on Kampong Nyabor Rd.

Places to Stay – bottom end
The majority of budget hotels in Sibu are pretty seedy places and there's little to choose between them. The *Government Rest House*, on Island Rd near the junction with Jalan Bridge, used to be great value (except it was always full), but now it costs M$50 for a double! And has plenty of room! Attached to the Methodist church on Island Rd, the *Hoover House* has excellent rooms from M$10 to M$24 and also dorm beds. It's just opposite the Borneo Company.

Otherwise there's the *Sibu Hotel* (tel 21784), 2 Kampong Pulu Rd, where rooms cost from M$12 with communal showers and toilets. The *Dipan Hotel* (tel 26853), 27 Kampong Nyabor Rd has rooms at similar prices plus more expensive air-con rooms from M$20. Or there's the *National Hotel* (tel 22727), 1 Kampong Pulu Rd with similarly priced rooms with and without air-con.

Even cheaper, more basic rooms can be found at the *Sing Hua Hing* and *Nan Kiew Hotels*, which are located side by side down a valley off Blacksmith Rd.

The most convenient mid-range hotels are the Miramar and the Rex, both popular with travellers. The *Miramar Hotel* (tel 22395), 47 Channel Rd, has pleasant fan-cooled rooms with their own bathroom and toilet. Rooms cost from M$18 or with air-con from M$30 and you even get towel and soap. The pleasant *Rex Hotel* (tel 21625), 32 Cross Rd, is next door to the Sarawak Hotel, and is similarly priced or a bit cheaper.

Other mid-range hotels include the *Today Hotel* (tel 26499), 40 Kampong Nyabor Rd, and the *Si Tai Hotel* (tel 21777), 5 Central Rd, which also have rooms from M$16 and up.

Places to Stay – top end
The enormous *Premier Hotel* (tel 23222), Kampong Nyabor Rd is, at present, Sibu's most prestigious hotel. It has 170 rooms, is air-con throughout and singles cost M$80 to 130, doubles M$100 to 150.

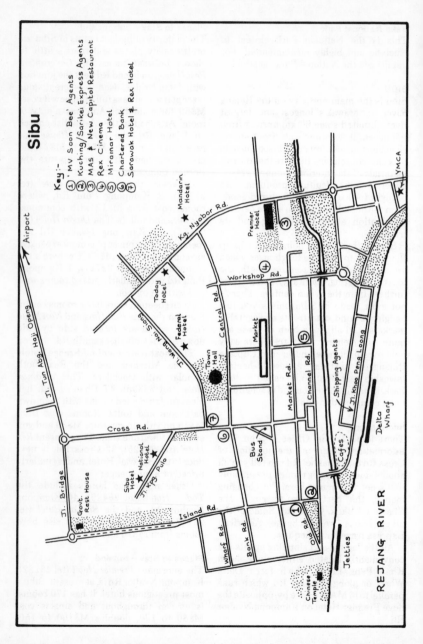

Sibu

Key:-
① 'MV Soon Bee' Agents
② Kuching/Sarikei Express Agents
③ MAS & New Capital Restaurant
④ Rex Cinema
⑤ Miranar Hotel
⑥ Chartered Bank
⑦ Sarawak Hotel & Rex Hotel

Top: Niah Caves, Sarawak (GC)
Left: plank walk to the Niah Caves, Sarawak (GC)
Right: shopfront in Kuching, Sarawak (GC)

Top: Sabah from the air, between Tawau & Kota Kinabalu (GC)
Left: lumber company in Kuching, Sarawak (GC)

Facilities include a nightclub, bars, coffee lounges and a travel agency.

The *Sarawak Hotel* (tel 23455), 34 Cross Rd is a much smaller hotel with 24 rooms with and without air-con at M$62 to 80 for singles, M$70 to 90 for doubles. Also in this category is the *Capitol Hotel* (tel 26444), 19 Jalan Wong Nai Siong where singles range from M$45 to 80, doubles from M$55 to 90. On the same road is the more modern *Merrido Hotel* which is popular with business people.

The *Li Hua* (tel 2400), at the Longbridge Commercial Centre, has singles at M$70 to 90, doubles at M$105. The *Hotel Malaysia* (tel 22298), 8 Kampong Nyabor Rd, has 21 rooms at M$45/60.

Places to Eat
Virtually all the restaurants in Sibu – as elsewhere in East Malaysia – are Chinese and very few of them have anything to recommend them. The vast majority serve only the standard, conservative, uninteresting, tasteless rubbish that will either provoke you into fasting or into spending hard-earned cash on a decent meal.

A place which escapes this category is the cafe on the corner of Kampong Nyabor Rd, opposite the Premier Hotel, which offers satay in the evening. Another is the restaurant opposite the Palace Cinema, Workshop Rd, halfway between Market Rd and Central Rd, which offers seafood. The only problem with the latter place is that the waitresses have an instant mental block when English is spoken so you have to put up with 15 minutes of giggling before anything happens.

If you can last through the day with just a snack then the best place to eat is at one or more of the street stalls on Jalan Lembangan, alongside the Miramar Hotel, which are set up there every evening – a good variety of food is available. *Hock Chu Leu* on Blacksmith Rd is good, M$4 to 8 per dish. If you'd like to splurge on a decent meal then the *New Capitol Restaurant*, opposite the Premier Hotel, is OK.

Getting There
Air If you're flying from Sibu to Bintulu note that this sector is usually heavily booked so plan ahead if you're on your way up the Rejang River. If you have no booking it's well worth trying standby at the airport since there are seven flights a day to Bintulu and MAS are notorious for 'fully-booked' flights which leave half empty.

Road – To Sibu The road from Sibu to Bintulu has been completed and this, being the last bit, means the entire coast of Sarawak is connected, right through to Brunei. This last section to Bintulu is a long, tough slog with the road often a joke. Buses don't yet run the entire trip, but do cover part of it. The rest can be done by hiring/sharing a taxi or hitching. I met a woman who did it by getting a ride with the police. Getting out and pushing is a definite possibility. The stretch between Tatau and Oya was the last to be completed and it's here that you're likely to have the most trouble finding transport. If you're determined to try it enquire at Hock Lee Travel Service, 015 Sarawak House, Sibu – their share-taxi costs M$45 per person.

You can go the long way round by trekking from Bintulu to Belaga and then taking the launches down the Rejang. This is a pretty rugged trek and not recommended for novices. For this reason and the fact that cargo/passenger boats from Sibu to Bintulu run on a very impromptu and irregular schedule, most travellers fly over this section. If, on the other hand, you have the time, it's worth waiting for a boat to Bintulu.

Buses – To Kuching See the Kuching section for details.

Road – Sibu-Sarikei-Kuching The fast launch to Kuching via Sarikei (where you change launches) departs from the Delta Wharf daily at 8 am, costs M$33 and takes about 7½ hours. Book at either Muara

Tebas Shipping, Channel Rd, which faces the bridge leading to Jalan Khoo Peng Loong, or simply go down to the wharf on the morning you want to go. Pay no attention to seat numbers.

There are several companies which offer cargo/passenger boats to Kuching and Sarikei via Binatang. Rajah Ramin Shipping Sdn Bhd (tel 21531), 18 Khoo Peng Loong Rd and South East Asia Shipping Bhd (tel 21424, 23231), 13 Khoo Peng Loong Rd both depart from Delta Wharf, cost M$24 and take 18-24 hours. For details see under Kuching.

Another company operates the ship *MV Soon Bee*. This ship does the run to Kuching twice weekly on Mondays and Thursdays and the fare is just M$15. The booking agent is located near the junction of Island Rd and Old Rd – there's a large sign in the street with 'MV Soon Bee' on it. You can't miss it.

Boat – To Kapit Getting to Kapit is the first leg of the journey up the Rejang River and the trip up there offers a fascinating insight into life along Sarawak's mightiest river and the rain forests which border its banks. The super-fast launches which do this trip, known as the 'Kapit Express' are narrow, steel-bottomed boats powered by enormous twin diesels which generate one hell of a thrust. They cover the 130 km or so from Sibu to Kapit in a mere four hours! Unfortunately the video craze has hit these boats – unless you sit outside you'll find no way of escaping from sleazy second-rate American films.

The launches depart Sibu daily about six or seven times from around 7 am to 1 pm – times are not exact since they like to leave full – and the fare is M$12. There's no need to book in advance: simply go down to Delta Wharf about half an hour before one is due to leave and pay on board. You can sit anywhere you like – on the seats inside, on the bench at the back, on the deck at the front or on the roof. The launches call at Kanowit and Song as well as a number of smaller settlements and

logging camps en route, but only long enough to let passengers on or off.

On arrival at Kapit you have a choice as to where you get off. If you intend to stay at one of the three hotels there then get off at the first 'jetty', below the Kapit Longhouse Hotel ('jetty' since it was in such an advanced state of decrepitude when I saw there that I wouldn't be surprised if it's been swept away by now!). If you're going to be staying at the Methodist Guest House then get off at the main (concrete) jetty.

Boat – To Bintulu & Miri There are no fast launches to either Bintulu or Miri. Cargo/passenger boats are the only ones which do this run and they do not operate on any regular schedule – departure times depend on demand – so you may have to wait around for several days. The fare to Bintulu is around M$35 and the journey takes about 18 hours. To Miri the fare is about M$50 and the journey takes around 32 hours.

If you're interested in a boat along this route enquire at Soon Ping Shipping Sdn Bhd (tel 24502), 2nd floor, 4 Khoo Peng Loong Rd; Hock Leong Shipping Sdn Bhd (tel 22616), 1st floor, 3 Khoo Peng Loong Rd (tel 22616) or Sibu United Shipping Agencies (tel 22403), 1st floor, 4 Khoo Peng Loong Rd. If nothing is going for several days it's worth asking around Delta Wharf to see if anything smaller is going that way.

Boat & Walking – To Bintulu See the Belaga section for details on the Sibu-Kapit-Belaga-Tubau-Bintulu trip.

Getting Around
If you arrive in Sibu by launch (from Kuching or Sarikei) or by cargo/passenger boat (from Kuching, Sarikei, Bintulu or Miri) then you will dock at Delta Wharf, which is only a few minutes' walk from all the main hotels and restaurants. Delta Wharf is also where the launches to and from Kapit dock.

If you arrive by air take either a taxi or bus No 1 to the terminus in the centre of town. The bus station in Sibu is located on Cross Rd at the junction of Market Rd. Few buses of interest to travellers depart from here. No 1 runs between here and the airport every 10-15 minutes. The fare is 50c and the journey takes about 15 minutes.

UP THE REJANG RIVER

Other than a visit to Kuching and one or more of the National Parks, the Rejang is the principal travel destination in Sarawak. All along this river and its tributaries, particularly the upper reaches, are scattered the longhouses of the Iban tribe. The Iban are famed for their hospitality and visitors are welcome. There's no need for an introduction – simply ask the boatmen for a suggestion and then, when you're dropped off, front up, smile and walk in. You'll undoubtedly be invited to join them for a meal and offered a place to stay for the night. If you want to get a real feel for life in the longhouses then you should plan on staying at least one night. Staying at a longhouse is one of the highlights of any trip to Sarawak.

Naturally the more 'authentic' longhouses are to be found on the upper reaches of the river, furthest away from 'civilisation', so head for the stretch of river between Kapit and Belaga. Going beyond Belaga tends to present difficulties in the form of red tape. Special permits for travel between Kapit and Belaga are a mere formality and will take up only an hour or two of your time at Kapit, but if you want to travel beyond Belaga then you will need another permit which isn't quite so easy to obtain. If you're planning on staying overnight at a longhouse or even just visiting for the day then it's a courtesy to take along a contribution towards your keep – canned or dried foods, cigarettes for the adults and something for the kids.

KAPIT

This beautiful, relaxing little town dating from the days of the White Rajahs and still sporting an old wooden fort built by Charles Brooke, will be your first stop on the journey up the Rejang. To anyone from outside it's just a sleepy riverside village tucked into the rain forest, but to upriver people it's the 'big city' to which they come to buy, sell and exchange goods as well as for entertainment – there are two cinemas.

There isn't a great deal to do or see in Kapit though the waterfront and the market are interesting and the Chinese temple works up a sweat on the big drums some evenings, but it's the terminus for the 'Kapit Express' launches from Sibu and the place to which you must come to obtain the permit for travelling between here and Belaga.

There are two longhouses about six to seven km from town along Jalan Selerik, but they're thoroughly urbanised and nothing like the more traditional ones you'll find further upriver. Posters of Abba, Peter Frampton and Harley-Davidsons are all you'll see here and it's not really worth the taxi fare to visit them. The old wooden fort – Fort Sylvia – near the main jetty is now a government administration office and no longer open to the public.

Information

If you need to change money (ie travellers' cheques) there's only one bank in town located in the same block as the Kapit Longhouse Hotel overlooking New Bazaar. Their charges for changing travellers' cheques are heavy. You can get good maps of the area on the top floor of the government complex. Iban weavings can be bought at the Methodist Guest House.

Permits for travel beyond Kapit The first step in this process is to go to the 'Pejabat Am' office on the 1st floor of the State Government Complex and collect the necessary forms. Fill them in and take them to the top floor of the Police HQ where they will be stamped and you'll be

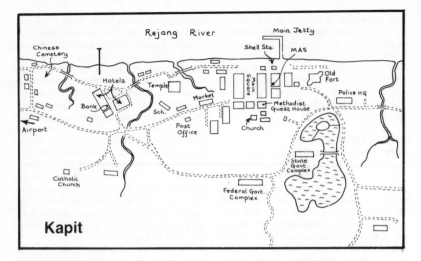

Kapit

asked to fill in a kind of visitors' book they keep there. Note that the forms will ask if you have a valid international cholera vaccination certificate, but they don't check this.

Take the stamped forms back to the State Government Complex and present them at the office of the 'Residen' which is next door to 'Pejabat Am'. Here the forms will be filed and a typed permit issued to you. There's no charge for the permits, but if you're planning on going beyond Belaga you'll need an additional permit – ask about it here. Unless you're going as far as Belaga, however, nobody is going to want to see your permit.

Places to Stay

There are only three hotels in Kapit, all of them on the bluff overlooking the river at the west end of town. The *Kapit Longhouse Hotel* (tel 96415), Berjaya Rd has air-con rooms with their own bathroom from M$30. The *Rejang Hotel* (tel 96356), 9 New Bazaar costs from M$18 for rooms with own bathroom, but without air-con. The *Hiap Chiong Hotel* (tel 96213), 33 New Bazaar is the cheapest with fan-cooled room with washbasins and clean

common bathrooms from M$12. They also have a few air-con rooms from M$25 and the management are friendly.

If you'd like somewhere cheaper to stay then head for the *Methodist Guest House*, which is a white two-storey building on the lefthand side of the green-painted wooden church near the centre of town. It's a very pleasant place and the people who run it are very friendly, but they only have two double rooms which cost M$10 (perhaps still less) per room – a real bargain!

Places to Eat

The two Chinese cafes on the riverside corners of the Rejang Hotel/Hiap Chiong Hotel block in New Bazaar serve fairly good, cheap meals and are popular with local people. The *Kah Ling Restaurant*, in the centre of town and very popular with local people in the evenings, is located on the top side of the basketball ground, close to the Methodist Guest House. It serves a much wider variety of food than the two cafes in New Bazaar including great sweet & sour pork. The places on top of the market hall are also good.

Beers and soft drinks are more expensive here than in Sibu or Kuching.

Getting There

Air When the river is really low you will not be able to get a launch or boat to Belaga so if this is your intended destination the only way of getting there is to fly. MAS fly Sibu-Kapit-Belaga and back on Fridays and Sundays. The free baggage allowance on the small Britten-Norman Islanders is officially just 10 kg.

Road The only local road transport is taxis and there are very few of those; which isn't surprising since there's hardly anywhere you can go by road. If you arrive by air you'll have to take a taxi the two km into town.

Launches & Boats – To Sibu The 'Kapit Express' departs for Sibu daily around 6.30, 7.30 and 11 am, and 1 pm – the times are approximate but if you want to catch the earliest launch get there at least half an hour before it's due to leave as it frequently goes early. The fare is M$12 and the journey takes around five hours. The launch calls en route at Song, Kanowit and a number of smaller settlements and logging camps.

Launches & Boats – To Belaga Launches and boats leave daily from the main jetty whenever the river is high enough to allow them to negotiate the several sets of rapids which are encountered between here and Belaga. The rapids are the main reason why there are no boats when the river is low. The launches to Belaga cost M$12 or more and take most of the day to get there. Make enquiries the day before at the Shell Station at the main jetty.

The Belaga launches and boats are the same ones you take to visit the Iban longhouses between Kapit and Belaga, except that when the river is low you'll have to make use of tribesmen's motorised dugouts. The latter are usually considerably more expensive than the launches so it makes sense to be part of a small group in order to share costs.

To recommend any particular longhouse as opposed to another would be to encourage a travellers' bottleneck and overload the traditional hospitality to be found at these settlements. Iban longhouse culture is very sensitive to such pressures from outside and although changes are inevitably being forced on these people from other quarters – development, commerce, government activity – there seems little justification for augmenting the process. Presumably you haven't come this far up the river just to see the plastic smiles of a tourist trap.

BELAGA

Belaga is just a small village and government administration centre on the upper reaches of the Rejang where the river divides into the Belaga and Balui rivers.

Places to Stay

Accommodation can be found here at the *Government Rest House* which costs M$25 per person. In the big line of shops there's a very clean lodging house with doubles at M$15. Or you could try the *Community Hall*.

Getting There

It's possible to trek in the dry season from Belaga to Bintulu – or in the opposite direction. To do this you'll need a permit from the Resident at Belaga (or Bintulu if you're coming in the opposite direction). The trek is pretty strenuous and shouldn't be attempted by novices to the jungle. The journey takes about four or five days and it's advisable to go as a small group – say, four or five people – since you'll have to hire guides at various longhouses as well as boats on the rivers.

The route you take will depend largely on how much water there is in the river, but the usual route is to head up the Belaga River until you get close to the Tibang Rapids where you get off the boat. From here walk a rough six hours over the mountains to cut out the rapids and then hire another boat up to one of the longhouses where you hire a guide to take you over the mountains to the Tabau River on the other side of the watershed.

The usual destination here is the longhouse at Long Unan. From here it's generally possible to hire a motorised boat down to Tabau for about M\$50 – a journey which will take all day. From Tabau there are launches down to Bintulu which cost M\$3 per person and take about nine hours.

One traveller's report on making this trip, from the Bintulu end:

After taking the boat up to Tubau you can continue on to Belaga via one of the logging camps set up along the Belaga River. They usually maintain daily Land-Cruiser connections with their dumping camps in Tubau. The loggers are friendly and co-operative and you can try to get a ride back to one of the camps with them. Their logging concessions are limited in time and place so the camps tend to move fairly frequently.

Once you get to the Belaga River it is possible to travel down to the town of Belaga, where the Rejang River starts, in one day of river paddling and jungle walking. There are several jungle paths you can choose from but you'll have to use the services of a local boatman at some point or other, either to travel along the river or to cross it. No matter how experienced a jungle walker you may be, you will find it helpful to take along a trustworthy local guide. He can help you bargain with the boatmen along the way. Even for local people there is no fixed price for hiring a boat on a given stretch of the river; the prices vary with the weather, the strength of the currents, the time of the day and willingness of the boatman to leave his farmwork to take you up or down the river. Nevertheless, when foreigners appear on the scene the locals are likely to ask for outrageous fares. And their bargaining position is certainly strong! Just for reference I paid M\$100 for two of us to travel from a logging camp all the way down to Belaga. This included three boat rides and the fees for two young Kenyah guides. The whole trip took seven hours. It turned out to be one of the most exciting jungle trips I have ever had, partly due to the Belaga River being rather swollen at the time.

Police permits are still necessary and are partly meant for your own safety. The police may tell you the story of the German guy who ventured on his journey without a permit and disappeared never to be seen again. Local touts will tell you the same story but stress that the unfortunate German didn't have the good sense to hire a guide! Bureaucratically the river seems to be a sort of one-way road because the permit is apparently easy to obtain in Bintulu for the Tubau-Belaga trek, but not so easy to to get in Kapit for Belaga-Tubau. We did not have a permit and nowhere were we asked to produce one.

I should think it is possible to do it alone, without guides and at the 'local price', even if you don't speak the local language. Make sure, however, that you have a good map, food, water, clothing, possibly a sleeping bag and maybe simple cooking utensils. Mosquito coils would be a good idea and mosquito net still better – Belaga is a bad malaria area. There are three rest houses (read stilted platforms topped by an attap roof) along the Belaga River, conveniently placed before and after the 'impassable' rapids. This is where you are most likely to get stuck if there is no boat or if it's too expensive. If you stay at the rest houses you are likely to meet small parties of travelling Kayans, perhaps families engaged in shifting agriculture or groups of young men who leave their longhouses in the Belaga basin and go to look for work in the logging camps. If they like you they may share their food with you and perhaps the boat they are going to charter next morning too. Be patient and be prepared to wait a few days for a passage which money could buy immediately.

This trip is likely to become easier as the logging roads are slowly pushed further down the river. There's even talk of a government plan for a Bintulu-Kapit road.

BINTULU

Bintulu is an air-conditioned boom town which it's best to get through as quickly as possible unless you want holes burned in every pocket. Construction is going on everywhere – a new international airport, deepwater port, residential suburbs, among other things – as a result of oil and lumber money which is pouring into the place. The town is jam-packed with migrants from all over Sarawak and abroad who have come here hoping for a piece of the action. Because of these

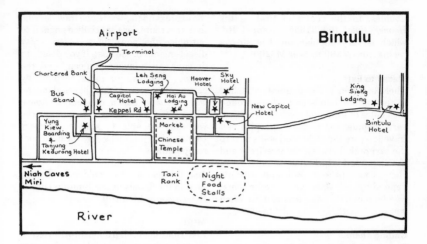

developments, prices have hit the sky and accommodation is really difficult to find. If you're heading east you'll have to stay overnight since there's only one bus per day to Miri and this is the same bus you take to the Niah Caves.

There isn't anything to see or do as such in Bintulu, except perhaps shed a lot of money in expensive night clubs, but the street markets which mushroom in the evenings are pretty lively.

Places to Stay

Everything is outrageously expensive and since all the hoteliers are trying to make a killing while the boom lasts there's nothing you can call a 'budget' hotel. Unfortunately, money is only half the story. The other half is finding a room at all, especially if you arrive in the evening, since many hotels are more or less permanently full with oil, lumber and construction workers and businessmen.

The *Hock Chuhn Lodging House* does, however, have pigeonhole-like rooms for M$12. It's a stone's throw from the Tubau Express pier if you're going upriver.

The cheapest and most convenient middle range hotel is the *Capitol Hotel* (tel 31167), 48 Keppel Rd – not to be confused with the New Capitol Hotel further along the street. It has one room under M$30, but most are M$50 or more and it's often full. There's a restaurant on the ground floor.

The next cheapest, and the one where you're most likely to find a room, is the *Bintulu Hotel*, a 10-minute walk from the centre of town. The cheapest rooms here start from M$33 but most of the 'rooms' are hardboard-partitioned cells with air-con, no window and containing a single bed and washbasin. The manager will allow two people to share a room. The communal bathroom facilities are very limited.

If you don't manage to find a room at one of the above then try one of the following although the prices are generally at least M$35: *New Capitol Hotel, Yung Kiew Lodging, Tanjung Kedurong Hotel, Leh Seng Lodging, Hai Au Lodging, Sky Hotel* and *King Siang Lodging*.

The 108-room *Aurora Beach Hotel* (tel 31622), Jalan Tanjung Datu, is located a long way from the centre of town on the coast. It's an international-class hotel with restaurant, bars, night club, swimming pool and even a helipad. Rooms here – all air-con – cost M$125/150 for singles/

doubles. In the centre of town is the *Hoover Hotel* (tel 31355), Keppel Rd, which is very popular and has air-con rooms from M$80 to over M$200.

Places to Eat

There are plenty of restaurants attached to the various hotels and others around the centre of town, but the best selection, very popular with local people and travellers, are the night food stalls next to the taxi rank, between the riverfront and the first road which runs parallel to it. Here you can eat well and cheaply depending on what you choose. Just wander round the stalls and sit down when you see something you'd like to eat.

Getting There

Buses – To Niah Caves & Miri There are a couple of buses daily which cost M$15 to either Batu Niah junction or Miri. If you're heading for the Niah Caves you get off at Batu Niah junction, which is 2½ hours out of Bintulu. The junction is about 12 km from the village of Batu Niah and there are no buses along this stretch so you'll have to hitch (easy) or take one of the occasional taxis which come through. It's advisable to book a seat on the bus the night before at the tailor's between Yung Kiew Boarding and Tanjung Kedurong Hotel – look for the sign 'Bas Suria Sdn Bhd Agent'. The shop is open from 7.30 am to 8.30 pm. A complete taxi would cost about M$120.

Buses – To Sibu See the Sibu section for details.

Boats It's sometimes possible to find cargo/passenger boats from Bintulu to either Sibu or Miri. The fare to either place is M$35 and the journey takes about 18 hours. Check with the agents along the waterfront.

There are also launches up the Kemena River as far as Tubau when there's sufficient water in the river. The cost is M$3 and the journey takes about nine hours. 'The kung fu video tapes played in

the express boats,' wrote one traveller who took this route, 'are specially designed to out-noise the powerful and very noisy diesel engines of the boat. If you decide to do your ears a favour, you can break the journey into two or more sections by getting off at some of the villages along the way'. Sebauh has a native rest house where you can stay for free. In other places you may be able to stay in Forestry Department barracks or local school compounds.

Boat & Walking – To Sibu See the Belaga section for details of the Bintulu-Tubau-Belaga-Kapit-Sibu trip.

MIRI

Like Bintulu, this is a boom town based on oil money and you'll see plenty of ex-pats wandering around with their children. Much of the town is being redeveloped and only the old centre remains. It's a pleasant enough town though there's precious little of interest to keep you here and, as in Bintulu, everything is air-con and expensive. Most travellers stay here only overnight on their way to Brunei if heading east or to the Niah Caves if heading west. If you're heading to the caves call at the National Parks office for a permit to visit the 'Painted Cave' at Niah – enquire at the Police HQ on Kingsway for the location of this office.

Everything in Miri is within easy walking distance of anywhere else so there's no need to take taxis or local buses to get anywhere. The only real point of interest in the town is the Chinese temple down by the waterfront at the end of China St.

Places to Stay – bottom end

The cheapest place in town is *Monica Lodgings* (tel 36611), 4 Kwang Tung Rd which has large, airy but scruffy fan-cooled rooms from M$18. The bathrooms are on their last legs but it's also the only place in Miri with anything you might describe as old Borneo atmosphere and

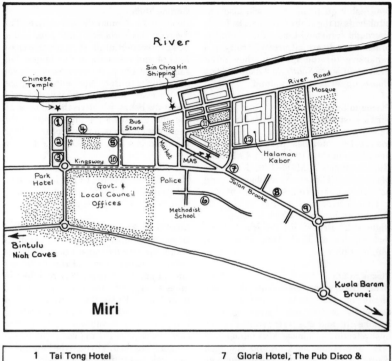

1	Tai Tong Hotel	7	Gloria Hotel, The Pub Disco &
2	Thai Foh Lodging		Miri Supermarket
3	Malaysia Lodging House	8	Miri Hotel
4	Borneo Hotel	9	Fatimah Hotel
5	SE Asia Lodging & Hotel	10	Chartered Bank
	Lover's Bay	11	King Hua Restaurant
6	Monical Lodging	12	Supreme Fried Chicken

the double rooms have a double and single bed so they'll sleep three people. It's either a reasonably quiet place (according to some visitors) or terribly noisy (according to others!) but the management are pleasant, despite its ramshackle and decrepit air and the fact that it also has short-time use.

If you can't get in here then the next cheapest places are the *Malaysia Lodging House* (tel 34300), 1-C China St, or the *Tung Foh Hotel* at 7 Brooke Rd, near the corner of China St, which has doubles with

fan for M\$18. *Hotel Miri*, a bit out of town, is also cheap as is the *Lodging House Yeo Lee*, which is kind of a hole, but OK for a night if you're desperate. At 17 China St the *Kheng Nam Lee* is OK at M\$25 for a bathless double with fan.

Most of the middle range hotels are nothing to write home about although the *Tai Tung Lodging House* (tel 34072), 26 China St is pretty good. A pleasant room with a view of the Chinese temple, market and river costs M\$30 and you get a fan, sink, towels and soap. It's clean and reasonably quiet and they will also put bunk beds in the lobby for M$5, OK for an overnight crash. Most other middle-bracket hotels are all pretty scruffy and expensive for the facilities they offer. They include the *South East Asia Lodging House*, opposite the bus stand.

Places to Stay – top end

Miri's best hotel is the *Park Hotel* (tel 32355), Kingsway where singles cost M$120-180, doubles M$135-195. The new *Fatimah Hotel* (tel 32255), 49 Brooke Rd, has singles at M$85-100, doubles at M$100-115. These two are all air-con and have restaurants, coffee bars and bars.

The *New Miri Hotel* (tel 34577), 47 Brooke Rd has rooms from M$60 to 100 while at 27 Brooke Rd the *Hotel Gloria* (has singles at M$82-105, doubles at M$107-120.

Places to Eat

Other than hotel restaurants there are plenty of good food places in Miri, especially in the new blocks between Brooke Rd and the waterfront. For the best selection – Chinese/Muslim/seafood – try any of the ones around Halaman Kabor. Also in this concourse *Supreme Fried Chicken* is an ex-pat hangout with pretty waitresses, high prices and small servings. Not far from here is an excellent Chinese restaurant – the *King Hua Restaurant* – which serves really good food, has a varied menu and is popular with local people. You can eat well here for M$6. For good dim sum and Korean food at night try the new air-con *The Kitchen* on China St. If you're waiting for a bus the *One Cent Cafe*, next to the big Park Hotel, is OK.

If you'd like somewhere to drink beer while listening to the endless monotony of disco music then try the *Pub Disco*, above the Miri Supermarket, in the same block as the Gloria Hotel, at the junction of Brooke Rd and Kingsway. There's a good open-air Malay food centre at the beach, where you can also enjoy beautiful sunsets.

Getting There

Road – To Bintulu & Batu Niah The Syarikat Bas Suria Sdn Bhd operates one bus per day to Bintulu at 7 am which costs M$124 and takes about five hours. The same company also operates two buses daily direct to Batu Niah village (for the Niah Caves) which cost M$9 and take about 2½ hours. It's advisable to book all the above buses a day in advance – the company's office is across the street from the main bus stand offices. It's a rough road.

If you would prefer to go by taxi to Batu Niah this will cost M$14 per person in an ordinary taxi and M$16 per person in an air-con taxi. Hitching is pretty good.

Road – To Brunei The Sharikai Berlima Belait bus company (office at the main bus stand) operate four buses daily to Kuala Belait – the first town in Brunei – from 7 am to 1 pm. The fare is M$10 and the trip takes about 2½ hours. The road is sealed from Miri to Kuala Baram where a river crossing is made. You unload everything from the bus here and walk on to the free car ferry or pay M$1 to take a motor boat across. They do this to beat the long line of cars waiting for the Shell car ferry. Small vehicles have priority, something to bear in mind if hitching.

Another bus on the other side of the Baram River takes you on the sand road to the Brunei border. After immigration and minimal customs formalities you board a third bus, a Brunei one, to the car ferry over the Belait River, just before Kuala Belait. The road from the border to Kuala Belait is bad, but if it's low tide you just drive along the beach.

At Kuala Belait you will be dropped at the Belait United Traction Co Ltd bus stand where you take another bus to Seria. There are 28 buses daily and the fare is B$1. The road is sealed all the way and the journey takes 30 to 45 minutes. If you need to change money – they're not very keen on Malaysian dollars – there's a branch of the Hong Kong & Shanghai

Banking Corporation just opposite the bus stand in Kuala Belait. From Seria you must take another bus to Bandar Seri Begawan, the capital of Brunei. Several bus companies do the run and there are many buses daily. The fare is B$4.50 and the journey takes 1½ hours. It's a good sealed road all the way. From Kuala Belait or Seria to BSB it's easy to hitch.

Boats Cargo/passenger boats operate between Miri and Bintulu, Sibu and Kuching. If you're interested in taking one of these start your enquiries at Sin Ching Hin Shipping (tel 3349), River Rd, Miri. There is a notice board on the wall outside the office with details of current sailings.

INLAND FROM MIRI

If you're heading out for a long trek into the mountains along the Indonesian border to Bario, Lio Matoh and Long Akah, the first stage of the journey will be by road to Kuala Baram – take the same buses that go to Brunei. From Kuala Baram there is a choice of fast launch (M$10, 45 minutes) or slow (M$6, two hours) up the Barum River to Marudi. Then there are regular launches to Long Lama further up river.

Beyond Long Lama and along the Tutuh River which passes by Gunung Mulu National Park (closed at present pending completion of accommodation facilities) there is no regular scheduled river transport and you will have to make use of tribesmen's boats. The price you pay on these boats is negotiable and journey times vary considerably. From Long Lama to Long Akah reckon on about M$25 and 1½ days and from there to Lio Matoh about the same.

There are airstrips at Marudi, Lawas, Limbang, Long Seridan, Long Lellang, Bario, Long Sukang, Long Semado and Bakelalan. MAS operates a network of flights between them. Permits are required to visit most of the places in the mountains. Apply for these at the office of the Resident, 4th Division, Miri.

Marudi

There are good views of the river from the hilltop Fort Hose, built in 1901. Permits for Bario, Long Lellang and Long Seridan are issued by the District Officer there. You can also get visas extended in Marudi and there are two banks for changing foreign currency. There is a road network around Marudi and you can visit longhouses by taxi or hitching.

Places to Stay The *Marudi Grand Hotel* is very nice and even meets launches with a car to drive you the four or five blocks to the hotel. Prices start at M$11/13 for singles/doubles with fan and bath. It's about the tallest building in town so the sunset views from the roof are good. The new *Mayland Hotel*, over the Mayland Cinema, is similarly priced and also good value.

There are some even lower-priced Chinese cheapies and a *Government Rest House*; ask at the District Office which is in old Fort Hose.

Getting There The Maju Yanmar Express boats from Kuala Baram to Marudi cost M$10, with no extra charge for kung fu videos.

Bario

Bario sits on a beautiful high valley floor in the Kelabit Highlands, close to the Indonesian border. A four-hour walk on a wide trail takes you to Pa'Lungan, a friendly longhouse with a pleasant river to swim in. The headman has a room for visitors with mats, blankets, pillows and mosquito net. From there you can hire guides and bearers to climb Gunung Murud, at 2423 metres (7946 feet) the highest peak in Sarawak. Or you can walk to Bakelalan and cross the uncontrolled Indonesian border to Long Bawan in east Kalimantan. The Kelabit people live on both sides of the border and ignore it. They are getting away from the traditional tattoos and stretched earlobes although you will still see these on the elders.

A six-day walk from Bario takes you to Long Lellang via Pa'Dalih and Ramudu with a night or two in the jungle with the nomadic Punan people. You can fly out from Long Lellang. The guest books in the longhouses are full of good information. Lots of the Kelabits are hard-core Christians and don't smoke so bring sugar, seeds, tea, kerosene or anything imaginative for the headman.

Places to Stay The *Bario Lodging House* is M\$8 per person but it's nothing special and you may want to head straight out to the longhouses.

Getting There MAS flies Twin Otters from Miri to Bario and from Marudi to Bario, Long Seridan (for Gunung Mulu National Park) and Long Lellang. Marudi-Bario is almost every day of the week. There are no roads there and getting there on foot takes a week or so.

THE NATIONAL PARKS

The Malaysian jungles are some of the oldest undisturbed areas of rain forest in the world. It's estimated they've existed for about 100 million years since they remained largely unaffected by the far-reaching climatic changes brought on elsewhere by the Ice Ages. In recent years, however, vast areas of this virgin forest – particularly in peninsular Malaysia and Sabah – have been devastated by the uncontrolled and thoughtless activities of lumber and mineral concerns. While the government is slowly moving in the direction of reforestation and forcing companies which negotiate concessions to invest in this, it's obvious that much goes by the board and that a more intelligent approach to these magnificent forests will be a long time in coming.

Fortunately quite large areas of some of the best and most spectacular of these rain forests have been made into National Parks, from which all commercial activities are banned. These parks are in effect the essence of a trip to Borneo, other than

visits to longhouses. A lot of effort goes into maintaining them and making them accessible to visitors, and you cannot help but be captivated by the astonishing variety of plant and animal life to be found.

In Sarawak itself there are six such parks at present – Samunsan at the extreme western tip near Sematan; Bako north of Kuching (2730 hectares); Similajau on the coast north-east of Bintulu (7452 hectares); Niah, of Niah caves fame, about halfway between Bintulu and Miri (3141 hectares); Lambir Hills just south of Miri (6926 hectares), and Gunung Mulu south-east of Marudi near the Brunei border (52,893 hectares). The Lambir Hills park is for day use only; no overnight lodging or camping. Because of the limited and often primitive road system in Sarawak, Samunsan and Similajau are difficult to reach for those without their own four-wheel drive transport. Similajau and Gunung Mulu are both temporarily closed to the public.

Gunung Mulu

When the Gunung Mulu park opens again it will, no doubt, vie with Bako and Niah as the number one travel destination in Sarawak. The park, with its 2377 metre (7798 feet) peak Mt Mulu, is particularly noted for its many caves. Cave explorers recently discovered the huge Sarawak Chamber and the 14-km-long Clearwater Cave, one of the longest caves in the world.

Bako National Park

This park is situated at the mouth of the Bako River, north of Kuching, and contains some 28 square km of unspoilt tropical rain forest. The coastline has many fine sandy beaches, cliffs and mangrove swamps while the interior sports seven very different types of vegetation. Because of this many animals – notably the rare and protected species of hornbill and the proboscis monkey – have made their homes in this park.

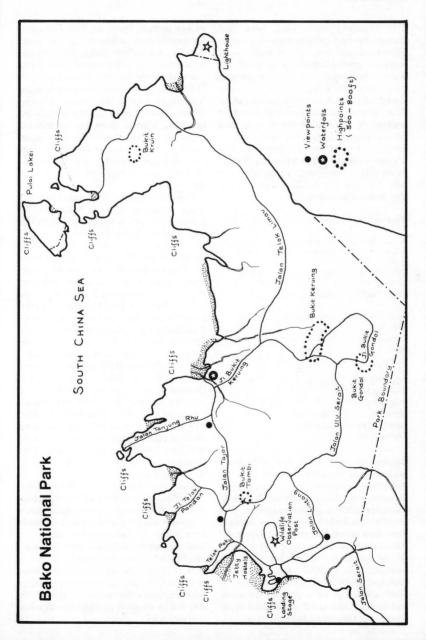

Bako National Park

- Viewpoints
- Waterfalls
- Highpoints (500 – 800 ft)

SOUTH CHINA SEA

Lighthouse

Cliffs

Pulai Lakei

Cliffs

Cliffs

Cliffs

Bukit Krun

Jalan Telok Limau

Bukit Kerung

Jt Bukit Kerung

Jl Bukit Gondol

Bukit Gondol

Jalan Ulu Serait

Park Boundary

Jalan Tanjung Rhu

Jalan Tajor

Bukit Tambi

Jl Telok Pondan

Jalan Lintang

Wildlife Observation Post

Telok Paku

Jetty Hostels

Cliffs

Landing Stage

Cliffs

Jalan Serait

Well-marked trails have been laid through the park to make it accessible and all of them are colour coded with a paint mark on trees adjacent to the path. On some of the longer walks you should plan your route before leaving and aim to be back at the hostels at Telok Assam before dark at 6.45 pm. If you're thinking of walking to the end of the longest trail (Jalan Telok Limau) you will need to arrange for transport to collect you since it's impossible to do the return trip on foot in one day. Transport can be arranged with the Park Warden. The main trails in the park are as follows:

Name of path	Destination	Time Req.
Jalan Lintang	circular path	3-4 hrs
Jalan Tanjong Sapi	cliffs/viewpoint	1/2 hr
Jalan Telok Delima	mangroves	3/4 hr
Jalan Telok Pandan	cove beaches	1½ hrs
Jalan Telok Paku	cove beach	3/4 hr
Jalan Serait	park boundary	1½ hr
Jalan Tanjor	waterfalls	2 hrs
Jalan Tanjong Rhu	cliffs/viewpoint	2½ hrs
Jalan Bukit Keruing/Jalan Bukit Gondol	mountain path	7 hrs
Jalan Ulu Serait/Jalan Telok Limau	Pulau Lakei (island)	8 hrs

Before you go to Bako you must book accommodation at the National Parks & Recreation Section (tel 24474), Forest Department, Jalan Gertak, Kuching. Telephone bookings are accepted, but must be confirmed and paid for at least three days before your intended departure. Remember that if you intend to stay in one of the hostels you must take your own bedding. Only a very limited selection of food and drink is available at the park – Coke and 7-Up, fried rice, noodle soup and canned food – so if you'd like a more varied diet take some food with you.

Places to Stay There are three types of accommodation available at the park. Rest houses include fridge, gas burners, all utensils and bed linens. Cost is M$22 per rest house for up to seven people. Hostel cabins sleep five to a room and are M$1.10 per person. Mattresses, kerosene stoves and a few basic kitchen utensils are provided. Lastly, there are permanent tents on raised platforms with open fireplaces at M$1.10 per tent. Bring your own supplies/utensils and sheets or sleeping bags. Tents can sleep two or three people.

From November to February the sea is often rough and at times it may not be possible for boats to approach or leave the hostel area at Telok Assam.

Getting There The park is 37 km from Kuching and can only be reached by boat. Two launches are available between Kuching and Kampong Bako (the village nearest the park). The *MV Juno* leaves the Long Wharf, Jalan Gambier, daily between 7 am and 9 am arriving at kampong Bako at about 11.30 am. It returns to Kuching daily at 1 pm. The one-way fare is M$2. The *ML Rahmat Bako* leaves the Shell Station Wharf, Jalan Tengku Abdul Rahman, daily except Sundays between 2 pm and 3 pm. The return trip leaves Kampong Bako at 8 am the following day. The one-way fare is M$1.50. The long wharf is called Pangkalan Panjang – you may find it easier using this name. The launches take 2 to 2½ hours to reach Kampong Bako.

From there you need another boat for the half-hour trip to the park headquarters at Telok Assam. The park seems to have stopped running their own launches which were relatively cheap – check when you book your accommodation. Private charters cost M$25 for one to five people, M$30 for up to 10 people. Arrange the time for them to come back and pick you up. During monsoon time – November to March – it may not be possible to make the trip due to rough seas.

Niah National Park & Niah Caves

A visit to the Niah Caves is one of the most memorable experiences available in East Malaysia. The Great Cave, one of the largest in the world, is located in the centre of the Niah National Park which is dominated by the 394-metre-high limestone massif of Gunung Subis, visible from far away.

Since 1958, when archaeologists discovered evidence that man has been living in and around the caves for some 40,000 years, they have been under the protection of the Sarawak Museum. The rock paintings found there in the 'Painted Cave' were the only ones known to exist in Borneo at the time and were associated with several small canoe-like boats which

were used as coffins, indicating that this part of the caves was used as a burial ground. A reconstruction of this cave together with some of the remains found there can be seen in the Sarawak Museum in Kuching.

More recent human activity in the caves has centred around the fact that they are the home of three species of swiftlet, numbering some four million, and 12 species of bat, of which there are also several million. The swiftlets construct their nests in crevices in the roof of the Great Cave and it's these nests which are used in the preparation of that famous Chinese dish, bird's nest soup.

The collection of these nests, which are sold for over a $250 a kilogram, is now

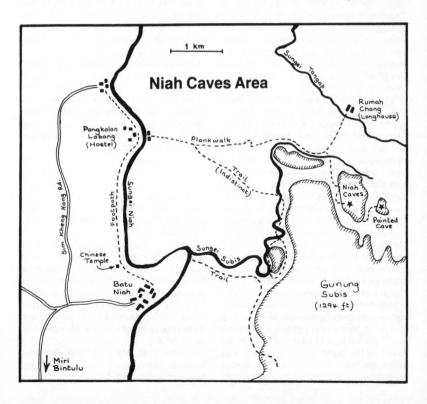

strictly limited to certain times of the year, but even if you're not here at those times you can get some idea of the hazards involved in collecting them. Scattered throughout the Great Cave are many flimsy poles – some of them well over 30 metres long – stretching from the floor to the roof, up which men have to scramble to get to the nests. Reportedly birds' nest collecting is now declining or has even stopped due to a drop in the quality of the nests.

The other activity which has been going on here since 1928 is the collection of guano – the bird and bat excrement which is used as a fertilizer. The guano is collected each week on Mondays, Tuesdays, and Wednesdays and carted laboriously along the plankwalk to the depot at Pangkalan Lubang where it is weighed, rebagged and boated down to Batu Niah for sale. If you're heading up to the caves on these days you may well have to give way to the collectors sweating it out down the plankwalk, each with a huge bag of guano on his back.

The millions of winged inhabitants of the caves provide an unforgettable spectacle as evening comes along. Swiftlets being day flyers and bats nocturnal animals, if you arrange to be at the mouth of the cave around 6 pm you can watch the shift change as the swiftlets return home and the bats go out for the night. You might even be lucky enough to see one of the large predatory birds, such as the bat hawks, swoop into the cave for a meal.

If you go up to the caves at this time be sure to bring a strong torch (flashlight) for the return trip. It's an exciting night time jungle experience, but made easy by the plankwalk. Though you are certain to hear and see plenty on the way you'll probably remember most the many luminous mushrooms that grow beside the plankwalk. If you go up to the caves at this time of day you'll probably find that the gate to the caves at the point where the plankwalk forks for the caves and the nearby longhouse is locked when you return.

There's a simple remedy for this which involves lifting the gate off its hinges – and, if you care to, putting it back on again. The technique was shown to me by two of the longhouse children! The alternative is to climb through the gap at the top of the gate.

The three-km-long plankwalk is made of belian wood, which is very durable and so heavy that it cannot be transported by water since it doesn't float. This plankwalk starts at Pangkalan Lubang about four km from the village of Batu Niah, opposite the Niah Park hostel, and passes through primary rain forest all the way to the Niah Caves. If you do the trip in the rainy season take care because the plankwalk gets very slippery at these times. The first part of the walk is also subject to flooding – if you stay at the park hostel ask if anyone has photographs or slides of what it's like when it really floods around here. Quite a sight!

Unfortunately, most visitors are so intent on reaching the caves that they miss out on the life in the forest around them. If you break your trek and spend some time just watching and listening you may be lucky enough to see such animals as the long-tailed macaque monkeys, hornbills, squirrels and flying lizards as well as the many hundreds of species of butterflies which inhabit this forest. Even if you don't, you'll certainly hear much more than you see.

No permit is needed to visit the Great Cave but if you wish to visit the 'Painted Cave' then you need a permit from the Curator's Office, Sarawak Museum, Kuching. The permit is free and takes about 10 minutes to issue if you're in Kuching. That's the official story, anyway. In practice, if you hire a local guide at the Park HQ at Pangkalan Lumbang to take you through the main cave to the 'Painted Cave', then it's unlikely you'll be asked for the permit.

Guides cost M$30 (shared between however many there are of you) and however much you fancy yourself as a

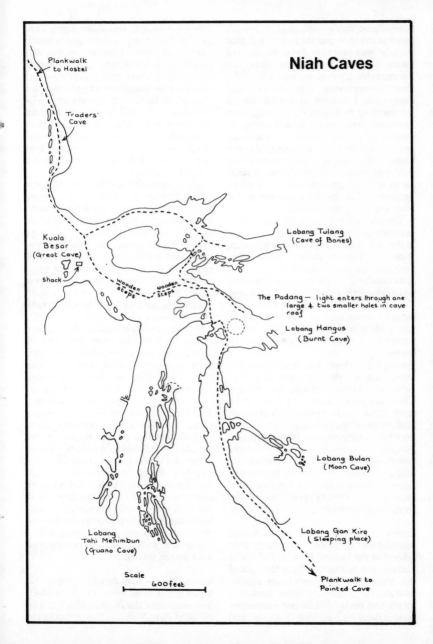

Niah Caves

Plankwalk to Hostel

Traders' Cave

Kuala Besar (Great Cave)

Shack

Lobang Tulang (Cave of Bones)

wooden steps   wooden steps

The Padang – light enters through one large & two smaller holes in cave roof

Lobang Hangus (Burnt Cave)

Lobang Bulan (Moon Cave)

Lobang Tahi Menimbun (Guano Cave)

Lobang Gan Kira (Sleeping place)

Plankwalk to Painted Cave

Scale
600 feet

speleologist they're well worth it. Sketch maps of the cave give the impression that it's relatively easy to find your way around inside, but this isn't the case. There are innumerable blind alleys which look like main thoroughfares – some of them quite dangerous. There are also a number of overhanging walls literally crawling with scorpions. Whether you go with a guide or not (we didn't – but it took us several hours to find the right path – and many hours to find our way out again!) you need a *strong* light and spare batteries. A pair of stout shoes wouldn't go amiss either – don't go in thongs. Ask the Park Warden or his assistant if you want a guide.

The area around the park hostel itself is not without interest. While you're relaxing in the cane chairs on the verandah four km from Batu Niah and about 17 km from the sea, keep an eye on the river. The river level can change by over a metre depending on the strength of the tides out to sea, and the current varies from static to quite strong – something you might notice as you paddle across to the shop in the waterlogged boat which belongs to the hostel.

Logging is widespread in this area and several times a day you'll see large, log-laden barges chug their way downstream. These barges are almost as wide as the river. Once at the river mouth they are loaded onto ships and exported to Japan, South Korea, Taiwan and the Philippines. Wildlife occasionally seen in the river includes monitor lizards (up to two metres long), crocodiles and snakes, but they're all extremely shy and, for the benefit of those who are thinking of swimming in the river, rarely seen around the hostel area.

Places to Stay It would be a strange traveller who would want to stay anywhere other than the *Visitors' Hostel* at Pangkalan Lubang, across the river from the start of the plankwalk. The hostel can accommodate 25 people in three dormitory rooms and costs M$2.50 per person per night. Bedding, cooking utensils and

crockery (latter in very short supply!) are provided and the hostel is equipped with toilets, showers, cooking stoves and electricity in the evenings until 10 pm. If you're lucky there may be an overseas volunteer working there who will put on a slide show for you in the evening. The hostel is rarely full so you can turn up without prior booking, but if you want to make sure then you can book in advance at the Forest Office (Pejabat Utan) in Miri (tel 085-36637). Weekends and holidays can get quite busy.

Meals cannot be bought at the hostel or across the river so you will have to prepare your own at the hostel. It's a good idea to bring canned foods, vegetables and cooking oil with you from Batu Niah although there's a store across the river from the hostel which sells a very limited range of canned meats, rice, noodles, onions, eggs, potatoes, soft drinks, beers and a few other things. They also have torches (flashlights) and batteries for sale in case you didn't pick one up earlier.

If for some reason you don't want to stay at the Visitors' Hostel or your time of arrival stops you getting there that night, there are three hotels in Batu Niah. The *Niah Caves Hotel* is clean, reasonably cheap at M$18 for a double and has good basic food in the restaurant downstairs. The *Yung Hur Lodging House* is similarly priced. The *Hock Sen Hotel* has a dormitory.

If you need to go into Batu Niah for supplies from Pangkalan Lubang you can either hail a boat going upriver (the one-way fare should be about M$2 though they'll naturally start higher) or walk there along the track which follows the river. If you walk there it will take about an hour, but be careful of the bridges along the way. Some of them are decidedly unsafe – though kids walk along them every day on their way to school.

Getting There – from Bintulu There are no buses direct from Bintulu to Batu Niah. You must take the Bintulu-Miri bus and get off at Batu Niah junction, about 12 km from the village of Batu Niah. For further info see the Bintulu section. From the junction to Batu Niah you must either hitch (easy) or take one of the occasional taxis which pass through (the fare should be about M$2 though they may ask for more). There are no buses along this stretch. If heading towards Bintulu from Batu Niah either hitch to the junction or take a taxi and then wait for the Miri-Bintulu bus which comes past here at about 9 am.

From Miri There are two daily buses from Miri direct to Batu Niah early in the morning and around noon. The fare is M$9 and the journey takes about 2½ hours. It's wise to book in advance. If heading back to Miri from Batu Niah you can either take one of the two daily buses or a taxi which will cost M$15 per person, slightly more with air-con. Taxis depart for Miri from the centre of Batu Niah up to noon each day. Don't bother looking for them; they'll find you.

On the way to Batu Niah you can stop at Lambir National Park, about 50 km from Miri. There's a pleasant waterfall about 20 minutes' walk in from the park buildings on the road. At the waterfall there's an empty house where you can stay for free – no beds or cooking facilities. Check with the Forest Officer in Miri or at the park.

Batu Niah to Pangkalan Lubang (Visitors' Hostel) Whether you come from Bintulu or Miri you will end up at Batu Niah. From here the best way to get to the Visitors' Hostel (or the start of the plankwalk if you're not staying at the hostel) is to take a motorised boat down the river to Pangkalan Lubang. The fare should be about M$2 per person (M$10 for the boat) though they'll start higher. Haggle. If you booked National Park transport in Miri someone will collect you from Batu Niah in the hostel's own longboat for M$5 per boat load per return trip.

The alternatives are to walk along the track which follows the river to the hostel (about 45 minutes to one hour) or, if you have your own transport, to drive to the end of Sim Kheng Hong Rd, leave your wheels there, and walk 10 minutes along the track to the hostel. It's possible to get a ride from Batu Niah to the end of the road for M$2 per person. It's about three km from Batu Niah to the hostel.

For crossing the river to the start of the plankwalk or to go to the store there is a (frequently waterlogged) longboat with planks of wood for oars which belongs to the hostel. Visitors are free to use it at any time. If it happens to be on the wrong side of the river when you need it just holler out. Someone will bring it across for you.

Around Niah

There is an 80-door Iban longhouse called Rumah Chang, about 40 minutes' walk down the plankwalk, where many of the guano and birds' nest collectors live. To get there take the left-hand fork where the plankwalk divides in two. Be warned though that they may charge you M$5 to look around.

In addition to the plankwalk there are a number of vague trails through the jungle which will take you to the summit of Gunung Subis. They're supposed to be marked with blue-and-white paint strips on the trunks of trees, but these are not at all obvious. Other walks in the area are also worth investigating.

Sabah

Until independence in 1963 Sabah was known as north Borneo and while its Borneo neighbour, Sarawak, was run by the Rajah Brookes, Sabah was operated by the British North Borneo Company. As with the Brooke family, administration was handed over to the British government after WW II and, again like Sarawak, Sabah became independent when it merged with Malaysia.

As in Sarawak there was trouble post-independence, but Sabah's existence was disputed not only by Indonesia but also by the Philippines. There are close cultural ties between the people of the Sulu Archipelago of the Philippines' Mindanao province and the neighbouring people of Sabah. To this day there is a busy smuggling trade operated from Sabah into Mindanao and Mindanao's Moslem rebels often scamper down towards Sabah when pursued by government forces. Recently, the Philippines government, looking for ways to divert attention away from domestic problems, has once again been making noisy claims to Sabah. Whether this will escalate into a major dispute is uncertain.

Post-independence Sabah was governed for a time by Tun Mustapha who ran the state almost as a private fiefdom and often at odds with the central government in Kuala Lumpur. In 1976 he slipped from power and since then Sabah has moved closer to the central government. Sabah's economic strength is based on timber and agriculture. For the visitor Sabah offers scenic grandeur, Mt Kinabalu and, like Sarawak, a variety of interesting tribes. Unfortunately Sabah, again like Sarawak, is an expensive place to travel around by peninsular standards. The population of Sabah is just over one million.

Tamus

The local weekly markets (known as tamus) held at various small towns all over Sabah are a colourful local attraction. *Tamu* days are:

Babaggon	Saturday
Beaufort	Saturday
Keningau	Thursday
Kinarut	Saturday
Kionsom	Sunday
Kiulu	Tuesday
Kota Belud	Sunday
Kota Merudu	Sunday
Kuala Penyu	1st Wednesday of month
Kundasang	20th of month
Mangis	Thursday
Mattunggon	Saturday
Membakut	Sunday
Mersapol	Friday
Papar	Sunday
Penampang	Saturday
Putatan	Sunday
Ranau	1st of month
Sequati	Sunday
Simpangan	Thursday
Sindumin	Saturday
Sinsuran	Friday
Sipitang	Thursday
Tambunan	Thursday
Tamparuli	Wednesday
Tandek	Monday
Telipok	Thursday
Tenghilan	Thursday
Tenom	Sunday
Tinnopok	15th & 30th of month
Toboh	Sunday
Topokom	Tuesday
Tuaran	Sunday
Weston	Friday

Visas & Permits

Sabah, like Sarawak, is semi-autonomous and has its own immigration controls, but they're much more relaxed about it than Sarawak. These days you are likely to be given a month's stay permit, as in Sarawak, and it's rare for you to be asked to show money or onward tickets. Permits can be renewed at an immigration office. There are immigration offices at most points of arrival – even at small riverine places like Merapok near Beaufort – but if you miss them there's no problem. Simply report to another immigration office, even several days later, and explain the situation.

No further permits are required to visit the interior. If you're going to Sandakan you're supposed to have a permission slip to visit the Orang Utan sanctuary outside the city at Sepilok, but when you get there no one asks for it.

General Costs

Sabah is an expensive place to travel around in. Only in Kota Kinabalu and at Kinabalu National Park will you find accommodation that could be classed as 'budget'. Elsewhere it's the familiar story of at least M$15 per night and often much more. Lodging is complicated too by the fact that many of the cheapest places are often full with semi-permanent boarders, which means you may well have to stay in places which would normally be outside the range of budget travel. If you're prepared to rough it there is the alternative in many places of staying overnight in churches, religious missions and schools – ask for permission first. The only trouble with this is that you have to cart your baggage around all day, but then most of these places are free.

The other alternative to budget accommodation in Sabah is the series of Government Rest Houses which cost M$12 per person per night. They're often full with government officials but are worth a try. Apart from those mentioned in the relevant sections of the text they are also found in Kota Merudu (tel 61321), Pitas Kudat (tel 61133), Semporna (tel 7781709), Sipitang (tel 426), Kuala Penyu (tel 231), Tambunan (tel 74339) and Tuaran (tel 788511). The rest house at Kota Belud is supposed to be for senior government officials only, but I heard of at least one traveller who had managed to get in there.

KOTA KINABALU

Known as Jesselton until 1963, Kota Kinabalu was razed during WW II to prevent the Japanese using it as a base, so it's now just a modern city of wide avenues and tall buildings without any of the historic charm of Kuching. All the same, it's a pleasant enough city, well landscaped in parts, and its location on the coast gives it an equitable climate.

One of Asia's fastest growing cities, with a population approaching 250,000, it's an interesting blend of European, Malay and Chinese cultures and worth hanging around in for a few days, if only to sample the excellent variety of cuisines available here – something which is sadly lacking elsewhere in the state. You must also come here to book accommodation and guides for the trip up to Mt Kinabalu – Sabah's number one attraction.

Orientation

Although the city sprawls for many miles along the coast from the international airport at Tanjong Aru to the new developments at Tanjong Lita, the centre itself is quite small and most places are within easy walking distance of each other. This includes the bulk of the hotels and restaurants, banks, travel agents, the Tourist Office, the National Parks Office and the General Post Office as well as the bus terminal and minibus stands. The city can be roughly divided into two halves split in the middle by the large pedestrian walkway or bridge. East of this is the older, cheaper part of town. The other side has the bulk of the better hotels and restaurants as well as offices, airline companies and the more western-type shops.

Information

Tourist Office The Tourist Office (tel 211732 or 211698) has a good range of information, with plenty of glossy leaflets and sketch maps available, but probably the most useful information they have is a loose-leaf folder packed with up-to-date

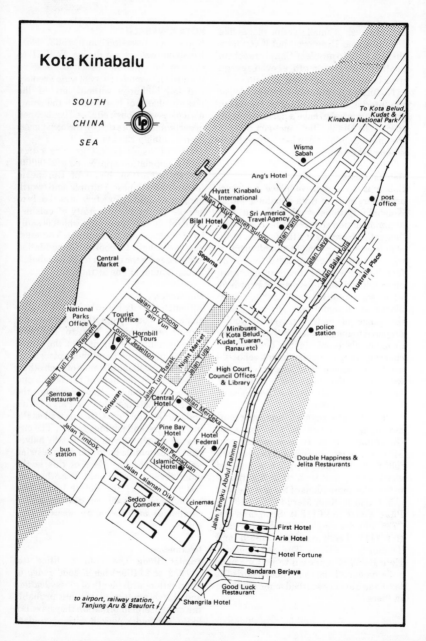

Kota Kinabalu

SOUTH

CHINA

SEA

To Kota Belud,
Kudat &
Kinabalu National Park

Wisma
Sabah

Ang's Hotel

Hyatt Kinabalu
International

Jalan Datuk Salleh Sulong

Sri America
Travel Agency

Bilal Hotel

Jalan Pantai

post
office

Segama

Jalan Gaya

Jalan Balai Polis

Australia Place

Central
Market

National
Parks
Office

Jalan Dr. Chong
Thin Vun

Tourist
Office

Lorong Jesselton

Hornbill
Tours

Minibuses
(Kota Belud,
Kudat, Tuaran,
Ranau etc)

police
station

Jalan Tun Fuad Stephens

Night Market

Jalan Tugu

High Court,
Council Offices
& Library

Sentosa
Restaurant

Sinsuran

Jalan Tun Razak

Central
Hotel

Jalan Merdeka

Jalan Timbok

Pine Bay
Hotel

Jalan Perbaduan

Hotel
Federal

Double Happiness &
Jelita Restaurants

Islamic
Hotel

bus
station

Jalan Laiaman Diki

Jalan Tengku Abdul Rahman

cinemas

Sedco
Complex

First Hotel

Aria Hotel

Hotel Fortune

Bandaran Berjaya

Good Luck
Restaurant

to airport, railway station,
Tanjung Aru & Beaufort

Shangrila Hotel

stuff on most of the hotels in Sabah, available transport in the form of taxis, buses, Land-Rovers, launch services, etc, and many other tid-bits of information you'd find hard to come across elsewhere. The staff are very friendly and helpful and will photocopy information for you if you need it. Hours are 8.30 am to 12.45 pm, 2 to 4.45 pm Monday through Friday, 8 am to 12.45 pm Saturday, closed Sundays. Kota Kinabalu has both a state and a national tourist office on either side of Hornbill Tours.

National Park Sabah National Parks Office, PO Box 626, Kota Kinabalu (tel 54452 for general enquiries and 51595 for reservations), is just around the corner on Jalan Tun Fuad Stephens. Before going to Mt Kinabalu or Poring Hot Springs you must come here to make reservations for accommodation (and guides, if required) and the further ahead you do it the more chance you have of being able to go there when you want. Mt Kinabalu is a very popular place both with overseas visitors and local people, and accommodation at the park HQ is often booked up a week in advance. The office is open Monday through Thursday from 8 am to 12.45 pm and from 2 pm to 4.15 pm, on Fridays from 8 am to 11.30 am and 2 pm to 4.15 pm and again on Saturdays from 8 am to 12.45 pm. In addition to handling reservations they stock a range of guidebooks on Mt Kinabalu, postcards and T-shirts.

Other Offices The Immigration Office is located in the Federal Buildings, Jalan Mat Salleh. If you need to go there take a taxi as it's some distance from the centre of the city. The Poste Restante service at the GPO is reliable. The clerk will give you the whole pile of letters to sort through. The Indonesian Consulate (tel 54100) is at Jalan Sagunting in the Wing On Life Building. Banking hours are Monday through Friday from 9.30 am to 2.30 pm and on Saturdays from 9.30 am to 11 am. Closed on Sundays and public holidays.

Airlines Airline offices: MAS, (tel 51455, 53560), 1 Jalan Sagunting; Cathay Pacific (tel 54733, 54758, 54759); Singapore Airlines (tel 55444); Philippine Airlines (tel 57870); Royal Brunei Airlines (tel 53211, 54028). Unlike Singapore, Penang or Hong Kong there are no real bargains to be found here in the form of discounted airline tickets. So if you're planning to fly on from Sabah to Hong Kong or Manila enquire about tickets in Singapore first.

Sri-America Travel (tel 57660, 57606) on Jalan Gaya have friendly staff. Kinabalu Travel Service at Block 5, Wisma yakim, Jalan Haji Samor has also been recommended. Or try Hornbill Tours (tel 57729, 53221), Sri Pelancungan Hornbill Sdn Bhd, Block L, Lots 4-6, Sinsuran Complex, next door to the Tourist Office. They also have a few handicrafts for sale.

The State Mosque

As an example of contemporary Islamic architecture at its best, this mosque is well worth a visit. It's located on the outskirts of town; you'll pass by if coming or going to the airport. It's much more interesting than the mosques at Kuching or Brunei. Visitors are allowed inside though naturally shoes must be removed before entering.

Sabah Museum

The new museum was completed toward the end of 1984. It's situated by the State Legislative Assembly Hall. The main building is a four-storey structure in longhouse style. Inside are good collections of tribal and historical artifacts, including ceramics. Another section has flora and fauna examples from around the country. There is also a restaurant, coffee shop, and views over the gardens and man-made lakes in the grounds. Definitely worth a visit.

Tunku Abdul Rahman National Park

The park is made up of the offshore islands of Pulau Gaya, Mamutik, Manukan, Sapi and Sulug. Only a short boat ride from the centre of the city, they offer good beaches, crystal-clear water and a wealth of tropical corals and marine life. Pulau Gaya is the biggest of the islands and aside from Police Beach has 20 km of marked hiking trails. If lucky you may see monkeys, pangolins or even what's known as the bearded pig. Close by is small Pulau Sapi, the other most visited island. It, too, has good beaches and trails and day-use facilities.

Places to Stay There is some basic camping on Pulau Mamutik and a guest house for up to eight people, but it costs M$160 per night on weekends. During the week it's 30% less. Make reservations through the park office in Kuching. You can also ask them about camping on the little-developed Pulau Sulug.

Getting There There are launches to the islands; one reliable operator is Hornbill Tours, next door to the tourist office. Boats are scheduled only on Sundays and holidays when the main islands get quite busy. Departures are at 7.30, 8.30 and 9.30 am; the latter only if an extra trip is required. The cost is M$10 and the return trips are made between 2 and 4 pm.

During the week you must charter the boat and this, unfortunately, is far from cheap. The boat can take up to 14 people and costs M$185 round trip. Other boat companies also do the trip; ask at the tourist office. Possibilities include House of Travels and Chong Brothers Shipping. Or you can strike up deals with local fishermen and boat owners although the half-hour trip is still costly – local boats cost M$40 to 50.

Tanjong Aru Beach
Several km south-west of the city centre is Tanjong Aru beach, adjacent to Prince Philip Park and close to the international airport. It's not bad as beaches go and the area is dotted with open-air food and drink stalls, but you can find much better beaches as well as Rungus longhouses at Kudat near the northern tip of Sabah.

Other
If you'd like a view over the city go for a stroll up Signal Hill at the eastern end of the city centre above the GPO. It's best at sunset. Prince Philip Park by the beach has some food stalls and is close to downtown.

You'll often see tourist literature in Sabah adorned with photographs of the Sabah Foundation's cylindrical, mirror-fronted, 31-storey building at Likas Bay, with its revolving restaurant and ministerial suites. The literature gushes breathlessly about this landmark and insists that you include it in your programme but it isn't worth the effort and anyway it can be seen from a distance en route to Kinabalu National Park, standing in the middle of a vast, devastated landscape.

There is also the market but it isn't very impressive at all. There are actually two locations for it – the waterfront area for fish and an area in front of the harbour for fruits and vegetables. There are some food stalls around the waterfront area.

Places to Stay
After Kuching and Brunei, Kota Kinabalu seems positively overflowing with hotels, but most of them are fairly expensive places and there are very few budget hotels.

Places to Stay – bottom end
Finding a decent budget hotel in KK is not easy. Essentially to get a good room here you have to pay for it. For many years the most popular budget hotel with travellers has been the *Islamic Hotel* (tel 54325) at 8 Jalan Perpaduan. It has 15 rooms at M$25.50. Rooms are very basic although you get a ceiling fan. The sink in the room likely won't work, nor the one in the toilet, nor the shower. A tap in the bathroom does, so with that and a plastic bucket you've got your shower. The restaurant downstairs serves OK Indian and Pakistani food.

An alternative, diagonally across the street, is the *Pine Bay* (tel 54900), but it's really no better. Singles are M\$28, doubles M\$33, with air-con M\$40/44. Some rooms are OK, some are totally airless holes where 'not even the cockroaches stay around'. Along the street the hotel is on there are numerous cheap restaurants – mostly Indian and Muslim. There's a Chinese one opposite the park. There are a couple of other cheap-looking hotels in this area like the *Central* at 5 Jalan Tugu, where there's always a bunch of people you wouldn't want to take home to mother hanging around the door, and the *Long House Hotel* on Jalan Tun Fuad Stephens, which is strictly a brothel and a very busy one at that. Across from the bus station is the pretty grim-looking *Hotel Golden Dragon*.

If you don't mind staying out at Tanjong Aru the *Victory Hotel* (tel 52640) at 9 Jalan Pinang has reasonable rooms at M\$20. You can get there on the airport bus, getting off at the bus shelter with 'Tanjong Aru' painted in big letters on the wall.

Places to Stay – middle
Hotels in this range are numerous, some of them not much more costly than the cheapies and yet much better.

Check the area in the streets of Bandar Berjaya across the large roundabout from the Sedco Complex (along Jalan Laiman Diki). The *Fortune* is friendly and M\$33 with fan, M\$41 with air-con. The *First Hotel* has been completely overhauled and is clean and comfortable. Rooms have air-con and own bath and there is a TV room. Prices have gone up accordingly and are now M\$50/60 for singles/doubles. A few doors down is the *Asia Hotel*, which is more modest and pretty good value at M\$33 without bath, M\$39 with.

Back in the main section of town the *Hotel Nam Tai* on Jalan Merdeka near Jalan Tugu in not bad. Reasonably clean and decently managed, they charge M\$33 single, M\$39 double.

As you head into the newer section of town near Jalan Datuk Sallah Sulong, you'll encounter another good close-to-budget hotel. It's the *Hotel Bilal* (tel 56709, 56488) where everything works and you even get soap. Singles or doubles are M\$35. The hotel is in the Segama shopping complex, across from the Hyatt Hotel on the second floor. Around behind it is the *Oriental*, which is a bit more expensive and nowhere near as friendly. Nearby are the *New Sabah* and behind the Bilal in the opposite direction the *Salamat* – all in the same bracket.

Once again in the older section of town is the *Eden* (tel 53577) across from the park at 1-2 Jalan Merdeka, where the clean rooms are good value at M\$48 with air-con, or M\$35 without.

Moving up the scale a bit the *Jesselton Hotel Inn* (tel 55633), Jalan Gaya is part of the *Jesselton Hotel* and offers cheaper rooms at M\$55-70 single, M\$70-85 double. The *Nim Hing Hotel* (tel 51433), 33-34 Jalan Haji Saman has air-con singles at M\$40 or M\$58 with bathroom. Doubles with bathroom are M\$70 to 75.

Others are the *Hotel Segama* (tel 221326), 16 Jalan Lubuk in the Segama shopping complex at M\$43-57. The *Diamond Inn* (tel 225222) on Jalan Haji Yakub has singles/doubles at M\$62/76. With rooms from M\$36 the *Hotel Rakyat* (tel 58536), Lot 3, Block 1, Sinsuran Complex is spotlessly clean and the staff are friendly. Or there's the *Sea View Hotel* (tel 54422), 31 Jalan Haji Saman and the *Federal Hotel* (tel 51191), 10 Jalan Haji Yakub.

Places to Stay – top end
Kota Kinabalu has a number of hotels with prices right up there with the Singapore-Kuala Lumpur-Penang places. Four of the top hotels are the centrally located *Hotel Capital*, the big *Hyatt Kinabalu International*, the *Hotel Shangri-La*, and the big, new and very expensive beachfront *Tanjong Aru Beach Hotel*.

Other top range hotels, but below this stratospheric level, include the *Jesselton Hotel*, which also has a more moderately priced annex; the *Sabah Inn*; the small

Ang's Hotel and, once again out at Tanjong Aru Beach, the *Borneo Hotel*. More top hotels are being built in and around town and the new airport, and several others are still in the planning stages.

Ang's Hotel (tel 55433), 25 Jalan Bakau, 35 rooms, singles M$84, doubles M$96
Borneo Hotel (tel 55255), 13 Jalan Selangor, Tanjong Aru, 31 rooms, singles M$90, doubles M$110-140
Hotel Capital (tel 53433), 23 Jalan Haji Saman, 102 rooms, singles M$150, doubles M$160
Hyatt Kinabalu International (tel 51777), Jalan Datuk Salleh Sulong, 344 rooms, singles M$210, doubles M$250
Jesselton Hotel (tel 55633), Gaya St, 49 rooms, singles M$140-155, doubles M$160-180; for annex rooms see middle bracket
Sabah Inn (tel 53322), 25 Jalan Pantai, 40 rooms, singles M$58, doubles M$78
Hotel Shangri-La (tel 56100), Bandaran Berjaya, 120 rooms, singles M$140, doubles M$155
Tanjong Aru Beach Hotel (tel 80752), Tanjong Aru, 300 rooms, singles M$210, doubles M$230

Places to Eat

For the variety of restaurants and the quality of food available KK is probably the best city in Borneo. Not that they're particularly cheap and – as everywhere else in East Malaysia – unless you're prepared to pay somewhat over the odds for a meal you'll have to settle for the usual indifferent Chinese fare of noodles and a parsimonious helping of fried vegetables and/or meat.

If you've had one too many of these meals, as most travellers have who have come through from Sarawak, then you're probably feeling like a splurge. The best place to go looking for restaurants – especially seafood restaurants – is the Sinsuran complex which is bounded by Jalan Timbok, Jalan Tun Razak, Lorong Jesselton and the waterfront (Jalan Tun Fuad Stephens). It's probably unfair to recommend one restaurant over another since all of them seem to be very good and popular especially in the evenings but for starters you might like to try the *Sentosa*,

behind the Sinsuran Centre at the corner of Jalan Tun Razak and Block 5. Another good place for seafood is the *Village House Restaurant* by the tourist office. At lunch times there's a set meal for M$11.50. At dinner main courses are M$10 to 16. The restaurant is open only at mealtimes, but the pub is open from 4.30 pm to midnight. Also in the Sentosa Centre is the *Golden Flower* for seafood.

If you'd like to try good Chinese food then go to the *Good Luck Restaurant* at the junction of Jalan Tengku Abdul Rahman and Jalan Laiman Diki near the Shangri-La Hotel. This place is extremely popular with local people and is open from 7 am to 2 am daily except Sunday, when it's open from 7 am to 2 pm. Prices are fairly reasonable and they also offer seafood in the evenings, but beware of unwanted extras on your bill like peanuts on the table or unasked-for hand towels. Other Chinese restaurants which are not as good, but very fair, include the *Double Happiness* and *Jelita Restaurant*, Jalan Merdeka, opposite the night market. The *Double Happiness* is one of the few places where I saw Peking duck. The *Golden Spring*, near the Shangri-La Hotel, has fresh fish in tanks. On the corner by the Elm Hotel is a very pleasant, but still reasonable, al fresco Chinese place.

There are now plenty of western snack places springing up around town. In the Segama complex there's the cafeteria-style *Tomato Restaurant* where you can get a beer. *Tidbits Cafe* upstairs is much the same. You'll see several fried chicken places, one near the *Hotel Jesselton*. They charge about M$3 to 4 for a meal.

Back in the Segama complex the *Ali Restaurant* has meals for about M$2.50, biriyani M$4. A few doors down is the *Bilal* which has good Malaysian food – quick and cheap. In both sections of town you'll find the usual cheapie Chinese and Muslim restaurants.

Getting There

To/From Peninsula Malaysia & Singapore
The cheapest way of getting from peninsula Malaysia to Kota Kinabalu is advance purchase (M$256) from Johore Bahru; regular fare is M$301. There are also economy night flights from Kuala Lumpur. Advance purchase tickets must be paid for 14 days in advance while the night fares only apply to certain flights. Similar fares are also available from Kota Kinabalu to the peninsula. MAS operate a special direct bus from their office in Singapore to Johore Bahru to make the flight from there not only rather cheaper but also quite convenient. The MAS office is located in the far western section of Kota Kinabalu, beyond the post office.

There used to be regular shipping services with Straits Shipping between Singapore and Sabah but these have now virtually disappeared. A new service, operated by Pernas National Shipping, is supposed to commence in mid-85 from Kuantan on the east coast of the peninsula to Kuching and Kota Kinabalu in north Borneo. Whether it will actually happen remains to be seen.

To/From Hong Kong MAS and Cathay Pacific each have two flights weekly between Kota Kinabalu and Hong Kong. The fare is M$658, but you will probably find cheaper tickets on Philippine Airlines. The flight time is a little under four hours.

To/From Philippines MAS and Philippine Airlines fly KK-Manila daily; the fare is M$413 and flight time is just under two hours. From time to time there have been flights between KK or other towns in Sabah and Zamboanga in the southern Philippines' island of Mindanao. At present they are, once again, out of operation.

Buses The main bus station in Kota Kinabalu is on the west side of the Sinsuran complex over the other side of Jalan Timbok. Most of the buses from here cover the routes south and west of Kota Kinabalu to such places as Papar, Kimanis and Beaufort. The road is paved and excellent for the 90 km to Beaufort. Beyond that it's gravel, generally getting worse the further you go. The road does now extend all the way to Lawas and even beyond that although it doesn't reach the border. The bus to Beaufort costs M$7 or M$8 with air-con in a new bus. Or you can take one all the way to Menumbok on the coast (from where boats run to Labuan) for M$14 air-con. The trip takes about three hours.

In addition to service buses there are several companies which operate fleets of minibuses to places east and north of Kota Kinabalu. They include Tuaran United Transport, Luen Thung Transport and Penampang Union Transport. Besides being faster and more comfortable than the service buses the minibuses differ very little in the price of the fare, so most travellers prefer them. Their terminals are shown on the map of Kota Kinabalu. There's no problem finding the minibus you want as you can hear the drivers shouting their destination from a long way off. They go when full but, for the long hauls, departures are only in the mornings. Because of road improvements and faster times some fares haven't changed much in a few years. Some examples from KK include:

To Kota Belud (77 km), departures up to 2 pm daily, two hours on a road that is sealed nearly all the way for M$8.
To Kudat (22 km), departures up to 8 am, four hours on a road which is partially sealed for M$15.
To Sandakan (400 km), two minibuses daily at 8.30 and 11 am, about 10 hours for M$40. The road is sealed as far as Ranau and then rough most of the way to Sandakan. It's paved in and around Sandakan. Going the other way from Ranau to Tenom, you'll travel on an all-weather gravel road. From KK to Tambunan the road is surfaced.

If you're heading for Kinabaju National Park from KK you can get there by taking either the minibuses for Ranau or andakan and getting off at the park HQ, which is right by the side of the road. Ask the driver to drop you off there. The fare to the park HQ should be about M$10 and the journey will take just over two hours.

Besides the minibuses there are also share-taxis to most places. Like the minibuses they go when full and their fares are usually about 20-25% higher than the minibuses. Journey times are about the same. There are some routes, however, which can only be covered by Land-Rover or share-taxi. The one you're most likely to come across is the route from KK to Keningau over the Crocker Range. The route first follows the sealed road as far as Papar, where it turns off and heads up into the mountains. From here on it's as rough as hell until you get to Keningau and if you like a degree of comfort then take a share-taxi in preference to a Land-Rover. The fare is M$15 for a Land-Rover and M$20 for a taxi – an expensive ride but then cars don't last too long over this kind of terrain!

Getting Around

Airport Transport The only occasion on which you'll need to use local public transport is to get to the airport at Tanjong Aru, south-west of the centre. To get there take a taxi or red bus No 12 or 13. The buses run every half hour from 6.15 am until late. The airport bus costs 60c. To get it turn right coming out of the airport, walk a few metres and there is a bus stand. A non air-con taxi to town will be M$6.20, with air-con M$7.70. From the airport they operate on a coupon system; buy one at the desk where prices are listed.

Note that there is no place to change money at the airport; you might get a taxi driver to change money for you. They'll only accept Malaysian money so try to bring some with you. The airport is small, hot and extremely crowded, but a new,

modern facility should be in operation sometime in early 1985.

Taxis Locally taxis are plentiful in the extreme. Fares are generally 10% more for air-con and 50% more from 1 am to 6 am.

Car Rentals You can try Sintat (tel 211221) in the Sinsuran complex. Price is M$125 for a Toyota Corona with unlimited mileage, or M$80 and 25c per km. Other outlets are Cantas Rent-a-Car (tel 55255) at the Borneo Hotel or Avis at the Hyatt.

Things to Buy

Though a major centre, KK isn't a great place to look for handicrafts. Hornbill Tours have a few items, mostly basket-work. The Handicraft Development Corporation above the tourist office also have some things – the odd weaving and maybe a Kadazan doll and jewellery, though the latter is expensive. I didn't see anything at the Sunday market, but sometimes in town a tribeswoman has something interesting. You might think that the best and cheapest place to buy these things would be at the *tamus* (weekly markets) held in such places as Kota Belud, but I didn't see any of these things for sale there so don't count on it. It's still possible to buy things like a Murut blowpipe (which are still in use by the tribe for hunting) but you'd have to shop around for something like that. All in all good local crafts are hard to find and expensive when you do come across something.

BEAUFORT

Beaufort is a quiet little provincial town on the River Padas with a fair amount of charm, although there's absolutely nothing to see or do here so it's unlikely you'll stay longer than overnight. If you're heading to or coming from eastern Sarawak by either the Brunei-Labuan-Mempakol or Lawas-Merapok-Sipitang routes then you will pass through Beaufort. The railway line

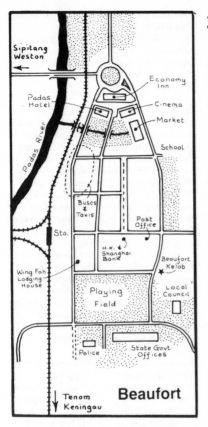

from Tanjong Aru (Kota Kinabalu) to Tenom also passes through Beaufort so you can take the train in either direction from here.

Information

There's a branch of the Hong Kong & Shanghai Banking Corporation in Beaufort which will change travellers' cheques. There is no bank at Sipitang. If you entered Sabah via the Lawas-Merapok-Sipitang route and missed immigration at Merapok (it's actually about a km beyond Merapok at Sindumin), there is no immigration office at Beaufort and you

will have to wait till you get to either Tenom or Kota Kinabalu.

Places to Stay

There is not much choice of accommodation in Beaufort although the (Wing Foh Lodging House), once permanently full of migrant workers, is now fairly easy to get into. Doubles are M$20 and spartan.

The *Economy Inn* (Hotel Ekonomi as one of the signs proclaims), is the cheaper of the other two places and has rooms from M$19 for a fan-cooled single up to M$38 for an air-con double. It's a very pleasant little place with clean communal bathrooms and though the staff are somewhat imbecilic they're very friendly. The other hotel is the *Padas Hotel* (tel 441/2) which has rooms from M$21 for a standard single up to M$50 for a double with air-con.

Places to Eat

The restaurant in the *Padas Hotel* is the most popular eating place in Beaufort with very good, albeit a little expensive, food. The restaurant under the *Economy Inn* is also pretty good and it's a little cheaper. English is spoken, but although drinks and cakes are available until late, meal orders are not accepted after 7 pm. If you're really on a tight budget there are several Chinese restaurants in town which serve she standard noodles-and-little-else meals.

If you're looking for something to do in the evening then you have the choice of Beaufort's only cinema (very popular) or attempting to talk your way into the upper social echelons of Beaufort society at the *Beaufort Kelab & Restaurant* where you can drink pink gins all night.

Getting There

Rail Sabah is the only place in East Malaysia where you will find railways and even here there's only one line. Unfortunately, this traveller's favourite has been cut back; the only link remaining is from

Beaufort to Tenom. The line formerly connected Beaufort to KK but this service was discontinued with the completion of the good road. Freight trains still chug the old route, though. The trip by rail between Beaufort and Tenom is a spectacular one following the Padas River gorge all the way to Tenom through steamy jungle.

Two types of passenger train are available: the railcars which are the best for comfort, speed and views, and the ordinary diesel trains which are the ones to take if you want a slower, more colourful journey packed in there with the local people and their produce. This route is unlikely to last long. The schedule is:

Beaufort-Tenom

diesel train:	Mon-Sat 10.50 am, 1.55 pm
	Sun 6.45 am, 2.30 pm
rail car:	Mon-Sat 8.25 am
	Sun 9.10 am, 3.40 pm

Tenom-Beaufort

diesel train:	Mon-Sat 7.30 am, 1.40 pm
	Sun 7.55 am, 3.05 pm
rail car:	Mon-Sat 3 pm, 10 pm
	Sun 7.20 am, 1.55 pm

Tenom-Beaufort the first-class fare is M$8.35, economy M$2.75.

Road There are now good bus services between KK and Beaufort; the fare is around M$8. Elsewhere there are minibuses or share-taxis – both forms of transport leave every morning for Papar/Kota Kinabalu, Mempakol – if you're heading for Labuan – (M$8), and Sipitang – if you're heading for Merapok and Lawas – (M$12). The road is now good all the way from KK to Beaufort.

There's no problem finding one as the drivers will approach you. Drivers who are heading for Mempakol will be shouting 'Labuan'. They connect with the launch to Labuan (M$7). If you're heading for Lawas you'll be able to get a taxi to Merapok from Sipitang (about M$3) in time to connect with a boat to Lawas.

AROUND BEAUFORT

Tiga Island

Off coastal Kuala Penyu, which sits on a peninsula, is Tiga Island. There is a good beach here and a government rest house. Boat charters are available, but, of course, are not inexpensive.

Labuan Island

Off the coast from Menumbok, Labuan is the jumping-off point for one way of getting to Brunei. It recently became a Federal Territory, and so is governed directly from Kuala Lumpur. How long this will last is not known and, come to think of it, the reasons for it aren't too clear either. Anyway, it acts as a duty-free centre and as such attracts many of Brunei's population as well as Malaysians for quick shopping sprees.

Victoria is the main town and it is here the ferries tie in. There really isn't anything to see unless you're into the bloody Sunday cockfights, though there are some nice beaches. Labuan is the place where the Japanese forces in north Borneo surrendered at the end of WW II. There's an appropriate memorial.

Places to Stay Accommodation is expensive. About the cheapest you'll find is the *Kim Soon Lee* on Jalan Okk Awang Besar or the *Victoria Lodging House* at 147 High St. Both are around M$50. The *Labuan Hotel* is the top hostel at M$100 single or double.

Getting There The ferry to Menumbok is M$7 or to Sipitang M$12. Several companies run regular shuttles to BSB (trips every day) and the 1½ hour trip costs M$12. Buses connect Menumbok to Beaufort and are M$8. The fare is cheaper if you get a through ticket to KK rather than get another in Beaufort.

TENOM

Tenom is the railhead on the line from Tanjong Aru (Kota Kinabalu) and a very pleasant rural town with much more old

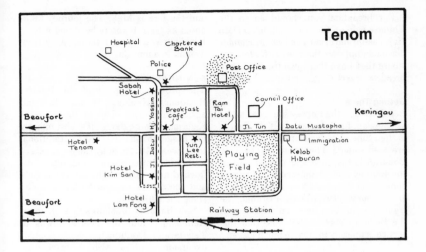

world charm than Beaufort. Nevertheless, although it has that perennial attraction of a 'backdrop of forested mountains' (as the tourist literature is fond of reminding you), there's absolutely nothing to do here unless you enjoy a game of pool. If you do then you're in luck because there's an excellent pool hall, but the game is very popular with locals so get there early and chalk your initials up if you want a game before it closes.

Information

There is an immigration office in Tenom where you can either check in (if you missed the checkpoint at Merapok) or get an extension to your permit. The staff here are very friendly and easygoing.

Places to Stay

If you can get in, Tenom has a four-room *Government Rest House* (tel 677) at the usual price of M\$12 per person or M\$5 for government workers. The cheapest hotels – the *Hotel Lam Fong* and the *Ram Tai Hotel* – will almost certainly be full with migrant workers. *Hotel Tenom* (tel 587) only has double rooms; they're fairly spartan but clean and cost from M\$33 for

a fan-cooled room without bathroom up to M\$50 for a room with bathroom and air-con. Downstairs there is a very spartan 'lounge' which serves cold beers; meals can be provided on request.

The next best is the *Sabah Hotel* (tel 534), Jalan Datu Haji Yassim (tel 534), which has clean doubles with fan and common bathroom for M\$22. The third place where you're likely to find a room is the *Hotel Kim San* (tel 611), Jalan Datu Haji Yassim, where rooms start from M\$22 (with bargaining), but it's poor value and best used only for emergencies.

At the top of the heap is the *Hotel Perkasa Tenom* (tel 088-56769), 65 rooms, all air-con, singles/doubles for M\$75/90.

Places to Eat

Probably the best place to eat is the *Yun Lee Restaurant*, Jalan Tun Datu Mustapha. It isn't the cheapest place to eat in Tenom, but it does have the best menu, the food is excellent and the staff are very friendly. You'll find everything from sweet & sour pork to nasi goreng. Downstairs in the *Sabah Hotel* there's a good and very reasonably priced Moslem restaurant serving excellent Indian-style food.

For breakfast you should go to the Chinese cafe on the corner of Jalan Datu Haji Yassim and Jalan Tun Datu Mustapha, diagonally opposite the *Yun Lee Restaurant*, where they have their own freshly baked bread, *hard* boiled eggs and speak English.

Getting There

Rail Although the railway line goes as far as Melalap, further up the valley, Tenom is the railhead as far as passenger trains are concerned. The journey down to Beaufort is the most spectacular part of the journey and recommended if you've come from Tambunan or Keningau and are on your way to Sarawak or Brunei. The train schedule and fares can be found in the Beaufort section, but note that this service is unlikely to survive much longer.

Road The only place there is to go by road from Tenom is up the valley to Keningau and Tambunan. Minibuses and share-taxis hang around outside the railway station and cruise around town in the mornings looking for passengers to Keningau. They go when full or almost full

and the fare is M$6. The journey takes about an hour. If you're heading for Kota Kinabalu you can get there easily from Tenom in a morning.

KENINGAU

The provincial capital of the Interior Residency, Keningau is a lumber and agricultural town deep in the heart of Kadazan country, though it's most unlikely you'll see anyone dressed in traditional tribal wear. Attracted by the prospects of well-paid employment, migrants have flocked here from neighbouring districts and the town's population has doubled since the 1960s.

Sabah tourist brochures rave on about Keningau – and the nearby towns of Tenom and Tambunan – being popular excursion centres with a fascinating cultural heritage, but they're really nothing of the sort. They're quite dull, uninteresting and expensive and it isn't long before you wonder why you came here at all. They're a perfect example of tourist organisations' over-enthusiasm for something which survives only as a fond memory.

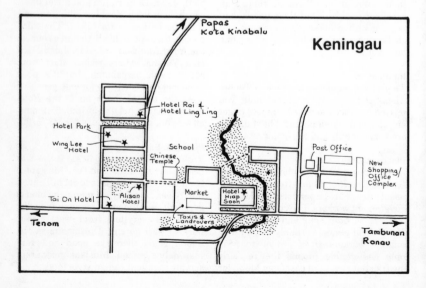

Top: Mt Kinabalu, Sabah (GC)
Left: pitcher plants by the Mt Kinabalu trail (GC)
Right: orang-utang sanctuary, Sepilok near Sandakan, Sabah (GC)

Top: Federal Secretariat, Kuala Lumpur (TW)
Bottom: Komala Vilas restaurant, Singapore (TW)

Keningau is simply a mini-boom town which is being torn apart to provide new business premises, shops, hotels, administrative offices and the like. The only worthwhile experience it offers is the journey there over the forested Crocker mountains, but get there soon if you want to see any trees because at the rate they're logging it there won't be any left in five years' time.

Places to Stay

Like other boom towns in East Malaysia, accommodation is expensive and the price you pay for a room doesn't necessarily reflect the facilities it offers. The *Government Rest House* (tel 31525/31177) has eight rooms at M$12 per person or M$5 for government officials. Probably the cheapest hotel in town is the *Tai On Hotel* on the main street, but it's often full.

Next up comes the *Park Hotel*, the *Wing Lee Hotel* and *Hotel Ling Ling*, but they're little cheaper than Keningau's better hotels. The *Hotel Alisan* is fully air-con and has rooms for around M$35, but has an unbelievably filthy entrance hall and stairs. Better hotels include the well-maintained air-con *Hotel Hiap Soon* with rooms from M$40. *Hotel Rai* has no single rooms and doubles cost M$33, or M$45 with air-con.

The *Hotel Perkasa Keningau* (tel 088-31044) is the most expensive hotel in town with 65 rooms at M$75/90 for singles/doubles.

Getting There

Share-taxis, minibuses and Land-Rovers are the only transport available and can be found around the central square where the market is also located. Keningau-Kota Kinabalu costs M$18 by Land-Rover and M$23 by share-taxi. The road over the mountains as far as Papar is rough as hell and unlikely to get better because it's constantly being churned up by enormous logging trucks. If the weather is fine there are superb views to take in, but if it's cloudy you'll see almost nothing. The drive to Kota Kinabalu takes two to 2½ hours.

Keningau-Tenom costs M$6 by minibus and takes about one hour along a good gravel road through forest and rubber plantations. There are also taxis and minibuses to Tambunan and Ranau. From Ranau you can go either to Sandakan or Kinabalu National Park.

KOTA BELUD

The town is the venue of Sabah's largest and most colourful *tamus* and as such is a magnet for travellers. The *tamu* takes place every Sunday – get there as early as possible. *Tamus* are not simply open-air markets where tribal people gather to sell their farm products of fruit and vegetables and to buy manufactured goods from the Chinese and Indian traders, but are also social occasions when news and stories are exchanged. The *tamu* here astracts all manner of traders from quasi-medical commercial travellers selling herbal remedies and magic pills to water buffalo owners who haggle all morning over the price of a cow or a calf.

For keen photographers the *tamus* provides a never-ending procession of colourful characters and situations and, if you're lucky, the Bajau 'cowboys' may turn up on their caparisoned horses looking like mediaeval knights at a tournament. Unfortunately, those looking for tribal handicrafts will be disappointed. I saw nothing of this nature for sale at the *tamu* I went to. If this is what you're looking for then you may have more luck at the Sunday *tamu* at Sikuati, 23 km from Kudat, which is attended by the Rungus who live in longhouses in the area.

Kota Belud itself is just a small, sleepy rural town with a vegetable and meat market; a town where everything except the pool halls closes down very early and bored adolescents roam the streets looking for something to do. Once a week on Sunday it comes to life as people from many miles around flock to the *tamu*.

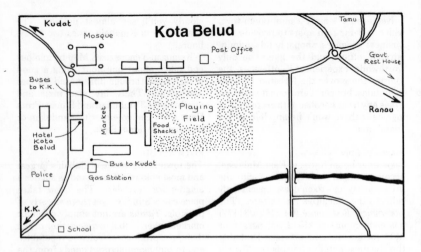

Places to Stay

The best place to stay if you don't want to rough it is the *Hotel Kota Belud* (tel 576) on the central square which costs M$30/35 for singles/doubles with air-con. Towels and soap are provided and the double rooms have two single beds and a handbasin. The communal bathroom is spotless and provided with an electric water heater which you need to switch on about 20 minutes before you intend to have a shower. You need to check occasionally over this 20 minute waiting period to make sure the management haven't switched if off! They're also prone to locking and barricading the place at 8 pm; it can be difficult to get back in if you've gone out for a meal.

If you can't afford to stay at the *Kota Belud* you can sleep free at the school near the police station – ask for the school teacher. Your 'bed' here will be the table tennis tables. There is also a faint possibility of staying at the *Government Rest House* (tel 67532) which costs M$12 per person per night, but it's officially for government officers only. The police station here can be most helpful if you're stuck for accommodation.

Places to Eat

Most of the restaurants here – and there are very few – close at the latest by 5.30 pm and unless you've eaten by then you're up for a 'meal' of peanuts, confectionery and beer bought from the stalls on the sports ground side of the central square/market.

Even the restaurant on the ground floor of the *Hotel Kota Belud* closes by 5.30 pm, however many people are staying in the hotel! They do serve good mee soup but asking for anything else is useless. An exception to the early closing hours is the *Indonesia Restoran*, in the gravel car park behind the Kota Belud Hotel, which does simple dishes like nasi goreng and is open until 8 pm. The standard of hygiene in other food stalls leaves much to be desired. All in all, Kota Belud has very little to offer in terms of good food.

Getting There

All the minibuses and share-taxis operate from the main square. Most of them serve the Kota Belud-Kota Kinabalu route which costs M$6 and takes about 1½ hours. The road is sealed all the way. On Sundays – *tamu* day – the number of minibuses and taxis has to be seen to be believed. On other days it's much quieter.

If you're heading up the coast from here to Kudat there is one bus daily which departs about 10 am from outside the petrol station, costs M$10 and takes about two to 2½ hours.

If you want to get to Kinabalu National Park from here then take any of the minibuses or share-taxis which are going to Kota Kinabalu and get off at Tamparuli about halfway there. The trip takes about 1½ hours and costs M$3. From Tamparuli there are several minibuses and taxis to Ranau every day up to about 2 pm. The taxis cost M$10-12 and the minibuses M$8-10 (you have to haggle and play a waiting game for the lower prices). The journey to the National Park HQ takes about two to 2½ hours along a good sealed road. Tell the driver to drop you off there.

AROUND KOTA BELUD
Mengkabong Water Village
About halfway along the coast from Kota Kinabalu to Kota Belud is the beautiful little Bajau water village of Mengkabong where the houses are built on stilts in the sea. Transport around the village is by canoe or sampan. It's well worth making a detour to see this place if you're passing by. First head for Tuaran and then take local transport from there. Remember if you happen to be in Tuaran on Sunday there is a *tamu* held here which is also worth visiting and where you might pick up native handicrafts. Transport to Tuaran from either Kota Kinabalu or Kota Belud is no problem. From Tuaran it's a short taxi ride to Pantadalit Beach, where there's a *Government Rest House* which costs M$15.

Kudat
Kudat, located near the north-eastern tip of Sabah, has some of the best beaches in Sabah. The beaches here are definitely for those who want unspoilt beauty and tranquility and who expect very little in terms of facilities; very few people find

their way up to this part of Sabah. For starters, try the beach at Bak Bak not far from Kudat.

The Kudat area is the home of the Rungus longhouse tribe – a people who prefer to continue living in the traditional manner. The black sarongs which the women wear and the heavy brass bracelets and beaded necklaces which accompany them are very characteristic. If you'd like to experience something out of the ordinary run of things try visiting one of the longhouses and ask if you can stay for a night or two. As with Iban longhouses in Sarawak, it's polite to take with you a contribution to your keep in the form of food, cigarettes, and sweets for the kids (or whatever else you feel is appropriate).

Places to Stay If you're planning on staying in Kudat there are three main hotels. *Hotel Sunrise* (tel 61517) is the largest and best with 20 rooms and its own good restaurant. Rooms cost from M$35 up to M$55/65 for singles/doubles with air-con and attached bathroom.

The *Kudat Hotel* (tel 61600), Little St has rooms for M$38-55; all air-con but the more expensive rooms have their own bathroom. The *Hasba Hotel* (tel 61959) is the cheapest of the three with rooms, without own bathroom or air-con, for M$25/30. The rooms are airless, hot and not very clean. There is also a *Government Rest House* (tel 61304) with seven rooms at M$12 per person, but the usual warning about 'government workers' only applies.

Getting There Several minibuses a day make the three to four hour trip from Kota Kinabalu for M$15. Bak Bak beach is 11 km from Kudat and difficult to get to without your own transport – count on M$6 for a taxi out there, M$12 to be picked up!

KINABALU NATIONAL PARK
Towering 4101 metres (13,455 feet) above the lush tropical jungles of North Borneo and the centrepiece of the vast

767-square-km Kinabalu National Park, Mt Kinabalu is the major attraction in Sabah. It is the highest mountain between the snow-capped peaks of the Himalaya and those of New Guinea and, although 50 km inland, its jagged granite peaks are visible most mornings from many places along the coast.

Yet, despite its height, it is one of the easiest mountains in the world to climb. No special skills or equipment are required. All you need is a little stamina. Given this, you will be rewarded with one of the most memorable experiences of your life. The views – even before you get to the top – are magnificent and the sunsets equally incredible. Where else could you see the rays of the setting sun shining *up* through the clouds below you?

Merely being able to climb to the top of this mountain – exhilarating though it undoubtedly is – isn't the only experience which awaits you here. Mt Kinabalu is a botanical paradise stocked with a phenomenal number of different plants, many of which are unique to the area. Apart from some of the more spectacular flowers belonging to the orchid family, of which almost a thousand species have been discovered so far with probably several hundred others blooming unnamed among still-unexplored gullies and ridges, there are many unusual rhododendron and the giant red blossoms of the *Rafflesia* which, at more than 70 cm in diameter, are one of the largest flowers in the world.

Even if you don't manage to catch sight of a *Rafflesia* you will certainly see one or more of the many types of insectivorous pitcher plants which grow in profusion here. You may well come across them elsewhere in Borneo – particularly in Bako National Park, Sarawak – but there's nowhere else they grow in such numbers. They come in all manner of elaborate shapes, sizes and colours, although you'll be lucky to find one 30 cm in diameter – a late-19th century botanist, Spencer St John, reported finding a *Nepenthes rajah* pitcher of this size which contained 2½

litres of watery fluid and a drowned rat! Most of them are only large enough to catch unwary insects which are attracted to nectar which the plants secrete, but then find themselves unable to escape up the slippery inner surface of the pitcher. While you're on your way up to the summit, try exploring a few metres in the undergrowth on either side of the trail – you're bound to come across a pitcher plant sooner or later.

From its immense size you might imagine that Mt Kinabalu is the ancient core of the island of Borneo from which more recent rocks have been eroded over millions of years, but in fact the mountain is a relatively recent arrival. Its origins go back a mere nine million years to when a solidified core of volcanic rock began swelling up from the depths below, pushing its way through the overlying rocks. This upward movement is apparently still going on and a team of Japanese geologists have estimated that the mountain continues to grow at the rate of about five mm per year.

Because of its youth very little erosion has occurred on the exposed granite rock faces around the summit, though the effects of glaciers which used to cover much of Kinabalu can be picked out by the trained eye. The glaciers have disappeared and only rarely these days does ice form in the rock pools near the summit though, as you might imagine, it gets pretty cold up there at nighttime so you need warm clothing to make the final ascent.

The first recorded ascent of the mountain was made in 1851 by Sir Hugh Low, the British Colonial Secretary on the island of Labuan and the highest peak is named after him as well as the mile-deep 'gully' on the other side of the mountain. In those days the difficulty of climbing Mt Kinabalu lay not in the ascent itself, but in getting to the base of it through the trackless jungles and finding local porters willing to go there. None of the Dusun or Kadazan tribespeople who accompanied Low had ever climbed the mountain before, believing

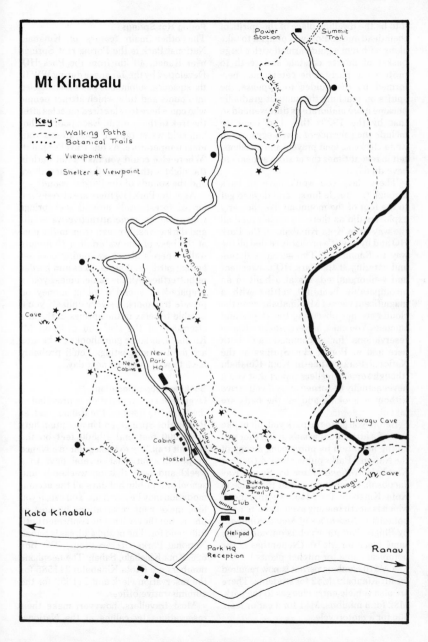

Mt Kinabalu

Key:-
- - - - - Walking Paths
· · · · · Botanical Trails
★ Viewpoint
● Shelter & Viewpoint

Power Station

Summit Trail

Bukit Ular Trail

Liwagu Trail

Mempening Trail

Liwagu River

Liwagu Cave

Cave

New Cabins

New Park HQ

Silau Silau Trail

Bukit Tupai

Kiau View Trail

Cabins

Hostel

Bukit Burong Trail

Liwagu Trail

Cave

Club

Helipad

Park HQ Reception

← Kota Kinabalu

Ranau →

it to be the dwelling place of the spirits of their dead and so Low was obliged to take along with him a guide armed with a large basket of quartz crystals and teeth to protect the party. The ceremonies performed by the guides to appease the spirits on reaching the summit gradually became more elaborate as time went on so that by the 1920s they had come to include the sacrifice of seven eggs, seven white chickens, loud prayers and gunshots, but in recent times the custom appears to have died out.

These days you won't have to hack through the jungle for several days to get to the foot of the mountain like the early explorers did as there's a sealed road all the way from Kota Kinabalu to the Park HQ and by now it's probably sealed all the way to Ranau too. The accommodation and catering at the Park HQ is excellent and well-organised. It's also built in an incomparably beautiful setting with a magnificent view of Mt Kinabalu when the clouds are not obscuring the slopes and summits. You must, however, make advance reservations for accommodation both here and at Poring Hot Springs at the National Parks office in Kota Kinabalu (though some travellers report that you'll never actually be turned away if you arrive without a booking and all the beds are taken).

Before you go to the park you might like to read a little about what's in store for you on the mountain by purchasing a copy of the National Parks publication, *A Guide to Kinabalu National Park* by Susan Kay Jacobson, which is on sale at the office in Kota Kinabalu for M$5. Another book which is worth reading even if you're not a botanist is *Nepenthes of Mount Kinabalu* by Shigeo Kurata which is on sale at the same place for M$10. (Nepenthes is the botanical name for pitcher plants.)

A M$10 climbing permit is now required for Mt Kinabalu, M$2 for students. There are also vehicle entry charges to the park, M$2 for a minibus, M$1 for a car or jeep, 50c for a motorcycle.

Poring Hot Springs

The other main feature of Kinabalu National Park is the Poring Hot Springs near Ranau, 43 km from the Park HQ. Developed by the Japanese during WW II, the steaming, sulphurous water is channeled into pools and tubs which attract people who come here to relax tired muscles after the trek to the summit. Each pool has hot and cold water taps so you can mix your ideal temperature. As one traveller put it, 'Where else could you take a hot bath in the night with the southern stars above and the sounds of the jungle around?'

As at the Park HQ there are also several km of forest trails around the springs which lead to some attractive waterfalls and dark caves. You can swim in the pool at the base of one waterfall, a 35-minute walk. There's also a swimming pool set among gardens, flowers, trees and hordes of butterflies. All the same, unless you're prepared to spend a lot of money on private transport, it's very unlikely you'll be able to relax in the springs in the late afternoon of the day you descend Mt Kinabalu, as some guidebooks to the area are fond of suggesting. You'll probably have to wait until the next day.

Booking Accommodation

Overnight accommodation is provided at the Park HQ itself on the Ranau road, at Poring Hot Springs, and in mountain huts at 11,000 feet and 12,500 feet on the summit trail. Try to book as far in advance as possible (at least several days to a week) and note that on weekends and school and public holidays all the accommodation may be taken up. You can, if you like, make your reservations by post or phone, but they will not be confirmed until fully paid for. The postal address is Sabah National Parks (Reservations), PO Box 626, Kota Kinabalu, Sabah. The telephone numbers are (Kota Kinabalu) 211585 for the reservation clerk and 211652 for the administrative officer.

Most travellers, however, make their reservations by calling at the National

Parks office, Jalan Tun Fuad Stephens, which is round the corner from the Tourist Office on the seafront in Kota Kinabalu. The office is open Monday through Thursday from 8 am to 12.45 pm and 2 to 4.15 pm; on Fridays from 8 to 11.30 am and 2 to 4.15 pm, and on Saturdays from 8 am to 12.45 pm.

In making up your mind how long you want to stay at Mt Kinabalu you should bear in mind that the weather on the mountain is very unpredictable. You can be in bright sunshine one minute and soaked to the skin the next though the first two hours after dawn is the most likely time to catch the summit free of clouds. You might be lucky and get a clear dawn the first morning you go up to the summit, but if you don't or it's raining you'll see absolutely nothing and will feel bitterly disappointed at having to go back down. So, if at all possible, book for four nights with two of them in the mountain huts.

You can shorten your walk by taking a truck up to the power station, saving about 500 metres of vertical climb. Cost is M$10 to 20 per person, depending on your bargaining power. One fit traveller wrote that he walked from the Park HQ to the summit and back down again in one day – but wouldn't recommend it as you get to the top in the afternoon when it's likely to be cloudy. In any case Mt Kinabalu is quite high enough for altitude sickness problems to occur; some acclimatisation is worthwhile. Another traveller suggested that it was worth spending extra days around the Park HQ to enjoy the trails there, as well as the mountain climb.

Places to Stay

Park Headquarters There's a variety of accommodation at the Park HQ, but prices have recently increased astronomically. The *Old Hostel* has 46 beds; nightly cost is M$10 or M$3 student. The *New Hostel* with 52 beds is M$15 or M$4 student. Blankets or pillows can be rented for 50c each.

Otherwise the park headquarters has a whole variety of chalets, cabins and rooms which have also become amazingly expensive. There are fireplaces and kitchens in the more expensive cabins. The twin-bed cabins are M$100, annexes for up to four people are M$200. Then there are chalets for six at M$200, cabins for five also at M$200, cabins for seven at M$300 and the lodge for eight at M$360. There are deluxe cabins too. A single-storey one is suitable for five people and costs M$200; a two-storey cabin for seven people is M$300. In some cases these prices have increased four or five fold since the last edition.

In addition to the above there are four suites in the Administrative Building good for four people each at a price of M$200 per room per night, but none of these have a fireplace or kitchen facilities. Also at the park the *Hotel Perkasa Kundasang* (tel 088-79511) has 74 rooms with singles/doubles at M$100/120.

There are two places where you can buy meals at the Park HQ. The cheaper and more popular of the two is the *Club Canteen*, down below the reception, which has an excellent range of Malay, Chinese and European dishes at very reasonable prices. There's also a shop here which sells a limited range of tinned foods (mostly fish), chocolate, beer, spirits, cigarettes, T-shirts, etc, but they don't have bread or butter or kerosene so you need to bring these from elsewhere (Ranau is the nearest town of any size).

The other place which sells meals is the *Steak & Coffee House* which is part of the very grand, new park HQ building beyond the hostel and the cabins. The decor suggests that food will be expensive, but it isn't that much more than the Club Canteen. Meals here cost on average about M$7 to 10, M$2 to 3 more per dish than at the Club, but it's excellent, you get larger helpings, and it comes complete with dressed salad and a small portion of chips. There's also a TV lounge for the use of anyone who wants to be bored stiff with Malaysian TV.

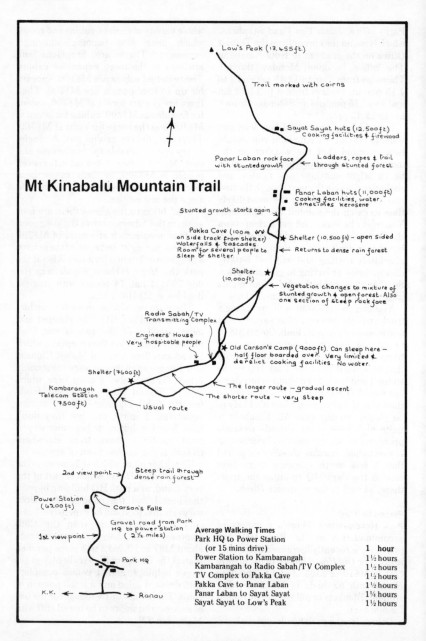

Mt Kinabalu Mountain Trail

Low's Peak (13,455ft.)

Trail marked with cairns

Sayat Sayat huts (12,500ft.)
Cooking facilities & firewood

Ladders, ropes & trail
through stunted forest

Panar Laban rock face
with stunted growth

Panar Laban huts (11,000ft.)
Cooking facilities, water.
Sometimes kerosene

Stunted growth starts again

Pakka Cave (100m on side track from shelter)
Waterfalls & cascades
Room for several people to
sleep or shelter

Shelter (10,500 ft) - open sided

Returns to dense rain forest

Shelter (10,000ft.)

Vegetation changes to mixture of
stunted growth & open forest. Also
one section of steep rock face

Radio Sabah/TV
Transmitting Complex

Engineers' House
Very hospitable people

Old Carson's Camp (9000ft.) Can sleep here -
half floor boarded over. Very limited &
derelict cooking facilities. No water.

Shelter (7600ft.)

Kambarangah
Telecom Station
(7500ft.)

Usual route

The longer route - gradual ascent
The shorter route - very steep

2nd view point

Steep trail through
dense rain forest

Power Station
(6200ft.)

Carson's Falls

1st view point

Gravel road from Park
HQ to power station
(2½ miles)

Park HQ

K.K. ←   → Ranau

Average Walking Times

Park HQ to Power Station (or 15 mins drive)	1 hour
Power Station to Kambarangah	1½ hours
Kambarangah to Radio Sabah/TV Complex	1½ hours
TV Complex to Pakka Cave	1½ hours
Pakka Cave to Panar Laban	1½ hours
Panar Laban to Sayat Sayat	1¼ hours
Sayat Sayat to Low's Peak	1½ hours

Lockers are available free of charge at the reception office so you can leave excess baggage here until you return from the mountain. Keep the key until you return. A small selection of crafts and books is also available here. Prices compare well with those elsewhere. As well as blankets and pillows you can rent foam mattresses, rucksacks and sleeping bags to take up the mountain. Sleeping bags are also available for hire from the caretaker at Gunting Lagadan mountain hut (Panar Laban).

On the Mountain Although the information sheet put out by the Sabah National Parks says otherwise, there are no raincoats available for hire. Being soaked to the skin in a cold mountain hut at 11,000 feet is no joke so *bring rain gear with you*. On your way up to the summit you will have to stay overnight at one or other of the *Mountain Huts*.

These are located at Panar Laban (3344 metres) and at Sayat-Sayat (3800 metres). Panar Laban has a total of 54 bunks dispersed over four huts and Sayat-Sayat has two huts with 20 bunks. Both cost M$6 per person per night or M$2 if you have a student card, and both provide wooden bunks with mattresses but no bedding. You must bring your own food with you, but Panar Laban now has plenty of cutlery, dishes and cooking utensils; you can even buy kerosene at M$5 per Guinness bottle! Don't expect a warm, Swiss-type chalet with a blazing fire at these huts. They're just aluminium sheds with the absolute minimum of facilities though Sayat-Sayat does have a pot-belly of sorts and some firewood if you're lucky.

Sayat-Sayat is the more popular of the Mountain Huts since it is only 1½ hours from the summit whereas Panar Laban is about 2¾ hours, so if you stay in the former you don't have to get up in the middle of the night to reach the summit by dawn. On the other hand, many people not used to climbing 1830 metres every day find

they've had enough for one day by the time they reach Panar Laban. Personally, I think the extra effort on the first day is worth the reward of a slightly easier day on the next. As far as sleep is concerned it doesn't really matter which you stay at; unless you've spent a lot of time in the mountains recently you'll probably sleep very fitfully – the air is quite thin up there. There is also a M$10 climbers' permit fee, M$2 for students. And a final warning: It's very cold up there in the early mornings. Take adequate warm clothing with you!

Hiring Guides & Porters
Hiring a guide (at least from Panar Laban to the summit) is supposedly compulsory although a lot of people get away without one. Porters are optional. Neither the guides nor the porters are employees of the National Park organisation, but they work closely together and when you book accommodation at the National Parks office the form you are handed will specify that you have 'requested' a guide to stand by at the Park HQ at 7 am on the day you intend to climb the mountain. The guide's fee is a minimum of M$25 per day (for one to three people), M$28 for four to six people, M$30 for seven to 12 (the maximum). A porter's fee is M$25 per day for a maximum load of 24 lbs up to the Panar Laban Huts and M$1 for every extra pound. For the second segment up to the Sayat-Sayat huts it's M$28 per day and M$1.25 for every pound over 24 lbs. It's advisable to pay in advance to avoid arguments later.

There are many conflicting opinions about the use of guides. The National Parks organisation says they're compulsory because climbers can 'easily lose their way on the rock surface when the fog and mist start covering the upper part of the mountain', which is probably true if you've never climbed mountains before. But most independent travellers dismiss them as a waste of time and money. The trail is generally so clear these days that getting lost would be difficult. They've installed a gate at the power station, manned to keep people going without guides, but if you start early you pass the gate before the guard gets on duty.

It's an expensive nuisance if you can't share the cost of a guide with other people. The best compromise you can make is to tell the National Parks office that you intend to share a guide with other people when you get there – this is no problem.

Poring Hot Springs Accommodation at Poring has also suffered from rapid price escalation. There's a campground costing M$2 per person, M$1 for students, in open-sided bamboo huts with about eight bamboo bunks per hut. Be prepared for the mosquitoes.

The new 24-person hostel costs M$8 per person, M$2 for students. The hostel has three bunkrooms, a huge kitchen and common room but, as at the headquarters hostel, you have to hire blankets or pillows. The *Old Cabin* has a flat rate of M$100 for up to six people; the *New Cabin* is M$80 for up to four people. As at Park HQ the prices have increased dramatically in early 1984.

There are cooking facilities at Poring with firewood provided, but you must take your own food as there's nowhere you can buy food here. There is a small shop at the entrance to the Springs, but it's expensive. Get your food in Ranau.

Getting There

From Kota Kinabalu There are several minibuses daily from KK to Ranau which depart up to about 2 pm. The fare is M$13 and the journey takes about 3½ hours. These minibuses go right past the Park HQ and are the cheapest means of getting there unless you are part of a group of at least 12 people. The fare to the Park HQ is M$11 and the journey as far as here will take about three hours. Reception is about 100 metres from the main road.

From Kota Belud/Tamparuli Tamparuli is where the road up the coast to Kudat

branches for Kota Belud and Ranau. If you've been visiting Mengkabong Water Village or Kota Belud and are heading for Kinabalu National Park, then first go to Tamparuli. From here there are several minibuses and share-taxis daily to Ranau which, like the ones from KK, pass right by the Park HQ. The minibuses cost M$8-11 and the share-taxis M$10-13 (you have to haggle for the lower prices). The journey to the Park HQ takes about two hours.

If you want to get from the Park HQ to Ranau then you can either wait at the side of the road for a minibus going to Ranau or Sandakan (they pass the Park HQ at least twice daily around 10.30 to 11 am and 2 to 2.30 pm) or hitch – easy except on Sundays when you'll probably have to take a taxi for M$6.

Ranau-Poring Hot Springs On weekends it's easy and cheap to get to the Springs from Ranau. Drivers in pick-ups cruise round the blocks shouting, 'Poring, Poring!'. The price is more or less fixed at M$3 per person and the transport leaves when it's full (which doesn't take long, as many Ranau people go there for the afternoon and return in the evening).

On weekdays it isn't quite so easy, especially if you arrive in Ranau during the afternoon, in which case you'll have to ask around the cafes and shops to see if anyone is going there with whom you can share the cost. Taxis *are* available – and the drivers will approach you muttering, 'charter, charter', but they want around M$15-20 for taking you there. If you're not willing to pay this price then you'll have to stay in Ranau overnight and try again the next morning when your chances of reasonably priced transport are much better. The road to Poring is a dead-end so hitching a ride is difficult.

Chartered Transport If you're part of a large group and are able to fill up a Land-Rover (up to 12 people) or a 28-seater minibus then you can charter vehicles from Kota Kinabalu to the National Park

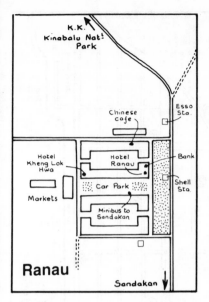

Ranau

road is now sealed past Sandakan, and the gravel road from there is pretty good halfway to Sandakan, after which it deteriorates incredibly until you get within sight of Sandakan. Along the way you'll be treated to the spectacle of devastated jungle landscapes raped to oblivion by the logging concerns.

RANAU

Ranau is just a small provincial town half way between Kota Kinabalu and Sandakan. Nothing much ever happens yet it seems to have some remarkably friendly people. We were offered unrequested discounts on food we bought at a Chinese store here, followed by an offer of free accommodation for the night and, at a cafe nearby, the owner fell over backwards to make sure we were perfectly satisfied with what we ate there. In the morning he refused to accept payment for the breakfast we had.

Few travellers stay here overnight since the big attraction is Poring Hot Springs about 18 km north of the town. If you arrive here late in the afternoon during the week, however, you may have to since the only transport available at that time to Poring are chartered taxis which are far from cheap. Although it's usually quiet, Ranau does have a big *tamu* market on the first of each month with, according to one visitor, 'some very funky tribespeople'.

Places to Stay

The best place in Ranau is the *Ranau Hotel* (tel 351) which is the first place you will see when you enter the town opposite the petrol stations. Rooms here start from around M$35 for singles without air-con and go up to nearly M$100 for an air-con double, despite which the hotel is nothing special.

The *Kheng Lok Hwa Hotel* is on the first floor above the cafe of the same name. Rooms cost from M$20. They're spartan but adequate, with fan, clean sheets and cobwebs. In fact the place looks virtually deserted and it's difficult to find anyone to let you in!

or the hot springs at competitive prices. Land-Rovers and minibuses depart KK for the National Park around 8 am and the National Park for KK around 1 pm.

National Park-Kota Kinabalu If you're heading back towards KK, minibuses pass the Park HQ around 8.30 am and 12 noon to 1 pm daily. Stand by the side of the main road and wave them down. The fare to KK is around M$9. If you get tired of waiting then hitch – there's quite a bit of traffic.

National Park-Sandakan The minibuses which leave KK at about 8.30 am and 11 am for Sandakan pass by the National Park HQ at about 10.30 to 11 am and 2 to 2.30 pm respectively. Just stand by the side of the main road and wave them down. They'll fit you in even if there are no seats (people always get off at Ranau so you'll have a seat from there if it's 'full').

The fare to Sandakan is M$25-30 (you must haggle for the lower figure) and the journey takes about seven hours. The

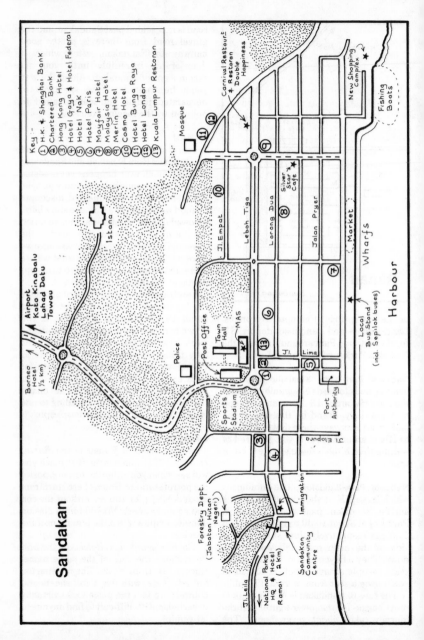

Sandakan

Key :-
1 H.K. & Shanghai Bank
2 Chartered Bank
3 Hong Kong Hotel
4 Hotel Gaya & Hotel Federal
5 Hotel Nak
6 Hotel Paris
7 Mayfair Hotel
8 Malaysia Hotel
9 Merlin Hotel
10 Cosmo Hotel
11 Hotel Bunga Raya
12 Hotel London
13 Kuala Lumpur Restoran

There is also a *Government Rest House* (tel 75534) which costs M$12 per person for rooms with attached bathroom and air-con. If you can show them an official-looking letter they'll let you stay at government official rates (M$5 per night). Very friendly people, but it's a little way from the centre.

Probably the best place to eat here is the Chinese restaurant around the corner from the Ranau Hotel on the top side of the first block. The food is good, the menu varied and prices very reasonable. The *Leang Leang* is very good and there are at least half a dozen others, but most close early – there simply isn't the clientele.

Getting There

To Poring Hot Springs On weekends there's no problem getting to Poring, as pick-ups cruise round the blocks with their drivers shouting the word you want to hear. They cost M$3 per person and go when full. You may also be able to get there for this price in the early mornings on weekdays, but usually you will have to ask around the cafes and small stores for a lift or hire a taxi (available anytime) for M$15-20.

To Kota Kinabalu Taxis and minibuses depart daily up to around 2 pm, cost M$12-15 and take about three hours.

To Sandakan There is one daily minibus from Ranau to Sandakan which departs about 7.30 am, costs M$25 and takes about seven hours. If you get there later in the day the two daily minibuses which ply between Kota Kinabalu and Sandakan arrive in Ranau about 11 to 11.30 am and 2.30 to 3 pm respectively and stop here for a meal or lunch break. They usually have spare seats and even if they don't are unlikely to refuse you.

SANDAKAN

The former capital city of Sabah, Sandakan is today a major commercial centre where the products of the interior – rattan, timber, rubber, copra, palm oil and even birds' nests from the Gomantong Caves – are brought to be loaded onto boats for export. The city lies at the entrance to a huge bay and its docks sprawl along the waterfront for many miles. The bay itself is dotted with islands, some of them with excellent beaches, and is always a bustle of boats, large and small.

Outside the city is the world's only orang utan sanctuary at Sepilok, the Gomantong Caves across the other side of the bay where edible birds' nests are collected for that famous Chinese delicacy, and, offshore, one of the world's few turtle sanctuaries where giant turtles come to lay their eggs. Unfortunately, the latter two are more or less inaccessible unless you have plenty of money to spend or are part of a large group which can charter its own transport.

Orientation

The centre of Sandakan is very compact and consists of three main blocks built between the seafront and the wooded hills on which the Governor's Residence sits. In these blocks are located many of the hotels and restaurants, banks, post office, MAS office, the local bus stand and the long-distance minibus stands. The minibus stands are located on Jalan Pryer, one street back from and parallel to the waterfront, round the back of the Mayfair Hotel. This is where you will be dropped off if arriving from outside the city.

West of the main area of the city off to one side or the other of Jalan Leila, the main road, lie other hotels and restaurants and, where a footbridge crosses the road, the Immigration Office and the National Forests Office. Considerably further along this road is the National Parks Office.

All the main trunk routes into and out of Sandakan start from the large roundabout at the junction of Leboh Tiga/Jalan Leila and Jalan Utara, just below the post office. Jalan Utara is a dual carriageway which heads north-west out of the city and passes the airport turn-off.

Information

If you're cashing travellers' cheques change them at the Hong Kong & Shanghai Banking Corporation rather than at the Chartered Bank where they charge commission.

The National Forest Office (Pejabat Ketua Pelindong Mergastua) is at Peti Surat 311, off Jalan Leila. If you intend to visit the orang utan sanctuary at Sepilok you're supposed to come here first for a permission slip, but when you get there no one asks for it. The permission slip is free but getting one is another matter. The people who staff this office are uncivil and often downright rude. Don't expect anyone to lift a finger for you until you've waited several hours.

The National Parks Office (Pejabat Taman Negara) (tel 42188) is located a 30c ride out of town along Jalan Leila – ask to be put down at the Kapitol Cinema (Punggung Kapitol) or the Hotel Ramai. In the new block next to the Hotel Ramai look for the 'SKE Carpet House'. Above this on the first floor is the National Parks Office; there are no signposts. If you'd like to or intend to visit the turtle sanctuary then you must come here for permission first, but see the warning below before you trail up to this office.

The Immigration Office is located next door to the Sandakan Community Centre, Jalan Leila, where the footbridge crosses the road. They are fairly easygoing. The MAS Office at Ground Floor, Rural District Council Building, Jalan Tiga (tel 2211/4) is often very busy.

Waterfront

The waterfront at Sandakan, with its motley collection of fishing boats, barges, ferries and ocean-going container ships as well as the vegetable and fish markets, is worth wandering around for a morning or afternoon, but apart from this there isn't a great deal else to see in Sandakan itself.

Orang Utan Sanctuary

Located at Sepilok, about 25 km from Sandakan, this is the only orang utan sanctuary in the world. Apes are brought here to be rehabilitated to forest life and so far the centre has handled about 80 of them. Only 20 or so of them still come back to be fed with any regularity, but it's unlikely you'll see anywhere near this number at feeding time. Three or four is a much more likely number.

Of the ones which have returned to the wild, two of the females still return when they're pregnant and stay near the sanctuary centre until they've given birth, after which they go back to the forest. The sanctuary was established in 1964 and now covers 4000 hectares. Entrance is free. Officially you need a permission slip to visit the sanctuary from the National Forests office in Sandakan.

Visiting hours are Monday through Thursday from 10 am to 12 noon and 3 to 4.15 pm; on Friday from 10 to 11.10 am and 2.30 to 4.15 pm; and on Saturday and Sunday from 10 am to 12 noon and 2 to 4.15 pm. To get to the centre take the service bus marked 'Sepilok Batu 14' from the local bus stand next to the central market on the waterfront. The fare is M$1.45 and the journey takes about 45 minutes. The 9.30 am bus gets you there for feeding time. This is the only bus which takes you right up to the gate. Buses are approximately hourly.

The apes are fed from a platform in the middle of the forest about 20 minutes' walk from the centre. Don't be in so much of a hurry to see the orang utans that you miss the forest! And if it's been raining watch out for leeches. If you're taking photographs you'll need to have ASA 400 film available (it's remarkably dark in the forest). Don't miss this place; it's well worth a visit.

There is now also a Nature Education Centre at the reserve that is open to the public. With Peace Corps and CUSO help a small museum has been established as well as a library and film theatre with information about the local forests. They have set up a self-guided nature trail and longer trails, one leading to a good spot for swimming.

Turtle Sanctuary

This is located on the island of Selingan out in the bay about 30 km from Sandakan. It's protected by the National Parks organisation and is the place to which the giant sea turtles come at night to lay their eggs. A turtle hatchery is also maintained here to help preserve the species. Before you can visit the sanctuary you must obtain permission from the National Parks Office. Unless you want to charter their boat, it's a case of waiting until it goes there on business and then paying their rather steep price.

You can stay overnight on the island if you like, but the only place to stay is a derelict hut which the National Parks Director disclaims responsibility for, but for which he's quite prepared to extract M$2 per night from you. You need to take your own bedding, cooking equipment, food and drink.

Gomantong Caves

These caves are located across the other side of the bay from Sandakan and about 20 km inland. They are famous as a source of swifts' nests, which are the raw material for that famous Chinese delicacy, birds' nest soup. Here you can see the nests being collected from the roof of the cave, as they are at Niah in Sarawak, by men climbing long, precariously placed bamboo poles.

The problem is getting there. Travel agencies will arrange a trip, but their costs are high and outside the range of most travellers' budgets. One way of getting there more cheaply would be to enquire at a place where you see the nests on sale or being unloaded and ask if you can go along on the next trip. If you haven't the time to do this or draw a blank, wait until you get to Niah Caves. This is another of the 'attractions' of Sabah about which the tourist literature neglects to mention the costs and difficulty of getting there.

Places to Stay – bottom end

The cheapest hotel in Sandakan is the *Hotel Bunga Raya* near the mosque. Rooms cost around M$20. Other base-price places include the empty classrooms of *St Mary's Catholic Church* (ask a taxi to take you there – M$1.50). Here you can sleep free, but look clean and tidy when you turn up, otherwise the old Chinese father may refuse you. Or there's the police station.

The place to head for if you're not on too tight a budget is the *Cosmo Hotel* (tel 2151) on Jalan Empat. This hotel has three floors of air-con rooms and a top floor of non air-con rooms, and despite the fact that it's cheaper than most it's very good value. Rooms here cost from M$30 to M$55 and have their own bathroom although the hot water system seems to be defunct. The disco on the ground floor is very well sound-proofed but the muezzin in the nearby mosque will wake you up well before dawn with his amplified wailing.

All the middle range hotels are of a similar standard and most offer a choice of air-con and non air-con rooms. There's very little to choose between these places. They fill up rapidly and if you get there late in the day you may have some difficulty finding a room (all the non air-con rooms will certainly have been taken by then).

At the cheaper end of the middle range the *Mayfair Hotel* (tel 5191-2), on the waterfront opposite the market and local bus stand, has non air-con rooms from M$30. It's often full because the long-distance minibuses park round the corner so it's popular. *Hotel Paris* at 27 Lorong Dua is similarly priced.

The *Hong Kong Hotel* (tel 2248), 18 Jalan Tiga costs from M$25 up to M$60 for an air-con double. *Hotel Kim Sam Sing* (tel 3244) at 51 Fourth St or the very popular *Hotel Paris* (tel 2288) at 45 Jalan Tiga are similarly priced. *Hotel New Sabah* at 18 Jalan Singapura has large air-con rooms with bathroom for M$50 to 70.

Or there's the *Federal Hotel* (tel 3251) at 8 Jalan Tiga and the *Malaysia Hotel* (tel 2277) at 32 Lorong Dua.

Places to Stay – top end
The *Sabah Hotel* (tel 213291) at Mile 1, Jalan Utara is on the hill out of town and has a considerable amount of old world charm. All 28 rooms are air-con and singles/doubles are M$95/110. There is an Indonesian and a Chinese restaurant.

Nearer the centre of town the *Hotel Gaya* (tel 2292) at 9-11 Leboh Tiga has 60 rooms at M$60/80. The *Hotel Ramai* (tel 58115) at Mile 1, Jalan Leila, has rooms from M$140. Right in the centre of town is the somewhat Alcatraz-like building of the *Nak Hotel* (tel 2171-6) with rooms from M$120.

Places to Eat
Eating in Sandakan depends on what you want to pay. The town is full of cheap Chinese restaurants and coffee houses serving the standard rice or noodles with fried vegetables, but none of them are worth recommending. If you'd like a break from this sort of high-carbohydrate fodder then go to the *Silver Star Ice Cream & Cafe* where, in the evenings, you can buy satay at 25c per stick with hot peanut sauce. It's a friendly place and popular with local people. They also have ice-cold beer!

If you're prepared to spend a little money then an excellent place to try is the *Kuala Lumpur Restoran*, first floor, Leboh Tiga, opposite the MAS office. Red table cloths, hovering waitresses and very good food. The menu has a bewildering selection of Chinese and Malay food. The helpings are large but bear in mind that the average price of a dish is M$6 to 8.

Other places you might like to try in this range are the *Carnival Restaurant* and the *Restoran Double Happiness*, at the far end of Leboh Tiga from the MAS office. Or try the *Yen Yun* at the Hsiang Garden Complex on Jalan Leila.

If you're looking for some cheaper night life than that offered by the top range

hotels then try the streets opposite the Hotels Gaya and Hong Kong, Jalan Leila. There are several night clubs, discos and restaurants in this area.

Getting There
Air Sandakan is on MAS's domestic network. If there are flights in operation, for they are notoriously unreliable, then the cheapest flights to Zamboanga in the Philippines operate out of Sandakan.

Road All the long-distance minibuses leave from round the back of the Mayfair Hotel, parallel to the waterfront. Most of them depart for their destinations early – between 5 and 6 am. There are buses to Kota Kinabalu (M$35, about 10 hours), Ranau (M$25, about seven hours), Lahad Datu (M$13, about seven to eight hours – very bad road), Beluaran, Tungku, Kunak and Semporna.

There may also be a direct bus to Tawau, but it's more usual to get another from Lahad Datu to Tawau. There's no problem finding the right bus – the runners will ask you where you're heading and direct you.

Getting Around
If you're arriving or leaving by air, the airport is about 11 km from the city. There are minibuses throughout the day connecting the two which tout for customers outside the Mayfair Hotel. The fare is M$2 and the journey takes about 15 minutes. A taxi costs M$8 to 10 depending on the age of the car.

LAHAD DATU
Lahad Datu is a busy little town of 20,000 population. There are very few tourists here but at least 10 hotels – all of them as expensive as the ones in Sandakan. Probably the only reason you would have for coming here would be to take a boat across Darvel Bay and explore some of the many islands between here and Semporna. They've recently been gazetted as a national park.

Places to Stay

For budget accommodation, the best place to stay is the *Government Rest House* (tel 81177/81536) which is located at the airport, less than a km from the town centre. If you're coming from Sandakan or Tawau by bus ask the driver to stop there. Overnight cost per person is M$12 or M$5 for people on official business.

If you can't get in at the *Government Rest House* then the *Liang Ming Lodging House* (tel 81419), Kampong Sawmill costs from M$22, more expensive with attached bathroom.

The middle range hotels include the *Ocean Hotel* (tel 81700), where rooms cost from M$45 without air-con, from M$55 with. The *Paradana Hotel* (tel 81400), Jalan Seroja has air-con rooms with attached bathrooms from M$65. The *Hotel Lahad Datu* (tel 81100), Canal St starts from M$35 and the *Venus Hotel* (tel 81900) is similarly priced.

Lahad Datu's best hotel is the *Hotel Mido* (tel 81800) at 94 Main St, where all the rooms are air-con, carpeted, have their own bathrooms and TV and cost M$90/120 for singles/doubles.

Places to Eat

As at Sandakan there are plenty of Chinese rice or noodle places, all more or less of the same standard. If you'd like something more interesting then try the *Good View Restaurant*, on the hill east of the town. There are other good Chinese restaurants if you're prepared to pay over the odds.

Getting There

Air MAS fly to Lahad Datu.

Road The long-distance minibus stand is located next to the Esso filling station by the market. Most depart for their destinations early – around 6 pm. Buses are available to Sandakan (M$13), Kunak (M$7), Semporna (M$13) and Tawau (M$22). Every second day a large bus leaves for Semporna and Tawau for the

same prices; it departs from 200 metres east of the Esso station.

The bus to Tungku, east of Lahad Datu, goes past a really fine beach about 20 km out of Lahad Datu which is worth visiting although it's a problem getting back.

Boats Boats are available going to Semporna (departs at 8 am daily, costs M$14) and Kunak (departs at 11.30 am daily, costs M$7). The boats leave from the old wharf at the back of the market. This trip is well worth the effort if you have the time. The water in Darvel Bay is crystal clear and there are many coral reefs. If you stop off in Kunak, which is just a small fishing town, there is only one hotel with rooms for M$22.

SEMPORNA

Semporna, between Lahad Datu and Tawau, has a stilt village and there's a cultured pearl farm off the coast here. There are some guest houses at M$5 and a more expensive hotel. The *Floating Restaurant* is good.

TAWAU

A mini-boomtown in the very south-east corner of Sabah close to the Indonesian border, Tawau is a provincial capital and centre for export of the products of the interior – timber, rubber, manila hemp, cocoa, copra and tobacco. There's precious little to do or see here, but the town has retained some of its old world charm and you'll pass through here if you're on your way south to Tarakan in Kalimantan.

Tawau is still a small, compact town with virtually everything located conveniently in or near to the centre. The only time you'll need to use public transport is to get to the airport (one km) or to the Indonesian Consulate, but you could walk to the consulate in 15 minutes.

Places to Stay – bottom end

So-called budget hotels in Tawau are, like those elsewhere in Sabah, outrageously priced and poor value for money. *Hotel*

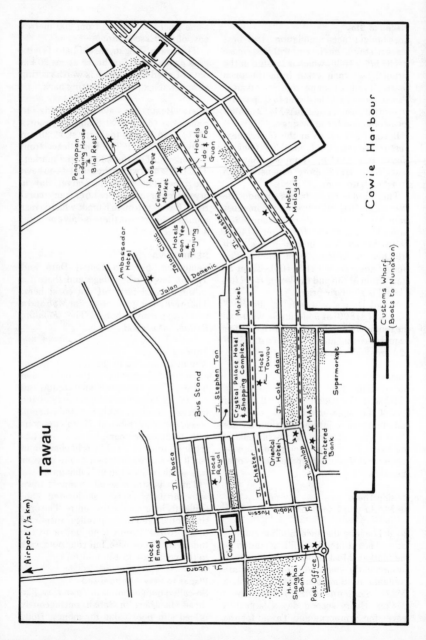

Lido (tel 74547), Jalan Stephen Tan, has rooms, all doubles and without attached bathroom, both with and without air-con, from M$30 to 50. At the same location the short time *Hotel Foo Guan* has rooms at M$25 for an interior double with fan. *Hotel Tanjung*, Jalan Stephen Tan, has doubles from M$25, if you haggle. A notice in the foyer says, 'No prostitutes', so now you know. *Hotel Soon Yee*, also on Jalan Stephen Tan, is a small, clean hotel with rooms from M$25 to 40.

Middle range hotels include the *Hotel Ambassador* (tel 72700/72718), 1872 Jalan Paya Tawau, which has air-con rooms with their own bathroom from M$35. The *Hotel Malaysia* (tel 72800), 37 Jalan Dunlop, is slightly more expensive. The *Wah Yew Hotel* (tel 71300), 117 Chester St, is fully air-con and has rooms from M$35 without attached bathroom, more expensive with.

Upper middle range places include the *Hotel Far East* (tel 73200 on Jalan Masjid, which is fully air-con and costs from M$50. The *Hotel Oriental* (tel 71500), 10 Jalan Dunlop, is also fully air-con and has singles/doubles at M$70/85.

Places to Stay – top end

The *Royal Hotel* (tel 73100) on Jalan Billian is fully air-con and has singles/doubles at M$110/130. *Hotel Emas* (tel 73300) on Jalan Utara is a larger hotel with 100 rooms at M$105-115 for singles, M$120-130 for doubles. The *Tawau Hotel* (tel 71100) at 72-73 Chester St has rooms at M$100/130.

Places to Eat

The choice here, as in many other places, is between a cheap meal in one of the many Chinese rice and noodle places or spending considerably more money on a decent meal. If you're looking for something in between try the *California Cafe*, Jalan Dunlop, opposite the MAS office. They serve very good mee soup and a few other dishes. The prices are reasonable.

Getting There

Road From Tawau to Semporna (110 km) you have a choice of taxis or Land-Rovers. The taxis depart up to 8.30 am daily, cost M$12 and take about 2½ hours. The Land-Rovers – one only per day – leave about 7.15 am, cost M$9 and take about the same time. For Tawau-Lahad Datu (176 km) shared taxis leave daily up to 7.30 am, cost M$25 and take about five hours. There's also a minibus which does the run to Lahad Datu for M$20.

Boats It's possible to get boats from Tawau to Semporna and Lahad Datu, but they don't run on any regular schedule – enquire down at the wharf.

To Kalimantan (Indonesian Borneo). Every day except Saturdays and Sundays a launch leaves for Nunakan Island at 10 am. It costs M$15 and takes about an hour. The boat leaves from the Customs Wharf at the back of the MAS office. From Nunakan you can get another boat south to Tarakan. Alternatively you can fly Tawau-Tarakan for M$150; at present it appears it's OK to fly but not OK to take the boat.

Tarakan seems to come and go as an officially recognised entry point into Indonesia. It appears that it is presently OK to enter Indonesia here although for a while it wasn't. It is not, however, on the list of places where you can be issued a visa on arrival. If you haven't got an Indonesian visa you can get one from the Indonesian Consulate (he's actually the Trade Representative), Batu 1, Jalan Kuhara (tel 72052). Take a taxi to get there (M$2 to 3); they all know where it is. If you find yourself stuck in Tawau for a day or two and are on your way south, try hanging around the Customs Wharf. Indonesian sailors often introduce themselves and you may be able to talk your way into a passage – if that's an acceptable means of entry.

The Indonesian visa/entry point question has always been a hazy one. At present it's complicated by the recent 'visa on entry' innovation. The Indonesian embassies themselves don't always seem to fully understand this. Basically there are now certain places where you can enter and depart Indonesia without obtaining a visa in advance. Just because a place is not on this 'approved list' does not mean it is not a valid entry or exit point. What it does mean is that you must have organised a visa before you get there. There are two additional important points to consider. You must enter and exit through approved points — even if you're coming in to Indonesia at an approved place (like Denpasar, Jakarta or Medan) you must still have a visa if you intend to exit through a non-listed place (like Jayapura or Tarakan). Secondly, although visa-on-entry people get a free extension, people with visas still have to pay the expensive landing tax to extend their visas.

A recent traveller's tale Tawau-Tarakan:

Still aren't allowed to overland from Tawau to Tarakan but we flew on Bouraq Indonesian Airlines, a 68-mile puddle jump in an eight-passenger Britten Norman Islander with 'Bali Air' markings. We used our Osaka-Bali mileage ticket, which meant the flight cost us about US$10. In Tawau they quoted M$150, in Tarakan the fare for flying back to Tawau would have been about M$100. Who knows what it would cost from Bouraq in Singapore? Anyway it operates four times a week and is often full – so book well ahead.

We tried to get our visas in Kota Kinabalu but were told they didn't do them and that we should get them in Tawau. In Tawau, which is just a branch of the KK consulate, we were asked why we didn't get visas in KK! Fortunately we had a letter from the KK office telling them to give us visas. They issued them in five hours; they cost M$35 each and required two photos.

To Philippines There are on-again, off-again flights between Tawau and Zamboanga. Check with Sabre Air Services in Tawau.

Getting Around
Probably the only time you'll need to use local transport is if you're going to or coming from the airport, which is a km from the centre. The best thing to do here is take one of the hotel buses into town. They are provided by the *Royal Hotel*, *Hotel Emas* and the *Tawau Hotel*. They're all free and you're under no obligation to stay at the hotel which runs the bus. If you take a taxi instead it will cost you about M$3. Hitching is also easy.

Brunei

Brunei is a tiny Islamic Sultanate sandwiched between the East Malaysian states of Sarawak and Sabah. It falls into that category of small states, remnants of empires and colonies and quirks of history that seem to captivate the imagination. And Brunei Darussalam, as it is formally known, lives up to this beguiling nature in its own way.

In early 1984 the immensely popular Sultan, Sir Muda Hassanal Bolkiah Mu'izzaddin Waddaulah, the 29th of his line, led his tightly ruled country somewhat reluctantly into complete independence from Britain. The 37-year-old leader rather enjoyed the English umbrella and colonial status so independence came almost unwanted.

It is not tradition nor romantic exoticism that makes this country fascinating. It is astounding wealth. The Sultan's gargantuan spending is the stuff of legends. In this skinflint world of penny-pinching it is unheard of, some would say sinful, to expend money as lavishly as this man does. It is also refreshing and few complain, for this population of only 220,000 is the second wealthiest per capita on earth, second only to Kuwait, and for the same reason – oil. The Sultan presides over a fortune of about US$15 billion and counting. The oil comes mainly from offshore wells at Seria and Maura; inland the country remains almost as it was. The enormous wealth is displayed in various ways, most obviously in the ostentatious, redundant public buildings of the capital. The airport is suitable for a country 10 times the size of Brunei. Everything is done big here.

Perhaps more outlandish are the Sultan's personal buys: a US$350 million palace; a fleet of Italian exoticars said to be serviced by a mechanic flown in from Italy; and a fabulous polo farm – his passion – with 200 Argentine ponies, some enjoying

air-conditioned stalls. But everybody benefits; there are no taxes, pensions for all, free medicare, free schooling, cheap loans, subsidies for many purchases including cars and the highest minimum wages in the region. The government with Brunei Shell Oil (the only oil company here in any substantial way) is by far the country's largest employer. And all government workers get subsidised holidays and trips to Mecca. All in all, not too shabby an arrangement. When there is any criticism, the government-owned newspaper stifles it. Some diversification plans for the economy are now being instituted for that fearsome day when the pump runs dry. These plans include more rice farming, some forestry and eventual self-sufficiency in beef production. To this latter goal the government has purchased a cattle station in Australia's Northern Territory which is larger than Brunei itself!

HISTORY

In the 15th and 16th centuries Brunei was a considerable power in the area and its role extended throughout Borneo and into the Philippines. The first European visitors began arriving in the 16th century in the form of the Spanish and Portuguese and though the Spanish actually made a bid to take over they were soon evicted.

The arrival of the British in the guise of James Brooke, the first White Rajah of Sarawak, in the first part of the 19th century, spelt the end of Brunei's power. A series of 'treaties' were forced onto the Sultan as James Brooke consolidated his hold over Kuching with the aim of developing commercial relationships and suppressing piracy – a favourite Bruneian and Dyak occupation. The country was gradually whittled away until, with a final dash of absurdity, Limbang was ceded to Sarawak, thus dividing the country in half.

On the point at which Brunei was about to be swallowed up entirely, oil was discovered in 1929. The Sultan's father, who abdicated in 1967, kept Brunei out of the Malaysian Confederacy, preferring that the country remain a British protectorate, which it had been since 1888. Since the 1960s, when there was a failed coup attempt, the country has been under emergency laws, but you'll see little evidence of this.

FACTS

The total population of Brunei is about 220,000 and is composed of Malays, Chinese, Indians and around 25,000 Iban, Dusan and other tribespeople of the interior. Brunei is quite a strict Muslim country; there is little alcohol and apparently government men prowl the streets after dark looking for unmarried couples standing or sitting too close to each other. Getting nailed for this crime, known as *khalwat*, can mean six months in jail.

Other than the capital, the oil town of Seria and the commercial town of Kuala Belait, the country is mainly jungle. About 80% of the country's food requirements have to be imported. The traditional pattern of agriculture is that of shifting cultivation which continues in the remoter areas. Farming is largely a part-time occupation and there are no large estates. A small amount of rubber is exported along with all the oil.

From November to January, during the north-east monsoon, temperatures are somewhat lower than the 28°C average. With an average humidity of 82% it's a pretty warm place. Singapore dollars are more or less equally exchanged and can be used. There's about a 9% difference between the Brunei dollar and the Malaysian ringgit. Banks give 10 to 20% less for cash than for travellers' cheques.

BANDAR SERI BEGAWAN

The capital, Bandar Seri Begawan, is the only town of any size and really one of the few places to go in the country. It's a neat,

very clean and modern city with some fine, overstated buildings. You won't see any bicycles, trishaws or even motorcycles here. Everybody has a car and they're nearly all new; you'll notice the quietness, because they all have working mufflers. The historical water villages surrounding the city offer some contrasting tradition. A big plus is the friendly people; even young women will smile and say hello. There are a few things to see and do around town but, unfortunately, the city can be expensive to linger in.

Information

There is a tourist information booth (tel 31794) at the airport which isn't bad and has maps, but although they are helpful they can't answer questions about the rest of the country. Another office is found at Customs Wharf. It's upstairs, around the back, facing the water, in the building closest to the bridge on Jalan McArthur over the canal.

Omar Ali Saifuddin Mosque

Named after the 28th Sultan of Brunei, the mosque was built in 1958 at a cost of about US$5 million. Designed by an Italian architect, the golden-domed structure stands close to the Brunei River in its own artificial lagoon and is the tallest building in BSB. For my money it's one of the most impressive structures in the east. As is customary the interior is simple though tasteful although certainly no match for the stunning exterior; but what other mosque anywhere has an elevator and an escalator? The small pools and quadrants surrounding the main building are also very fine. The ceremonial boat sitting in the lagoon/moat is used for special occasions, including Koran-reading competitions.

The elevator to the top of the 44-metre (146 feet) minaret was broken last visit, but ask in the mosque and someone will open the door and let you walk up the long, winding staircase without charge. The view over the city and nearby Kampong

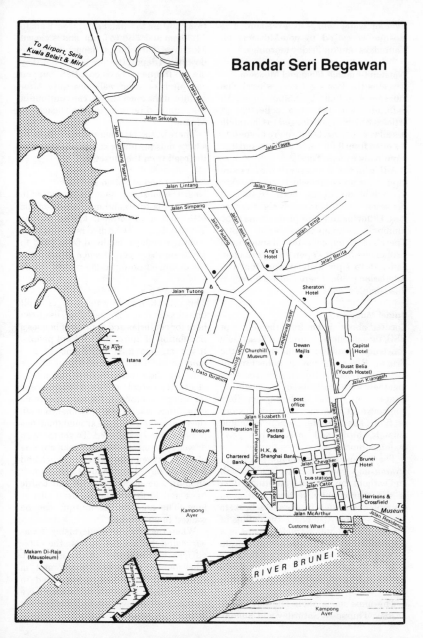

Bandar Seri Begawan

Ayer or water village is excellent. The mosque is closed to non-Moslems on Thursdays and on Friday mornings.

Winston Churchill Memorial Museum
It seems the Poms get everywhere! The museum was built by Sultan Omar Ali Saifuddin and houses a collection of articles which once belonged to Churchill. It's all very boring, but if you're desperate it's open from 9.30 am to 12 noon and 2 to 5 pm daily except Tuesdays.

Adjacent to this museum is the far more interesting aquarium which has a total of 47 exhibition tanks, both fresh and seawater, one of them nearly eight metres long. Unfortunately, the place seems to be running down; many tanks are now empty. There's still a fair collection of small, local Brunei reef fish. It's open 9 am to 12 noon and 1.15 to 7 pm daily except Mondays. Admission is 30c. There is also a library in this complex.

Brunei Museum
Located about six km from the centre of BSB, the museum is housed in a beautifully constructed building on the banks of the Brunei River. It has a collection of historical treasures from the 15th century together with artifacts of the cultural heritage of Brunei, including an Iban longhouse. It also has a natural history section. The wildlife section including animals, birds and insects, has good mammal dioramas.

There is an extensive section on oil with an amusing vignette showing local life with and without the 'benefits' oil brings. Best is the ethnography section with good examples of musical instruments, baskets and brassware. Also check the coffins of the Kenyah people's chiefs. There is a large collection of Chinese ceramics from 1000 AD to more recent times. Brunei's first gunboat is on display under a traditional roof by the riverbank in front of the museum.

The museum is open Tuesday, Wednesday, Thursday, Saturday and Sunday from 9.30 am to 5 pm; Friday from 9 am to 11.30 am and 2.30 to 5 pm; and is closed Mondays. City buses depart from the downtown depot; the fare is 50c, but they are not frequent. Taxis cost B$6, but you can hitch or even walk one-way. After culture at the museum you can continue in the same direction to the beach at Muara.

There is, so a last-minute postcard says, a huge mosque under construction across the road from the museum.

Ancient Tomb of Sultan Bolkiah
Near the museum, about a km closer to town, is the tomb and mausoleum of the fifth Sultan of Brunei, known as the 'Singing Admiral' who died returning from a voyage to Java. He lived from 1473 to 1521, during a period when Brunei was the dominant power in the region.

Kampong Ayer
This collection of 28 water villages, built on stilts out in the Brunei River, has been here for centuries and at present houses a population of 20 to 30 thousand people. It's a strange mixture of ancient and modern; old traditions and ways of life are side by side with modern plumbing, electricity and colour TVs. A visit to one of the villages is probably the most rewarding experience you'll have in Brunei, though the garbage which floats around them has to be seen to be believed. To get there go down to the main wharf and take any one of the many launches which ply back and forth all day. Bargain over the fare, it shouldn't be more than 50c and traffic back and forth continues busily all day long. The area by the mosque can be walked to on planks.

When the city was modernising it was suggested that the people from the water villages be re-located to the mainland. The people refused to move and in enlightened fashion were permitted to stay. Schools, hospitals and so on were instead built in the villages – but of cement rather than wood.

Handicraft Centre

The preposterously large and grandiose handicraft centre was built to help develop local craftwork. It's along the waterfront toward the museum, visible from town and an easy walk. However, if you are interested in traditional crafts, it is disappointing. Only new silverwork and weaving are available and everything is very expensive, even hundreds of dollars. There's not much variety either. You can visit workshops upstairs.

A Short Town Walk

From town it's a short walk to a small waterfall and a view. Past the Ang's Hotel, going away from the town centre, turn right at the next traffic light. Go up the road to the parking lot, through the gate by the parking lot and continue for about 15 minutes. Continuing past the flowers and picnic tables follow the stream to the falls. They are best in the wet season when the water is deeper; you can swim here. Another road by the gate leads to a 15-minute walk uphill to a view over the water reservoir.

Brunei's Gift to N.Y.

The sultan of Brunei, which became the 159th member of the United Nations last week, presented the city of New York with a check for $500,000 over the weekend. The money will be used to feed the city's elderly shut-ins.

In official acceptance ceremonies, **Mayor Edward Koch** returned the gesture by presenting a representative of Brunei with a brass key to the city.

Oil-rich Brunei, which has $13 billion in currency reserves, also gave $1 million to UNICEF.

Other

There is a Chinese temple on the corner of Jalan Chevalier and Jalan Sungai Kianggeh with some colourful, pictorial tilework and plenty of carved, gilded wood. The recently completed Sultan's palace, said to be due for inclusion in the *Guiness Book of Records* for its nearly 1800 rooms, which makes it larger than the Vatican Palace, has plans to open a portion for public viewing. Ask if this has yet occurred. It has to be impressive; you can be sure nothing was spared.

All over town you'll notice the oversized federal buildings – the post office and the government complex which you can visit, for example. It's across from the Youth Centre. Try to see the Royal Ceremonial Hall (Lapua) where traditional events are held and the Sultan's golden throne sits. The Dewan Majlis, the Legislative Assembly, is also here.

Visitors are invited to see traditional Malay weddings; ask at the tourist office for more information. The small market is outside, behind the movie theatre on Jalan Roberts; walk through the theatre area. For books and magazines try the third floor of the Teck Guan Plaza Building, on the corner of Jalan Sultan and Jalan McArthur. There are also STP distributors at the corner of Jalan Chevalier and Jalan Sultan and the Rex around the corner on Jalan Sungai Kianggeh.

Lastly, note the meter maids all over town wearing green suits, white gloves and usually sporting umbrellas. They ticket cars incessantly with parking charges and collect the money when the driver returns.

Places to Stay – bottom end

The only place to stay in this range is the very controversial Youth Centre or *Pusat Belia* (tel 23936), on Jalan Sungai Kianggeh a short walk from the town centre. The problem with the place has been getting in. It's not easy for men, possibly harder for single women. There are two large dorms, both generally nearly empty, one for each sex, and beds are sometimes rented to travellers.

The place was set up for local and visiting youth groups and registered clubs, and this is its main function. If one of them is staying you likely won't be given permission even if all the beds are not taken. I spent nearly an hour with the manager of the place trying to figure out the criteria and learned the following. First, look as respectable as possible. Second, be very polite, courteous and calm. Remember that in letting you stay, the management is doing you a favour, not helping you exercise your God-given right. It is not a hotel. I was told some horror stories of tantrum-throwing, screaming western travellers behaving like spoiled brats. Remain calm and quietly state why you would like to stay. Your odds will be greatly increased if you have a Student Card, Youth Hostel Card or any Youth Organization or Association membership. Most importantly, be friendly and do not start a confrontation which will only make things more difficult for travellers in the future.

There are two men in charge, one with a desk in the office front room and the boss with a desk in the private office at the back. Both respond to a handshake (light) and smile and a little formal decorum. Unfortunately, locating these gentlemen is not always easy and may require some waiting. Be patient. It's best to try in the early morning. There is somebody on duty every day so ask to see the officer on duty.

There is room for 60 men and 20 women in dorms that have seen better days. Maintenance is non-existent. Fans don't work, showers are broken, the pool is closed and the water is shut off at night – take your shower early or you won't get one. However, the price is only B$10 for one to three nights (same price for one, two or three nights) and then B$5 for each night after that. Don't stay one night and then demand B$6.66 back! It's B$10 flat rate. Downstairs there is a small cafeteria-type restaurant for cheap, fairly well-balanced, passable meals served up by friendly women and girls and supervised by numerous straggly cats.

Good luck. No matter what, getting in still relies heavily on the officer's whim. Despite stories you may hear there is really no accommodation at St Andrew's Church, although the minister is friendly. If you're really desperate, he has a very small, old shed you can use but there are no beds and no screens. The mosquitoes will love having you.

Places to Stay – middle

The older place in this range is the *Capital Hostel* (tel 23561), off Jalan Tasek Lama just at the back of Pusat Belia. It's the one you'll most likely have to use if you're on a budget and cannot get into the Pusat Belia Youth Hostel. It's undergoing an external facelift and some internal renovations. Rooms here cost B$70 single, B$85 double. All the rooms are air-con with TV and fridge. The restaurant and bar downstairs serve relatively reasonably priced meals at B$7 to 8. The continental breakfast is B$3.50 or B$6 with eggs and is handy if you're at the youth centre.

A more recent middle to top addition is the *National Inn* (tel 21128) on Jalan Tutong, out of the town centre, across the Brunei River behind the mosque. It features fine, modern rooms, all air-con, but with prices of B$69-99 single, B$69-109 double. The hotel offers free transport to the airport and a regular shuttle service into town. The restaurant serves lunches for B$10.50, dinners for B$17.50.

Places to Stay – top end

There are more hotels in this category than in any other. The relatively new *Sheraton-Utama* (tel 27272) is the country's top hotel and has all the modern amenities, including a pool. It is centrally located on Jalan Bendahara. The 170 rooms cost B$185-225 for singles, B$205-245 for doubles.

Ang's Hotel (tel 23553) on Jalan Tasek

has its own restaurant and bar and is fully air-con, of course. The 84 rooms cost B$108 single, B$118 double. Right downtown is the *Brunei Hotel* (tel 22372) at 95 Jalan Chevalier. Each room has air-con, private bath and TV and the hotel has a restaurant and bar. Rates are B$97-125 single, B$112-141 double.

Places to Eat

All the hotels and the *Pusat Belia* have their own restaurants. The meals at the *Capital* are pretty good and relatively cheap. The same goes for the *Pusat Belia*, but arrive early so the food is warm and fresh and don't rely too heavily on the meat. The best place to eat, especially in the evenings, is at the food stalls down at the riverfront near the bridge. Looking out to the stilt villages while you eat is a very pleasant experience. Soups are a specialty and cost B$2. Various rice and noodle dishes also cost B$2. Soft drinks are B$1, as they are all over town.

Along the main street, Jalan Sultan, you'll find a few places to eat. *The Creamery* has ice cream, milkshakes, pastries and the *Wisma Bahru* has cheap Muslim-style food. Also here are other cheap Chinese and Indian places. The *Darussalam*, toward the McArthur end, is the only place in town I saw fresh Indian breads being made.

On Jalan McArthur the *Seri Indah* has the usual items; nasi goreng is B$3.50. It's quick and the local office crowd frequents the place. On Jalan Chevalier near the river is a take-away bake shop. On Jalan Roberts across from the cinema the *Sin Hup Leong* seems to be the place for beer. Nearby is the *Chop Chuan Huat*, an Indian place where you can get a good, tasty meal for under B$4. Drink a refreshing lemon ping for B$1.20.

For a better meal try the *Lucky Restaurant*, where Chinese food may be had at about B$40 for two without alcohol. The *Grill Room* has a set lunch for B$20. Main courses at dinner in this western restaurant are B$30 to 35; the menu includes some seafood. Note there are very few bars and only Chinese restaurants carry a liquor licence. Muslims are not allowed to drink. Nevertheless beer, wine and spirits are *much* cheaper in Brunei than in Sarawak or Sabah. Enough cheaper that you can make a little profit on exporting. Or, recommended one visitor, take a six-pack for the Niah Caves hostel refrigerator!

Getting There

Air Airlines which fly into Brunei include Royal Brunei, MAS, SIA, Cathay Pacific, Qantas and British Airways. Qantas have direct flights between Brunei and Darwin while British Airways have a weekly flight between London and Australia which goes via Brunei. Royal Brunei flies to Bandar Seri Begawan from Singapore, Hong Kong, Manila, Darwin (!) and other destinations. It's actually cheaper to fly Manila-BSB than Manila-Kota Kinabalu, even though it's further. Being a good Muslim airline Royal Brunei serve no alcohol on their flights.

None of the airline offices offer student or other discounts but some of the travel agents (such as the one next door to the Brunei Hotel) will offer small discounts. SIA and Royal Brunei are on Jalan Chevalier. MAS is also, but at the other end just off Jalan Pretty. On Royal Brunei, standard fare to Singapore is B$320, B$510 return. To Kuching costs B$185, KK B$65, Manila B$444, Kuala Lumpur B$372, Bangkok B$504. For Qantas, Pan Am and Cathay Pacific, tickets can be bought at the Borneo Company Travel at the corner of Jalan Cator and Jalan Sungai Kianggeh.

Road The only roads which exist in Brunei are the ones linking BSB to Seria, Kuala Belait and the Sarawak border near Kuala Baram. There are no roads to the eastern Sarawak towns of Limbang and Lawas or to Sabah. The only way of getting to the latter is by direct launch or by launch-taxi combinations. It has been said that the government purposely keeps the roads out of Brunei in such miserable condition to make any invasion by land difficult!

The bus station in BSB is located next to the central market, near Britannia House at the back of the Brunei Hotel. There are many buses every day to Seria. The fare is B$4 and the journey takes 1½ to two hours. From Seria to Kuala Belait there are 28 buses daily and the fare is B$1. The journey takes about half an hour. On both of these legs beware of bus conductors trying to charge you extra for your bags. It's very easy, however, to hitch from BSB to Seria and then Kuala Belait because there are plenty of air-con cars and very few hitch-hikers.

If you want to reach Miri in one day from BSB then start out early in the day although there are now four or five buses daily from Kuala Belait to Miri. These are operated by the Sharikat Berlima Belait bus company. The fare is B$10 and the journey takes about 2½ hours and involves several river crossings.

Just out of town you cross the Belait River; you must get out of the bus and walk on to the ferry so you won't be trapped in the bus if the ferry sinks. The worst stretch of unsealed road (it's a private Shell Oil road) leads from here to the border but at low tide they drive along the nice smooth beach.

After clearing immigration you change buses to a Sarawak one and drive over more sandy, unsealed road to the Baram River. Here you again leave the bus, together with all your gear, and cross the river, either free on the Shell vehicle ferry or for M$1 in a motor boat. The bus people try to hurry you on to the motor boats so they can leave faster for Miri, but they'll wait if you insist on taking the free ferry. Across the river in Kuala Baram you board your third bus (all on the same ticket) for the short run on sealed road to Miri.

Launches & Boats Unless you are going to fly to Labuan or Kota Kinabalu the only way to get to Sabah or the isolated eastern Sarawak outposts of Limbang or Lawas is to use riverboats or riverboat/taxi combinations. If you really want to know what makes this part of Borneo tick then take the riverboats. It's a fascinating journey whichever route you take. Some of the possibilities include:

Brunei-Limbang There are several private speed boats which do this run at various times of the day – departure times depend on demand. The fare is B$5. The trip takes about a half hour, ask around at the dock. There isn't much to see or do in Limbang and the town has a bit of a reputation as a sin spot. You can either stay at Limbang overnight or take another boat to Punang, further up the coast. Boats for Punang depart every day about 11 am except Sunday. From Punang you can get a connecting share taxi to Lawas. Total fare from Limbang to Lawas will be about B$13.

Brunei-Labuan Labuan is a duty-free island off Brunei from which you can get ferries to Sabah and then a bus into Kota Kinabalu. For more details, see the section under Sabah. From BSB there are four boats to Labuan, all costing B$12. The *Serai Sungai Express* leaves at 8 am every Sunday, Tuesday, Thursday and Friday. Get tickets at the boat or at Oriental Travel, down a little alley off Jalan McArthur, opposite the dock area. The alley is beside G L Amour, a store selling sporting goods. The agent is beside the Borneo Hardware.

You can also pre-book tickets here for the *Duta Muhibbah Express* which leaves Mondays, Wednesdays and Saturdays at 1 pm and returns at 8.15 pm. The *Sri Labuan Dua Express* departs Mondays, Wednesdays, Fridays and Saturdays at 8 am and returns at 2 pm. The *Raji Wali Express* does the same trip, also leaving in the morning. All take about 1½ to two hours and it's usually a good idea to book a day ahead. You can get private boats to take you; they charge B$15 or so, but will ask for B\$20. With triple outboard engines they're very fast. Just stand around the dock area and touts and boat owners will approach you or call out.

The *Serai Sungai* docks at the end of the wharf near the tourist office; the others leave from beside the tin-roofed building with the yellow sides, just before the market stalls. Normally you can get tickets the morning of departure, but on holidays and weekends it can get busy. You can book ahead at Oriental Travel. The cheaper government launch doesn't run any longer.

Labuan is a pretty expensive place to hang around in and there is virtually nothing of interest there so if you don't want to shed a lot of money on partially duty-free consumer items then catch a launch to Menumbok on the Sabah mainland. There are several launches every day and the fare is M\$7. They depart from the dock opposite the Hock Hua Bank, several blocks to the left after you clear Labuan immigration. It is intended that government car ferries will soon start operating this service. From Menumbok share taxis and minibuses are available to either Beaufort (M\$7 or 8 per person) or Kota Kinabalu. All in all this route to Kota Kinabalu from Brunei adds up to over M\$30.

Brunei-Lawas There are usually one or two launches daily to Lawas which cost B\$15 and take about two hours. The one which most travellers take is scheduled to depart at 11 am. Runners will accost you as you enter the wharf – no problem finding it, just ask around the area near the bridge over the canal.

You can stay the night at Lawas, in which case the *Government Rest House* on the airport road is good, but recently all Sarawak rest houses have had their prices for non-government workers increased dramatically and the cost is now M\$30. Failing that there's the *Federal Hotel* which is similarly priced. Or you can take another boat to Merapok, which will cost

M\$4 and take about 3/4 hour. The road to Beaufort and KK now connects down to Lawas, but there is not a lot of traffic. You can apparently get lifts with trucks. If you're lucky and have no particular interest in going to Lawas you may find that the launch which is bringing you from Brunei will hail a motorised longboat in mid-river on the way to Lawas and transfer you onto it so you get to Merapok without having to wait around in Lawas.

Merapok is a strange one-street hamlet in the middle of nowhere and you get the distinct impression that you could be here forever trying to get out. At least that's the case if you arrive by somewhat unorthodox methods – as we did. But there are two billiard halls – with beautiful tables made in Australia – and a cafe while you wait! From here it's a question of hassling for a lift to Sipitang (the usual price is M\$2.50 per person for the half hour journey) which isn't difficult – *someone* will be going there so long as you don't arrive too late in the day.

Note that the Sabah immigration and customs post is a few hundred metres out of the hamlet and that you're supposed to report there for immigration formalities. If you happen to drive past it – like we did – it doesn't really matter. Sabah immigration is pretty easygoing, unlike Sarawak immigration, and you can report to another office inside Sabah, such as Sipitang, Tenom or KK (but not Beaufort) even several days later.

If you took the 11 am launch from Brunei to Lawas then you'll arrive in Sipitang too late for any scheduled transport (taxis or buses) out of there so if you want to get to Beaufort or KK that night you'll have to hitch – not easy as there's very little traffic. If you have to stay in Sipitang for the night there's a *Government Rest House*, about a km from the centre on the Merapok road, which costs M\$12 per person. A more basic flea-pit in the centre of the village costs less than this. Share-taxis depart for Beaufort every day around 7 to 8 am and cost M\$7 per person. From Beaufort there are buses, taxis and trains to KK or Tenom.

Getting Around

Airport Transport There are no buses to the airport so if you're flying into or out of Brunei you will have to hire a taxi. Or hitch, which is quite easy. Taxis do not have meters so fix the fare in advance. Taxis to or from the airport and town are B$15; very expensive for just four km. The airport is big, new and modern and you can change money there.

Buses Local buses around BSB are few and far between and only leave when full. The bus station is next to the central market, behind the Brunei Hotel.

Rent-a-Cars At the airport are two car rental agencies, Sharikat Yuran (tel 24054) and Avis. Other offices are located in town. Rates for a car are B$75 a day (Toyota or Datsun 1600cc) or B$150 a jeep. Gas, need I say, is ridiculously cheap. Sharikat can be found at 144 Jalan Chevalier.

AROUND BRUNEI

Muara

This is a small town north from Bandar Seri Begawan at the top of the peninsula. It's a new oil centre with not much to see but there is a pretty decent beach. The World Wide club is basically for expats and is a good place for a beer and maybe to meet someone who lives in the country. There are also a lot of yachts here, for you opportunists. The bus from BSB takes about 40 minutes and costs B$2 or you can try hitching. There are other beaches on the north coast, but these are not as pleasant and the buses are less frequent.

Bangar

Bangar is another small town, but it is reached only by boat. You can get launches there from BSB. Bangar is the district centre and is east of BSB, toward Sarawak, located on the Temburong River. There is a government rest house here, but I don't know if travellers can use it. Apparently you can organise some sleeping arrangements in town, perhaps through the tourist office in BSB.

A road follows the river upstream for a distance to the village of Batang Duri. There are several Iban longhouses in this upper river area. While there are some basic restaurants in Bangar, take food with you if you're going upstream.

Seria

Seria is the main town on the north coast, situated between Tutong and Kuala Belait, quite close to the Malaysian border. Before Seria a road branches off inland to Labi. About halfway to Labi is Luagan Lalak with good views and a lake. From Labi there are several Iban long-houses it is possible to visit. The main one is called Rumah Panjang Mendaram Besar. There is a road, but you may have to walk it. Take some small presents. On the way at Rampayoh you can view a waterfall.

Places to Stay The *Hotel Seria* has non-air-con doubles for B$15. If you're just passing through Brunei from Sabah to Sarawak, and can't stay in the Pusat Belia, then it's quite a saving to spend your last Brunei night here rather than at a more expensive BSB hotel.

At the other end of Seria's price scale the *Sea View Hotel* is completely modern at B$85/90 for singles/doubles.

Getting There The road from BSB is good; there are about 10 buses daily taking two hours. The last one leaves Seria at 4 pm. From Seria there are buses to Kuala Belait for B$1.

Kuala Belait

The last town before Malaysia, Kuala Belait is where you get buses for Miri in Sarawak. You can hire a motor launch by the market for trips up the river to Kuala Balai, a small river village. The 45-minute trip (one way) goes by good, jungle vegetation at the river's edge. Near Kuala Balai you'll see sago palms growing. Along the way ask the driver to stop at the wooden case of skulls mounted on stilts, left over from the head-hunting days.

Places to Stay At the cheap end of the scale there's a *Government Rest House*. Or the *Sentosa Hotel* at 92 Jalan McKerron is all air-con and has singles/doubles at B$54/70.

Getting There For Malaysia there are quite a few buses daily, mostly in the morning, and the fare is just under B$10 for the three-hour trip. Just out of town the road ends and you take a ferry over the Belait River. The road then continues along the coast to the border. This stretch is rough and sometimes the beach is used instead of the road – of course when the tide is out! At the border you change to a Malaysian bus and head to the Beram River. Here there is another ferry crossing and from here on into Miri it's a good road.

Other

There are walking trails to various villages and their longhouses in the interior jungles, particularly along the Belait River. Three such villages are Buau, Punan and Melilas. These are all south of Batu Sawat, which is on a branch of the main road leading from the coast to Labi. Getting enough time on your visa for such extensive touring could be a hassle, however. These villages see few visitors.

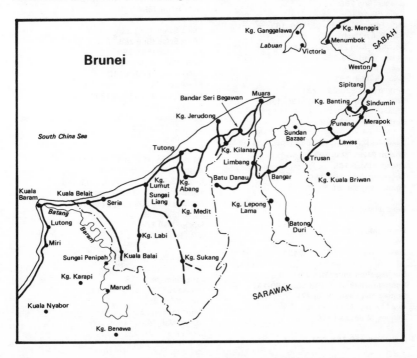

Index

Thanks

Thanks to all these people who wrote to us:

Sumner Adams (UK), Trevor Akerman (UK), Ilene Alastaire (USA), Garry Allan, Robert Armstrong (UK), Bob Aronoff (USA), Wayne Asquith (NZ), Barbara & Neil, Caroline Bartlett (UK), Andrew Bartram (UK), Klaas Bisschop (H), Martin Bode (D), Chris Bollam, John Bowman (UK), Richard Braczor (NZ), Stefan Braunwalder (CH), Judy Brichetto (USA), M L Bridge (UK), K Brophy (UK), Trish Browning (Aus), David Bryant (Aus), Maxine Burney (NZ), Sue Bush (UK), Amy & Neil Carpenter (USA), Eva D Casmirro (C), Jack Carling (Aus), Joanne Celens (B), Bill Chappell (C), B J Clapton (Aus), J Clayton (Aus), Ade Colley, Stuart Collinson (UK), Joe Corrigan (UK), Wendy Cotton (UK), Garry Cowley (Aus), Patrick Creedon, Angel Dew (Nep), George Dodd, Cathy & Anne Doherty (Aus), Kevin Dwyer (USA), Lau Hwai Eng, Martin Ellison (Aus), Vic Esbenson, Kiri Evans (S), Richard Evans, Ann Faraday, Tim Foster (SA), Tony Francis (Aus), Hans Jurgen Frundt, Jo Gardner (UK), Jill Garlick, Ian Greenwood (Br), Bjorn Grinde (N), J J Hai (Aus), Carole Haligan (UK), Ned & Robert Hall (Aus), Ann Hardcastle (UK), Tom Harriman (USA), Marcia Harris, Bill Harvey (NZ), Wolfgang Hauger (A), Dennis Heazle (Aus), Eli Heimann (Isr), Lucy Holder (UK), John M Houlahan (USA), Chris Howe (UK), Cathryn Hugh, Ruth Jaeger, Jay (UK), George Jelinek, Eugenie Jenkins, Rob Kay (NZ), Sarah Kellet (UK), S G Ketkar (Ind), Jan King (USA), Bill Kitchen (Aus), Erik Klingzell (Sw), Poh Lek, Jeremy Levy (UK), Peter Loosemore, Candace Lowe (USA), Tony Luys, Babs MacLeod, Rene Marx (F), Lee Masters, Jenny McRae, John Mewma, Trevor Millum, Rob Mitchell, Mick Moser, John Nettleship, John Newman, Georg Neumaier (CH), Morten Nielsen (Dk), Ole Winther Nielsen (Dk), Mary Peckham (Aus), Fabian Pedrazzini (I), Anthony J Percy (UK), A Phillips, H Keith Pierce, David Pinkerton (USA), Franziska Planzer (T), Charles Pollard (UK), Brian J J Powell (Aus), Sergej Presern (UK), Bill Pries (NZ), Mr Rajanayagam (M), Murray Reinhart, Bruce Reznik (USA), Adrian Rice (M), Huw Robson (Aus), B Rowsell (Aus), Richard W Ruff (HK), Karen Sagstetter, Tom Sawyer (Aus), Brian Schaeffer, Jocelyne Sephord (F), Peter R Slocombe (UK), Brian & Lesley Smith, Grant Soosalu, Terry Stein (USA), Nick Stephens (USA), D J Stip (H), Wayne Stockdale (NZ), Helen Stockley (UK), Jeannet Straagaard (Dk), Paul Suhler (USA), T N Tan (S), Ann Tipton (UK), Neil Thompson, Rosemary Thomson (Aus), Chris Tollast, Johannes Trilling (D), Ruud van Wijnen (H), C J Van der Horst (H), Teunis van der Veen (H), Martin & Kathy Van der Voorn, Waipang Au (S), Ann & Ernie Wallbank, Hugh R Waters (S), Richard Waye (UK), C J White, N E Whitehead (NZ), Anne Whybourne (Aus), William E Widrig (USA), Steve Wilbur (USA), J Woodell (Aus), Michael Woodhouse (Aus), John Wren Lewis, Steve Wyn-Harris (NZ), David Yost

A – Austria, Aus – Australia, B – Belgium, Br – Brunei, C – Canada, CH – Switzerland, D – Germany, Dk – Denmark, F – France, H – Holland, HK – Hong Kong, I – Italy, Ind – India, Isr – Israel, M – Malaysia, N – Norway, Nep – Nepal, NZ – New Zealand, S – Singapore, SA – Saudi Arabia, Sw – Sweden, T – Taiwan, UK – UK, USA – USA

LONELY PLANET NEWSLETTER

We collect an enormous amount of information here at Lonely Planet. Apart from our research we also get a steady stream of letters from people out on the road – some of them are just one line on a postcard, others go on for pages. Plus we always have an ear to the ground for the latest on cheap airfares, new visa regulations, borders opening and closing. A lot of this information goes into our new editions or 'update supplements' in reprints. But we want to make better use of this information so, we also produce a quarterly newsletter packed full of the latest news from out on the road. It appears in January, April, July and October of each year. If you'd like an airmailed copy of the most recent newsletter just send us $7.50 for a years subscription, or for $2 each for single issues. That's US$ in the US or A$ for Australia, write to:

Lonely Planet Publications
PO Box 88, Sth Yarra, VIC., 3141 Australia
        or
Lonely Planet Publications
PO Box 2001A, Berkeley, CA 94702 USA

Lonely Planet travel guides
Africa on a Shoestring
Australia – a travel survival kit
Alaska – a travel survival kit
Bali & Lombok – a travel survival kit
Burma – a travel survival kit
Bushwalking in Papua New Guinea
Canada – a travel survival kit
China – a travel survival kit
Hong Kong, Macau & Canton
India – a travel survival kit
Japan – a travel survival kit
Kashmir, Ladakh & Zanskar
Kathmandu & the Kingdom of Nepal
Korea & Taiwan – a travel survival kit
Malaysia, Singapore & Brunei – a travel survival kit
Mexico – a travel survival kit
New Zealand – a travel survival kit
Pakistan – a travel survival kit kit
Papua New Guinea – a travel survival kit
The Philippines – a travel survival kit
South America on a Shoestring
South-East Asia on a Shoestring
Sri Lanka – a travel survival kit
Thailand – a travel survival kit
Tramping in New Zealand
Trekking in the Himalayas
USA West
West Asia on a Shoestring

Lonely Planet phrasebooks
Indonesia Phrasebook
Nepal Phrasebook
Thailand Phrasebook

Lonely Planet travel guides are available around the world. If you can't find them, ask your bookshop to order them from one of the distributors listed below. For countries not listed or if you would like a free copy of our latest booklist write to Lonely Planet in Australia.

Australia
Lonely Planet Publications, PO Box 88, South Yarra, Victoria 3141.
Canada see USA
Denmark
Scanvik Books aps, Store Kongensgade 59 A, DK-1264 Copenhagen K.
Hong Kong
The Book Society, GPO Box 7804.
India & Nepal
UBS Distributors, 5 Ansari Rd, New Delhi.
Israel
Geographical Tours Ltd, 8 Tverya St, Tel Aviv 63144.
Japan
Intercontinental Marketing Corp, IPO Box 5056, Tokyo 100-31.
Malaysia
MPH Distributors, 13 Jalan 13/6, Petaling Jaya, Selangor.
Netherlands
Nilsson & Lamm bv, Postbus 195, Pampuslaan 212, 1380 AD Weesp.
New Zealand
Roulston Greene Publishing Associates Ltd, Box 33850, Takapuna, Auckland 9.
Pakistan
London Book House, 281/C Tariq Rd, PECHS Karachi 29, Pakistan
Papua New Guinea
Gordon & Gotch (PNG), PO Box 3395, Port Moresby.
Singapore
MPH Distributors, 3rd Storey, 601 Sims Drive #03-21, Singapore 1438
Sweden
Esselte Kartcentrum AB, Vasagatan 16, S-111 20 Stockholm.
Thailand
Chalermnit, 1-2 Erawan Arcade, Bangkok.
UK
Roger Lascelles, 47 York Rd, Brentford, Middlesex, TW8 0QP.
USA
Lonely Planet Publications, PO Box 2001A, Berkeley, CA 94702.
West Germany
Buchvertrieb Gerda Schettler, Postfach 64, D3415 Hattorf a H.